Immanent Critique

ESSEX STUDIES IN CONTEMPORARY CRITICAL THEORY

Series Editors: Peter Dews, Professor of Philosophy at the University of Essex; Lorna Finlayson, Lecturer in Philosophy at the University of Essex; Fabian Freyenhagen, Professor of Philosophy at the University of Essex; Steven Gormley, Lecturer in Philosophy at the University of Essex; Timo Jütten, Senior Lecturer in Philosophy at the University of Essex; and Jörg Schaub, Lecturer in Philosophy at the University of Essex.

Essex Studies in Contemporary Critical Theory. This series aims to develop the critical analysis of contemporary societies. The series publishes both substantive critical analyses of recent and current developments in society and culture and studies dealing with methodological/conceptual problems in the Critical Theory tradition, intended to further enhance its ability to address the problems of contemporary society

The Political Is Political, Lorna Finlayson
The Spell of Responsibility, Frieder Vogelmann; translated by Daniel Steuer
Social Suffering: Sociology, Psychology, Politics, Emmanuel Renault; translated by Maude Dews
Critical Theory and Social Self-Understanding, Robin Celikates; translated by Naomi van Steenbergen
Debating Critical Theory: Engagements with Axel Honneth, edited by Julia Christ, Kristina Lepold, Daniel Loick and Titus Stahl
Immanent Critique, Titus Stahl

Immanent Critique

Titus Stahl

Translated with John-Baptiste Oduor

ROWMAN & LITTLEFIELD
Lanham • Boulder • New York • London

Published by Rowman & Littlefield
An imprint of The Rowman & Littlefield Publishing Group, Inc.
4501 Forbes Boulevard, Suite 200, Lanham, Maryland 20706
www.rowman.com

86-90 Paul Street, London EC2A 4NE

The book was first published by Campus Verlag under the German title "Immanente Kritik" by Titus Stahl
Original © Campus Verlag GmbH, Frankfurt am Main 2013

The translation of this work was funded by Geisteswissenschaften International – Translation Funding for Humanities and Social Sciences from Germany, a joint initiative of the Fritz Thyssen Foundation, the German Federal Foreign Office, the collecting society VG WORT and the Börsenverein des Deutschen Buchhandels (German Publishers & Booksellers Association).

Copyright to the English translation © 2022 by The Rowman & Littlefield Publishing Group, Inc.

All rights reserved. No part of this book may be reproduced in any form or by any electronic or mechanical means, including information storage and retrieval systems, without written permission from the publisher, except by a reviewer who may quote passages in a review.

British Library Cataloguing in Publication Information Available

Library of Congress Cataloging-in-Publication Data
Names: Stahl, Titus, 1979– author. | Oduor, John-Baptiste, translator.
Title: Immanent critique / Titus Stahl ; translated with John-Baptiste Oduor.
Other titles: Immanente Kritik. English
Description: Lanham, Maryland : Rowman & Littlefield, [2022] | Series: Essex studies in contemporary critical theory | "Campus Verlag under the German title "Immanente Kritik" by Titus Stahl Original, Campus Verlag GmbH, Frankfurt am Main 2013." | Includes bibliographical references and index.
Identifiers: LCCN 2021030042 (print) | LCCN 2021030043 (ebook) | ISBN 9781786601797 (cloth) | ISBN 9781538199190 (paper) | ISBN 9781786601810 (epub)
Subjects: LCSH: Social sciences—Philosophy. | Social sciences—Methodology. | Critical theory. | Frankfurt school of sociology.
Classification: LCC H61.15 .S69 2022 (print) | LCC H61.15 (ebook) | DDC 300.1—dc23
LC record available at https://lccn.loc.gov/2021030042
LC ebook record available at https://lccn.loc.gov/2021030043

Contents

Preface to the English Translation — vii
1 Introduction — 1
2 Social Critique — 9
3 Interpretation and Immanent Critique — 33
4 Immanent Critique and the Critical Theory of Society — 75
5 Collective Intentionality — 117
6 Norms and Social Practices — 157
7 The Immanent Norms of Social Practices — 197
8 The Possibility of Immanent Critique — 229
9 The Critique of Reification — 257
10 Conclusion: Social Conflict and Social Hope — 283
Notes — 289
Bibliography — 329
Index — 345

Preface to the English Translation

This book is a revised and substantially shortened translation of the monograph *Immanente Kritik*, which was published in German by Campus in 2013, itself a revised and substantially shortened translation of a PhD thesis that I submitted in 2010. While a great amount of literature that covers related issues has been published since the original text was written, I hope that this text continues to offer an argument that is not available elsewhere, and I remain convinced of the overall line of reasoning I defend. I have therefore only made revisions where it became necessary in the course of shortening the text and at some points where the original German version was less clear than I had intended.

Throughout its various iterations, I have incurred many debts to those who have supported the project. The PhD thesis could not have been written without the unwavering support of my advisors, Axel Honneth and Nicholas H. Smith, as well as Rahel Jaeggi and Jean-Philippe Deranty. At the Frankfurt Institute for Social Research and the Department of Philosophy at Goethe University, Frankfurt, and at the Department of Philosophy of Macquarie University, Sydney, I found a community of colleagues who have deeply shaped me and the present book. Hannah Bayer, Robin Celikates, Kristina Lepold, Jasper Liptow, Andreas Maier and Frieder Vogelmann were kind enough to provide feedback on various iterations of drafts, from which I learned a lot. I am also grateful for the questions and suggestions I received at colloquia in Frankfurt, Berlin, Munich, Cologne, and Sydney. In addition, I was fortunate enough to have been supported while working on the manuscript by project funding from the Volkswagen Foundation and by a Macquarie Research Excellence scholarship.

The English translation of the book was funded by a stipend from the Geisteswissenschaften International program of the Börsenverein des

Deutschen Buchhandels. Its publication would not have been possible without the help of the editors of the Essex Studies in Critical Theory series. In particular, I am deeply grateful to Fabian Freyenhagen and Frankie Mace at Rowman & Littlefield and to the Campus editors for guiding the translation project through a series of obstacles we could not have anticipated. John-Baptiste Oduor took over the translation project at a critical moment, and I am deeply grateful to him and to Carolyn Benson for invaluable help with the manuscript.

As always, my greatest debt is to Babette. Without her, none of this would have been possible.

Chapter One

Introduction

In September 1843, Karl Marx wrote a letter to his friend Arnold Ruge from Bad Kreuznach, where he had married Jenny von Westphalen only a short time prior. In it, he complained of the state of the philosophical social criticism of their time. In the past, Marx wrote, philosophy had always been under the sway of the idea that

> philosophers have had the solution of all riddles lying in their writing-desks, and the stupid, exoteric world had only to open its mouth for the roast pigeons of absolute knowledge to fly into it.[1]

Although Marx described it as an improvement that philosophy was overcoming this dogmatic view of its own role, he notes that a certain 'anarchy' had broken out among the reformers of the day. This 'anarchy' prevailed in particular in confusion over the proper content of philosophical critique. In Marx's view, however, these confusions were owing to *methodological progress*, which he intended to bring to completion. This methodological progress consisted in the development of a *new form of critique*. It is the distinguishing principle of this new form of criticism, Marx writes, 'that we do not dogmatically anticipate the world, but only want to find the new world through criticism of the old one'.[2]

On Marx's account, therefore, the new kind of critique does not proceed dogmatically. It does not begin by developing normative or moral principles purely theoretically, without reference to empirical reality, and then proceed to apply these principles to the social world. Rather, this new form of criticism takes social reality seriously and extracts the norms by which the 'new world' should be governed *from this social reality itself.* Such nondogmatic criticism must thus understand itself as a critique that develops its critical principles from the existing social and political conditions. And these conditions, in a sense yet to be clarified, must already *contain* the critical principles.

At the same time, in order offer a *real* criticism, critique must still transcend existing conditions. In writing these lines, Marx certainly did not have the intention of criticizing preceding philosophy for being *too radical*. In Marx's view, nondogmatic criticism can (and often must) reject prevailing social norms entirely. As this new form of critique is to develop its norms out of criticism of the old world, it cannot proceed by merely *picking up* existing ideas of how people should live. Rather, it should draw out *new* norms from the unrealized potential of existing social conditions. How exactly this is to be understood, however, Marx's letter does not explain.

Although the precise nature of the method by which these new forms of critique may be distinguished is by no means clear, Marx's remarks on the relationship between theory and reality proved pivotal for critical theory. The various generations and approaches of this tradition do not share the same normative principles, and nor do they seek the same political changes. Rather, they share a *methodological* assumption. This is the methodological stipulation that, rather than developing its principles independently of social reality, critical social philosophy must treat them as an *elucidation [Aufklärung] of that social reality, including its own commitments and potential*. This is the method of *immanent social critique*.

Although a commitment to immanent critique has formed the methodological core of critical theory up to now,[3] only rarely have critical theorists tried to reconstruct in their own vocabulary precisely what this commitment amounts to.[4] Its underlying metaphysical, epistemological and political assumptions have never been translated into the vocabulary of contemporary philosophy. As a result, explicitly elaborated models of immanent critique in Marx's sense do not play a role in contemporary philosophy, outside of those theories that, on political grounds, verbally emphasize a commitment to immanent critique.

So why revisit the question of what immanent critique is? If answering this question is to be more than merely a matter of faithfulness to a tradition, it must be shown that the model of immanent critique can solve philosophical, social-theoretical and political problems better than other theories. Only once this has been shown will it be at all meaningful to enquire into which aspects of the idea of immanent critique require further explanation; only once this has been shown can the idea of immanent critique form a productive point of reference in current philosophical debate.

What could a theory of immanent critique actually achieve? First, it is notable that for several years there has been a resurgence of interest in the philosophical foundations of social critique, even though the idea of an 'immanent critique' has played no role in it. These debates about the foundations of critique were occasioned by the work of Michael Walzer and controversies over John Rawls's theory of justice.[5] Some of the problems that drive this debate could possibly be solved if we were to succeed in reformulating the idea of immanent critique such that it could meet the demands that we currently place on philosophical theories of social criticism.

The central problem in these debates lies in the assumption that the claims raised by social critique must be justified to those to whom the critique applies. Insistence on the necessity of justification is not – as one might suspect – a purely normative demand on what social criticism *should* be: in modern societies, at least, public discourse is constituted in such a way that any critical approach that has not worked through this problem in a credible way will not elicit agreement from its audience. The requirement that social critique must make explicit how it takes itself to be justified is irreversibly institutionalized in the social practices of these societies. Social critique *should*, then, not only justify itself to its audience (for moral reasons) but *must* justify itself if it wants to achieve anything.

In many cases, it is not sufficient for such justification that critics of a society simply disclose their reasons for advancing their critique. Whenever individuals or social groups put forward specific reasons for why their societies should be changed, they are inevitably asked why precisely *these* reasons should be seen as relevant by all of the members of the society in question and not some other set. Social critique therefore requires not only an answer to the question of *which* concrete reasons are given for criticism of specific social practices, but also an answer to the more general question of what *kinds of reasons* are appropriate as grounds for criticism of practices in a society or social group.

Once we have begun to discuss with others what appropriate reasons there could be for criticism of our society, social critique has already started to thematize its own foundations and to become *reflexive*. Sooner or later, social critique must scrutinize its own criteria and the practices on which it rests.

This problem becomes notably urgent if critics do not limit themselves to *applying* specific, already universally accepted norms, but rather pose the question whether these norms (or the way they come into being, are interpreted, or make demands) are not *themselves objectionable*. In sum, the problem becomes urgent when, rather than merely measuring a particular practice against an already recognized norm, the correctness of both elements – norms *and* practice – is brought into question.

If the possibility of criticizing practices *and* norms comes under scrutiny, it appears that social critique is faced with a dilemma. On the one hand, if we assume that we are only justified in criticizing others for failing to observe those norms they have previously explicitly accepted, then this not only leads to the objection that very few norms are shared by everyone in this sense in a pluralistic society but also the objection that social critique will then apparently have no leverage against the multifarious forms of oppression, discrimination and injustice which are a matter of shared practices that involve people accepting objectionable norms of behaviour. If we think of racist or sexist practices, those who enforce them often also accept racist and misogynist norms. This fact is part of why we reject such practices as bad. We therefore cannot simply content ourselves with measuring people against the norms they accept.

If, on the other hand, we assume that we need not fulfil the requirement of showing that our audience has accepted the relevant norms, and if we assume that we may criticize social practices by drawing on norms that the participants in those practices do not share, then it appears that we have opened the door to a dogmatic introduction of norms from a paternalistic perspective that is difficult to justify. Such a strategy also seemingly gives up on the requirement of showing that the norms that motivate the critique are norms that are in some sense socially relevant for the society at issue. Effectively, we then appear to exercise that dogmatic form of criticism which, in Marx's words, always already knows the solutions to all its riddles.

If we take this dilemma seriously, it is clear that progress in these debates can only be made if we succeed in showing that there is a form of nonexternal critique that does not simply underwrite socially accepted norms (and that therefore does not proceed purely 'internally'). That is, we need to show that there is a form of critique that draws on the normative potential of the society it criticizes and is therefore not simply dogmatic, 'external' criticism. Put simply, progress in these debates is only possible if immanent critique is possible. Immanent critique would be a form of critique that reconstructs norms from social reality that can then serve as a basis for demands that transcend the reality the critique is targeted at. This would be an attractive option if it could be methodologically justified.

If we understand immanent critique as relating to normative potentials that, while already inherent in social reality, are not yet recognized or realized in it, then this form of critique can complement both the idea of an 'internal' explication of the already recognized norms and the 'external' justification of independent normative principles. Such an immanent critique can not only avoid the suspicion that what counts as critique is merely an attempt to push through the critic's preferred ideology – a suspicion that would be appropriate if the critic claimed superior insight into independently valid norms, which does not require those affected by their critique to agree to them – but also take up the insight that through social critique, we can only demand of one another that we meet those obligations we already reciprocally accept.

Immanent critique can, however, *also* take up the intuition that the socially accepted norms in a society are not always entitled to the last word when criticizing that society. The model of immanent critique can therefore accommodate the plausible idea that we are not required to limit our demands to what is already accepted. We are entitled to demand of our society that new, hitherto unrecognized claims be recognized as justified.

Even if the idea of taking up the methodological commitment to immanent critique seems attractive, the traditional understanding of immanent critique – developed in different ways by the theories of Hegel and Marx and the first generation of critical theorists, in broad continuity – cannot be uncritically revived.[6] Not only have the previously plausible political assumptions about the agents of social criticism and the relevant practices on which such a critique could draw proved questionable in the course of the twentieth century,[7] the philosophical plausibility of the these models has furthermore been called into doubt. The traditional conception of immanent critique cannot readily be reconstructed in the vocabulary of contemporary philosophy. This is due both to the metaphysical assumptions regarding the normative facts allegedly reconstructed by immanent critique and the strategies of justification that these models employ. An endorsement of the method of immanent critique that dogmatically ignores these problems would therefore be self-defeating. This is because the justification of the method of immanent critique should not require that we abandon the methods and insights that the best contemporary self-understanding of philosophy makes available, assuming an external position in the process.

For these reasons, I intend to defend the idea of immanent critique in a new way. I will attempt to make the underlying assumptions of this method comprehensible on the basis of contemporary philosophical theories. My suggestion is that immanent social critique can find the normative potential on which it relies in the *social practices* of social groups or communities[8] and societies and that, on this basis, radical social critique is possible. The view of social practices that I will advance in what follows is that social practices as normatively regulated patterns of interaction only exist by virtue of the fact that the individuals who reproduce and enact them encounter each other with a specific attitude of *recognition*. The main thesis of this book is that we cannot understand the force of immanent norms that (at least in principle) transcend the 'official' rules of the relevant groups without reference to this attitude. To justify this claim, it is not sufficient to bring into view the classical questions of social criticism from the tradition of critical theory. Rather, I will engage with the problem from the perspective of *social ontology*. This is for the following reason: when we consider whether there is something 'in' society that the critic can use as a basis for a form of critique that goes beyond applying the explicitly accepted norms of that society, we must first clarify *which* social phenomena, facts or entities are meant by this and how claims about them can be justified. It must first be established that there is *a class of facts available at all* that is appropriate as a basis for immanent social critique.

The topic of this book is this social ontological justification of immanent critique. My basic question is this: in what sense does social reality contain normative potentials on which immanent social critique can rely? My claim is that these normative potentials can be found in social practices that are constituted through reciprocal recognition. This proposal should be understood as an attempt to give expression to the intuition that it is up to human beings themselves which norms they give to themselves and which norms they use to critically evaluate their own societies. At the same time, it also follows from this that the social existence of norms, which is a product of human action, is never fully cognitively transparent and intentionally accessible to its authors, although it always constrains the range of our acting and thinking.

I develop this argument in three steps. In the first part (chapters 2–4), fundamental concepts will be clarified, but above all two possible models of immanent critique – the 'hermeneutic' and the 'practice-based' models – will be presented and discussed in detail on the basis of the most important positions in each. For the discussion of hermeneutic immanent critique, Michael Walzer, Charles Taylor and Alasdair MacIntyre will be the main interlocutors, while for practice-based immanent critique Jürgen Habermas and Axel Honneth, as the most important contemporary representatives of critical theory, will serve as examples. With regard to both theoretical models, I will show that both the idea that immanent norms must be recovered through a process of interpretation and the idea that norms 'are immanent' in forms of interaction only make sense if we assume the existence of specific forms of social practice. However, the exact nature of these practices and the manner in which they give rise to immanent norms remains unclear in all of these approaches.

In the second part of the book (chapters 5–7), I will attempt to remedy these deficits. I will rely on two theoretical debates that do not belong to critical social philosophy in the narrow sense but that are highly relevant to the question of immanent critique. First, by considering current debates on *collective intentionality*, I will attempt to show that phenomena related to collective commitment regarding beliefs and intentions, which may be sufficient to ascribe the acceptance of particular norms to groups, can best be understood as normative phenomena established through social practices. Building on this idea, I will examine the question of what it actually means to claim that people who engage in a *social practice* are oriented by a norm.

This question, originally raised by Ludwig Wittgenstein, leads to the idea of a *recognition model of social practices*. Put concisely, the basic idea is that there are immanent norms in social practices whenever members of those practices ascribe *contestable default evaluative authority* to each other, which is internally related to their *collective acceptance* of particular norms.

In the third part of the book (chapters 8 and 9), I will focus on whether the idea of immanent critique can be made plausible on the basis of a practice-based model and whether more radical forms of critique can thereby be made comprehensible.

Chapter Two

Social Critique

What is social critique? Social critique is an everyday practice in which nearly all members of modern societies participate at one time or another. Social critique clearly takes place when, as part of an organized movement, people explicitly criticize social conditions. Examples of such *organized* social critique can be found in the feminist movement's criticism of discrimination against women, or in the labour movement's criticism of exploitation. However, the criticism of modern liberalism by religious fundamentalists, the various forms of anarchistic critique of domination and ecological critiques of modern production methods are also instances of social critique. These clear cases should not, however, conceal the fact that social critique can also be undertaken by individuals even without the background of a comprehensive theory. This can happen when individuals wish merely to air individual grievances and perhaps only occasionally express this explicitly in the form of a critique of social conditions.

Critique is only *social* critique when the *objects* of critique are social practices or institutions and when the critique is aimed at those aspects of practices or institutions that have a *social nature*. Therefore, neither criticism aimed at individual people nor individuals being asked to stop participating in certain social practices are cases of social critique. Social critique aims at changes to practices *as social practices*. This can easily be shown: when I criticize a friend for arriving late to our meeting, this is obviously not a case of social critique, as what is criticized here is an isolated case, both in terms of the person and in terms of the situation itself.

However, even if we criticize a larger number of people for recurring actions, this only amounts to social critique if that criticism is about social practices or institutions. If I denounce the general bad habits of tardy people, this is only social critique if I suppose that their behaviour amounts to a *social practice* of tardiness, and not merely an aggregate of many isolated, unrelated cases of tardiness. Only if particular patterns of behaviour constitute social practices – if a "culture of tardiness" exists – or if their causes are to be found in a social practice – for example, in a work culture that places excessive demands on people – are they appropriate objects of social critique. These criteria are not fulfilled by every consistent and widespread pattern of action: if the frequent occurrences of tardiness are caused by a scoundrel who regularly introduces soporifics into the water supply, for instance, then social critique would be inappropriate, as the object of criticism does not have a social cause. The same is true for patterns that reflect nonsocial causes like the innate depravity of human nature, genes or acts of God. If the adverse phenomena can be explained through such nonsocial causes, then social critique can at most launch the criticism that society failed to put in place possible countermeasures to effectively defend against them. The object of criticism in this case, however, is neither the cause of the actions that are characterized as reprehensible nor the actions themselves, but society's failure to establish institutions to counteract them.

These arguments suggest a specific, ontologically characterized area of possible objects of social critique, namely, those circumstances and regularities that are socially constituted and therefore socially changeable. The object of all forms of social critique is therefore social conditions, broadly speaking. That is, it is directed neither at nonsocial facts, nor at individual actions lying below the threshold of social relevance, nor at the psychological conditions, habits and dispositions of individuals, but rather at ways of acting that are socially constituted and have social significance. In what follows, I will call these ways of acting *social practices*.

Furthermore, we normally only use the term 'social critique' to refer to a critique of practices that can be found in large parts of a society, or that are relevant to society as a whole. We do not include those practices that only exist in small groups or without social consequences. We only call a critique of religious practices a 'social critique', for example, when a society as a whole is affected by the influence of that religion. The critique of the practices of a small religious group would not, by contrast, be termed 'social critique'.

Because as a rule social critique refers to recurrent, widely shared ways of acting that have a social character, it stands to reason that the *motivation* or the *reason* for social critique must also have a general character. Wrong social conditions are wrong from the perspective of social critique not only because in each isolated case they could be improved in some specific, particular way, but because these conditions should be better *in principle*. Their failings therefore have a systematic character. Whether their defects are characterized by a negative principle – in the form of condemnation of a particular social practice – or through confrontation with a positive principle – through comparison with an ideal state of affairs or with a positively formulated rule – they can in both cases be best described as having failed to meet a *norm* or an *evaluative standard* in the widest sense.

Social critique measures a social situation against a norm. This norm must also be applicable to the situation at issue, however: the respective social ills must be able to be *changed*. It is pointless to criticize the ineluctable. Only those social facts that are under the control of human beings, and that therefore in principle could be changed so as to satisfy a norm, can be criticized at all. This means that neither those outcomes that in principle occur independently of human action, such as natural processes, nor fully determined events are potential objects of social critique. Social critique is reserved for individual and collective actions (insofar as they express social arrangements).

Social critique in the widest sense includes all criticism of social practices and institutions that assumes that these institutions and practices can be changed for the better. It is not necessary for social critique in this wide sense to be guided by the intention that those who participate in the criticized practices and institutions should or could be *convinced* or *motivated* through this criticism. When people criticize the behaviour of others in a way that is not understood by or comprehensible to those others, and that therefore cannot motivate a change in their behaviour, this does not necessarily show that these critics are mistaken about anything. Their criticism can, for example, represent a mere discussion among uninvolved third parties about the failings of a society with respect to certain standards. Engaging in such a discussion is in no way irrational, even if it does not provide those whose behaviour forms the subject matter of these discussions with a reason to change their practices.[1] When, for example, people discuss why they hold the alleged precolonial Aztec practice of human sacrifice to be reprehensible, this is a case of social critique in the widest sense, even if it is uncertain whether the arguments they produce would have convinced precolonial Aztecs. But this is obviously not the aim of such discussions. Such discussions more often result in people's acquiring a better *self-understanding* of their *own* norms and in their assessing the merits of other systems of norms. Social critique in this widest sense can therefore serve not only to change behaviour but also to inform critics about their own norms.[2]

Just as social critique in the widest sense does not have a particular *function* predetermined from the outset, neither are the *addressees* of that criticism predetermined: both the activity of coming to an understanding of the merits and failures of a given social practice and the activity of seeking change can address societies or groups in which the critic is a member, but they can also address those societies or groups to which the critic does not belong. Critics, and those whose actions the social critique is about, need not necessarily be members of the same society, or of societies with similar normative systems.[3]

The commonly held view that social critics should always address their *own* society, or should only address those who participate in the practices they criticize, thus pertains not to the question of what social critique *is* but to ideas about what *good* social critique amounts to. Even if one were to agree that the sole *legitimate* aim of social critique is to change one's own society, or that such criticism must always convince those it criticizes to change their practices, it must be admitted that this is not the sole *possible* aim.

Among those forms of social critique that address themselves to those whose actions they criticize, a central case emerges, which I will call *social critique in the narrower sense*. This is a form of critique in which the addressees are the ones who have the power to change or maintain the practices in question, and which aims, through critique, to give them reasons to do one or the other.[4] In this narrower sense, social critique always involves an attempt to effect social change. In this sense, it aims not only to clarify which social changes are desirable according to certain criteria, but also to act as a *cause* of these social changes.[5] In the characteristic 'moves' of the practice of social critique in this narrower sense, which I will be concentrating on in what follows, three elements are always linked: first, a *descriptive* element, which comprises statements about the object of criticism (the social practices); second, an *evaluative* element, in which this object is measured against a particular standard; and third, a *practical* element, which comprises either a demand for the continued existence of those objects it judges to be good, a demand for improvement, or even a demand for comprehensive change. The last element, the demand to realize a certain normative standard, sets social critique in the narrower sense apart from forms of criticism that are not immediately practical, such as aesthetic or literary criticism.[6] The first (descriptive) element, which makes a claim to at least a certain standard of objectivity, sets social critique apart from purely expressive utterances of discontent. The evaluative standard, which represents the core of any form of critique, ultimately has an intersubjective form through its connection to the third element of the demand for change, which at least in principle should be able to address other actors. Social critique not only expresses an evaluation but also addresses others in an attempt to bring them to share and accept it. It aims at *intersubjective validity* – at least between those who exercise the criticism and those to whom the criticism is addressed.[7]

In the case of 'reflexive' social critique – where the critics form a subset of the addressees of the criticism – the attempt to achieve intersubjective validity receives its paradigmatic form: for anyone who is a member of a society or community characterized by the acceptance of specific norms, additional resources are available that he or she can draw on to identify reasons that may motivate other members of that society to join together to bring about the relevant changes. In particular, such a person can assume that many reasons that they have found to be convincing will not be inaccessible to others. However, this reflexivity is not itself necessary for social critique in the narrow sense.[8] Social critique as rationally motivated criticism in the narrow sense can also be applied 'from the outside'. The criticism that members of a colonized society apply to the contradictions between the normative claims of the colonizers and the actual reality of colonization is a criticism that fulfils all the requirements of social critique in the narrow sense, without being reflexive criticism. Any such criticism in the narrower sense (that argues 'from the outside') is, however, committed to the idea that it *could also* be made reflexive (if members of the criticized group took up the arguments and became critics themselves) – in contrast to social critique in the widest sense, which need not make this assumption.

Social critique is ultimately to be distinguished from *moral* criticism in light of two characteristics: moral criticism need not necessarily refer to institutions or practices. In the paradigmatic case, moral criticism is directed towards the actions of both individuals and groups; social critique, by contrast, refers solely to *social practices and social structures* and only indirectly to actions.[9] The range of the possible objects of social critique is therefore more restricted than that of the objects of moral criticism. Its normative basis is broader, however. While moral criticism only recognizes particular kinds of reasons as valid – namely, *moral* reasons – in social critique, instrumental, aesthetic and religious norms, together with others, can play a role as well.

Social critique in the narrow sense – social critique that aims to motivate changes to the object of criticism through the activity of criticism – is ultimately characterized by the fact that it claims to have *rational motivating force*. It usually aims not only to bring about actual changes but to do so in a way that brings its addressees (the criticizing subject included) to recognize its arguments as *reasons* for such change. It thus operates under the assumption that, if its addressees are rational, its arguments will generate both a motivating and a normative reason for bringing about the desired changes.

In the following, the concept of 'social critique in the narrow sense' will therefore only be used to refer to those forms of criticism in which those who carry out the critique aim to provide reasons to those addressed by the criticism. As mentioned above, this is not the only possible form of social critique or the only promising or normatively good form of social critique. Nevertheless, my choice to focus on this form of criticism is not merely arbitrary. Addressing others by providing them with reasons to change social reality is not merely one of many forms of critical discourse in modern society but rather its paradigmatic form. Only this form of social critique can claim not only to try to motivate its addressees but also to justify the normative demand that its addresses *should* proceed in the way the social critic considers justified.[10] The normative dimension of the justification of demands is thereby inseparable from the related assumption that such reasons could also actually be motivationally effective. While something like aesthetic criticism can be carried out without the intention of leading to the creation of more accomplished artworks, it is essential for social critique in the narrow sense that it be motivated by the intention to actually be effective with regard to its object. Therefore, this kind of social critique must always consider whether it can be rationally motivating for those to whom it is directed.[11]

2.1 INTERNAL AND EXTERNAL CRITIQUE

The question whether social critique can be rationally motivating for its addressees can serve to structure an overview of the field of existing theories of criticism. However, this is a question that has only recently become a central point of contention. The first generations of Frankfurt School critical theorists were still able to adopt the idea of social critique with relatively little hesitation from the Enlightenment tradition on the one hand and from Marxism on the other; by contrast, in the second half of the twentieth century, under the impact of the disastrous consequences of political experiments, the normative foundations of social critique as a whole came into question. The question of the justification of social critique has therefore become a focus of debate in political philosophy over the last thirty years.

A common distinction in this debate is that between *internal* and *external* critique.[12] External critique is criticism that – put roughly – does not assume that it depends on assumptions about the normative beliefs, practices or relationships of its addressees in order to be justified.

External critique relies on standards that are taken to be valid independently of context and, in principle, to apply universally.[13] In particular, it is assumed that the validity of the norms it appeals to does not depend on their acceptance by the people it criticizes. Its standards therefore refer to norms that are taken to be 'objectively valid', applicable beyond those who implicitly or explicitly agree with them.

External criticism is, in short, criticism that can in principle be exercised without consultation with and without knowledge of – even 'from the outside' – the normative convictions of those it criticizes. Although not all models of external, or 'strong', critique that follow the 'path of discovery'[14] exhibit all of these characteristics, they nonetheless rest on the central claim that such critique is feasible and legitimately applicable even if the subjects of that criticism do not share the standards on which it is based.

Internal, 'weak' social critique, however, is critique that always (at least) refers to local, context-specific standards that are presupposed not because of their *objective* validity but because they are implicitly or explicitly *accepted*. To be justified, this form of critique need not assume that its norms are 'objectively valid' but only that they are de facto accepted. This form of critique therefore presupposes knowledge of the accepted normative standards of those it criticizes. It argues from the perspective of the members of the criticized practices and accordingly cannot claim universal validity.[15]

This difference between internal and external critique is well established in the literature, but different authors have justified it in different ways and have in fact run several distinctions together: that between normative realism and normative subjectivism, between universalist and particularist moral values, distinctions relating to the motivational force of normative arguments and possibly other distinctions.

One immediately encounters problems in finding a real case of 'external critique'. On closer inspection, all candidate models of supposedly 'external' critique turn out to assume, more or less covertly, that the standards they apply are implicitly shared by the subjects of that criticism. Were this not the case, then their activity would not count as an instance of social critique in the narrow sense. This is because criticism cannot claim to aim to deliver motivating reasons to change the behaviour of its targets if it remains completely disconnected from them.[16]

Suppose, for example, that a social critic draws their standards from the self-understanding of their own society and is confronted with a hitherto unknown culture whose social practices they find wrong, inhumane and indefensible to the highest degree. We might describe such a critic as accepting that the standard they are using is not de facto shared by the people to whom it is being applied and as nonetheless insisting that the latter's practices are false from a 'universally valid perspective'. This would then indeed be a form of 'external social critique' in the wider sense, but no longer in the narrow sense; such a critic must realize that this alleged universal perspective – on the basis of which they are reasoning – cannot be a source of motivating reasons for those they are criticizing (assuming, for the moment, that there are no means available to make them switch to the perspective of the critic). The alleged objective reasons are 'intrinsically unavailable' to them.[17] If we understand such an approach as a case of purely 'external' critique, it therefore does not belong to social critique in the narrower sense.

We can describe this critic's conduct more precisely if we assume that they are operating on the conviction that the wrongness of their addressees' actions *can be made available* in a more or less complicated way to those addressees. How can this be, however, if the addressees cannot *in principle* take up a perspective that makes these reasons available to them? Even if one admits that there are cases where wholly new reasons that were previously unavailable to people can only be disclosed through critique, social critique still needs to refer in some way to the 'internal' normative dispositions of those whom it criticizes. Therefore, it cannot fulfil the requirement that external critique be entirely independent of such a connection.[18] This explains why it is so difficult to find genuine cases of external social critique. Any form of critique that initially appears as external criticism and that wants to belong to social critique in the narrower sense is necessarily put in the awkward position of having to accept 'internal' elements.

Things are different with internal critique. One can undoubtedly find examples of this form of critique in many actual social conflicts. Any form of criticism that takes up laws, statutes, moral rules or religious texts and that employs these accepted standards to evaluate concrete practices without more than trivial reinterpretation is a case of internal critique. Even if interpretative differences can never be wholly ruled out, there are still clear cases of arguments in which such an application of accepted norms is possible in an almost automatic way – for example, in the many cases in which clear violations of human rights statutes are criticized. These simple cases hardly play a role in the philosophical debate, however.

The theories that are usually classified as models of internal critique, such as Michael Walzer's, go beyond this simple model and focus on the more theoretically complex cases in which norms are not merely *applied* but must first be *interpreted* as part of a social conflict. As soon as the question of interpretation arises, so too does the question of the standards of *correctness of understanding*. If we take this problem seriously, it becomes apparent that the question of the extent to which an 'internal' critique draws *only* on the normative resources already accepted in the community it is being applied to is by no means trivial.

This shows that a vague distinction between 'internal' and 'external' critique is unhelpful. It leads to external critique's becoming a mere residual category of forms of criticism that are not in a position to make their implicit premises explicit. Furthermore, various strategies are often combined under the label 'internal critique', the 'internal' character of which is by no means obvious. It is thus more helpful to make the following distinction:[19]

- Forms of criticism should be called *external* if, with respect to the structure of the reasons they bring forth, they do *not* only depend on assumptions

about which normative obligations are *accepted* by the addressed persons. External critique can therefore in principle be aimed at introducing *new* normative standards into the practices it criticizes.
- *Internal critique*, by contrast, is criticism that refers *exclusively* to the *explicitly recognized normative standards* that are present in a community, practice or group of people and that presumes their validity for the project of criticizing them.[20]

This distinction is conceptually precise and has the advantage of corresponding to the main intuitions in the literature: forms of critique that are exclusively based on constructivist justifications of norms or on religious revelation can be placed in the category of external critique, while the usual case of a normative discussion conducted in a group with a shared understanding represents an instance of internal critique. That means, however, that some models that are often regarded as examples of 'internal' critique – such as Walzer's – can no longer be understood as exclusively conducted 'internally' and must rather be seen as examples of a yet to be explained form of immanent critique.[21]

2.2 RATIONALITY AND CRITIQUE

All forms of critique must fulfil certain minimal requirements in order to be comprehensible as forms of criticism at all. Criticism is always a *normative* undertaking that applies normative standards to particular beliefs, attitudes, actions or action-contexts, such that the relevant norms (at least initially) apply to its object independently of whether that object already complies with them.

In almost all actual cases, however, social critique is not a matter of applying *any* norms whatsoever. Rather, those engaged in social criticism are ultimately always motivated by their *own* normative convictions. That is, social critique is not a matter of norms as abstract objects; it always proceeds from the critic's active attitude towards the world. This attitude is expressed through their critical activity. Insofar as this attitude is reflexive, one can say that critics must be committed to the norms they apply and that these norms must necessarily appear to them as *justified*.[22]

Counterexamples to this claim are seemingly found in those cases of internal critique where a critic only points out an inconsistency between someone else's actions and normative convictions, without necessarily being committed to the norms at issue themselves. Although such cases are of course possible, we are dealing here with borderline cases that should not be raised to the position of paradigmatic examples. It is only rarely the case that people criticize another person's inconsistency without further normative goals and while remaining fully indifferent to the further question of *which* norms are at stake. The atheist who points out the inconsistency between the moral postulates of the Bible and the actual behaviour of their fellow citizens who claim to be Christians is not indifferent to which direction the resolution of this inconsistency takes. Rather, their hope is that, by referring to the Bible, they will motivate others to change their behaviour in a way that the critic prefers for other (their 'own') reasons. As the critic may have reason to believe that their fellow citizens will not easily accept these reasons, they draw on those reasons that their audience already accepts, without sharing them themselves. This, however, raises the question of the extent to which such argumentation still deserves to be called 'critique'. For anyone who has abandoned hope of convincing others through offering reasons they can accept, but who still desires to see a particular change in others' behaviour, there is ultimately no choice but to make use of those arguments that de facto offer the greatest chance of changing others' behaviour in the desired way, even if the critic views these arguments as not only unconvincing but morally reprehensible. Someone who is threatened by right-wing, racist violence, for example, could perhaps successfully appeal to ideas of 'manly honour' that the attackers accept and that disallow attacking the defenceless. This would no longer be criticism, however, but manipulation (as understandable and justified as such manipulation might be given the situation).[23]

Social critique (in the narrower sense) is therefore always connected to the objective of bringing other actors to change their behaviour, practices or social circumstances *through making good reasons available to them*. By this I mean not only that the objective is to have these others act in a way that is motivated by particular reasons, but also that the change in their behaviour should be accompanied by a change to the 'structure' of their reasons for action, either such that new, good reasons become effective or the relative weight of reasons in their motivational structure changes, or such that good reasons, which are already available but ineffective, are motivationally 'activated'.

But this criterion is not yet sufficient to distinguish genuine criticism from manipulation. One could imagine a group of pacifists publicly advocating a small war in the hope that its terrible effects will open the eyes of the public to reasons to avoid war at all cost. They would thereby 'make available' reasons to others that the pacifists themselves take to be normatively convincing. This is clearly not a case of criticism but of political manipulation, even if the critics' actions aim to allow (good) reasons to take effect.

Therefore, a further requirement must be fulfilled for criticism to become genuine social critique in the narrower sense. Social critique in this narrower sense is a process that is essentially accomplished with the assistance of speech acts in the widest sense, in which the reasons the critic views as sufficient for the change in behaviour are *thematized*. Such a speech act does not necessarily need to consist in the explicit articulation and discussion of reasons. Literary, artistic and performative acts are also appropriately called acts of critique so long as they not only *result* in the thematization of the corresponding reasons but (also) make these reasons *available* through the act itself.

As reasons do not have a context-free existence and can only ever be reasons *for somebody*, it follows immediately from the premises just set out that for social critique in the narrower sense, the reasons must be such that they can in principle become motivating reasons both for the critic and for the addressee (who is often identical to the subject of the criticism). The reference to the future is appropriate here because the reasons at issue need not be reasons for all involved from the outset. This would unduly limit criticism to what has thus far been termed 'internal critique'. Rather, through changing the perception of particular phenomena such that new, previously unaccepted reasons are disclosed, certain forms of critique show that we can bring other people to accept as reasons considerations that they would have previously rejected.[24] Different forms of moral constructivism, for example, do not hold that their principles of justice are acceptable a priori but rather attempt to establish them – through the very process of construction – as *reasons* for the creation of particular institutions.

This characterization of social critique in the narrower sense does not make it trivial. That certain considerations are or could be reasons for the addressees of criticism is always a disputable claim in need of justification. Any strategy that does not include the accepted self-understanding of the parties concerned from the outset must, if it is to count as a model of critique in this narrower sense, prove that its reasons could also function as reasons for those to whom it is addressed.[25] Social critique (in the narrower sense) can therefore be characterized in the following ways:

Social critique (in the narrower sense) is an activity

1. in which social practices are thematized that are relevant to an entire society or large parts of that society;
2. in which these practices are deliberately described and measured against norms or evaluative standards, in a way suited to making reasons for a (negative) assessment of and change to these practices accessible;

3. that is characterized by a belief on the part of the critics that the reasons they are offering are rationally sufficient to justify the proposed change to the practices;
4. that is characterized by the belief and the aim, on the part of the critics, that those who can change these practices could in principle be rationally motivated, through the thematization of these reasons, to change these practices to better realize these norms or evaluative standards.

2.3 RECONSTRUCTIVE AND IMMANENT CRITIQUE

Even when adequately revised, this chapter's opening distinction between 'internal' and 'external' critique remains problematic. This is because it conveys the false impression that we have to decide between an external form of criticism that is independent of *all* recognized norms and an internal form of criticism that is only supported by *explicitly recognized* norms.

However, there appears to be a range of forms of social critique that do not easily fit this alternative. For example, scholars have drawn on the work of Friedrich Nietzsche and Michel Foucault to develop forms of genealogical critique. Genealogical critique, in this context, reconstructs the origin of a particular form of normative order in a way that discloses that order as objectionable for those subject to it. Such a reconstruction does more than merely deploy accepted norms against this order.[26] Richard Rorty – to take a second example – proposes that we supplement traditional forms of critique, which he understands as solutions to problems, with forms in which new 'vocabularies' allow us to develop new forms of moral perception, which then lead to critiques of existing practices.[27] Both genealogical and disclosing criticism bring established norms partly into question, but they understand their task not solely as measuring prevailing practices against the norms they claim to fulfil. They aim rather at transforming the whole normative situation, which comprises both norms and practices.

In what follows, I will focus on a further alternative. A central claim of all classical forms of critical theory is that they provide a further form of social critique beyond internal and external criticism. This is most often called 'reconstructive' or 'immanent' social critique.[28] Reconstructive or immanent social critique is not content to incorporate the explicitly recognized norms of a community but attempts, in addition, to reconstruct the *normative commitments that are implicit* in social practices.

The 'objects' of any such reconstruction are therefore the *real conditions, de facto social practices and implicit understandings of a social community*, which go beyond explicit beliefs. In this sense, Axel Honneth describes reconstructive critique as being based on the notion that only those principles or ideals which have already taken some form in the present social order can serve as a valid basis for social critique. In this case, normative claims or ideas internal to social reality are merely reconstrued, their transcendent character permitting the extant social order to be subjected to a justified critique.[29]

That critique should take this form is not only a central requirement from the perspective of the self-conception of critical social theory.[30] This model is also a live option for a theory of social critique because we can only understand many cases of actual critique as featuring critics who refer to norms that are neither reducible to explicitly recognized standards nor introduced independently of the social conditions.

Even though a detailed discussion of actual cases of political criticism clearly cannot be attempted here, an example makes clear that such forms of criticism in fact exist. The debate currently being conducted in both Europe and the United States on the future of healthcare,[31] for example, cannot be understood solely as an argument about the application of socially accepted principles. Nor is it the case, however, that the moral or other normative calls for justice by the agents in these debates are raised from the standpoint of externally justified theories. Rather, two fundamentally different understandings of the character of the healthcare system clash in this debate.

One can therefore better understand this debate if one recognizes that one side of the conflict – which is pleading for the expansion of the principle of solidarity – represents principles that give rise to an understanding of members of society as reciprocally reliant on each other's aid and is motivated by the principled conviction that our existential needs raise moral demands on each other. The other side – which argues for the strengthening of individual responsibility – relates to the institutionalized principle that other people are allowed to compel our continual cooperation only insofar as we consent, and only insofar as we can understand these obligations as an expression of our own decisions.

These two understandings of the normative social context of the healthcare system are not contingent cultural artefacts, however, but rather expressions of fundamentally different *practice-based forms of communal life* (governed by ideals of solidarity between members and of the freedom of autonomous market participants) which are *both* grounded in the institutional structure of society. We must therefore understand the demands of those involved as demands for change with respect to both the existing practice of healthcare and the norms that apply to it, which are based on what they understand as the guiding principles of our common practice – principles that are not explicitly accepted by all but that are *already institutionalized* in that practice. Both sides in this debate appeal to our practical disposition towards solidarity or, respectively, to our practical understanding of autonomy. Both sides therefore attempt at least to appeal to immanent norms and – insofar as they aim to make their normative foundations explicit – to reconstruct them.

Reconstructive or immanent social critique is therefore not merely an abstract model but gives us resources for understanding actually existing forms of criticism. The motivating idea behind any such model of critique is, quite apart from its analytical strength, also attractive from a normative point of view. The model of immanent critique avoids the obvious problems that affect external forms of critique, such as the suspicion that the social critic is claiming an ideologically founded authority that is unintelligible from the perspective of those they criticize, or the problem of how those who are being criticized could be convinced or motivated by arguments that are cognitively unavailable from their standpoint. It also avoids the shortcomings of internal forms of critique: it need not exclude from criticism those practices that result in the production of systematically unacceptable normative beliefs. Unlike internal critique, immanent critique can also criticize practices that consist in oppressing social groups through denying them the means to develop their demands in the form of explicit principles.

Yet the attractiveness of the idea that critique can refer to immanent norms seems to come at the cost, at least in part, of ambiguity. It is difficult to determine exactly what it means to reconstruct normative claims from the practices or the self-understanding of a community. In particular, it is unclear what the *object* of such a reconstruction could be, how we might *cognitively grasp* the norms contained therein, and in what way such a reconstruction makes 'new' normative *reasons* available.

To clarify these questions, it is necessary to differentiate between two methodological options when it comes to immanent or reconstructive social critique. I will call these the *hermeneutic model* and the *practice-based model*.

The hermeneutic model of immanent social critique is based on two assumptions: first, that immanent critique reconstructs its norms from the *self-understanding* of a community, and second, that this reconstruction amounts to a process of *understanding or interpretation*, which can be described as broadly analogous to our understanding of linguistic utterances. This model, as represented by Michael Walzer, Charles Taylor and others, is relatively close to the internal critique model insofar as the hermeneutic model is primarily oriented towards eliminating inconsistencies in the 'actual' (that is, explicit) normative self-understanding of a community through criticism, and, if appropriate, towards making conflicts among individual elements of this self-understanding explicit.

By contrast, representatives of practice-based immanent critique proceed on the assumption that social reality also allows for the discovery of new normative resources that can serve as points of departure for critique *beyond the self-understanding* of the members of a given practice. They therefore assume that critique is more than participation in the process of self-interpretation on the part of a community and that independently acquired *knowledge of social reality* may also be a necessary component of reconstructing critical standards (even if such knowledge alone may not be sufficient).[32] The fundamental assumption of such practice-based forms of immanent critique is that social criticism need not justify its standards from an independent, external perspective; instead, social criticism can show that standards are already contained *in social reality itself*. This assumption is one of the few elements shared not only by the Frankfurt School and Marx but also by all three generations of Frankfurt School critical theorists and by forms of social critique inspired by Marxism in the widest sense. These *classical* approaches to immanent critique share with hermeneutic models the general assumption that the norms that they apply are in some sense immanent in reality. They go beyond this general assumption, however, as they assume not only that every social practice carries a normative standard in itself, by which it can be measured, but that in modern practices, especially the practices of bourgeois society, norms can be identified that are in some sense *contradictory*. This classical approach is therefore a specific form of what I would like to call the basic model of immanent critique, which adds further stipulations that are not already given in the idea of practice-based immanence itself.

It is therefore necessary to carefully examine the justificatory burden borne by specific theories of immanent critique in each case. To this end, it seems reasonable to distinguish between basic questions concerning the immanent existence of normative potentials – questions that all theories of immanent critique must answer – and a series of further questions that only relate to specific theories of immanent critique.

2.3.1. Fundamental Questions: Immanent Normativity, Epistemology, Progress

Both hermeneutic and practice-based models of immanent critique assume that either the *self-understanding* that is constitutive of the social practices of a society or those *practices themselves* contain normative commitments that can be reconstructed and taken up by the critic.

From the perspective of an idea that many find self-evident – namely, the idea of a 'value-free social science' – this immediately raises the question of what exactly is meant by the claim that norms are 'contained in the practice itself' or in the self-understanding of that practice, which go beyond the explicitly accepted norms of the members of the relevant society. Most approaches in social science accept the idea that there are norms towards which agents in a practice are *subjectively orientated*. Depending on their stance on issues in philosophy of science, many approaches also recognize that the values that underlie any particular description of a practice form a part of that description. Both 'acceptable' forms of normativity – referring to the subjective norms of the participants and the subjective norms of the observers – do not, however, relate to that which the concept of the immanent norms of a practice aims to pick out. These assumptions are therefore not sufficient to make the possibility of immanent critique comprehensible.

On the one hand, reference to the norms that guide the theorist's analysis of a social practice is insufficient for a theory of immanent critique because these norms remain external to the practice at issue, even if they influence the description of the criticized reality. If those norms are applied in critique, they derive from the perspective of the critics and not from the reality that is being criticized. If, on the other hand, critique takes up norms that are found in the actual subjective value orientations of those agents whose behaviour it investigates and criticizes, this basis only allows for an internal form of critique.

Immanent critique, by contrast, aims to transcend the self-understanding of the members of a practice, which is why it is essential not to search for normative potentials only in the empirically discoverable, subjective beliefs or value orientations of individual actors but to go beyond them. As already suggested, there are two options: on the one hand, one can start with their self-understanding and attempt, using hermeneutic methods, to achieve a *better* understanding of its meaning than is currently available to the agents themselves, taking the resulting difference between the self-ascription and this better understanding as a basis for critique. On the other hand, the self-understanding of the agents can be construed by social science as part of a more comprehensive context of actions, beliefs and dispositions, which I have called 'social practice'. This second option implies that the normative content, which underlies immanent critique, can be found in *structures of social practices*. This thesis, on which critical theory has always relied but which it has rarely spelled out, is a *social ontological* thesis that has yet to be given a more precise meaning.

The central problem that motivates this discussion can be summed up as follows: w*hat does it mean to claim that social practices can have a normative content beyond the actual, subjective self-understanding of the agents?* Answering this question is the primary and central problem of the theory of immanent critique, which in the following will be the focus of my discussion.

Apart from this first problem, there are two further problems that arise from this social ontological question. The second concerns how we can *gain knowledge* about the normative potentials to which immanent critique refers. The answer will obviously depend on the answer to the first question. Which form of knowledge is possible depends on the nature of what there is to be known. I would like to term this problem the *epistemological problem of immanent criticism*.

Finally, the third problem concerns the question of how criticism, by means of these norms, can determine changes in social practices as *better* or *worse*. To achieve a full concept of immanent critique, the social ontological model must be able to reveal not only the norms that can be used to legitimately criticize and change a concrete practice, but also how, in concrete disputes, the realization of particular alternatives can be *rationally demanded* of the parties involved. It must also show that there are cases in which these immanent norms, alongside the fact of their – yet to be explained – existence, can also have *action-orienting normative force*.

Even if one does not have to endorse the claim that the best option in a practical conflict must always be derived purely deductively from empirical facts and normative principles, one must justify, in the course of an argumentative controversy, why one believes that one concretely demanded change to a practice is *better* than the available alternatives and not merely *different*. It does not help to point out that a particular change could be *retrospectively* seen as justified – the function of a call for progress is a function of justification, not merely of retrospective description. I will call this the *problem of progress*.

2.3.2. The Classical Model of Immanent Critique

These fundamental questions concern the idea of immanent critique in its most general form. In the history of philosophy, the problem of immanent critique has been thematized above all in the tradition of critical social theory, which has its beginnings in Hegel and which found its first paradigmatic expression in Marx's work, before, in the twentieth century, being further developed by Western Marxism, the Frankfurt School as well as other theories drawing inspiration from this tradition.

When taking up this tradition, we face not only the problem that we must interpret these historical models (which we no longer find immediately plausible) so as to reappropriate their rational content, but also the problem that these models each take on such specific justificatory burdens that it is difficult to develop a unified theory of immanent critique that can subsume them all. For this reason, I will not attempt to reconstruct these classical models in the following. Nevertheless, it is worth spelling out a number of specific questions that arise with regard to this tradition. To this end, I will briefly sketch

(a) the role of conceptions of immanent normativity in Marx and Hegel and (b) the essential characteristics of the 'classical' form of immanent critique.

(a) Excursus: The original model of immanent critique. What are the theoretical assumptions that lie in the background of the history of the development of immanent critique? As will be shown, these are assumptions that cannot simply be expressed in a contemporary philosophical vocabulary and that therefore can only inform the discussion from the outside – yet precisely for this reason it is worth casting at least a brief glance at both Hegel's and Marx's fundamental premises.

(i) Hegel. Hegel's notorious remark that what is actual (*wirklich*) is also rational (*vernünftig*)[33] expresses the fundamental premise underlying Hegelian methods of immanent critique: namely, that 'actuality', or social reality, itself contains rational norms. This thesis of the immanent normativity of social reality clearly does not mean that Hegel assumes that every empirically encountered, subjectively accepted normative belief is rational or justified. Hegel instead proceeds from specific concepts of actuality and rationality. What Hegel terms 'actual' always refers to concepts and commitments that, in the course of rational investigation, prove to be *justifiable* and that we therefore distinguish from 'mere' opinions (just like in ordinary language, where saying that something is 'actually' an X means that we are referring to a particular quality that is contrary to appearances).[34] Furthermore, according to Hegel, commitments that grasp 'actuality' (*Wirklichkeit*) are not statements about any facts whatsoever but rather represent knowledge regarding the justification of particular forms of *institutionalized conceptual practice and knowledge*. To say that something is *actual* (a state, for example) is to take ourselves to be justified – by our best standards concerning a particular institutionalized form of conceptual engagement with reality – in believing that this form is the most appropriate conceptual form to capture our reality (in the case of a state, we must take ourselves to be justified with regard to a self-understanding that captures a specific structure of rights and obligations that make up that state).

Hegel's definition of 'actuality' (*Wirklichkeit*) is thus concerned with capturing something about those socially shared standards of reasoning that result from our best available understanding of knowledge and justification. Behind this insistence on the importance of the social, institutional reality of the relevant norms for conceptual thought stands the conviction that a constructivist method, which attempts to create the conceptual standards of our thought from nothing (without falling back on already existing institutions and theories that allow us to determine what, in concrete cases, are justified and true statements), is equivalent to attempting to learn to swim before getting in the water.[35] In contrast to this 'external' method, Hegel proceeds on the basis that the standards that philosophical criticism should employ must already be found in social reality, namely, in the institutionalized, rule-governed and reciprocally supporting practices of justification that he calls '*Geist*'.[36] If we want to conduct science (*Wissenschaft*), according to Hegel, we have no choice but to proceed from the best contemporary forms of such structures.

This does not mean, however, that a given historical form of such institutional practices is a quasi-transcendental conceptual scheme, which is not accessible to our critical judgement. Rather, those rules that constitute the structure of '*Geist*' are *themselves* assessable according to the standards of justification they contain and are therefore *themselves changeable through those standards*. '*Geist*' therefore has a reflexive structure.

This ultimately leads to a model of immanent critique: within the self-understanding that a particular community adopts regarding its practices of justification and knowledge, there are always normative standards that allow us to examine whether what is characterized *by* this self-understanding as a *sufficient, good reason* only *appears* to be such, or whether it indeed *is* such a reason.[37]

But *to be able to pose* such a critical question about the justification of one's own standards at all, a practice must have already brought its own rules and foundational principles to the level of conceptually explicit formulations. This means that it must make its own constitutive standards *explicit*. When a practice becomes explicit in this way, its members can develop a form of self-consciousness that goes beyond a purely practical or intuitive recognition of the practice's standards. If this level of reflexivity is achieved, the conceptual relations that are constitutive rules of the practice can be *thematized* on the level of propositional statements. Practices that achieve this level of self-consciousness and make their own rules explicitly assessable will therefore allow agents to perceive *contradictions within these practices*. If a given formulation of those rules that, as a form of self-consciousness, are essential to the relevant practice is no longer justified according to the practice's own standards of justification in a given case, the practice's entire ability to authoritatively decide on questions of justification comes into question.

This complex picture of institutionalized criteria of justification has two consequences for the resulting understanding of 'critique'. First, a theoretical discussion of the rules of practices that are capable of producing knowledge must always take up their own reflexive concepts; that is, it must make use of those propositional statements in which the constitutive conceptual distinctions of the practice can be made explicit. Second, our endorsement of the concepts of any such practice always falls under the caveat that its own standards of justification could turn out to be unfulfillable and to lead to sceptical dilemmas. This is what Hegel calls the 'negativity of concepts';[38] if the rules of a practice of justification, which are initially only practically grasped by those engaged in it, are brought into the form of an explicit, systematic rule system, those norms, which at the level of action may have only raised *incompatible* demands, become propositional *contradictions*.[39] If such a contradictory structure is made explicit, this constitutes a *crisis* in the justificatory practice.[40] Such a crisis is a condition in which contradictions are disclosed, and thereby the present self-understanding of the practice not only becomes unsustainable but must become actively committed to its own replacement.

Hegel understands his method of immanent critique as bringing two elements into view at the same time: on the one hand, the *social practices* that underlie any form of 'objective spirit' and any form of knowledge, and on the other hand, the *systems of propositional statements and rules* in which any such practice describes its own commitments and thereby becomes conscious of itself. Critique must always proceed from the given self-understanding of any such practice but does not merely abide by this self-understanding; it can always *additionally* raise the question whether this self-understanding is an accurate description in light of its own standards of knowledge. In addition to this, immanent critique can further question whether the self-understanding is *justified* by its own standards. This second aspect points to a possibility not afforded by a purely internal form of critique – namely, that the self-understanding of a community, as soon as it is checked against its own standards, may end up being inconsistent and hence in need of revision according to those standards.

This (very brief) account of Hegel's method discloses two elements that are definitive of the classical form of immanent critique: first, the question of the extent to which explicit self-descriptions of semantically rich practices are accepted not only as standards for critique but also as testable with regard to their accuracy; second, the idea that the standards to be found in the implicit norms that are constitutive of a particular practice can be inconsistent in a particular way, and that this inconsistency demands not the adaption of the practice to the norms but rather a revision of both norms and practice.

(ii) Marx. Marx employs both of these characteristics of immanent critique. Like Hegel, he demands of his contemporaries that, rather than merely confronting reality with standards justified *independently of it*,[41] they show that the preconditions of a given form of social critique are contained in the criticized practices themselves. Unlike Hegel, however, Marx does not want to approach practices through the *self-understanding* of a particular form of '*Geist*'. Instead, Marx believes that this mode of critique gives too much room to the preexisting self-understanding of a society – which, in his opinion, is nothing more than a reflection of an underlying, *nontheoretical*

practice. Moreover, unlike Hegel, he does not assume that there is a substantive, unified model of justification and reason to be reconstructed from actual social practices. He understands the social practices of all historical societies as fundamentally divided and ruptured, such that a given self-conception always only expresses the viewpoint of the currently victorious party in practical conflicts.

Marx therefore devises a model of social critique that refers to the norms that underlie the given social practices of a society but that does not – as Hegel does – rest with an evaluation of their internal rationality. Rather, Marx claims, social critique can reveal an opposition between the supposedly *universal form* of historically specific self-conceptions and their actual *partisan content* to create a basis for a more thoroughgoing critique that transcends the practices at issue and that demands a transition to different social practices.

As already implied, Marx will demonstrate that *necessary antagonisms* (or 'contradictions') can be found in the objective normative structures of concrete social practices and that such antagonisms form a basis for immanent critique.[42] This also means that Marx's understanding of immanent critique as an explication of implicit normative commitments differs from Hegel's. That is, Marx understands immanent critique as an explication not of those normative commitments that underlie a particular form of *knowledge and justification*, but of those norms that are at the root of the internal contradictoriness of particular *forms of material social practice*. This explication is at the same time critique when it accurately describes these norms in their problematic structure.

Marx writes that his criticism

> includes in its positive understanding of what exists a simultaneous recognition of its negation, its inevitable destruction; because it regards every historically developed form as being in a fluid state, in motion, and therefore grasps its transient aspect as well; and because it does not let itself be impressed by anything, being in its very essence critical and revolutionary.[43]

In this sense, for example, Marx analyses the fact that the practices of the capitalist economy, on the one hand, are structured by norms that demand and functionally necessitate particular normative orientations on the part of its members – towards ideals of formal freedom and equality – but, on the other hand, are constitutively incapable of satisfying these norms.[44]

Here we can distinguish between an argument that, on a purely *descriptive* level, reveals the functionally problematic character of these arrangements and a *normative* argument that confronts the normative orientations that are constitutive of a given practice with incompatible conditions of the existence of that same practice, normatively condemning the practice on that basis.[45]

According to Marx, this form of (immanent) critique is distinct from any 'vulgar criticism' that argues merely 'internally' (for which Proudhon is his favoured example) by virtue of the fact that it can clarify *why* the contradictions between necessary normative orientations and actual practice *must be systematically produced*. That is, while immanent critique employs the contradiction between normatively generated orientations and practices in order to criticize both norms and practice (by showing the necessarily problematic structure of these relationships), internal critique merely shows that these norms have not been fulfilled and does not take an interest in the fact that this failure of fulfilment is not merely contingent but a necessary part of the social practice itself (like the norms themselves).[46] Marx accordingly criticizes 'vulgar criticism' as a form of internal criticism:

> Vulgar criticism falls into an opposite, dogmatic error. Thus it criticises the constitution, for example. It draws attention to the antagonism of the powers, etc. It finds contradictions everywhere. This is still dogmatic criticism which fights with its subject-matter in the same way in which formerly the dogma of the Holy Trinity, say, was demolished by the contradiction of one and three. True criticism, by contrast, shows the inner genesis of the Holy Trinity in the human brain. It describes the act of its birth. So the truly philosophical criticism of the present state constitution not only shows up contradictions as existing; it explains them, it comprehends their genesis, their necessity.[47]

Marx's conception of immanent critique therefore calls not merely for a *comparison* between norm and reality but for an *elucidation of the necessity* of the mismatch between norm and reality, based on an explanatory theory. Immanent critique does not naively assert that certain norms could and should be met but rather uncovers *why* the violation of these norms is necessary rather than contingent.

As Georg Lohmann observes,[48] this model of immanent critique is not fully satisfactory. Marx achieves sociological credibility through distinguishing his position from internally dogmatic critique because he does not consider the existence of moral and social norms independently of the social dynamics of their nonfulfilment, and because his account does not present merely a normative demand but rather a theory-based analysis. But it remains unclear which *critical consequences* follow from this model. As long as immanent critique only *observes* the contradictoriness of its objects of enquiry, it can only draw the relatively abstract conclusion that contradictory practices should be replaced by less contradictory practices. It cannot, however, justify why a *particular* resolution of the contradiction should be demanded. Marx can no longer make use of the resources afforded by reference to a better form of justification, which is available to Hegel's analysis of forms of consciousness in the *Phenomenology of Spirit*. This raises the question whether Marx's model of immanent critique can justify any normative judgements that go beyond the mere disclosure of contradictions. This model of immanent critique is missing the element that would allow it to justify the demand for *particular* changes or – put differently – that would allow it to call the results of any such classically immanent critique a *learning process*.

(b) A model of the classical form of immanent critique. A modernized version of the Marxist model of immanent criticism can be found if one connects the (general) thesis of the implicit normativity of social practices to a methodology of the demonstration of *constitutive contradictions*. In addition to the idea of immanent normativity, the classical model further assumes that it is at least sometimes the case that there are norms that constitutively give a contradictory structure to social practices – that is, it is constitutive of a practice that participants *orient themselves to certain norms*, but at the same time the *realization* of this orientation is *systematically prevented*.[49] The contradictoriness of social practices is therefore not immediate – it is not the case that the norms of a practice simply prescribe incompatible courses of action. Instead, the contradiction is *practically mediated*. This means that a practice is constituted by an array of normative orientations that are essential to the description and functions of the practice, but, at the same time, the practice that is thereby constituted must systematically frustrate these normative orientations.[50]

As we saw in our discussion of Marx, a further third claim must be added to the theses of immanent normativity and constitutive contradictoriness in order to actually arrive at the classical concept of immanent critique. Immanent critique cannot stop at the *description* of the contradiction. Rather, it must show that this contradiction can at least in principle be resolved. It can only demand that these practices change when they can be changed for the better. Therefore, immanent critique must presuppose that there is a potential in these social practices that can justify hoping for a particular resolution of these contradictions.[51]

Immanent critique on the classical model can therefore be characterized in the following way:

- It justifies the demands it raises by drawing on norms that are neither external to the criticized practice nor restricted to those that are explicitly accepted in that practice. Rather, it draws its justification from norms that are laid out in the practice itself (this makes it immanent critique in the general sense).
- It assumes that there are norms that are constitutive of the practice at issue and that prescribe certain normative orientations for its members.

- It assumes that the practice's failure to fulfil these norms is not merely contingent.
- It aims to effect concrete changes that can resolve the criticized practice's contradictions.

While this classical model of immanent critique is not the focus of this investigation, it is an important part of the background to what follows.

Chapter Three

Interpretation and Immanent Critique

Immanent critique, I argued in the previous chapter, is a form of social practice in which people use speech acts to disclose what they take to be reasons for others to change their practices. Critique proceeds immanently when it refers to *immanent potentials* in the self-understandings or practices of those to whom it is addressed. When critique aims to forego an 'external' leverage point in this way, it raises the question of whether such a critique is capable of going beyond the explicit self-understanding of those it criticizes, or whether in fact it is confined to merely reproducing those norms that are already explicitly accepted.

One possible answer to this question will be discussed by examining 'hermeneutic models' of social critique. I use the term 'hermeneutic models' to refer to all models of social critique that attempt to explain the transcendent – and, at the same time, immanent – reference of social critique to norms in social practices as a *process of coming to a better understanding*. The first premise from which these models proceed is the claim that we cannot understand people's normative commitments if we do not recognize how these people *themselves understand* these commitments. Unlike a purely internal model of critique, however, this model does not take their self-understanding simply as a given but – and this is the second premise – holds that people's understanding of their commitments itself has a transcendent moment that critique can disclose.

Hermeneutic models further hold that the self-understandings that are to be interpreted are always already constituted by previous interpretations, which can be further developed and improved. Immanent critique therefore does not refer to 'raw data' but rather amounts to an improvement of the understanding that the interpretive community has of itself.[1]

In what follows, I will present three models of hermeneutic immanent critique that differ from each other in how they weigh the internal perspective on interpretative practices against the external perspective. The first model, exemplified by Michael Walzer's approach (section 3.1), views interpretation as an aspect of political critique that cannot be characterized from an external perspective. The second model, laid out by Charles Taylor (section 3.2), offers a comprehensive methodological characterization of the social role of interpretation. In the third model – exemplified by Alasdair MacIntyre's work (section 3.3) – the interpretive process is linked to social and historical dynamics that can be usefully characterized from an external perspective.

3.1. MICHAEL WALZER: THE CONNECTED CRITIC

Michael Walzer is the best-known advocate of the idea of 'interpretive social critique'.[2] He advances the idea that the core of social critique consists in an interpretive, hermeneutic approach to the values and norms of a community. Walzer claims that if we understand social critique not as detached from concrete everyday life but rather as participating in one way or another in discussions that are already occurring in a community, we cannot understand the social critic as a distant observer but must understand her as a partial member of the community who is developing an argument as a participant in an ongoing conflict. An interpretive or 'connected' critique is, from Walzer's perspective, a superior alternative to two other ways of conducting social critique, which he terms 'discovery' and 'invention'.

I will first briefly lay out these other two ways (section 3.1.1) before then examining Walzer's argument for interpretive critique (section 3.1.2). In a third step (section 3.1.3), I will examine the epistemological assumptions and the model of social change that lies at the heart of his theory.

3.1.1. Discovery, Invention and Interpretation

Walzer assumes that there is a comprehensive and ubiquitous practice of critique within all societies and that the various forms of self-understanding of the participants in this practice are reflected in the various theoretical models that can be used to comprehend it. He describes 'discovery', 'invention' and 'interpretation' as the three forms of self-understanding that can be found in philosophical discussions of critique.[3]

In short, the first approach ('discovery') consists in drawing moral norms from an independent source that does not necessarily have a connection to the moral practice of the community. The paradigmatic example of this strategy is religious epiphany, but there are also secular forms of criticism that claim to have discovered objective moral principles.[4]

Walzer claims, however, that the strategy of discovery must always fail to fulfil its claim to independence from established morality. As it is indispensable to our moral discourse to make decisions about which principles count as *candidate* moral principles by measuring them against strong intuitions we already have about central cases of their application, the strategy of discovery can never lead us very far from our already established morality.[5]

John Rawls's philosophy represents a paradigmatic example of the strategy of 'invention' or moral constructivism:[6] 'inventive' methods are those that generate new moral standards by means of a *method* that is held to guarantee the correctness of the resulting moral standards. Walzer does not claim that such a procedure is impossible or that no interesting outcomes could result from it; he only claims that it does not go far enough. Constructivism, which removes all reference to the assumptions of specific moral systems and begins, as it were, 'from scratch', can only ever establish a weak universalistic morality because it neglects the normative resources that are exclusively laid out in existing moral systems. So long as the moral constructivist cannot show that a connection to already established principles is impermissible, it remains unclear why a functioning and convincing moral system should be replaced by such an 'invented', weak morality.[7]

Walzer therefore assumes that the approaches of both discovery and invention are so heavily dependent on the strategy of interpretation whenever they aim to produce substantial results that they must, in such cases, be understood as forms of interpretation themselves.

3.1.2 Interpretation as Paradigm

In contrast to the strategies of invention and discovery, interpretation begins not with a tabula rasa but with an already existing morality.[8] Interpretive critique consists in arguing, in the context of an existing moral tradition, about the meaning of that tradition for specific cases. Social critique in this sense is, in Walzer's view, typically delivered by 'marginal' critics,[9] who can keep a certain distance from the prevailing interpretation of social norms and practices but who are nonetheless still members of the group that is united by a common recognition of these norms.[10]

In Walzer's view, the fact that social critique typically takes this form speaks in favour of reconstructing critique on the model that hermeneutics offers. If this fact is recognized, Walzer claims, it shows that it is not only *improper* to replace this interpretative practice with the strategies of discovery or invention – due to the problems with these strategies discussed above – but also *unnecessary*. If we do not dogmatically equate a *critical* position with a *disconnected* position, but rather identify it with the position of a *distanced* or *marginal connection*, then it turns out that the practice of interpreting a given morality from such a position can be sufficiently critical.

To justify this claim, Walzer wants to show, on the one hand, that the interpretative procedure not only reproduces the prevailing norms but also takes a certain distance from them. On the other hand, he wants to show that we can still also present this distance as a form of connection. In this context, he refers to Antonio Gramsci:[11] any cultural interpretation is, according to Gramsci, always an expression of the interests of dominant social groups, but it also contains a normative surplus that never allows for full congruence between 'official' morality and the actual behaviour of the ruling classes. Precisely because the purpose of 'official morality' is the *justification* of the prevailing conditions, this morality carries the intrinsic potential for critique. The standards expressed in moral principles must always – to be able to be at least remotely convincing – be so general that they allow interpretations that cast the justification of the prevailing practices into doubt.[12] This is because – among other reasons – expressions of moral self-understanding that are intended to legitimize social practices can only develop the necessary persuasiveness if they at least minimally respect the interests of everyone involved. Therefore, they cannot be fully adapted to the contingent interests of power but always have a surplus validity, which critics can take up and use.

The common complaint[13] is the primary way the critic can deploy this surplus for their purposes. Within the scope of the common complaint, the critic can bring into focus specific, previously marginal aspects of the dominant morality and thereby attempt to not only offer an interpretation of the existing moral discourse but also effect a gradual transformation of it. Such a transformation, however, can only appear as justified if it presents itself as an *authentic clarification* of the extant morality.

Walzer's argument for understanding critique as interpretation is therefore directed not so much against the concrete models of discovery and invention themselves but rather against one of their apparent assumptions – namely, the idea of disconnected critique – and therefore against the idea that criticism of a society is better the more radically it breaks with that society's values in an attempt to solve moral problems from a putatively 'objective' standpoint.[14]

In *Interpretation and Social Criticism*, Walzer introduces numerous examples of critics who have practised 'disconnected' critique. Walzer claims that these examples of 'external' critique are (1) problematic *internally*, as their motivation cannot be rationally justified; (2) problematic *externally*, because they cannot motivate those they address; (3) problematic *morally*, because they tend to claim expert moral knowledge;[15] and (4) problematic because they ignore the moral resources already laid out in the morality of society.[16]

Successful critique – in both the empirical and the normative senses – is criticism that emphasizes the critical aspects of everyday moral discourse, which is formulated in the language of the people and that proceeds with moderate boldness and a sense of proportion.[17] It is therefore not a break with already established moral values but rather a better utilization of them – and thus, in an important sense, a form of immanent critique.

Here, however, we encounter a central and problematic assumption of this strategy: despite his anticonventionalist reading of the strategy of interpretation, Walzer must assume that societies have a *single* substantive moral structure upon which critics can draw.[18] He suggests that critique typically only discusses those alternatives that are present within a widely shared normative paradigm or normative tradition. This model is therefore insufficient if a society contains competing and incompatible traditions.[19]

3.1.3. Interpretation and Social Progress

Can Walzer's analysis of interpretive criticism put forward a form of immanent critique that goes beyond internal critique but is still not *external* criticism? In what follows, I will give four reasons to doubt that he can: *first*, Walzer incorrectly runs social and moral critique together; *second*, he can only with difficulty give any sense to the idea of critique as a justified demand for a particular change in situations of disagreement; *third*, he proceeds in a reifying and homogenizing manner from the assumption of a single, substantially shared morality; *fourth*, his model is unable to properly account for the 'form' of critical discourses.

The first critical point concerns Walzer's conflation of social and moral critique.[20] Walzer writes about the critique of ideology: 'We wait for some angry or indignant neighbor or friend or former friend, the private version of a social critic, to tell us [that our private moral beliefs do not ring true]. . . . This account of morality can be recapitulated at the level of collective life.'[21] Basically, the argument is that the method of social critique is the same as the method of private moral criticism. Such a description of social critique leaves out those essential ways in which social critique differs from 'private' moral criticism. Social critique does not primarily criticize the actions of particular people but rather social structures.[22] Accordingly, the standards of morality are often inappropriate for social critique, as they are based on the attribution of actions to persons, which is not unproblematically possible in the context of social structures, which are more or less anonymous. For this reason, social critique – unlike moral criticism – does not directly address other members of society in order to ask them to change their *individual* actions, but is rather a demand that they reflect on their *common practice*. Walzer fails to draw out this distinction, however.²³

A second problem emerges from this conflation of moral and social critique, concerning the idea of progress. This is the central idea that criticism consists in giving those it criticizes good reasons to change their behaviour in specific ways. While moral critique normally consists only in applying the correct norms to concrete actions, social critique usually aims not only to criticize individual actions but also to criticize socially accepted norms themselves. Moral critique therefore proceeds *from* socially accepted norms, while social critique brings just such norms into question. On these grounds, it seems obvious to object that Walzer's model – which takes the interpretation of norms as the central practice of social critique – is conventionalist, or even conservative.

Walzer continuously tries to ward off this impression. According to him, interpretive critique always refers to the contribution of the prevailing ideas to the justification of the prevailing practices and therefore can also demand that the norms should be interpreted in such a way that they are *actually* acceptable and capable of grounding actual justifications. Norms can be changed in the process of their application and can always be improved through new interpretations and 'narratives', and so moral changes – and therefore a change to norms – can be demanded by the 'connected critic'.²⁴ Walzer therefore also ascribes a potentially transformative function to his model: 'Social criticism in maximalist [i.e., interpretive] terms can call into question, can even overturn, the moral maximum itself, by exposing its internal tensions and contradictions.'²⁵ By demanding the *realization* of a particular system of norms, the critic can show that this system cannot be realized and is therefore not viable. Through forcing this insight, Walzer seems to argue, a normatively conservative critique can nonetheless have subversive consequences. However, this does not justify the conclusion that Walzer draws – that his model can also reconstruct the *self-understanding* of subversive critics. The subversive effect of the connected critic on local norms – if Walzer's model correctly describes the self-understanding of these critics – can only ever be an *unintended consequence*, as the 'connected' critic by definition only *applies* local norms and does not seek to undermine them. If the subversive consequences are intended, by contrast, the critic must take up a standpoint that goes beyond the local norms, as his relationship to these local norms – the inconsistency of which is already clear to him – must be of a merely tactical nature. In just this way, the connected critic takes up precisely the elitist position that Walzer wants to avoid.

Perhaps Walzer could avoid this dilemma by acknowledging that the interpretation of local norms is not immediately subversive and by instead ascribing a transformative function to such interpretation only over the long term.[26] The continual reinterpretation of shared norms can, in the long run, lead to major changes (even if not intentionally – though also not unintentionally in the narrow sense). He interprets Gramsci in this way, for example. According to this interpretation, the underdeterminedness of the respective hegemonic models of justification and the necessity of adapting the ruling ideologies to the needs of the ruled, open up the possibility of subversive readings of the ruling ideology. Through such a reading, this ideology – through a shift in emphasis – abruptly receives a prosecutory rather than a legitimatizing function.[27]

This description of the critical function of interpretation can indeed refute a simple accusation of conventionalism. The model is still unsatisfactory, however, as it says nothing about how criteria that pick out *specific* interpretations as correct can be acquired. It is not plausible to assume – especially in situations of social conflict – that a critical interpretation of norms can hope to find general acceptance automatically and thereby be absolved of the need to provide justification. In situations of social conflict, a revisionist interpretation will always be controversial. Therefore, critics cannot avoid bringing forward *reasons* as to why one interpretation excels over the others.

It is precisely the critics who argue against a mainstream interpretation of the extant norms that need to be *justified* in their interpretation. Such a critic proposes to society not only a *different* self-understanding but what is in their view a *better* self-understanding.[28] Because Walzer does not accept that it is possible to speak of reasons at all outside of the interpretation of social norms, however, he does not have much to say about this essential component of the self-understanding of all social critics.[29]

An alternative to this view consists in attempting to find critical potential not in the *explicit* values or ideas of a society but rather in the *implicit moral values* of the social practices in which particular goods are produced. Despite his express emphasis on the primacy of ideas, this appears to be Walzer's position in *Spheres of Justice* (and other texts).[30] However, the method of identifying and interpreting shared norms by means of practices has also been met with scepticism by Walzer's critics. Joshua Cohen, for example, argues that the idea that norms could be interpretively gleaned from practices leads to a 'simple communitarian dilemma':

If the values of a community are identified through its current distributive practices, then the distributive norms subsequently 'derived' from those values will not serve as criticisms of existing practices. For example, if we determine what goods a community understands as needs by considering what goods the community now distributes according to need, then we will never be in a position to judge that a community ought to distribute a good according to need, but does not. On the other hand, if we identify values apart from practices, with a view to assessing the conformity of practices to those values, what evidence will there be that we have the values right?[31]

If norms should be derived from social practices, Walzer must provide us with a method of reconstruction that clarifies how the reconstructed norms could in principle serve as authoritative reasons for people to change their practices. The model of interpretation – as Walzer understands it – is not suitable for this task.

The problem of the lack of justification of specific interpretations is also exacerbated by a broader, third ambiguity. Even if critics can convincingly argue that a particular norm should be interpreted in a particular way, they must then prove that their audience also *shares* the norm so interpreted. Whenever a conflict about the interpretation of a norm breaks out, the immediate suspicion is that this is not in fact a conflict about a shared norm at all, and that two different, similar norms have always existed side by side in the community in question. Together with the problem of competing interpretations, such a theory therefore also faces the problem of the possibility of competing norms.

This problem becomes particularly pressing when an argument is not merely a matter of different emphases within a homogeneous tradition but occurs between different traditions with their own standards of justification.[32] It is precisely in such cases that it cannot be unproblematically assumed that taking an interpretive approach to each tradition via the interpretation that is dominant in it is appropriate, as the interests expressed in *minoritarian* interpretations will then not be taken up,[33] and because the predominant self-understanding may not offer any purely internal resources to which the critic could refer.[34]

Walzer repeatedly suggests that social critique always finds a unified and clearly bounded morality as the object of its interpretation. In so doing, he overlooks the insight that an objectionable social injustice can also consist precisely in the fact that the internal, interpretive discourses of a community, on the basis of their assumption of a broad consensus concerning the themes of discussion,[35] fail to acknowledge that the validity of their interpretations is limited to a specific, particular moral tradition.

The notion of a single, uncontroversial basis of interpretation can also be contested on broader grounds. The idea of a single morality that encompasses an entire society is – at least in modern societies – at best an illusion, and at worst an ideology.[36] Beate Rössler puts the objection in the following way: '[Walzer's] fundamental concept of a political community is therefore a phantom: communities in his sense are constituted precisely not through a harmonious accordance of their members, but rather through the repressive exclusion of all those who do not want to share the desired agreement.'[37] As Walzer rightly responds to objections along these lines, not every disagreement can be taken as evidence that there are no shared norms or conventions to be interpreted. Rather, it could in principle be possible to distinguish between cases where two different interpretations of *a single* shared norm are in play and cases where *two different* norms are in play.[38] However, even if such an argument is possible in principle, Walzer offers no criteria for differentiating between cases of *interpretive difference* and deeper cases of *normative difference*.

Even if one agrees with Walzer's criticisms of invention and discovery, there is a fourth objection that follows from these arguments concerning the way Walzer fails to distinguish between two questions that should be answered separately. The first is whether the reflexive attitudes of members of a society should be the *basis for critique*. The second is whether the critics themselves *must share these attitudes*.

The first question accordingly asks whether the critic must pay attention to the attitudes of the members of a given society at all, or whether the critic's norms should be exclusively drawn from independent resources. Without a doubt, one can agree with Walzer – for the reasons already discussed – that it is problematic for a model of social critique to ignore the self-descriptions of those it criticizes. As for the second question – of whether critique should not only *recognize* the explicitly recognized norms of a community but also *make them its own* – it is not so clear how this must be answered. Even if the critic takes the explicit normative attitudes of the members of society as a starting point, there is still the possibility of a type of distance that does not amount to the 'view from nowhere' that Walzer criticizes.[39]

We can bring both our explicitly recognized principles and our social practices into view from an objective (i.e., not purely interpretive) perspective and thereby learn new things about ourselves. Even if such 'discoveries' about the potential of social practices can obviously never be fully independent of the self-description of a moral practice, it is not true that *we cannot discover anything fundamentally new* about these matters from the perspective of an observer. It is only because Walzer equates the moral practice of a society with its explicitly recognized moral ideas and norms that he can assert that any new knowledge concerning that moral practice must be understood as an *interpretation of ideas*. Even if moral discoveries – like all discoveries – never dispense with interpretive elements, such discoveries do not always only concern new interpretations of already shared beliefs, but often introduce claims about previously unacknowledged normative potentials into the interpretive discussion.

If there are other normative resources in this – still relatively vague – sense that the critic can draw on besides the explicit morality of the society at issue, this opens up not only the important possibility that people could have new experiences in relation to their moral situation from a subjective perspective, but also the more important option of critically examining, from an objectifying perspective, whether or not the explicit normative attitudes of the members of a society are expressions of their moral feelings, their habitual reactions, or even the implicit norms of their practices. The answer to these questions may well be a discovery, which may have consequences for moral practice.

3.1.4. The Prospects of Walzer's Model of Immanent Critique

In his examples, Walzer always focuses on what he takes to be the paradigm case of moral argument, in which several parties argue about the correct interpretation of their shared principles and do so without the need for an elaborate theory. However, moral argument is different from social critique: first, social critique always starts from the claim that social practices of a particular type are the cause of an allegedly suboptimal state of affairs; secondly, not only individual but, in a strong sense, *shared* norms underpin the demands to change these practices. Walzer's theory has two weaknesses with regard to shared norms. First, it cannot explain, on the basis of a model that views critique as exclusively drawing on what is explicitly given in our conversations, how certain interpretations acquire social and normative force, while others lack such force. Second, he cannot accommodate the thought that we can discover anything about our socially shared norms that is not already evident in our explicit conversations. Both weaknesses stem from the lack of a substantive theory of how normative commitments are instituted in social practices. To avoid these weaknesses, social critique must be informed by (at least) a middle-range social theory.[40] Only a social theory allows the moral attitudes of members of a society to come into view from something other than a hermeneutic point of view. A theory of immanent critique – even if one, like Walzer, wants to ascribe a certain priority to interpretation – must be concerned in this sense with mediating between an internal understanding of and external access to the norms that are valid within a community. Walzer's theory does not provide such an alternative, however.

3.2. CHARLES TAYLOR'S STRONG HERMENEUTICS

The weak model of immanent-interpretive critique developed by Walzer is unsatisfactory because it does not provide us with standards to determine when critics are justified in their interpretation of collective norms. This problem does not amount to a reason to abandon the project of understanding immanent critique as a practice of interpretation, however. This is because it is less the idea of interpretive critique in itself that is responsible for the weakness of Walzer's model and more the lack of explanation of how hermeneutic critique can become transcendent critique, that is, how it can go beyond the existing normative beliefs of members of the society in question. It is therefore worth investigating whether Walzer's model of critique cannot be supplemented by a more plausible model of interpretation. Charles Taylor has developed such a model over the last four decades.

Taylor's theory is especially well suited to clarifying the potential of the hermeneutic model as he places a *social theory of meaning* at the very centre of his work. Already in his early writings on the theory of action, Taylor argues that no account of human action that fails to integrate the irreducible dimension of the meaning that actions have for the acting subjects can be sufficient. Taylor takes a decisive step beyond Walzer's vague model of the meaning of actions by analysing this dimension of meaning within the framework of an 'expressivist' model.[41] 'Expressivism' refers to theories that do not clarify the meaning of statements or symbols through the concept of reference, or by reference to truth-conditions. Expressivist theories instead start from human action – both linguistic and nonlinguistic – and understand such action as an *expression* of meaning. The meaning of a speech act or an action therefore consists in the fact that these activities express a certain content. The content expressed by an action is not independent of that expression, however. Rather, it is only created through its expression.

For a theory of social action, this entails that the meanings of norms of social practices and institutions are only clarified and determined through the *actions* with which a community *expresses* its *commitment* to those norms. Contra Walzer's assumption, the content of a practice is not simply given and does not simply 'wait' to be interpreted. Rather, through every action that claims to give expression to the norms of a practice, the meaning of the practice is reconstituted, and thereby continually changed and expanded. This also applies conversely, however, in that every specific expression that a community gives to its norms can always be subsequently questioned as to whether it expresses the underlying content *authentically* and *articulates* it *sufficiently*, or whether it can and must be improved *as an expression* of it. Every interpretation is therefore subject to the normative demand, stemming from the interpreted and already expressed meaning, to attempt to find new and better forms of expression, which then in turn constitute new aspects of that meaning and thereby bring to light new materials for interpretation.

Because the question of meaning in an expressivist model only arises when there is an action expressing this meaning, and because any expression always raises the question of its own appropriateness, the interpretation of human action is not something that happens in addition to such action only occasionally, or in exceptional cases. Taylor, rather, assumes that the concept of action cannot be understood without reference to interpretation because, through their actions, people always react to the perceived meanings of their situation. Therefore, every form of action must be understood as already containing judgements about meanings, and therefore interpretations.

An interpretation that is brought forward in the context of a *critique* of action must therefore be understood as an improvement on an already existing interpretation, which it aims to replace with a putatively better understanding of the *same* meaning. Put differently, social critique that relies on such a model will be a form of critique in which the actions of a community are taken as to some degree defective expressions of underlying commitments, and in which critics propose a change in action that will remedy these defects. On such a model, the interpretation of social practices and the norms present within them cannot be understood as unproblematically reconstructing a meaning that is already and clearly present. Rather, immanent critique participates in *constituting* this content through interpreting it. This constructive moment of interpretation, however, must not be understood as suggesting that the interpretation of social practices imposes arbitrary meaning:[42] the object of interpretation – human actions on the one hand and pretheoretical understanding of them on the other – are always themselves interpretations. They therefore carry internal standards for reinterpretation which must incorporate the content of the original interpretation and re-present it more clearly, and which therefore cannot simply replace the original interpretation but must always attempt to improve it.

3.2.1 A Hermeneutic Theory of Action as Social Critique

Taylor consequently identifies *human action* as the object of interpretations that allow us to gain clarity about our norms. This object, however, does not exist independently of the interpretations that the agents *themselves* give of their actions. With these self-understandings, which are expressed in action, social critique is not dealing with unproblematic objects that need only be interpreted 'correctly'; the activity of critical interpretation is itself one of the conditions that determine the meaning of these objects, as the explicit practice of interpretation is only a continuation of the everyday practice of self-interpretation, through which the meaning of actions is constituted. At the same time, however, an interpretation can only be critical if it – at least potentially – goes beyond the self-interpretations of the relevant actors. A critical interpretation of human action must therefore take as its 'material' the extant *preconceptions* of social reality, and above all the more or less articulated self-understandings of agents. On a hermeneutic approach, these ubiquitous, everyday interpretations are picked out as the object of interpretation. At the same time, they serve as standards of the success of new interpretations in that the quality of these new interpretations is measured by the extent to which they can clarify and articulate the original understanding.

One could object that this approach exacerbates the conservatism of Walzer's form of critique. Is it possible to formulate a radical critique of a society if our starting point is not only the moral standards of that society but the *interpretations of those standards* available in that society? This objection is misleading, as can be shown if one looks at two aspects of the concept of 'articulation' in Taylor's work. An articulation of a given semantic content is justified *as* an interpretation if it can be accepted and recognized as a (better) articulation of an *existing understanding* and if it *corresponds*, in a certain sense, to that understanding. However, an interpretation can only emerge as a *better* reformulation of an understanding if it makes better insight into the *object* of this understanding possible. Furthermore, articulation – as already shown – does not leave its object unchanged[43] but gives it a new form, which also changes its content.

As will be shown in the following, a new understanding of the reasons that guide actions is not all that can be achieved through an articulation of the goods to which actions, as we must assume, are always oriented. Such an articulation can also produce a new *connection between* the goods that underlie an action. This discloses to agents new or different motivational potentials, which can in turn be expressed in social changes. Accordingly, the articulation of insufficiently clear understandings of goods in Taylor's model is not at all conservative, but is rather a primary means of social change.[44]

Before turning to the question of how Taylor's hermeneutics relates to social critique, it is therefore necessary to briefly examine his theory of how the meaning of actions is constituted by their reference to goods, and how interpretations of that meaning can transcend the given self-interpretation of agents.

Taylor wants to claim not only that the concept of meaning is *methodologically* indispensable to understanding actions but also that a particular way of constituting the meaning of actions is both *anthropologically essential* for subjects and *ontologically indispensable* for their existence as persons. It is this thesis that has consequences for how social critique can reconstruct norms from actions.

Taylor introduces the concept of a 'strong evaluation' to characterize the relation of actions to values.[45] Unlike 'weak evaluations', which consist in judging certain courses of action as more or less desirable, 'strong evaluations' describe qualitatively different conceptions of the good, in reference to which actions are able to appear attractive *at all*. Each of these conceptions is identified by a distinctive set of *qualitatively contrastive descriptions*. Someone who sacrifices their free time in favour of studying because they desire to 'be a hardworking person' and not to 'waste their life' applies a *qualitative* judgement about the worth of the desire to have a meaningful life and about the desire to have free time, respectively.[46] A *quantitative trade-off* between the two desires is (for such a person) not possible because the desire for free time and the ideal of industriousness are essentially incompatible. From the perspective of a particular outlook on life, the choice between two forms of life that are fundamentally determined by these two desires is a choice between two alternatives that are *necessarily incompatible* at the level of fundamental values.

According to Taylor, many theories of action and decision falsely assume that there are only weak evaluations and accordingly assume that options for action are always weighed against each other in terms of fundamentally commensurable qualities. The concept of 'strong evaluation' goes beyond this limited perspective by allowing us to understand how in every decision, agents potentially commit themselves to a new interpretation of their fundamental values and goods – which are essential to their *self-understanding as agents*. In this way, the concept of strong evaluation is at the same time connected to the concept of a person's 'practical identity'. A person's strong evaluations are constitutive of how they integrate their own actions into a self-conception over time and are therefore constitutive of this self-conception itself. Taylor therefore not only argues that there are such 'strong evaluations' and that we cannot understand many human actions without them, but also that we can only have the capacity for action in the full sense – and thus be persons at all – when we are in the position to determine our identity in terms of strong evaluations. From this it follows not only that human actions are only to be understood against the background of a self-understanding that is already articulated in some way, but also that human actions themselves must always be conceived as *articulations* of these self-understandings.

3.2.2 Social Critique as Interpretation

Having examined Taylor's account of the meaning of actions, the implications of this account for social critique in a narrower sense can be examined. Even if Taylor does not explicitly develop his account in this way, it is doubtless possible to construe an argument similar to his view in terms of the shared self-understanding not of individuals but of a community. Social groups, one could argue, must also always understand their social norms and practices with reference to the previously perceived meaning of situations and actions. Therefore, a social critique of the *norms of a group* – and therefore its practices – can also be understood as a reinterpretation of this meaning, which, through the improvement of the self-understanding of the corresponding community, simultaneously articulates the semantic content of those practices, clarifies them and changes them.

A model of social critique that is more substantial than Walzer's results from the fact that, according to Taylor, disputes in a community about the *correct* interpretation of its norms must be understood as disputes about the correct interpretation of its fundamental 'strong evaluations', which have been expressed in the previous decisions of the community. The correct interpretation of the norms – and therefore the basis for justified criticism of different interpretations – would then be the interpretation of the social practice that can *most clearly capture the strong evaluations* that underlie it.

This idea assumes that the strong evaluations that determine our identity always constitute specific forms of social practice at the same time,[47] such that – in the case of individuals – criticism of *false understandings of our personal identity* must always at the same time be criticism of *false practices*. This relationship between personal identity and practice can be understood in two different ways. One can assume, first, that some evaluative choices that we make as individuals have consequences for how we live with others and that the interpretation of our personal identities therefore usually also has an effect on our common practices. Taylor argues, however, for a second, more powerful thesis: we cannot *understand* our social practices (as with any other form of action) if we do not understand the strong evaluations that underlie them. Social practices are therefore only comprehensible if we grasp *the vocabulary of strong, contrasting distinctions* on which they are based.[48] How the members of a practice understand that practice, and the articulations they give to this understanding, determines the practice's form. The thesis of the *indispensability of strong evaluations for our moral identity* can therefore be supplemented by a second thesis: *the indispensability of strong evaluations for social practices*. Therefore, any criticism of a moral identity, and any argument for articulating it in a new way, is always also a corresponding critique of the social practices that are based on it. This results in a form of social critique that is identical to a hermeneutically understood social science.[49] Immanent critique would therefore consist in criticism of our given individual and collective understandings of our moral identity – and therefore a critique of their inextricably interlinked social practices – in which we recommend an improved understanding of this identity that better articulates our underlying strong evaluations, the general acceptance of which would lead to different forms of social practice.

However, there are two obstacles standing in the way of developing Taylor's theory into a theory of immanent critique. First, in the case of moral self-conceptions, it is unclear which concrete criteria are suitable for deciding whether a particular change to one's interpretation of one's strong evaluations is the *best* option in the event of a conflict between interpretations. In the case of the specifically *social* norms to which immanent critique must refer, it further needs to be shown with what right a critic could demand of *others* that a particular demand for change – and the interpretation on which it rests – should be accepted. Second, it is unclear whether the social norms of a community can be treated analogously to moral self-conceptions. We are accustomed to thinking about the personal self in such a way that – at least in nonpathological cases – a certain unity may be assumed a priori which makes the question of its central structuring values, goods or evaluations meaningful. With regard to social practices, however, which develop through the cooperation of multiple subjects, both the assumption of consensus and the demand for integration are far more difficult to justify.

But there is also a second social theoretical idea in Taylor that reverses, as it were, the direction of the argument. Taylor assumes that the *conditions of the development of strong evaluations*, and therefore of authentic (individual) self-understandings, are constitutively based on *the existence of a common language*: 'We can . . . say that all the institutions and practices by which we live are constituted by certain distinctions and hence a certain language which is thus essential to them.'[50] A common language (and a common space of meaning) is therefore an 'irreducibly social good'[51] that makes the development of strong evaluations possible. However, this good is only possible on the basis of certain *intersubjective relationships*. If strong evaluations are an irreducible part of our identity, and if a common language and social relations of a certain kind are necessary preconditions for strong evaluations, it follows that these social relationships are themselves indispensable for our identities and our interpretations.

As a result, we have the following options for a model of immanent critique. First, we can criticize social practices not only in terms of the interpretations of identities that form part of their implicit content, but also with regard to whether they make possible a language that allows us to understand our own identities sufficiently clearly. We can therefore imagine a critique of social practices that relies on the argument that we can only fully understand our identity if we change these practices.

Second, the same argument also leads to the possibility of a critique that refers to *pathologies* of social relations that obstruct the availability of a language in which we can understand ourselves meaningfully. Such pathologies cannot consist in the absence of social relationships that are constitutive of a language – as there would be no moral subjects at all in such a case – but only in their *incomplete articulation*. A path is opened here for social critique, which leads directly to the goal of a critique of social practices without taking a detour through the concept of personal identity. If we accept the idea that social practices are constitutive of the availability of meaning, then the pathologies of these practices must consist in the fact that they are structured such that these meanings do not play their proper role and cannot be articulated in them. Immanent social critique would then be a critique of the inability of certain forms of practices to provide the enabling conditions for full articulation.

Hartmut Rosa has similarly distinguished between three versions of immanent critique in Taylor:[52] first, *a critique of alienation*, which concerns practices that are not sensitive to changed values and articulations, and in which the self-understanding of the agents and the material conditions of the practice develop in isolation from each other. Second, there are practices in which some members purposefully *distort the articulation in ideological ways* in order to secure their own power. Third, there are *conflicts* that cannot reach the level of consciousness.

All these forms of critique, however, presuppose not only that we can recognize the value of the articulation of self-understandings independently of the concrete content of such self-understandings, but also that social agents can refer to this value in concrete processes of criticism in such a way that they can *demand* of other agents that they accept a corresponding critique. Therefore, this value must also be institutionalized in social practices, so that it can serve as the basis of mutually binding obligations that members of these practices can have in relation to one another. To clarify this, we must examine how, exactly, the model of social practice to which Taylor refers is constituted.

3.2.3 Validity and Truth in the Interpretation of Human Action

To understand the first form of immanent critique – that is, the critical elucidation of collective identities – we must ask which criteria could be available to differentiate between correct and incorrect interpretations of those evaluations that are fundamental to our social practices. The justification of a form of critique that puts forward a claim to rationality depends crucially on the fact that interpretations brought forward by critics about the 'real' meaning of the norms accepted by their community can be shown to represent *objective improvements* to the self-understanding of a group.

Taylor proposes a combination of three criteria. These are the criteria of *progress in understanding*, the *success of practices* and an *increase in the capacity for articulation*.

(i) Progress in understanding. The first strategy for demonstrating the possibility of objectively justified hermeneutic judgements is based on the assumption that the claims of objectivity in hermeneutic discourses should only be understood *locally*. According to this strategy, an interpretation is objectively correct if the transition to that interpretation, compared to other interpretations available at the time, can be shown to enable progress in understanding the interpreted objects.[53] The criterion for comparing two interpretations, and thus the criterion for distinguishing between better and worse interpretations, is therefore formulated with reference to the *epistemic benefits* and *reduction in errors* that these interpretations make possible.[54] It remains unclear, however, what *exactly* produces such progress in understanding. Taylor says only that it must be an increase in clarity[55] and persuasiveness.[56] Good interpretations make clear what was previously unclear: 'A successful interpretation is one which makes clear the meaning originally present in a confused, fragmentary, cloudy form. But how does one know that this interpretation is correct? Presumably, because it makes sense of the original text: what is strange, mystifying, puzzling, contradictory is no longer so, is accounted for.'[57] Taylor rightly notes that the hermeneutic method rules out a context-free criterion of what 'clarity' consists in. He therefore assumes that we can only answer the question of which of two alternative interpretations of the norms by which a community must be measured is 'clearer' against a shared background of meaning or – should this not be available – through shared intuitions.[58] We should not, however, accept the claim that it is the *actual intuitions* or an *actual willingness to consent* that determines the correct norms of critique. It is precisely in objectionable situations that the willingness to accept certain interpretations can be twisted by pathological social conditions, such that these criteria *systematically validate false interpretations*.

(ii) Practical success. The rather unclear criterion of progress in clarity is supplemented by two further criteria, which Taylor formulates in terms of the *practical success* that an interpretation exhibits, together with its *ability to produce greater levels of articulation*. The first of these has interesting consequences, especially with regard to social practices: Taylor initially claims that the correctness of an interpretation of social practices is demonstrated by the fact that the self-understanding that informs it is *practically successful* and can *solve problems*.[59] Conversely, practices that are informed by false interpretations are 'self-defeating'[60] and therefore lead to practical failure. However, this criterion is hardly suitable for remedying the vagueness of the concept of a 'better understanding'. As Taylor himself admits, the success of an interpretation sometimes consists in the stability of the practice, but also sometimes in its dissolution:

We should note that attaining clairvoyant practice is not the same thing as being more successful in our practice. It may be that there is something deeply muddled and contradictory in our original activity.... [W]e can abandon this self-defeating enterprise, and turn to another goal.... Of course, if we bring this off, we shall have been more successful overall; but not in the practices we originally set out to understand.[61]

However, if the success of a practice is understood as the *survival of the right practices* and *the replacement of the wrong practices*, then we can only know when a practice is successful if we already know what the *right* practice consists in.

(iii) Increase in the capacity for articulation. Even if Taylor rarely talks about an 'increase in the capacity for articulation' as an independent criterion of the quality of interpretations – especially when the question of when an interpretation allows for 'more' or 'less' articulation is always run together with the question of its correctness – he always emphasizes that modernity is 'unarticulated' in ways that demand critique and thus refers to the second, previously discussed understanding of immanent critique – that is, to a model that critiques practices for their failure to fulfil the general preconditions for making collective self-understandings available.

One could therefore understand the *capacity for the articulation of a practice* as a normative criterion for the correctness of interpretations that are constitutive of it. An increase in the ability to provide an articulation that is achieved by the fact that a particular interpretation of a practice is accepted *in* that practice strengthens, in Taylor's view, our motivational connection to its goods – and the stronger our ability to articulate them, the more clearly we can recognize the 'correct' meaning of these goods.[62] It is therefore obvious that interpretations that allow for a more explicit articulation of the normative distinctions of a practice are of a higher quality, because greater articulation always leads to a more authentic understanding of that practice.

But the fact that we need a *minimum* of articulation in order to maintain 'contact' with the central goods of our lives does not entail that an *increase* in the capacity for articulation is (always) progress. It does not follow from this that increasing the ability of practices to provide articulations should always be treated as valuable, as Taylor describes the minimal degree of articulation that matters to us as a 'transcendental' condition. This seems to suggest that the minimal standard of articulation designated in this way cannot be violated by a practice if it is a practice *at all* in the relevant sense.[63] The idea that we should always aim for an increase in articulation beyond this minimum cannot be justified by citing the necessity of articulation – rather, Taylor would require a new, independent argument that shows that an increase in the ability to articulate beyond the transcendental minimum always amounts to progress.

No matter how plausible this thesis appears in the framework of Taylor's theory, it proves unclear on closer inspection. It is not at all clear that an interpretation of the values of a practice is necessarily better if it is able to articulate more aspects.

A practice's capacity for articulation therefore cannot immediately be identified as a good. What needs to be determined is whether the practice of interpretation itself does not presuppose a commitment to the articulation of *certain* aspects, and whether the value of articulation as an ideal could be drawn not from the ontology of the person but from a *theory of practices of social interpretation*.

Taylor attempts to show how, in situations of conflicting interpretation – situations in which reference to a common background or common intuitions cannot help – critics can justify their own positions such that they raise rationally binding claims against their opponents. As he does not take on the challenge just outlined, however, Taylor's attempts are ultimately unsatisfactory.

3.2.4 A Model of Progress

The following objection could be levied against this negative conclusion: hermeneutic critique can forego a general criterion for determining the quality of interpretations if it limits itself to offering criteria for determining whether the transition between two specific interpretations is rational *in specific cases*.

But how might such an assessment of particular, competing interpretations proceed? Taylor's rejection of proceduralism[64] closes off the obvious possibility of answering this question by specifying a *process* through which conflicts between interpretations could be decided. A better interpretation cannot be distinguished – according to Taylor – by the fact that it has been achieved by science or any other privileged method, but only through evaluating the substantive question of whether it better fits the content of what is being interpreted.

In this context, it is worth looking at a second model of justification which Taylor proposes following Alasdair MacIntyre, and which gives social practices a considerably higher significance than moral hermeneutics. It is a model that assumes that the correctness of normative interpretations can emerge from the very *dynamics of the social practices of interpretation*. In his essay 'Explanation and Practical Reason',[65] Taylor adopts MacIntyre's view that interpretative alternatives have always competed with one another in the historical development of the prevailing self-understanding of specific societies, and that against the background of an agreement about what is considered to be a good argument, some of these alternatives were successful against each other. They therefore have at least a claim to be seen as justified, as we can understand this historical process as *progress*.

Taylor distinguishes between two models, each of which describes processes of transition from one self-conception to another. The first model explains the transition from one set of beliefs to another through *the learning process* that is achieved by this transition. A learning process is characterized by the fact that the new belief system has *fewer internal inconsistencies and problems*. Such a statement, according to Taylor, is still possible even if one does not want to create a universal, external standard for the quality of a worldview. This model is still based, however, on the claim that from both standpoints – from the 'old' and the 'new' self-understanding – there is agreement about what is generally *considered to be a problem*. This assumption, however – according to Taylor – cannot be made during comprehensive upheavals in socially shared self-understandings, in which the *criteria for the justification of worldviews* (or interpretations), and therefore the *criteria for identifying problems*, always also change.

He therefore proposes, as a second model, that the criterion for a rational transition should in fact be whether one of the models can *explain the success of the other*. So, for example, the success of modern natural science, according to its own criteria (of technical control) must remain completely inexplicable to the medieval and ancient understanding of nature.[66] Seen retrospectively, there is a transition that is only rationally comprehensible *from one side*, namely, from the side of modern science, the development of which is thus considered progress.

But isn't the converse also true, that from the perspective of modern natural science the 'success' of medieval theories in their 'discovery' of a cosmic order must remain inexplicable? There is in fact a difference in that, from the perspective of the modern natural sciences, the issue is not so much that it is impossible to discover any such order but rather that, from that perspective, the search for a cosmic order is a meaningless enterprise, while conversely, for a medieval scholar, the goal of mastering nature as a lower-order goal was at least comprehensible. But wouldn't this oblige us to argue that it is an 'advantage' of modern science that it recognizes as few other goals as possible? Or do we have to admit that modern natural science would be less rational than medieval theories if the latter had had resounding success on their own terms? Both consequences seem untenable.

Moving to the problem of normative interpretation, there are in Taylor's view only two relatively weak possibilities for justifying judgements of progress. With the first model, he can explain the unproblematic phenomenon of certain interpretations or assumptions being replaced by others, and he can show that this replacement is justified by means of a criterion shared by both standpoints (consistency, for example). Second, he can explain how – from the standpoint of a worldview that has already been transformed – the replacement of the old worldview can be seen as justified, insofar as the criteria that form the ultimate basis of validity in the new worldview are already incompletely recognized in the old. It must be emphasized, however, that this narrowing of argumentative focus can only appear justified *retrospectively*, from the point of view of the new position: 'The superiority of one position over another will thus consist in this, that from the more adequate position one can understand one's own stand and that of one's opponent, but not the other way round. It goes without saying that this argument can only have weight for those in the superior position.'[67] Such a purely retrospective criterion – even if it proves helpful for the understanding of previous reinterpretations of human self-understandings – is not suitable for reconstructing a method of social critique. This is because hermeneutic social critique demands a transformation of normative self-understandings that has *yet to be implemented*. As long as those to whom social criticism in the narrower sense applies cannot 'yet' understand the reasons that *should compel them* to accept the better interpretation, these reasons cannot be motivating.[68] In such cases, critique appears to be no different from manipulation, from the perspective of those to whom it is addressed.

3.2.5 Arguing with Taylor against Taylor

Taylor's model of immanent critique builds on several substantial assumptions. He always assumes that the criterion of the successful articulation of our (individual or collective) moral identities is decisive for the assessment of our practices; that the possibility of a better, clearer understanding of these practices justifies us in undertaking a new interpretation of these practices; and that the fact that a new interpretation or articulation of a practice undermines this practice is a reason to change it rather than to revert to a previous interpretation of it.

These assumptions are in no way counterintuitive, but it should not be overlooked that Taylor's overall position receives relatively little argumentative support. In particular, the idea that the criterion of successful identity formation must always be the most important one – even if one takes both individual and collective identities as the object of this criterion – appears to not reflect a universally shared worldview but rather a *modern* view, even if Taylor attempts to find analogies with premodern societies.[69]

The idea that the most important value should always be that people should have the potential to develop a nonpathological relationship with themselves either as individuals or as members of a community is not entailed by the nature of moral practices as such. Rather, it is – as Taylor acknowledges elsewhere – an idea that developed in a specifically modern form of moral practice, in which all members can demand to be allowed certain possibilities for development.

Accordingly, one can use Taylor's own arguments against him: just as he demonstrates that many forms of modern philosophy ontologize and assume as paradigmatic the form of life they attempt to justify, so his own theory could be criticized for introducing the criterion of transparent and complete articulation and a focus on the successful identity formation of individuals as normative premises without examining whether the particularly modern self-understanding that privileges these criteria is itself a valid normative basis. Further, the validity of his claims about the value of articulation depends on the normative assumption that only *certain* forms of self-understanding have value – namely, those that are strengthened rather than destroyed by articulation. This assumption appears to presuppose rather than justify the intrinsic value of articulation. The same argument applies, mutatis mutandis, for the account of social practices that are undermined or strengthened through articulations.

3.2.6 The Prospects of Taylor's Model of Immanent Critique

Taylor (like Walzer) assumes that a critique of social practices must refer to the values that the members of the practice already recognize in some way, and that critique must therefore take place from a participant perspective that is linked, in particular, to the evaluative categories in which participants in social practices understand their own experience.[70]

The model of critique that Taylor suggests is therefore also a model of the articulation and interpretation of already 'given' goods and moral sources, which already play a role in the identity of those addressed by the critique. Taylor thereby qualifies as a genuine representative of the immanent critique approach: the practices and implicit values of those addressed by critique are indispensable, but critique is not exhausted in reproducing them, as it would be in a purely 'internal' critique.

Within this model of immanent critique one can – as already discussed – distinguish between a more 'internal' strand and a more immanent strand. Taylor's model of critique has two levels – the material level of concrete interpretations of the particular practices or evaluative commitments of moral identities, and the level of formal critiques of practices the structures of which are defective insofar as they do not allow us to articulate their underlying evaluations.

An immanent critique in the latter sense – a critique that is therefore not so much directed at identity-determining goods but rather at the structural properties of the community's relation to these goods – is doubtless the most interesting aspect of Taylor's theory of social critique. It opens the possibility of shedding light on those aspects of the *practice of critique* that can be made comprehensible independently of specific contents and goods, and that can explain how the rationality of the transition from one self-interpretation to another can be analysed. It suggests that the idea of the 'success' of a self-interpretation – which remains quite vague in Taylor – is based, among other things, on whether it is capable of liberating practices from such structural pathologies.

Just why articulation should be thought to have intrinsic value – to which such a model of strong immanent critique must refer – remains, however, notoriously unclear. Instead of simply referring to the ontological constitution of personhood or the human form of life – which could make the significance of an increase in the capacity for articulation comprehensible but does not yet provide a concrete normative argument for why progressive changes must occur in one direction rather than another – what is needed is *a model of social practices of interpretation*, one that can explain how and why increasing these practices' capacity for articulation plays such a specific normative role.

The following objection is more crucial, however: a theory of critique can only give an interesting answer to the dilemma of social critique if it can show how reference to the practices and beliefs of a community can *rationally motivate* the members of that community to *change* these practices or beliefs – this is needed, in particular, if it aims to allow for more than merely internal critique, that is, for more than a mere demonstration of inconsistency. Taylor no doubt pursues such a project, as the reference to implicit, underlying evaluations is suitable for developing such a model. But it must also be shown, then, how critics can criticize the given self-conception of a community not merely in retrospect, but by providing arguments for interpretations that are yet to be accepted. In order to show how new interpretations can be concretely justified, Taylor must, however, fall back on inadequately analysed shared background beliefs, or implicit self-understandings. It is therefore necessary to explain how the argumentative reference to a shared background functions as a concrete discursive 'move' in the process of critique and to explain how the constitution of those commonalities to which critique necessarily refers is to be understood, as well as how these commonalities can demand movement beyond the current self-conception.

3.3 'PRACTICE' AND 'TRADITION' IN ALASDAIR MACINTYRE

Hermeneutic models of immanent critique can methodologically draw on a mature tradition in the literary and human sciences but must as a consequence expend much energy clarifying which *social* prerequisites must be in place such that its model of social critique is possible. This is why the most important question that such models must address is which premises regarding their social theory are to be introduced, and which new assumptions about the mechanics of social practices must be made, so that the hermeneutic method can also be applied for the purposes of social critique.

In this respect, Alasdair MacIntyre's work can be understood as radicalizing the difference between Taylor and Walzer: MacIntyre, even more than Taylor, places the fact that interpretations are always grounded in socially institutionalized discourses, traditions and practices at the very centre of his work. Both with regard to the concrete content of critique, which he elucidates by means of a critique of modern moral philosophy, and with regard to forms of critique, he begins by diagnosing a crisis: he argues that substantive standards of critique (more specifically, moral critique) can only apply and function in a particular form of a practice or tradition. This assumption clearly shows his commitment to immanent critique, but he then further argues that no adequate form of such practice exists in the modern world. Therefore, every project of substantive (immanent) critique and every attempt to justify the possibility of this kind of critique that refers to today's form of critical practice must fail. MacIntyre thus proposes a *negativistic* theory of immanent critique, which formulates the counterfactual conditions under which immanent critique *would* be possible. In short, he offers two models of immanent normativity on which social critique could draw – if only they existed: one is the model of substantive ethical *practices*, the other of substantive ethical *traditions*. While in Taylor suprahistorical, anthropologically ineluctable demands still form the basis of critique, MacIntyre grounds the normative standards of critique not in the general preconditions for successful identity formation but in a historically specific configuration of practices and interpretations.

The dialectical entanglement of substantive critique and methodological reflection on the forms of critique that results from this argument is made yet more complicated by the fact that MacIntyre propounds two different models of critique. In his best-known work, *After Virtue*, modern moral philosophy is criticized as the result of the fragmentation and partial destruction of a holistic, ancient conception of the good life founded in specifically ethical *practices*. In *Whose Justice? Which Rationality?* this is supplemented through the concept of *tradition*. The modern conception of morality is here understood as *one specific* tradition of moral enquiry which, in contrast to other traditions, disowns its own traditional character. Genuine normativity on this model is therefore localized in specific moral-philosophical traditions, which (ideally) contain a successful form of reflexivity. In *Three Rival Versions* of *Moral Enquiry*, this account is developed further: the modern conception of morality is no longer understood merely as one tradition among others; 'tradition' is construed together with the competing theoretical paradigms of the 'encyclopaedia' and 'genealogy' as the result of the establishment of normative-theoretical alternatives in philosophy. In order to cut a path through this dense theoretical web, I will present MacIntyre's theory in two stages. First, I will analyse MacIntyre's theory of social practices; second, I will outline the role of traditions in his model. In both cases, the question arises whether these rich models of how norms are instituted in social reality are sufficient to make immanent critique possible.

3.3.1 Social Practice and Critique

In *After Virtue*, one already finds two tightly interwoven models of normativity: the model of a normatively substantive practice, and the model of tradition. In order to clarify the often confusing relationship between these models, I will first examine the contribution that the practice concept can make to a theory of immanent critique.

MacIntyre's fundamental idea is that the possibility of moral interpretation and critique, and therefore the precondition of a hermeneutic approach to immanent norms, is bound to a specific form of practice that only exists in certain historical contexts. MacIntyre locates the paradigmatic form of such a practice in ancient, post-Homeric Greece, which saw the development of social practices of a kind that not only had a substantive, immanent normative structure but that were also reflexive and allowed for criticism.[71] These practices had *internal norms* that allowed for a distinction between what *appears to be good* and what is *objectively good*.[72] Such practices, one can assume, allowed for immanent critique when their members applied these norms to criticize the *explicitly recognized* values and ideals of the practices, which perhaps only imperfectly captured their internal norms.

MacIntyre thereby binds the possibility of immanent critique to a form of social practice that must allow for critique of a community's self-interpretation, even if this critique is only possible through that practice. Accordingly, he shares with Walzer the idea that moral critique does not consist in an absolute distancing from social normative standards but rather in providing new interpretations of them. Unlike Walzer, however, he assumes that *objective criteria* for such interpretations exist at any given point in time.[73] These objective criteria, which go beyond the beliefs of the members of the society, result from the fact that the relevant standards are *socially actualized* in relationships of reciprocal ascription of normative authority; these relationships precede the interpretation of the respective standards but can themselves be changed through reflexive interpretation and critique, and can thereby be improved.[74] If we assume such an interaction between social institutionalization and reflexive self-discovery, it follows that any given self-understanding can be criticized as a whole by recourse to the objective criteria that are partially independent of it.

What do the objective standards of critique consist in? In MacIntyre's view, the internal standards of classical, ancient forms of practice can only be understood by means of the idea of *virtue*, which – he claims – is indispensable for genuine morality. Moral norms – to summarize – only exist together with virtues, and virtues are only comprehensible in the context of specific social practices. Practices are therefore a necessary but not omnipresent condition for morality.[75] MacIntyre initially defines the concept of 'practice' in the following way:

> By 'a practice' I am going to mean any coherent and complex form of socially established cooperative human activity through which goods internal to that form of activity are realized in the course of trying to achieve those standards of excellence which are appropriate to, and partially definitive of, that form of activity, with the result that human powers to achieve excellence, and human conceptions of the ends and goods involved, are systematically extended.[76]

This complex definition brings together a series of properties that MacIntyre holds to be necessary for explaining the meaning of virtues as the internal, objective standards of such practices.

Practices are primarily forms of cooperation – but, interestingly, only those cooperative relationships that are aimed at obtaining a particular kind of good are eligible as candidates for moral practices. MacIntyre understands the concept of a good in such a way that the exercise of a practice for its own sake is not merely a possible good; the attempt to obtain such an 'internal good' is actually the *paradigmatic* case of the exercise of a fully normative practice.

On MacIntyre's view, practices are determined by their *normative content*. This is due to their institutionalized standards of action, which he terms their 'standards of excellence'. Finally, practices essentially consist in a certain form of intersubjective relationship: 'Every practice requires a certain kind of relationship between those who participate in it.'[77] This is because 'its goods can only be achieved by subordinating ourselves within the practice in our relationship to other practitioners'.[78] In these intersubjective relationships, which – as it were – create the material substrate of normative beliefs, the standards of the practice are institutionalized.

The conditions under which our moral (or, more generally, normative) vocabulary has objective meaning therefore consist in our being located in social practices in which we cooperatively strive for and realize their internal goods with others. The objective, normative content of these practices arises from the shared standards of excellence applied in the pursuit of these goods, this standard being constituted by intersubjective relationships of authority and experience. Moral evaluation and moral critique of a society's self-understanding therefore refer to the objective social practices that provide the background for its normative vocabulary. Even if these social practices are not fully independent of the self-understanding of those involved, primarily because their self-conceptions shape the relations of authority that are part of the objective structures of practices, their meaning is not exhausted by the interpretations of their members. A substantive model of immanent critique therefore appears to be within reach.

But even if MacIntyre's account of social practices at first blush suggests a substantive social theory of the practical foundation of normative standards that could serve to justify such a model of immanent critique, his approach is marred by several problems that prevent him from systematically developing the idea of a normative practice. He instead merges it with the concept of tradition, resulting in an approach that remains a form of interpretive, internal critique. It suffices in this context to point to two objections that touch on (a) MacIntyre's implausible distinction between external and internal goods and (b) his lack of a convincing conception of social critique and social change.

(a) On the distinction between internal and external goods. To justify the thesis that modern society is no longer in a position to explain its own moral principles and principles of virtue – although it obviously still contains social practices – MacIntyre must distinguish between different types of practice; that is, between normatively substantive and normatively deficient forms of social practice. From the very beginning, he is committed to carrying out this distinction by means of the concept of 'internal' and 'external' goods.

What is the difference between internal and external goods? The internal goods of a normatively substantive practice are first characterized by the fact that they are not comprehensible independently of that practice.[79] Second, it is characteristic of internal goods that they are recognizable *as* goods not only for the individual but also for the community that constitutes the practice.[80] Finally, one can only genuinely pursue an internal good by attempting to match or exceed the degree of excellence displayed by prior practitioners.[81] External goods, by contrast, are characterized by the fact that they are only contingently connected with the practices through which they are obtained.[82] Accordingly, they are also comprehensible without reference to this practice; there are always possible alternative means of obtaining them, and they can mostly be understood as possessions or properties of individuals who can be in competition, as they are only available to a limited extent.[83]

Not only does MacIntyre fail to provide reasons for the thesis that only 'internal' goods can constitute points of orientation for normatively substantive practices, but there are many counterexamples that can be raised against it. Many meaningful practices that we know of are characterized by externally comprehensible goods in MacIntyre's sense, which create corresponding virtues: the practice of medicine, for example – which is doubtlessly accompanied by specific virtues of medical ethics, care and so on – is determined by its focus on the good of healing illness;[84] the practice of managing a household is determined by its focus on the satisfaction of needs; the practice of academic teaching is determined by its focus on the good of the enlargement of knowledge and skills. All of these goods are – at least in part – more or less comprehensible without reference to the practices in which they are pursued.[85] The notion that striving for the respective goods in these cases is the basis of the values of the respective practices is – one might assume – justified by the fact that *the value of these practices* and their corresponding activities is only comprehensible through their *internal connection* to more or less external goods, but *not* by the fact that the *goods are only comprehensible through those practices*.[86] Many valuable practices are constituted through rules and standards of excellence that prescribe the pursuit of goods that are comprehensible independently of them. Only a minority of practices are determined through rules that constitute completely new goods.

The plausibility of MacIntyre's distinction is further weakened by the fact that he is bereft of the possibility of recognizing normative qualities that are laid out in instrumental practices, which he could have opened up with the concept of 'cooperation'. He understands that the fact of successful cooperation and the common commitment to standards of excellence (whether externally or internally) already require significant moral preconditions, which are always implicitly realized in such practices. Given his commitment to the notion that the 'actual' moral values of society always lie in those goods that necessarily transcend instrumental cooperation, however, his focus is so constricted that he cannot make this productive for his theory.[87]

(b) The lack of a convincing conception of social critique. These problems also make it difficult to assess the critical force of MacIntyre's model. He is of the opinion that his approach can and must be critical of practices: 'That the virtues . . . are defined not in terms of good and right practices, but of practices, does not entail or imply that practices as actually carried out at particular times and places do not stand in need of moral criticism. And the resources for such criticism are not lacking.'[88] MacIntyre justifies his claim about the critical force of the internal standards of practices that are expressed in virtues with a *success argument*: a nonvirtuous life must *necessarily fail*. The reason for this is that, in the absence of virtues, such a life is shaped by

omnipresent conflict and by a lack of integrated goals and integrity. These criteria, however, seem to presuppose an Aristotelian conception that requires argumentation.[89] It is also surprising that he understands the existence of conflict as a symptom of a lack of virtue, insofar as one of the objections he levels against the traditional Aristotelian position is its lack of a conception of moral conflict as a necessary component of practices. He repeatedly points out that conflicts are necessary components of social life and that the misery of modernity is caused not by the fact that conflicts exist but by the fact that they are no longer rationally solvable.[90]

One would therefore expect that the superiority of his position would be demonstrated through the fact that a practice-based theory and virtue ethics together show that suitable practices contain the resources necessary not so much for avoiding interpretative conflicts as for *solving them rationally*, especially as practices are defined from the outset as temporally extended phenomena that are to be understood through a narrative of change – one within which we stand in dialogue with contemporary and historical members of a practical community on the topic of objective yet interpretable standards[91] (a dialectic that must also contain conflict and changes). No solution is to be found here in MacIntyre, however, save for a platitudinous demand that balanced solutions be found in each individual case.[92]

Even if MacIntyre can provide a model of immanent normativity, this model cannot be integrated into a plausible conception of normative change, or indeed normative progress, much less into a social theoretically plausible description of social conflict.

3.3.2 Tradition and Critique

The approach that MacIntyre lays out in *After Virtue* has the benefit of enriching the hermeneutic perspective with a substantive model of social practices, but MacIntyre does not succeed in developing this theory into a convincing model of immanent critique.

It is therefore worth considering the second strand of argumentation in MacIntyre's work: the idea that we can draw the normative standards of critique from tradition. In *Whose Justice? Which Rationality?*, and yet more clearly in the later Gifford Lectures, which were published as *Three Rival Versions of Moral Enquiry*, MacIntyre distinguishes two (and later, three) fundamentally different models of normative discourse, and thus three fundamentally different models of critique.[93] In addition to *genealogy*, which ultimately represents only a pathological phenomenon, the two modes of *encyclopaedia* and *tradition* stand for the range of moral reasoning in the modern world. The encyclopaedic mode – which is only explicitly designated in *Three Rival Versions*[94] – is a product of the Enlightenment. It is a form of moral questioning and argumentation that assumes that moral arguments are universally comprehensible in principle, that they can be presented in a context-free fashion, and that they put people in a position to find universal and rational solutions to moral problems. In this respect, the encyclopaedic mode of enquiry can be identified with Walzer's modes of 'discovery' and 'invention', which are also characterized by the fact that they are context free. The encyclopaedic mode of moral enquiry is not without alternatives, however. Indeed, there is an alternative that consists in developing a self-conception that sees moral discourse as part of a tradition.

What is a tradition? MacIntyre uses the concept of tradition to elucidate the fact that the normative meaning of an action in a social practice can only be comprehended if we assume that the standards of social practices to be applied to actions (their 'standards of excellence') cannot be described in a context-free way but are rather part of a narrative that includes and describes the past *history of the practice* and the past *attempts to articulate the leading good of the practice*. The internal good that determines a social practice – for example, self-determination as the determining internal good of a democratic community – cannot be described objectively, that is, in abstraction from the history of the practice, which is always a history of disputes *over what this good is*. Rather, the meaning of such goods which is accessible to us presently can only be grasped if we understand it as resulting from a history of arguments about that meaning and if we understand the *current* articulation of this good as an answer to the problems of earlier articulations. For MacIntyre, as for Taylor, every articulation of a good is always already an interpretation. Furthermore, the actual social history of all preceding, superseded interpretations and their problems is *part of the meaning* of that which is interpreted.

MacIntyre uses 'tradition' to refer to comprehensive narratives in which the history of the articulations of a community with regard to their central goods, norms and criteria of rationality is expressed and which are linked to the concrete practices in which these arguments occur:[95] 'A living tradition is a historically extended, socially embodied argument, and an argument precisely in part about the goods which constitute that tradition.'[96] Traditions are therefore those practices and discourses in which the fundamental normative conceptual questions of a community are negotiated, continually newly reconfigured by recourse to their own history, and newly interpreted in response to specific problems. Traditions furthermore carry *their own standards of rationality* in the form of their history and their explicit metacriteria of argumentation. Normative claims in radically different traditions are therefore fundamentally incapable of being translated into one another, as the criteria for their application can only be learned within their own originating traditions.[97] MacIntyre insists – against the conservative implications of the word 'tradition' – that traditions are uncompleted processes that are shaped above all by conflicts over the correct understanding of goods, rules and values.[98] Through this idea of a temporally extended negotiation of the normative content of social practices, an important lacuna in hermeneutic theory of the constitution of norms is filled, as it makes clear that MacIntyre only refers to those practices that include standards that ensure that new developments are consistent with the preceding history of the tradition – more specifically, practices in which new answers to the tradition's characteristic conflicts and problems are developed. By means of this argument – as will become clear – standards for rational social change can be developed.

Although the idea of historical embeddedness could in principle strengthen a practice-theoretical conception of immanent normativity, the idea of tradition is at the same time – at least as MacIntyre employs it – also connected to something of a departure from the assumption of the constitution of norms through practices, which played a role in *After Virtue*. He defines traditions first and foremost as *narratives* and – in an entirely literal sense – as discourses and conversations in which arguments and thoughts are exchanged; in other words, as traditions of thought,[99] which are to be understood on the model of philosophical arguments, even if the arguments are not always conducted as lucidly as in philosophical discourse.

Traditions are therefore debates about meaning, understandings, ideas, criteria of rationality, self-understandings and theories. This definition of the concept of a tradition is not incompatible with a practice-based theory, but it suggests a departure from a different conception of practices in which *cooperation*, and not *argumentation*, is central. By referring to traditions in this way, the practice concept is displaced from what was its central position.[100]

With the concept of tradition, MacIntyre presents his own positive concept of how first morality, and then criticism in a more general sense, can refer to an immanent normative basis which allows for objectively justified judgements. If MacIntyre's model of traditions is to be developed as an alternative to universalist-constructivist or objectivist models of critique (and also as an alternative to a practice-theoretic model), he must show that it is superior to these other models. That is, he must prove that the tradition model can better explain, first, how the normative standards of critique are constituted; second, how people can rationally recognize these standards; and third, how critique can be legitimated as bringing about justified social changes, and therefore how progress can be produced by reference to these norms.

The reference to traditions as narratively structured and conceptually substantive 'temporally extended conversations' is based – among other things – on the assumption that the first and second of these questions have only one answer: the question of the normative content of a tradition is, on the one hand, a question of the self-description, self-knowledge or self-consciousness of whole communities – that is, the narrative self-reconstruction of their norms and beliefs. On the other hand, the question of what the content of a tradition consists in cannot be answered only by reference to the currently dominant interpretation of that tradition, but must also make reference to the social history of conflicts regarding that question. The third question, however, demands a different answer: if critique is not ultimately merely a *reproduction* of the internal contents of a tradition – as in Walzer's theory – but can aim at genuine *progress*, then it must be shown that traditions possess a content that can transcend the current self-understanding of a community.

Like Taylor, MacIntyre assumes that the question of the normative content of traditions cannot be posed independently of the actual beliefs and self-descriptions of the agents involved. In conflicts in which the norms of a tradition come into play, agents must always begin from their own, everyday beliefs.[101] Unlike on a purely internal approach, MacIntyre understands these beliefs not as static but as *structured by conflict*. This concerns not only their history, in which these meanings and norms have prevailed against others, but also the present, in which they are the object of continuous debate. The norms and beliefs that form standards for critique are therefore those actual interpretations that constitute the hitherto most convincing *option in light of all past and present conflicts*.[102] MacIntyre's dialectical model of criticism therefore departs from the existence (at any given time) of unquestioned beliefs but takes them to be justified only insofar as they are able to fend off all objections that can be formulated in the same vocabulary: 'That thesis which most successfully withstands all attempts to refute it – characteristically, of course, such a thesis will have had to be modified and reformulated in the course of its encounters with a variety of objections – is that which claims our rational allegiance.'[103] The claim that there is a temporally extended argument that supports any given interpretation assumes that there is a certain prior agreement about *which* arguments are objections, which standards determine when a thesis must be modified and so on. Indeed, while these metastandards are always revisable, their basis always remains contingent in a sense. This attachment to an already existing consensus about what counts as an objection or a sufficient reason for revision cannot be replaced by an objective starting point, as even the meaning of nonsemantic facts can only be disclosed in the light of such arguments:[104]

> Only for the inhabitants of such a community, who already possess some established theory or theories and who have so far characterized the data in terms of it or them, can the question be put: In the light of the norms of evaluation which we now possess, which of the presently competing theories is the best, or can we

conceive of a better? That there is a true theory to be found is a presupposition of the ongoing activity of the scientific community.[105]

A tradition is characterized not only by the fact that it can *justify* the norms and beliefs it embodies against earlier assumptions, but by the fact that it can also present a convincing narrative that explains the earlier mistakes in its self-description and the processes by which they were overcome. The rationality of beliefs and norms is therefore based not on their agreement with an external criterion but on the role they play in the narrative structure of the tradition – although all these elements can always in principle be further revised and developed. The rationality of a tradition is accordingly always a question of degree. The further a tradition can make its internal structure explicit in its own vocabulary and understand itself as a tradition, the better it can intentionally develop higher-level criteria of rationality and offer standards up for debate, checking both these standards and its own first-level assumptions against competing possibilities, and thereby at least temporarily validating them.

> A tradition which reaches this point of development will have become to greater or lesser degree a form of enquiry and will have had to institutionalize and regulate to some extent at least its methods of enquiry. It will have had to recognize intellectual virtues, and questions lie in wait for it about the relationship of such virtues to virtues of character. On these as on other questions conflicts will develop, rival answers will be proposed and accepted or rejected.[106]

This picture of the internal normativity of discourses and belief systems is significantly more complex than the picture offered by Walzer, and in its concretization of the historical dimension and its elucidation of the intrinsic value of explicit articulation, it also goes further than Taylor. It is easy to see how an attractive picture of immanent critique can be developed from this model. As soon as a system of meanings, beliefs and norms is no longer understood as given statically, but rather seen as a moment in an internal process of revision in which competing standpoints struggle with each other, it is clear why participation in such a process can be called 'critique'.

Immanent critique, on this model, would then be a form of critique that departs not from *all* the actual normative beliefs of a community but only from those beliefs for which a plausible narrative of their prevailing against all the available alternatives can be construed. The actual normative beliefs of a community can then be criticized as part of a normative practice if they do not fulfil these criteria in their dynamics of change, and if they are unable to present a plausible narrative of their own historical success.

Nevertheless, open questions remain: on the one hand, the starting point of traditions and their narratives remains arbitrary, such that a multiplicity of rational systems of belief can be developed depending on the starting situation in a pluralistic community.[107] There is therefore the danger that this criterion will not ultimately exclude anything, as *any* belief or practice can be justified at least as part of *some* narrative. On the other hand, it is not entirely clear how the process of development should be understood, as the question whether a certain argument prevails against others in the framework of a narrative in a justified or unjustified way is not easily answered. The assumption of an infinite regress of higher-level norms of rationality does not seem plausible, and nor is a criterion of coherence a good solution, as every incoherence can be remedied through ad hoc modifications.

There are two further questions connected to the question of progress. Since it is to be assumed that 'better arguments' do not emerge immediately but are found in debates that proceed from an existing problem in a tradition, it must be shown what an insufficiency in previous arguments or a 'problem' within a tradition amounts to. Finally, it must also be clarified whether not only *gradual changes* in a tradition but also *fundamental upheavals*, or even *replacements* of entire traditions, are possible as rational processes, and therefore as results or goals of critique.

(i) The first model of progress – improved understanding. If a tradition can be described as a sequence of argumentative conflicts and solutions, then this sequence cannot be a mere random series. However, for such a sequence to become a history that is comprehensible as progress oriented towards a goal, later positions must improve on how earlier positions are understood, not only *solving* conflicts through progress but also making these conflicts *comprehensible*, such that over time the object of the conflict (and thus the 'goal' of the argumentation) and what it could mean to achieve this goal become clearer.[108]

A tradition can become more rational not only in its content, however, but also in its *form* if it can make the greater part of its assumptions and procedures explicit:

> Progress in rationality is achieved ... when the adherents of that point of view succeed to some degree in elaborating more comprehensive and adequate statements of their positions through the dialectical procedure of advancing objections which identify incoherences, omissions, explanatory failures, and other types of flaw and limitation in earlier statements of them, of finding the strongest arguments available for supporting those objections, and then of attempting to restate the position so that it is no longer vulnerable to those specific objections and arguments.[109]

Through combining the criteria of hermeneutic progress with the conception of expressive rationality determined in this way, a criterion for critique can be achieved which allows one to distinguish between traditions without determining an absolute hierarchy. This conception of rationality is again – according to MacIntyre – applied internally within the practice of rational questioning ('enquiry').[110] In this practice, there is necessarily a sequence of various stages that are recognizable across all traditions. The first stage consists in the existence of contingent norms, institutions, and practices that are historically given at a particular time. In such a community, there is always simultaneously a particular *ascription of authority* to texts and persons: the authority to interpret and lay down common norms. In a second stage, conflicts in this system become evident, which then lead, in a third stage, to a reformulation of norms and standards of rationality.[111]

The criterion of rationality applied in this history of progress is retrospective and negative.[112] A particular stage in the development of a tradition can only claim to be rationally justified if it can prove that the previous stages had a distorted relation to reality. The benchmark of justification is therefore not an absolute, timeless ideal of truth[113] but a relative improvement against other formulations of the same tradition. MacIntyre distinguishes the development of a tradition from the gradual changes to which any body of beliefs is subject, on the one hand, and from abrupt changes of belief on the part of entire communities, on the other. On his view, development only counts as progressive development of a tradition if it proceeds reflexively and systematically, and therefore only if the members of the tradition arrive at a *theory* in which they can describe their own activity.[114]

(ii) The second model of progress – providing solutions to crises. This continuous improvement of understanding of a certain domain of meaning is only necessary, however, and not sufficient, for producing progress in a tradition. A tradition in the full sense must be able to describe changes in its own narrative that go beyond the normal adjustment of beliefs within the framework of a hermeneutic self-understanding: a tradition – MacIntyre claims – must also be in a position to *reflexively overcome epistemological crises*. For this reason, the idea of an epistemological crisis is central to his theory of traditions.[115]

MacIntyre characterizes an epistemological crisis as a situation in which a tradition must recognize that its normal methods for handling conflicts and questions cannot lead to further progress. Such a situation occurs when a form of stagnation emerges, or even when these methods merely tend to raise new and more difficult questions.[116] In such a situation, in which a tradition has forfeited its 'vitality', its confidence in being able to overcome new and existing problems in the future with the existing means available is no longer justified: 'One of the signs that a tradition is in crisis is that its accustomed ways for relating *seems* and *is* begin to break down. Thus the pressures of skepticism become more urgent.'[117] Such a crisis really only serves to show whether a belief system is *actually* a rational tradition. An affirmative answer to this question is only justified if the tradition succeeds in reacting to the crisis with a process of fundamental change that fulfils three specific criteria. These three criteria are fulfilled when a tradition (1) arrives at a *solution* to an *epistemological crisis* through a *conceptual innovation* that can offer a coherent solution to the problem; (2) if this solution at the same time provides a *clarification* of why the now obsolete conceptual system could not solve the crisis; and (3) if, despite the transformation of the beliefs and methods, the new approach can still also be understood as a *further development* of the established tradition.[118] MacIntyre therefore insists that narrative continuity must be retained even in radically new conceptions of a tradition's norms and that a solution to the problems affecting a research tradition must not merely constitute a change of paradigm but must always involve a reconceptualization of the past: 'When an epistemological crisis is resolved, it is by the construction of a new narrative which enables the agent to understand both how he or she could intelligibly have his or her original beliefs and how he or she could have been so drastically misled by them.'[119] Crucially, MacIntyre – unlike Walzer and Taylor – can plausibly understand not only the reconstitution of a tradition but also its breakdown and replacement by another tradition as a result of such a crisis, and he thus allows for transformative critique, at least in principle. If a tradition falls into insoluble crisis and there is a competing tradition whose solution to the same problems can be *understood* by the members of the first tradition,[120] then within the framework of the first tradition it may be rationally necessary to recognize the superiority of this other tradition.[121] The members are thereby given a reason to revise their own fundamental norms – and in this MacIntyre finally achieves the transition from an internal-reconstructive critique to an immanent-transformative critique:

> When they have understood the beliefs of the alien tradition, they may find themselves compelled to recognize that within this other tradition, it is possible to construct from the concepts and theories peculiar to it what they were unable to provide from their own conceptual and theoretical resources, a cogent and illuminating explanation – cogent and illuminating, that is, by their own standards – of why their own intellectual tradition had been unable to solve its problem or restore its coherence.[122]

If, however, it is rationally necessary in these cases to recognize another tradition as superior, and therefore also to adopt its vocabulary, then, conversely, a community can also be criticized for *not* taking this step. This critique is appropriate when the members of the original tradition continue to insist on their tradition in light of obvious contradictions and pathologies, even though another tradition is available that solves their problems and even though its ability to do so can be recognized according to the criteria of their own tradition. According to MacIntyre, it is therefore possible to rationally demand a change of tradition from the point of view of a tradition that proves deficient. He can therefore allow for the possibility of a fundamental critique of moral beliefs in a more radical sense than Walzer or Taylor. This model of crises allows MacIntyre to understand the fundamental form of critique of the totality of moral practice as 'interpretation', insofar as such critique is based on the internal dynamic of the given moral world. Accordingly, on the one hand, the range of interpretive critique can be greatly expanded. On the other hand, MacIntyre *limits* a fundamental critique of normative practices to those traditions that are no longer productive, or that can no longer solve their internal problems in a satisfactory way. Transformative critique, in other words, is only justified when a tradition can no longer successfully practice internal reconstructive self-critique.

According to this model, we can therefore distinguish *hermeneutic critique* from *radical critique*. The first can be understood as the gradual improvement of beliefs against the background of a consensus on the criteria of rationality. This idea is largely consistent with Taylor's model. In the case of radical critique, however, a fundamental revision of the criterion of rationality is initiated by a crisis. Both forms of critique give the members of the tradition reasons to revise their norms.

Even if MacIntyre's model proves superior to a simple hermeneutic approach based on Walzer's model with regard to the possibility of critique and also supplements Taylor's model through the idea of an epistemic crisis, thus allowing for more fundamental critique, it is nonetheless not fully satisfactory.

First, MacIntyre remains oddly vague about the causes of normative conflicts within traditions.[123] Conflicts are – in his opinion – essential parts of traditions; indeed, discord is constitutive of them.[124] But what is the driving force behind these conflicts? MacIntyre simply points towards 'new developments' – for example, the discovery of incoherence among the beliefs of a community, or confrontations with new situations or other belief systems. However, he also has a fundamental cause in mind, independent of such developments: the fact that authoritative texts, or the utterances of authorities, always require interpretation, and interpretations necessarily carry the risk of divergence. While the first type of cause is contingent, the second is a systematic source of conflict, which *per definitionem* is not exceptional but rather a ubiquitous property of moral practice. If this systematic potential for conflict (which lies in social practices' irreducible need for interpretation) is taken seriously, however, a criterion of progress can be derived from it: a form of life is more rational than another if it can better handle *the constitutive and permanent risk of disagreement it engenders*. But this possibility is discarded by MacIntyre insofar as he conceives of all kinds of normative conflict as being first purely contingent and then – once a tradition has developed – as conflicts that are rooted in the specific preconditions of rationality within that tradition. This understanding, however, does not allow for a characterization of a common content of such conflicts across traditions.

Second, the criterion of the successful solution of conflict is too weak. Narrative continuity, which creates a tradition, is always construed retrospectively, and thus construed from the standpoint of a particular solution. This retrospective point of view, however, cannot be a basis for a rational reconstruction of the self-understanding of practitioners of social critique, as was already mentioned in the analysis of Taylor's model. There can be a whole range of solutions available for every conflict, which can be represented as continuity in some narratives, even those that are insignificantly novel interpretations of the self-understandings to date. The critics who are in a crisis must be able to justify their critique with reasons that cannot *presuppose* a solution as already acceptable. The same applies to radical change that takes place through the replacement of one tradition by another: MacIntyre states as a criterion for the replacement of rationality criteria that the new tradition must also provide a solution to the problems of the old that is *recognized as* a solution from the standpoint of the old tradition.[125] But this is only a negative criterion, as the old tradition must only be able to recognize that the new tradition *does not exhibit* the old tradition's unsolvable problems. The old tradition will, however – due to the presumed untranslatability of traditions – typically be unable to describe in its own vocabulary *how* the new tradition solves its problems. This criterion therefore does not provide a *positive* reason for the replacement of a crisis by means of some *specific* alternative tradition. MacIntyre must therefore assume that, in any case, only *one* alternative tradition is available. This is hardly convincing in modernity, where countless answers to moral problems from different traditions compete with each other in the same society.[126]

Third, the focus on traditions of moral *discourse* is an unnecessary constriction. As MacIntyre does not tire of emphasizing, the tradition of moral enquiry is always part of a more comprehensive tradition of *moral life*, in which there is a place for normative standards to be made explicit.[127]

The relationship between theory and social practice is reciprocal as far as this idea is concerned: not only are theories the expression of normative practices,[128] but they are also conversely constitutive of these practices, in

72 Chapter Three

which they are embodied. A tradition can therefore only arise when its theoretical commitments can also be correspondingly institutionalized in social practices. With this idea, MacIntyre approaches a practice-based theory that conceives of theoretical obligations as practically founded. However, because, he ultimately privileges discursive forms of expression over practical forms of normativity, he limits the set of traditions (and thereby of social practices) that are eligible as resources for critique to those that have already created social institutions in which normative claims can become explicit. This is inevitable, as he exclusively emphasizes those internal standards of rationality that can *only* appear in discursive practices. This commitment comes along with two significant decisions: first, those traditions and communities that lack institutionalized forms of explicit moral deliberation are rejected as possible sources of competing norms because they cannot function as self-conscious advocates of their norms. Second, it entails that the *best way to access* the norms of a community is to interpret the norms already *made explicit* within it. It follows that the participant's perspective in a tradition is the best standpoint from which the claims of that tradition can be made explicit. Therefore, MacIntyre must finally always present critique of normative commitments as a discursive disagreement between members of different moral traditions.[129] Moral principles are therefore not grounded in a social practice as a whole but in the specific part of a social practice in which disagreements about the correct understanding of human actions and goods take place. At this point, MacIntyre makes no room for the idea that norms can also be institutionalized in nondiscursive, comprehensive practices and instead exclusively attempts to locate the reason for the validity of norms in *discourses about norms*. Nevertheless, his method remains an immanent method, as he does not accept that the explicit beliefs of the members of a traditional community provide the final reference point for moral debate.

3.3.3. The Prospects of MacIntyre's Model of Immanent Critique

MacIntyre – with his practice-based model – puts forward a proposal that appears to add a social theoretical foundation to Taylor's approach, as the focus is shifted away from 'strong evaluations' and towards goods that are constituted by practices. As has been shown, however, his model of practices remains incomplete and has not been worked out systematically. With respect to its sociological strength, his later recourse to a strong hermeneutical approach with the concept of tradition is a step backwards: the earlier concept of practices at least had the potential to locate a systematic source of the incongruence of interpretations in the nondiscursive, institutional and cooperative preconditions of moral discourse. MacIntyre's concept of tradition, however, must treat the disagreement, contradictoriness and inconsistency of semantic content merely as a given, not as socially conditioned. Furthermore, his model of practices opens up the prospect of enabling a general understanding of social conflicts (on which social critique could draw) to a larger degree than a model of disagreement within moral traditions.

Only when MacIntyre brings into view the connection between traditions (which at least can serve to partly explain the idea of normative progress) and social practices (which form the basis for implicit normativity) can he aim at a productive connection between hermeneutic understanding and social theory. However, this is at the same time the point at which his model comes up against an internal boundary.

3.4 HERMENEUTIC IMMANENT CRITIQUE AND SOCIAL THEORY

This survey of three theories of hermeneutic immanent critique has shown that the question of how the role of the interpretation of normative commitments is construed within the framework of those social practices in which *disagreements about interpretations* have their place is decisive in determining whether these models can solve the problems of immanent critique. Both Taylor and MacIntyre take seriously the demand that this social context of interpretation be made explicit, and both attempt to define more precisely Walzer's idea that interpretation of normative commitments is a social practice that can also be at least partially described 'externally'.

There are two issues which emerge from the examination of these accounts. The first is that it is obvious that the hermeneutic models need a criterion that does not require us to ignore the plurality of existing interpretations for recognizing which interpretations conform to the 'actually meant' sense of a practice. The second is that it remains unclear how the *practice of interpretation* can be conceived of as a specifically *social practice*. After all, the critique of the self-interpretations of a certain action context is only a genuinely *social* critique when it applies a certain type of argument: it must describe these self-interpretations as criticizable social practices.

Taylor's and MacIntyre's models fulfil this requirement. Taylor assumes that societies must answer existential questions about their shared social self-understanding but does not clarify how we should understand specifically *social* conflicts about its interpretation. MacIntyre assumes that social practices or traditions are the paradigmatic site of such disagreements. However, once the plurality and conflict-laden nature of social practices is accepted, it is no longer clear why social conflicts are always best described as conflicts about the interpretation of shared *conceptions or ideas* about values. This makes it clear that the idea of a hermeneutic approach to immanent norms faces a dilemma: either it posits in advance – without justification – that the object of the interpretive analysis displays an internal unity on the model of consensual morality (Walzer) or moral identity (Taylor), or it recognizes that the reference point of social critique is social practices that are always controversial and shot through with conflict – but it is then unclear to what extent the privileging of a specific interpretation of the content of the practices can be justified by hermeneutic means.

This gives rise to a second problem: the fact that a particular interpretation of a self-understanding – which at the same time revises this self-understanding – represents progress means nothing other than that a critic who proposes this revision is *socially entitled to demand* that other members of that society *recognize* their proposal as being an adequate interpretation of their shared commitments. This social entitlement to demand (in the process of interpretation) the recognition of a particular position is only comprehensible if we can view the collective acceptance of a particular self-understanding as part of a social practice in which agents have certain *claims* against each other. It must then be shown how such claims are grounded in the specific social practices in question, which, again, requires more social theory than the hermeneutic conceptions can offer.

A plausible hermeneutic theory that is strong enough for immanent critique therefore presupposes a complex model of social practices. This means that the interpretive dimension of critique must be underpinned by a social ontological model of its normativity.

Chapter Four

Immanent Critique and the Critical Theory of Society

As I argued in chapter 2, practice-based models of immanent critique of the kind that is distinctive of critical theory in the tradition of the Frankfurt School assume that immanent critique does more than just uncover the potentials that are implicit in our self-understandings. We can only understand the nature of the norms to which immanent social critique refers, such models argue, if we know how those norms are socially institutionalized beyond the beliefs of individuals, and beyond an unproblematic consensus in a community's self-interpretations. This means that social theory and social critique cannot be conducted independently of one another. This assertion, which ultimately merely establishes that a certain kind of critique is only possible if certain assumptions are also made in social theory, is presumably uncontroversial.

In the history of critical theory, however, this claim has always come together with a stronger thesis: not only is the *possibility of critique* dependent on certain objective social preconditions, but the discovery of normative potentials in society only becomes possible through adopting the critical perspective. The assumption of normative potentials is therefore bound to a particular, critical research program. In classical critical theory, as paradigmatically articulated in Horkheimer's essay 'Traditional and Critical Theory', these two ideas are linked – that is, the idea of *the normative interest of theory* and the idea of the *normative constitution of its objects*. In particular, Horkheimer assumes that immanent normative demands can be found in the social *practice of work*, which points beyond the current society.[1] Unlike in classical Marxism, however, he does not assume that these demands create their own subject – the proletariat – such that the value judgements of the members of society and the immanent demands of the practice ultimately coincide.[2] Rather, he claims that these normative demands are only disclosed through a *theory* that is understood as a part of this practice. As innovative as this idea was, it owed a great deal to the assumption that the structure of human work can be understood without difficulty such that the claim that it contains immanent demands becomes plausible. This assumption has since proved both empirically problematic and theoretically unclear.[3]

Contemporary critical theory therefore cannot take over this strategy of locating the basis of immanent critique in social reality. Rather, it must find a new way of establishing the interconnection between social critique and social theory.

In this chapter, I will examine two models in contemporary critical theory: Jürgen Habermas's theory of communicative action and Axel Honneth's theory of recognition. Both of these theories, I will argue, are committed to the idea of immanent critique. They understand social critique not as the mere application of moral or otherwise independent norms but as grounded in the commitments instituted in social practices. There are, however, some fundamental disagreements between these two theories. Crucially, the theory of communicative action and the theory of recognition disagree about the best way to conceptualize what social practices and immanent norms are. Furthermore, their commitment to immanent critique often remains implicit and obscured by their more substantive social theoretical claims. In order to bring into view their distinctive approaches to immanent critique, I will therefore first attempt to reconstruct them as theories of immanent critique, before subjecting their claims to critical scrutiny.

4.1. THE MODEL OF COMMUNICATIVE RATIONALITY

Jürgen Habermas's work is one of the most elaborate attempts to account for the normative standards of social critique on the basis of a social theory. Even if we limit ourselves to his social theoretical and philosophical writings in the narrower sense, the complexity of his work makes a comprehensive examination impossible here. Therefore, this section will merely provide a rough outline – by means of the fundamental idea that Habermas presents in his main work, *The Theory of Communicative Action*[4] – of the resources his work offers in dealing with the problem I have sketched.

First, a misunderstanding must be cleared up concerning the concept of immanent critique. In the essay 'Technology and Science as "Ideology"', published in 1968, Habermas explicitly rejects the Marxist idea of immanent critique, which he understands as a form of critique that uses the *normative components of bourgeois ideology* to criticize the reality of capitalism. In Habermas's view at the time, this program can no longer be pursued: the ideology of free exchange to which Marx refers in his analysis of the contradictions of capitalist practices has been replaced by a new technocratic ideology that no longer carries the same potential for emancipation.[5] Immanent critique can therefore no longer be supported by this potential but must go beyond bourgeois ideology to 'disclose the fundamental interests of mankind as such, engaged in the process of self-constitution'.[6] Habermas applies the concept of 'immanent critique' in a relatively narrow way here, however: he refers only to a *particular* interpretation of this concept, one that is bound to a specific interpretation of Marx, which locates normative potentials solely in the explicitly normative components of *ideologies*. This narrow understanding does not relate to the conception of immanent critique employed here, which leaves open how, exactly, the immanence of norms in practices is to be understood.

After 1968, Habermas – although he later decisively modified his social analysis – did not comment explicitly on the theory of immanent critique. As I will show in the following, his work can nevertheless be understood as a theory of immanent critique that focuses not on ideologies but on the *form of practices*.[7] Even if his criticism of classical ideology critique does not entail that he must reject every form of immanent critique, it follows from his pessimistic account that he cannot share the hermeneutic paradigm that locates the normative foundations of criticism in the *self-understanding* of a society. He must – if these self-understandings are themselves part of an objectionable context of power – rely on a different basis.

4.1.1 Communicative Action and Immanent Critique – an Overview

If we wanted to condense *The Theory of Communicative Action* into a slogan, we could say, first, that the immanent potential on which a critical theory should be based can only be explained through the concept of *rationality* and that, second, rationality is based on the formal characteristics of the practice of *communicative action*.[8] According to this model, immanent critique is a form of critique that refers to objective criteria of rationality within a specific form of communicative practice, thereby gaining a kind of access to socially institutionalized norms that is partially interpretation-independent.

The first step in this argument is as follows: reflexive critique can only make its claims comprehensible as *rationally justified* assertions. It can therefore only refer to social reality as the source of the norms it applies if it also reconstructs the actions and beliefs of the members of the society from which these norms are derived such that their rationality is assumed. Second, Habermas wants to show that we should understand this assumption of the rationality of social actions with reference to the internal norms of the *communicative coordination of action*. To substantiate his model of rational action, Habermas first presents a diagnosis of the failures of previous attempts, which tried to explain the immanent rationality potential of society via a truncated concept of the rationality of actions. His theoretical-historical excursuses seek to demonstrate – above all via the example of Max Weber – that a model that contracts rationality into *formal instrumental rationality* leads to the *aporiae* that ultimately find expression in the problems faced by the first generation of the Frankfurt School.[9] Habermas's project differs from Weber's attempts – and those of early critical theory – to understand rationality via the category of instrumental action, as Habermas *widens the concept of rationality*: he assumes that rational actions cannot be understood merely as instrumental actions. Rather, we can only fully understand the nature of rationality by reference to the *practice of communication* – that is, *the establishment of validity claims* in the context of the intersubjective coordination of actions.

For this reason, he treats 'communicative action' as the central phenomenon of intersubjective rationality. As the 'original mode' of language use,[10] communicative action is an irreducible type of social practice[11] in which an irreducible normative potential can be found in the form of *validity claims* that must necessarily be raised in a particular form of communication. At the same time, communicative action allows for the emergence of a type of *unabbreviated rationality*, which is disclosed by reflection on the validity claims raised in communicative acts.[12]

Habermas distinguishes communicative rationality from the complementary types of *instrumental* and *strategic* rationality. With this distinction, he lays the foundation for a social theoretical model that relies on a social ontological distinction between two modes of social reproduction, which Habermas refers to as 'system' and 'lifeworld'. The 'lifeworld' stands for those kinds of social integration that are shaped by a continually communicative and renewed understanding and that make this integration possible in the form of sedimented and shared self-understandings. The 'system', by contrast, serves as shorthand for those forms of noncommunicative social action-coordination that develop from processes of social differentiation, through which social interaction is relieved of the need for communicative justification. As this distinction shows, it is therefore possible to differentiate between two aspects of social practices: those from which immanent potentials for communicative rationality can be reconstructed, and those in which these potentials have been replaced by substitutes that do not allow for immanent critique.

Therefore, immanent potentials exist in those social practices in the 'lifeworld' that are structured communicatively such that their participants must assume that everyone is committed to the acceptance of a specific range of validity claims. Immanent critique can reconstruct these claims by examining which (yet to be elucidated) norms people *necessarily* – that is, independently of their self-understanding – have already committed themselves to by virtue of participating in communicative practices.

This cursory overview of key preliminary conceptual distinctions shows that *The Theory of Communicative Action* provides the basis for a form of immanent critique in the sense discussed here.

4.1.2 Communication and Critique

Before any arguments from *The Theory of Communicative Action* can be examined in detail, I will briefly lay out the structure of Habermas's social ontological argument. This argument establishes the claim that the normativity that immanent critique can take up is, on the one hand, immanent in a type of practice of communicative action and, on the other hand, immanent in the form of social integration of the 'lifeworld' that is related to this form of action.

As already mentioned, the normativity that underlies Habermas's model of critique is localized in a specific mode of social practice: *communicative action*. The basis of normativity is therefore not an abstract structure of language 'in itself' but rather the specific form of the *practice of communication*. Communicative action is a mode of language use – the carrying out of speech acts – which is *structured by an orientation towards agreement*.[13]

Because communicative action contexts are necessarily oriented towards this goal, any practice characterized by them can be assumed to be oriented towards specific norms. In addition to expressing some content in our speech acts, we must also – in order to intentionally come to an agreement – raise *validity claims*: we must act with the intention that our speech acts are recognized by others as *serious* and – in the case of assertions – *true*. This goal must be implicit in any attempt to reach agreement in a minimal sense. In a strong sense, communicative action only occurs if this agreement also serves to coordinate *actions* in such a way that not only the *truth of the assertions* but also the *correctness of the resultant actions* is an object of the agreement. This distinguishes communicative action from other forms of communication in which the raising of claims of truth and sincerity allows for the coordination of strategic actions oriented by purely individual preferences.[14]

According to Habermas, communicative action only plays this crucial role in modern societies. Whereas traditional societies are integrated through a 'basic normative agreement'[15] in the framework of a unified symbolic order, modern societies are so functionally differentiated that they do not have such a basis for integration at their disposal. Therefore, in order to ensure the integration of their constituent action contexts, they are at least partially dependent on communicative action – that is, the coordination of actions by means of *communication*. With this thesis, Habermas diverges from the model with which modern systems theory conceptualizes the functional differentiation of modern societies. Systems theory assumes that coordination within individual action systems in modern societies is ensured not through shared action orientations but through 'functionally intermeshing action consequences'[16] and, more specifically, through noncommunicatively structured *steering media* (money or power, for example). Habermas rejects this assumption, at least in its generalized form.

In addition to assuming systemically integrated spheres of action – whose existence he concedes – Habermas also assumes the existence of a sphere in modern societies which is *normatively integrated through consensus*, which the members of society refer to as their 'lifeworld'. This refers not to a social sphere that is separate in a strong sense but rather to a 'perspective of acting subjects'.[17] The lifeworld is actualized as a frame of reference when subjects rely on shared certainties, which form the unquestionable and ultimately insuperable background to linguistic understanding.[18] The lifeworld is constituted not only by cultural conventions – as classical sociological theories of the lifeworld assume – but also by narratively constructed meaning resources, social belonging, institutions and personal identities, which are produced by communicative processes.[19] Furthermore, Habermas does not identify the lifeworld with a perspective on society as a whole, but rather excludes from this perspective those areas that are not dependent on communicative reproduction but which – like the market, for example – can reproduce themselves through systemic processes that are not governed by communication.[20] The consequences of this theoretical move for immanent critique are that it can no longer develop a comprehensive approach to 'society' as a unified object, as the theories of hermeneutic critique assumed. Society must rather be, at least in part, reconstructed from the *specific perspective of the lifeworld*, which is only one part of the social self-description. Nevertheless, this need not mean that a model of immanent critique that builds on this reconstruction is only *applicable* to phenomena that can be reconstructed from the perspective of the lifeworld.

The concept of the lifeworld is not only normatively but also social theoretically central to Habermas's account, as the fundamental processes of communication are both dependent on the lifeworld as a condition of their possibility and necessary for reproducing this lifeworld and its symbolic resources.[21] Communication and lifeworld, or communicative interaction and the sedimented symbolic background of the normal relations to the world, are the two components that together create the substratum of normativity in society.

As already mentioned, Habermas does not himself understand his theory as an attempt to justify a model of immanent critique. Nevertheless, the conjunction of his theories of communication, rationality and society can be used to develop such a model: Habermas reconstructs the normative potentials of society in such a way that agents' explicit beliefs do not have the last word and, at the same time, no external normative premises need be introduced. The fundamental assumption of his model is that a specific form of social integration comes into being through the rationalization of modern lifeworlds. This form of integration is based on communicative action. Its immanent norms demand the actualization of the normative potentials contained in these forms of action. Critics can therefore – as *members* of discourses *in the lifeworld* – demand the realization of the potentials that are presupposed in it; as *theorists*, they can also diagnose pathologies of the lifeworld, with these pathologies serving to systematically block the actualization of existing rationality potentials. The two standpoints of 'normal' participation in, and theoretical analysis of, discourses refer to the same foundation, namely, the (yet to be clarified) ineluctable presuppositions of communicative action, which can always be presupposed as an effective integrative moment in modern societies.

The focus of Habermas's model is the second aspect – that is, the critical diagnosis of distortions in communication and the sociological diagnosis of repressive and pathological processes, as Habermas does not regard 'ordinary' participation in discourse as a task in which knowledge of philosophical or sociological theories gives intellectuals any special advantage.[22] For this reason, this specific kind of immanent critique – to which Habermas must be committed as a consequence of his theoretical programme – is a critique that does not raise a claim to argue for substantive norms. It is a proceduralist critique of communicative processes and governing conditions, which assesses the quality of the ways norms are established by communicative agreement but does not evaluate those norms themselves.[23]

4.1.3. Universal Pragmatics as a Normative Epistemology

With this brief sketch of the concept of communicative action and the perspective of the lifeworld in hand, we can now turn to the method by which Habermas seeks to reconstruct the normative potentials of communicative action: universal pragmatics.

On Habermas's model of critique, the immanent normativity of social practices is based on the always-supposed preconditions of those communicative actions in which validity claims are raised. In particular, these are claims about the *comprehensibility, truth, truthfulness* and *normative correctness* of speech acts or their contents.[24] In the communicative coordination of actions, all parties must raise these claims, mutually assume an orientation towards their fulfilment and assume that their counterparts likewise make these assumptions. As this may be assumed in the process of communication without further proof, it is clear that all parties immediately have a reason to demand and accept that such claims be redeemed in cases of doubt. Habermas therefore says that speakers always take on *obligations* through their speech acts the satisfaction of which is *socially demandable*.[25]

This social normativity of communicative action is only visible, however, when the assumption of the fulfilment of validity claims becomes *problematic* – that is, when *communicative disorders* occur. In these cases, Habermas argues, there are always two strategies that people can adopt: one can relinquish the communicative attitude together with its correlative assumptions and switch from the mode of communicative action to the mode of strategic action, or one can make the claims explicit and discursively thematize the question of their satisfiability.[26] This second alternative is not a theoretical-scientific undertaking but rather part of everyday discursive practices that constitutively include the possibility of becoming thematic to themselves. This self-thematization can be reconstructed theoretically, however: in this sense, Habermas envisages 'universal pragmatics' as a project that is internal to the philosophy of language, which is aimed at reconstructing the necessary assumptions underlying communicative action.[27] In this sense, universal pragmatics takes on the role of what I have previously called a 'normative epistemology'.[28]

But how can we know in advance what qualifies as communication? If we assume that communicative action is action that is coordinated through the raising of validity claims, we are only able to count as instances of this form of practice those actions in which a series of (more or less counterfactual) 'procedural conditions' may be assumed as accepted – because only they can be understood as practices of raising justified validity claims.[29]

> Anyone who seriously engages in argumentation must presuppose that the context of discussion guarantees in principle freedom of access, equal rights to participate, truthfulness on the part of participants, the absence of coercion in adopting positions, and so on.[30]

This naturally has implications for how discourses can proceed: from these presuppositions resulting from the pragmatics of justification, *a principle of universalization* can be derived,[31] which stipulates that the consequences of any valid norm must be accepted by all concerned.[32] This *principle of universalization* is not effective at the level of the norms themselves; it merely establishes the rules for a discourse *in which* norms can be demonstrated as justified. At the material level of normative validity, however, it corresponds to the well-known discourse principle, from which Habermas wants to draw discourse ethical conclusions in a narrow sense: 'Only those norms of action are valid to which all possibly affected persons could assent as participants in rational discourses.'[33] Habermas's discourse ethics, which relies on this principle, does not need to be discussed here – it is sufficient for our purposes to note the methodological assumption that the *conditions of the constitution of normative validity* can develop a normative force through the assumption of an idealized universal communicative community, which is an idealization that is necessary for comprehending that validity. This force affects actual discursive behaviour insofar as it is incorporated in accepted norms of justification. At the same time, whether these conditions are satisfied becomes a criterion for the normative validity of the consensus that is achieved in concrete discourses.

Can we derive a model of social critique from this? The answer to this question depends on what exactly can be understood as the object of the kind of critique that applies norms reconstructed through universal pragmatics. Is it the *norms* on which people agree in discourse, is it *their communicative actions* in discourse, or is it the *norms of discourse*?

None of these answers is persuasive. On the first level of *communicative content* – that is, the norms that become thematic in communication – Habermas's theory is largely unenlightening.[34] The discourse principle does not fix *which* norms people should agree on. Rather, it only spells out the conditions that discourses must meet through which people can come to a valid agreement about first-order norms. Communicative interaction *in* discourses can, by contrast, be the object of a discourse-theoretically informed critique: agents can be criticized, for example, if they are unable to redeem the implied validity claims; if their speech acts are incomprehensible; if their statements are not true or not meant seriously; or if their normative claims are unjustified. But this cannot yet be a model of immanent critique, because such speech acts, as *individual* actions, can hardly be the object of *social* critique. On a second level, however, the *rules of a discourse* that are presumed in a given situation can be the object of critique. If participants in a discourse assume that making false claims, excluding potential participants, or denying the status of 'participant' to others is not in conflict with the ideal of communication, this assumption can be shown to be false. However, this form of critique also remains relatively abstract and insubstantial, as it must be limited to clarifying the *presuppositions* of discourses in general. Above all, however, as a critique of assumptions made by *individual participants*, it is again not a form of *social* critique. The critique of communication overcomes this barrier to becoming a form of social critique only if it is assumed that the aforementioned violations of the rules of discourse are *not failures of individual members* but *false institutionalized modes of conduct*. Only in such cases can critique begin to address a practice in which the *violation* of the presuppositions of communicative action is *institutionalized* in the form of social rules.

Yet the normative significance of the reconstruction of the preconditions of discourses cannot be made clear from the perspective of universal pragmatics alone. It does not necessarily follow from the simple observation that the assumptions that are essential for communication are violated by a given practice that these assumptions also constitute the most relevant overall criteria for *that kind of practice* (especially for those components of a practice that cannot be subsumed under the label 'discursive'), as 'normativity in the more restricted sense of a binding practical orientation is not identical with the rationality of action oriented to reaching understanding as a whole'.[35] The idea that Habermas develops as an answer to this problem – the idea that only *real discourse itself* and not the *form of discourse alone* can ground the necessary normative force – is only persuasive if it can be shown that communicative practices are in a relevant sense crucial components of all essential social action contexts, and only if the question of when we can legitimately assume the existence of social practices for which norms of communication are both relevant and substantive is made clear. Therefore, the full model can succeed only in combination with the social ontological thesis, which we have yet to develop.

4.1.4. The Social Ontology of Communicative Action

This short journey through Habermas's methodology shows that it can serve as a basis for social critique only if the mode of communicative action is understood to be constitutive of central social practices as a whole. Otherwise, Habermas would be exposed to the criticism that his model of social criticism remains restricted to those practices that structurally come closest to the explicit expression of normative commitments. Put differently: the essential function of the concept of 'communication' for an analysis of society as a whole, as Habermas understands it, must not be merely an *assumption*. Communication must prove to be *actually necessary*, as a matter of social theory, for understanding central social practices. This means that Habermas must complement his methodology with an ontology of social practices in order to arrive at a critical program. This ontology remains largely implicit in his social theory. His theory of the lifeworld, however, contains numerous stipulations that allow these social ontological foundations to be understood.[36]

The concept of the lifeworld primarily refers to a *relation to the world*, namely, the horizon of unquestioned situation definitions, with which acting subjects relate to their social actions from a participant's perspective.[37] As Habermas explains, most classic social theorists, such as Mead and Durkheim, commit the error of reducing the lifeworld to *only one* of its structural components. Durkheim only provides the lifeworld with elements of the normative regulation of belonging, compared to which culture and personality take on auxiliary roles;[38] Mead only considers the elements of *personality*. By contrast, Thomas Luckmann's analysis – which draws on phenomenological conceptions of the lifeworld – commits the error of reducing the lifeworld to *cultural* commonalities.[39] Habermas assumes that the inadequacy of these classic approaches stems from the fact that they ultimately do not adequately capture the way the lifeworld is differentiated into three structural components[40] – culture, personality and society.[41] He proposes as an alternative a *comprehensive* conception of the lifeworld that consists of the three aforementioned components, which are jointly constitutive of the possibility of communication.[42]

The function of this conception of the lifeworld consists in explaining the *normative force* of the idealizations that are always assumed in communicative action, as well as the normative force of specific validity claims.

Habermas's conception of the lifeworld remains relatively vague because it appears to assume that we need not reconstruct the normative force of communicative assumptions through a *social ontological analysis of the institutionalization* of norms through interactions or relationships. He appears instead to assume that a *reconstruction of the participant's perspective* on the lifeworld makes all the salient facts about this normative force available to us.

It accordingly remains unclear whether such a reconstruction can only describe the *formal* preconditions for communicative acts or facilitates a *sociologically substantive* analysis of the normative force of communicative processes. Concerning the latter, Habermas was soon confronted with the question whether his theory of the lifeworld as an entity that is exclusively communicatively reproduced must not necessarily neglect issues of power and domination, which accompany any actual institutionalization of norms.[43]

Habermas responded to this criticism by introducing a distinction between the *formal-pragmatic* and the *sociological* conception of the lifeworld.[44] The formal-pragmatic conception of the lifeworld recognizes how, *from the first-person perspective* of participants in communicative action, a background of lifeworld resources can always be *unproblematically* assumed.[45] By contrast, the *sociological perspective* describes the reproduction of the necessary resources from the external standpoint of a sociologist, who is able to recognize the force of noncommunicative processes in the empirically existing lifeworld and can problematize the normative validity of the norms of the lifeworld. Habermas assumes that this distinction allows us to clarify why we can conceptually capture the *binding force of communicative normativity* (which can only be seen from the perspective of a potential participant in communication – that is, from the formal-pragmatic perspective) *independently* of the *sociological perspective*. In other words, as soon as we have grasped the historical emergence of the logic of communication via a theory of social evolution, *the binding force of communicative actions can be fully explained from the perspective of this logic, without the need for an additional social ontological explanation* of its institutionalization.

The distinction between the formal-pragmatic and the sociological conception of the lifeworld on which this argument is based is ultimately untenable, however, as it leads to the following dilemma. *On the one hand*, Habermas cannot rely solely on the formal-pragmatically reconstructible participant perspective in order to explain what contribution the normative resources of the lifeworld make to the possibility of communicative action. Because norms cannot become *thematic* from this perspective, it cannot generate any sociological insights regarding norms and therefore also no social scientific explanations. As Habermas furthermore assumes that we can only understand the normative force of communicatively produced normative constraints from the participant's perspective rather than the sociological observer's perspective, he introduces, in addition to the formal-pragmatic concept, the 'everyday concept of the lifeworld' as a third conception,[46] where the lifeworld is described neither exclusively from the perspective of participants (as in the formal-pragmatic conception) nor from the perspective of observers, but from the quasi-participatory perspective of *narrators*.[47] From this perspective, norms can be thematized, and thus also described with regard to their normative force.

It is unclear, however, to what extent this third perspective actually constitutes an independent standpoint.[48] If, as Habermas suggests, the narrator perspective in which the lifeworld can actually become thematic – in contrast to the participant's perspective – can actually be 'theoretically oriented' such that it makes 'statements about the reproduction or self-maintenance of communicatively structured lifeworlds'[49] possible, then it is unclear not only how it is marked off against the sociological perspective but also whether we can still assume that the norms of the lifeworld have *an unproblematic* character from this perspective. If it really were possible to reconstruct the lifeworld from an independent perspective exclusively based on the logic of its communicative reproduction, in such a way that questions with regard to its normative constitution can be addressed, then the question arises as to whether the *same perspective* would also allow us, in principle, to *criticize* such norms

Immanent Critique and the Critical Theory of Society 87

as mere effects of *power and domination*. Yet if this is impossible – and if, therefore, Habermas must assume norms as unproblematically given in the context of an *explanation* of the normative force of the lifeworld – then he falls victim to the same critique he directed at the hermeneutic theories in the social sciences: the explanation of the normative force of lifeworld norms is always based on the assumption of their legitimacy and thereby makes ideological distortions and discursive exclusions systematically invisible.

On the other hand, if Habermas answers this question in the affirmative, allowing for a description of the normative force of the lifeworld that is rich enough for social explanations and for social critique (for example, descriptions that explain the force of such norms with recourse to power, ideology or material necessity), then it is no longer obvious that we can actually understand the force of communicative action solely through the *logic of the communicative reproduction* of the lifeworld.[50] In particular, the question whether we should disregard the possibility that the institutional foundations of communicative normativity might also consist in noncommunicative and noncommunicatively reproduced relations would remain unanswered.[51] Put differently: if this dilemma leads us to acknowledge that a pure communications-theoretic analysis of the lifeworld does not provide an adequate explanation of the social force of its norms, then there is no longer any argument as to why *noncommunicative* sources of normative obligation couldn't also appear in such an analysis. But then Habermas cannot assume that the theory of communication is sufficient to answer the fundamental social ontological question faced by any theory of immanent critique: namely, the question of which social structures underlie the force of the social norms that the theory reconstructs. This question cannot be answered without reference to a more developed social ontological theory than that offered by Habermas.

A social ontological theory of this sort would have to answer, rather than evade, the question of how exactly social practices are capable of generating normative force. This normative force is, as I have discussed above, already presumed to exist in Habermas's analyses of communicative action and, correspondingly, in his theory of the lifeworld. Instead of simply assuming that the formal properties of communicative interaction explain everything we need to know to understand how immanent normativity, and thus immanent critique, is possible, such a social ontology theory would have to explain what specific features must be present in the social practices of a given society for the form of communicative action to acquire the social relevance that Habermas assumes it must have in modernity. Furthermore, it must explain which social norms account for the structural properties of that form of interaction. In short, to answer these questions, and in order to explain how the norms he reconstructs in his formal pragmatics acquire their specific force, Habermas would have to provide a *social ontological account that explains how normativity in general emerges from intersubjective interaction*. As I have argued, there is little reason to assume that communicative practices are the only kind that are structured by immanent norms of the sort presupposed by immanent critique.

Insofar as Habermas maintains that the combination of a theory of social evolution and formal pragmatics is sufficient for understanding the normative constitution of the lifeworld, however, he implicitly commits himself to a radical version of *social ontological monism* regarding the lifeworld, that is, the idea that all practices that figure in an explanation of the social norms and institutions of the lifeworld are communicative. This is because he assumes that the symbolic consensus of premodernity has been replaced with the communicative reproduction of the lifeworld,[52] and that the formal-pragmatic reconstruction of the lifeworld is sufficient for understanding the existence of the norms institutionalized there.[53] This entails that *we can answer all questions concerning the constitution of the lifeworld with a theory of communication*. Insofar as he further identifies the possibility of communicative rationality as the normatively relevant achievement of the lifeworld and understands the mechanisms behind the normative force of communicative rationality only according to the model of raising of validity claims, he must confine his analysis of the institutionalization of lifeworld norms to those social ontological elements that can be understood through the language of a theory of communication.[54] Habermas therefore implicitly accepts the premise that from the participant's perspective, *only those norms that can be made communicatively available* can claim normative binding force – a premise from which he derives social ontological implications for his theory of the lifeworld, namely, that the foundations of the lifeworld are exclusively provided by communicative processes. The social ontology of immanent normativity is therefore extremely narrow. From the outset, this approach excludes the question whether there could also be normative potentials that are institutionalized through noncommunicative practices, even if they can be communicatively reconstructed and validated. This exclusion prepares the ground for a further distinction between practices that are relevant to the constitution of immanent norms (namely, those practices that can be reconstructed by a theory of communication) and those that are irrelevant to this purpose – a distinction that ultimately culminates in the system–lifeworld distinction.

From a normative point of view, the lifeworld concept also causes a further confusion: the normative claims that find their objective form in the self-evident certainties of the lifeworld are clearly not identical to the normative demands that arise directly from the discourse principle. Rather, normativity *in* the lifeworld must be meticulously distinguished from other norms, including those that perhaps demand the reproduction *of* the lifeworld.

There are therefore three ways to analyse pathologies of the lifeworld: (a) without recourse to the concept of the lifeworld, as a violation of the *conditions assumed in all communicative acts* (i.e., the preconditions of sincere communication); (b) as a violation of the *norms that constitute the lifeworld* in a specific society and that therefore are de facto preconditions for the persistence of socially necessary processes of communication in that society; and (c) as a violation of the presuppositions of those *processes of communication that reproduce the lifeworld* of a specific society. These three descriptions of problems have varying 'depths': in the first case, the norms that are violated are the general rules of any communication C; in the second case, they are the norms of lifeworld L, on which C is dependent; and in the third case, the norms of communication processes C' are violated, which are necessary for the reproduction of L.[55] If we take these three descriptions as offering an analysis of the norms of immanent critique, then case (a) represents a 'hard' transcendental-pragmatic analysis of immanent normativity; case (b) identifies immanent norms through a sociologically informed reference to the actual norms of a given lifeworld, but always presupposes the intrinsic value and an independent – not directly communicatively realized – normative content of that lifeworld; and case (c) represents a model of a 'soft' transcendental-pragmatic critique.

It is my opinion that Habermas always has all three forms of critique in view, which to him represent different levels of complexity in a single model. Only the latter two forms can claim to be models of social critique in the strict sense, however, because here it is not only the source of the violations of norms but also the *norms themselves* that have a socially institutionalized character.[56] Yet as soon as the norms institutionalized in empirically existing lifeworlds are given a systematic place in the analysis – as is the case with these two forms – a social ontological account is needed to clarify how we should understand the mode of existence of these norms.

Habermas's proposal – that we explain the existence of these norms solely from the perspective of the participants in communicative practices – leaves this social ontology underdetermined in three respects. First, it remains unclear how we should understand the general mode of social normativity, on the basis of which the particular practice of communicative obligation can first evolve (or, alternatively, whether the practice of communication by virtue of its unique properties does not require a more general basis). Secondly, it is unclear to what extent intersubjective obligations, on which a critique could be based, can be derived from the general conditions of the

90   Chapter Four

institutionalization of lifeworld norms. Thirdly, it ultimately remains open whether the idea that the communicatively reproduced lifeworld could alone form the basis of critique is an idealized picture of social norms that conceals the intrinsic vulnerability of all social practices to power and domination.

4.1.5 Rationalization and Reification: The Model of Critique

These problems with Habermas's foundation for social critique, however, should not obscure the model of critique he attempts to establish. Habermas's theory can be understood as a form of immanent critique in two senses: first, it seeks to uncover the normative potentials of social interaction (which is the subject of *The Theory of Communicative Action*) and to reconstruct how processes of one-sided rationalization can violate legitimate normative expectations arising from forms of communicative action. Second, it aims to show that a reconstruction of critical theory can only succeed if it explicitly acknowledges that it is based on a demand that has thus far remained implicit in the self-conception of modernity: a demand for the unconstrained development of communicative rationality.

The first argument is supplied by Habermas's theory of colonization. Habermas assumes that the replacement of the sacred origins of morality comes along with the 'institutional embodiment and motivational anchoring of postconventional moral and legal representations',[57] which is ultimately the appropriate expression of proceduralized, communicatively constituted rationality. At the same time, however, social modernization follows 'a pattern such that cognitive-instrumental rationality surges beyond the bounds of the economy and state into other, communicatively structured areas of life and achieves dominance there at the expense of moral-political and aesthetic-practical rationality, and this produces disturbances in the symbolic reproduction of the lifeworld.'[58] Habermas therefore negativistically sketches a model of social change from the perspective of violations of the normativity immanently presupposed in the communicatively structured lifeworld.

Without going into the details of the colonization thesis, it can be summed up in the following way: the media-steered subsystems of the economy and state are 'formally organized domains of action' that 'are no longer integrated through the mechanism of mutual understanding . . . and congeal into a kind of norm-free sociality.'[59] As far as the strategic imperatives institutionalized in these domains invade the lifeworld, the communicatively structured mechanisms of the integration of the lifeworld are thereby undermined, and the unity of everyday consciousness is destroyed. This tendency toward the colonization of the communicative lifeworld through systemic imperatives leads to the fact that in modernization, the 'old' models of consensus are destroyed without allowing for the full development of new possible forms of communicative rationality.[60] Not only are these losses *not* compensated for by a corresponding increase in efficiency,[61] but they lead, above all, to the destruction and 'desolation' of entire areas of life.[62] Both tendencies taken together ultimately lead to the central object of Habermas's immanent critique, namely, the dissolution of the legitimation of a social order that systematically violates the immanent norms of the lifeworld and for which no more legitimation is ultimately possible.[63]

However, it is at the same time clear to Habermas that a critical theory cannot aim – as classical Western Marxism did – at *overcoming* systemic rationalization; rather, the question is whether systemic imperatives can be *limited* to the areas in which they can efficiently organize material reproduction such that they can at least avoid endangering the social preconditions of communicative rationality as such.

There is a certain ambivalence in Habermas between formulations that suggest that this colonization *replaces* or *destroys* communicative rationality[64] and those that suggest that it *violates* the immanent norms of communicative practices.[65] Only the second alternative can be Habermas's view, since it is only when communicative rationality is not merely *dropped* but has its norms violated that we can detect the potential in communicative practices that makes rationally motivated resistance against this colonization possible.

For Habermas, the question of which forms of critique are relevant in this context can be relatively clearly answered, at least at the political level: these are the communicative disputes in the political public sphere, in which citizens can draw on the discursive resources of the lifeworld to criticize the described pathologies.[66] Critique is therefore a protest by a public that brings to the political system's attention a call to solve normative problems that have been established as insufferable. As already suggested, Habermas's theory of critique is not suited to justifying the content of these demands on the 'object level' of social norms, but only to allowing us to understand the *form* of the justifications that need to be provided by citizens themselves. On a metalevel, however, he can justify the formal demand that the destruction and colonization of the lifeworld's structures must be opposed – which is to say, his theory must be able to understand itself as providing the groundwork for a critique of processes that involve the proliferation of systemic imperatives to such an extent that the symbolic reproduction of society is threatened.

Accordingly, what counts as progress are those changes to social practices that thwart dangers to the lifeworld by influencing the political system such that it imposes appropriate limits on systemic rationalization. This criterion is again derived from the conditions necessary for the discursively produced legitimacy on which this political system is dependent, and whose deterioration can be described as a pathology.

However, the description both of colonization and of the kind of social progress that is produced through critique remains unsatisfactory. The pathologies of the colonization of the lifeworld are not automatic results that emerge without the involvement of human subjects; rather, they are only possible if, at least for the time being, *critique is absent* and agents *follow norms* that must appear to them as appropriate, and even subjectively reasonable, from the viewpoint of systemic rationality. The pathological character of this colonization can therefore never be immediately *apparent* as a normative problem. On the contrary, the boundary between appropriate and pathological states of the lifeworld is always contentious.[67] Similarly, Habermas understands systemic rules as *communicatively instituted*, but not as *dependent on communication*[68] – due to his social ontological self-limitation. Therefore, he cannot conceive of the possibility of internal, communicatively explicable conflicts in systemic spheres and thereby forfeits the possibility of understanding the possibility that conflicts around colonization might also emerge from within systemic contexts.

Furthermore, Habermas only draws on arguments concerning the pathological or dysfunctional *consequences* of the colonization process for the normative foundation of his critique of the colonization of the lifeworld. That is, his critique focuses on the undesirable *consequences* of the colonization of the lifeworld for subjects or society as a whole. He never considers the possibility that such a critique could also take up *violations of normative claims* that are already institutionalized in the corresponding practices themselves.[69] It is sometimes objected, against this functionalistic argumentative strategy, that such a critique is neither in a position to clearly distinguish between legitimate and illegitimate delinguistification nor in a position to use the norms of communicative action as a basis for critique.[70] This problem is connected to the fatal narrowing of the account of social normativity in the communications-theoretic monism already explored, which does not allow for immanent critique of noncommunicative socialization.

Accordingly, it is not surprising that Habermas withdraws to the position according to which the question of where the boundary between normality and pathology is to be drawn is not one that allows for an objective answer by critical theory[71] but must be relinquished to the argumentative discourse of the citizens themselves. The question therefore remains open whether recourse to the structure of communicative action that is accessible via universal pragmatics, in conjunction with Habermas's social theory, can ever accomplish more than merely representing the *form* of the questions through which protests against the colonization of the lifeworld proceed.[72] This purely formal reconstruction of immanent critique would not amount to what a model of immanent critique would have to accomplish – namely, allowing us to understand how the justification of specific demands for social change can emerge from social reality. In particular, Habermas's portrayal of the colonization of the lifeworld as an overloading and emptying of the lifeworld is ultimately based on assumptions about its functional role, but it does not indicate which normative basis a specific critique of the colonization of the lifeworld would argumentatively draw on.[73]

4.1.6 Habermas as Immanent Critic

To summarize, Habermas's work can be read as a model of immanent critique. It faces two weaknesses, however. First, with regard to his social ontology, it remains unclear how communicative norms are institutionalized as social norms within the wider context of social practices. By restricting his analysis of immanent normative potentials to the internal reconstruction of the logic of communication, Habermas foregoes the opportunity to embed the analysis of communicative action in a broader theory of social normativity, which would allow him to thematize the structural preconditions of discourse in general. Second, this restriction also leads him to designate the general norms of communicative action as the only relevant sources of immanent normativity. Therefore, his theory does not have room for the idea that particular normative potentials might be found in other kinds of social practices. As the discussion of the colonization thesis has shown, this leads to a form of social critique that, for the entire range of those practices of the 'system' that are not structured by a commitment to reach communicative consensus, only allows for a critique of their dysfunctional effects but cannot allow that these practices may violate demands that are internal to them.

Finally, Habermas's model turns out to be normatively thin: it can indeed reconstruct normative discourses from the participant's perspective, as it does not claim anything that could not in principle be cognitively available to a participant in a discourse. But precisely this democratic virtue means that it has less room for one of the most attractive properties of models of immanent critique: the idea that there is more for critique to say, normatively, than that on which everyone can already agree beforehand. Habermas therefore goes beyond the hermeneutic approaches insofar as he is able to provide a social theoretical model of one particular kind of social practice in which immanent normativity can be found. Nevertheless, the unclear social ontological foundation on which this model is founded hinders the full realization of his theory's potential.

4.2 THE RECOGNITION-THEORETIC MODEL

Honneth's theory of recognition is, in the context of more recent critical theory, the best-known alternative to Habermas's theory of communicative action. I will therefore use this theory as a second exemplary test case for examining the problems that a theory of immanent critique must solve. Put briefly, Honneth's theory is driven by the notion that the normative potentials of society are to be found not in the *conditions of the communicative coordination of action* but rather in the *precommunicative demands* with which people approach their social relations and which are decisive for their self-relation[74] – claims that he defines more precisely as *claims of recognition*.[75]

In what follows, I will briefly outline Honneth's criticism of Habermas (section 4.2.1), before reconstructing his model of the struggle for recognition in social practices (section 4.2.2). I will then go on to consider and answer the question of whether Honneth's model of immanent critique is best understood as primarily anthropological or as founded on a conception of social practice (section 4.2.3). Finally, I will consider which concept of progress underlies Honneth's approach (section 4.2.4).

4.2.1 Honneth's Criticism of Habermas

Habermas introduces a fundamental interest in communicative understanding as the principle of a sphere in which social normativity is embodied in a particular way. In Honneth's view, this conceals an ambivalence. On the one hand, Habermas identifies communication as a necessary element of *all* complex social practices. Honneth characterizes Habermas's early works approvingly in this respect: 'Together they supply guidelines for a comprehensive concept of society in which the process of material reproduction is seen as dependent upon a process of intersubjective understanding mediated by social norms.'[76] On the other hand, communication for Habermas increasingly becomes an *independent principle of a specific mode of interaction*, which is opposed to the principle of strategic interaction. This tendency, in Honneth's view, amounts to the reification and splitting off of communicative action. According to Honneth, Habermas draws a distinction 'on the level of social domains of action' based on the 'structural differences between "labour" and "interaction"',[77] thereby falling victim to a 'falsely placed concretization'[78] by redescribing structural differentiations within *a single* kind of normative practice as the dominant interaction patterns of *different spheres of action*.

Even if Honneth concedes that after the publication of *Knowledge and Human Interest* Habermas gives up distinguishing between two modes of action and no longer posits communication as a separate principle but rather understands it as the foundation of a comprehensive conception of rationality,[79] this dualism is still at work in *The Theory of Communicative Action* – no longer with respect to two types of action, but rather to two forms of the coordination of action and two dynamics of rationalization. Accordingly, Habermas foregoes the chance to arrive at a uniform model of human practice:

> Work and interaction are not thereby intertwined with one another in the history of the species. . . . But he could have found such an alternative conception if he had consistently followed one of his own interpretive proposals and had understood social interaction also as a struggle between social groups for the organizational form of purposive-rational action.[80]

This criticism of Habermas makes it easy to recognize which alternative Honneth has in mind: instead of understanding communicative action as the only source of normativity, he sees the *general practice of interaction* as the ontologically relevant basis for explaining immanent normativity, this general practice comprising the interactions bound up with both the material and the symbolic reproduction of society. But how should we then understand the institutionalization of immanent norms in such a general practice?

4.2.2 Struggle, Injustice and Disrespect

(a) The struggle for recognition. In his essay 'Moral Consciousness and Class Domination',[81] originally published in 1981, Honneth presents (for the first time) the core of his alternative to Habermas's account of normative practices. There, he argues that the discursively structured moral systems that Habermas has in mind inadequately reflect what Honneth calls 'consciousness of injustice': the inconsistent normative attitudes within the social morality of the economically disadvantaged, where the main explanation of such inconsistency is that the relevant attitudes are not shaped by the need to provide explicit justifications. This consciousness of injustice remains mostly implicit[82] and therefore represents a source of normative demands that cannot be disclosed by any Habermasian theory that focuses exclusively on explicit validity claims.

Honneth, in opposition to Habermas, assumes that the central normative conflicts in modern Western society are not so much *displaced* by subsystems of media-driven interaction but rather *made invisible* in the form of this consciousness of injustice. The economically underprivileged are deliberately and structurally blocked in various ways from the possibility of articulating their normative claims, a process that Honneth calls 'control [over] the consciousness of social injustice'.[83] Too narrow a focus on argumentative communication therefore runs the risk of reproducing this social blockage in the theory itself. This also means, however, that Honneth cannot be content with the communications-theoretic social ontology that is laid out in Habermas but must develop an alternative answer to the question of how the normative potentials of the social can be conceptualized.[84] This answer is systematically provided in Honneth's *Struggle for Recognition*[85] and in the inaugural lecture based upon it, 'Integrity and Disrespect'.[86] Honneth explicitly states that the objective of *Struggle for Recognition* is the elaboration of a theory that is able 'to explain processes of social change by referring to the normative demands that are, structurally speaking, internal to the relationship of mutual recognition'[87] – and therefore to provide an answer to the question of which immanent normative potentials can explain social change.

In *Struggle for Recognition*, Honneth proceeds from both the social philosophy of the young Hegel and Mead's social psychology. He finds in both theories the idea that subjects' fundamental moral expectations towards society are based on those experiences in which they realize that their relationship to themselves is dependent on their relationships to others. Based on this idea, Honneth then argues that the pretheoretic moral consciousness that finds expression in both moral theory and practical moral conflicts reflects those *basic demands for recognition* that subjects must inevitably raise towards their environment in order to achieve an undamaged relationship with themselves. It follows that an agent's *subjective experiences of injustice* in social struggles – that is, what Honneth calls 'consciousness of injustice' – are symptoms of a *lack of recognition*, which in turn causes damage to an agent's self-relation.[88] The *suffering* this brings about is, in Honneth's view, both the normative and the motivational foundation of social conflict.

It is therefore the concept of recognition that is key to analysing the social basis of those norms at issue in social conflicts. These norms concern the quality of the intersubjective relationships that are so essential to the self-relation of individuals that their absence or distortion leads to social suffering and the frustration of normative expectations. The constellation of the (relatively universally conceived) preconditions for successful self-relation, for the central types of social relationships, and the corresponding forms of violation are the material that makes immanent critique possible in Honneth's view (even if he does not use this term explicitly). Social critique can draw on the concept of recognition to relate to those forms of suffering that motivate social struggles and thereby take up normative experiences theoretically without necessarily imposing on them the same form they take in the self-understanding of social agents.

(b) The epistemology of 'disrespect'. In order not to prejudge the question of which social ontology lies in the background of this model, I will first tackle

Honneth's approach with regard to its normative epistemology. Honneth proposes a middle way between a hermeneutic and a traditional social scientific model: the 'material' of critique comprises empirical social struggles, on the one hand, and social pathologies resulting from the suppression of consciousness of injustice, on the other. The normative demands that underpin these phenomena must be *clarified* by critique insofar as critique examines which social processes lead to which empirically determinable deformations in the self-relation of individuals; this clarification can, however, only be successful if it also clarifies which culturally determined conceptions of value are at play in these social processes.

Just which particular recognitive needs underpin conflicts – according to Honneth – cannot be directly determined by a positive, substantive conception of what a successful self-relation is. Rather, recognition theory must approach the demands implicit in struggles by means of a negativistic strategy that ascertains the content of normative violations by means of observed phenomena of 'disrespect'.[89] 'Disrespect' is therefore a central concept of Honneth's normative epistemology, as it is not only hermeneutically but explanatorily central to understanding social conflicts. Honneth accords priority to social conflicts – as concrete forms of the expression of normative demands – over and above the explicit self-definitions of agents. Such conflicts are primarily to be understood through the articulated and unarticulated moral motivations with which participants react to experiences of disrespect, and which can therefore be made explicit with reference to these conflicts. This epistemic strategy has the advantage, in comparison to Habermas, that it does not have to exclude inarticulate self-definitions.

The fundamental epistemic role of 'disrespect' is not yet sufficiently defined, however. The idea that identities are threatened by disrespect – an idea that Honneth develops on the basis of Mead's and Hegel's intersubjective theories of identity – is sufficient to explain how demands for recognition can be integrated into an analysis of social pathologies, but it is unclear why it is *only* disrespect that motivates claims to recognition. A desire for a broader form of recognition could also emerge, it seems, from other sources – for example, in the context of utopian references to *new* forms of recognition.

'Disrespect' plays such a fundamental role in Honneth's model because he assumes that there must be a motivational basis for participation in *social conflicts* that goes beyond mere consciousness of possibility.[90] An analysis of social struggles therefore allows us – indirectly, via a consideration of what motivates them – to understand, on the one hand, which moral demands underlie them. Such an understanding is not dependent on an interpretation of the subjective normative beliefs of the individuals involved in these struggles. To the contrary, an analysis of social struggles can only serve to justify statements about the immanent normative potentials of social practices if one can also convincingly explain how such struggles are *brought about* by the normative deficiencies of those practices themselves (and not by unrelated, idiosyncratic motives). This means that we can only learn something about the fundamental normative structure of society independently of the (potentially distorted) self-interpretations of participants if we have an analysis of social struggles at our disposal that understands these struggles as resulting from a failure of social integration that is explained by the fact that certain normative expectations, that were already somehow contained in these social practices themselves, have not been met.

Such an explicitly social theoretical thesis is initially difficult to reconcile with the fact that 'disrespect' appears to represent an individually attributable, basic emotional phenomenon of moral experience, which, as an 'inner feeling', provides the motivation for struggles for recognition but is not yet intersubjectively structured in itself.[91] As Honneth explains[92] with reference to Dewey, however, the experience of disrespect is, in fact, essentially an intersubjective phenomenon: disrespect is not primarily an 'inner state' but rather the experience of a failure of intersubjective interaction.[93] Experiences of disrespect are therefore not only *outcomes* but primary *parts* of the failure of certain forms of interaction. As disrespect is always experienced together with the violation of a social norm, experiences of injustice must always be embedded in normatively regulated practices. Disrespect and struggle as features of social interaction are therefore ineluctably linked with each other as conceptual components of Honneth's model of critique.

This link between social struggle and experiences of disrespect has consequences for the entirety of Honneth's social theory: as social struggles are understood as essentially and irrevocably part of social practices and not as pathologies which are in principle eliminable,[94] experiences of disrespect – as *parts* of these struggles – make it possible for the social critic to acquire knowledge of the normative content of social interactions. Honneth therefore aims to identify a range of normative demands *directly* in contexts of social interaction that are not imposed on them from the outside but rather provide immanently justified standards as the internal criteria of the success of interactions in these contexts.

Accordingly, if immanent critique wishes to reconstruct the content of normative self-understandings, it has to be more than an interpretive reconstruction of how people explicitly argue in their normative debates. It must go beyond their explicit assertions and also reconstruct unarticulated experiences of disrespect, and thereby implicit norms, through a *sociological analysis of social struggles*, and provide a broader basis for arguments over what a self-understanding could be that adequately recognizes the normative expectations of members of a society.

4.2.3. Formal Anthropology or Social Practice?

(a) Formal anthropology. Honneth derives the idea that norms are implicitly contained in social forms of interaction or practices from his interpretation of Dewey.[95] The (at least implicit) strategy of analysing the social ontology of immanent norms in such a way that these norms are seen as institutionalized through struggles for the recognition of aspects of people's identities appears, however, to stand in tension with some of Honneth's arguments, in which he seems to rely on anthropological assumptions and to argue for the importance of recognition by virtue of the fact that experiences of recognition are necessary for any subject's successful *self-relation*. This appears to imply that, in the form of such anthropological preconditions for successful self-relation, there must be a foundation that *precedes* the intersubjective practices of justification in society, which explains the (derived) value of these practices for the subjects. When criticizing the model proposed by Nancy Fraser, Honneth writes, for example:

> But, on the other hand, this restriction to only a form of justification seems to entirely lose sight of the normative perspectives from which individuals decide how far they can follow the established principles of public justification in the first place. It is as if the generally accepted reasons need not correspond to the normative expectations that the subjects bring – *in a certain way on their own* – to the social order.[96]

These remarks suggest that the structure of human subjectivity – or, more specifically, *the form of human subject formation as such* – already carries claims for recognition which are not bound to specific practices but which allow for critique from an independent standpoint.

This anthropological model – which directly contradicts attempts to interpret Honneth as suggesting that struggles for recognition play a social ontologically constitutive role – was largely met with scepticism. Nancy Fraser, for example, criticizes Honneth by observing that taking *the success of identity development* as a criterion reduces social critique to moral psychology.[97]

It would be a mistake, however, to treat Honneth's recognition theory merely as a form of 'anthropologized morality',[98] for Honneth does not accept the idea that moral feelings are brute facts, as Fraser suggests.[99] An experience of disrespect is rather understood as a reaction to a violation of an 'already normatively structured need',[100] and therefore a need that plays a normatively fundamental role not in itself but only in virtue of its social role. By referring to 'normatively structured experiences', Honneth suggests that, rather than being a purely individual matter, individual experiences of injustice have a social, normative structure (as he argued previously with reference to Dewey). Accordingly, the crucial question is as follows: how is this normative quality of experiences constituted in such a way as to go beyond the subject's self-understanding? This is the question that Honneth must answer to distinguish his theory from a purely psychological theory of empirical suffering. One can find two alternative answers to this question in Honneth: on the one hand, the idea of a *formal anthropology* that justifies statements beyond pure psychological empiricism about what accounts for the successful development of subjectivity; on the other, the idea of a form of interaction that is *normative in itself*, which suggests a genuinely social ontological argument.[101]

With regard to the foundation of normativity, both of these models are in a certain tension; either Honneth succeeds in showing the source of norms in specific properties of *human existence* – above all with regard to the requirements for the successful development of personal identity – or he succeeds in localizing them in structures of *human interaction*, as his objection to Habermas suggests. Honneth's criticism of the role played by the quasi–a priori preconditions of communication in Habermas applies analogously to the idea that anthropology has an a priori role. It makes a big difference whether *human existence itself* produces normative expectations or whether it is thanks to *specific forms of interaction* that normative elements enter into human life.

At first glance, the anthropological model carries greater weight in Honneth's work. However, Honneth later considerably clarifies the role of anthropology in response to the criticism already mentioned. He makes clear that anthropological assumptions only provide a formal framework for understanding the normative importance of the conditions of the constitution of subjectivity. Only the *existence* of recognitive needs is assumed as an anthropological foundation – the historically contingent configuration of the spheres of recognition follows directly not from anthropology but from needs that are in their exact shape culturally, and thus historically, determined.[102] This model, however, unifies not only the advantages of a 'strong' anthropological and a 'weak' hermeneutic conception but also their disadvantages: such a model runs the risk of being unable to ground any substantive form of critique as long as the question of *which* normative demands are justified in relation to a given practice remains underdetermined by a merely formal anthropology. It seems to follow that, in order to arrive at a justification for critical claims, we must always apply further criteria for determining which needs count, criteria that Honneth leaves unspecified. At the same time – and this is an even more important objection – the 'formal' idea that the normative contents of critique are always accessible to the critic in the form of suffering and experiences of injustice remains exposed to an obvious objection: even if it is true that all forms of social suffering can be explained by reference to a violation of deep, anthropologically defined needs, the *anthropological rootedness of these forms of suffering* does not by itself justify the normative conclusion at issue – namely, that this suffering should be avoided for that specific reason. Any anthropologically founded criterion – whether it be naturalness,[103] integrity, successful identity formation or 'undistorted self-realization'[104] – must have been *previously* established as the *normatively most relevant* criterion in order to amount to a privileged critical standard.[105] However, this normative valorization of an anthropological requirement is always in need of justification. For these reasons, confidence in the direct or indirect necessity of recognition established by the anthropological thesis with reference to human identity is not sufficient to justify a recognition-theoretic form of immanent critique. It therefore seems desirable for a recognition theory to avoid putting too much emphasis on its anthropological assumptions in its normative project and instead to look for purely practice-immanent sources of normativity.

(b) Social interaction as a normative element. The fact that Honneth justifiably rejects Habermas's overly rationalistic model of social reconstruction clearly does not entail that an alternative to communicative reason must be sought in a nonsocial source. Against Habermas, a practice theory of immanent critique can object that the normative aspects of the social order are not exhausted by practices of discursive justification: localizing experiences of disrespect in an anthropologically characterized particular sphere in which subjects can experience normative demands sui generis is not the only alternative to Habermas's proposal. It is also possible – following Honneth's originally proposed alternative to Habermas – to search for the source of experiences of disrespect in the general structure of nondiscursively structured *interaction contexts*.

This alternative to a model based on a strong anthropology would then be a *model of social practices* that takes social norms to be the result of the establishment of common attitudes in processes of interaction. In this sense, Honneth originally attempted to determine how the experiences of suffering of entire *social groups* can be expressed in social struggles.[106] A theory that localizes the source of normative demands in individual subjectivity cannot do this immediately. It would first have to explain how initially individual and ultimately incommensurable experiences can subsequently merge into a collective motivation without already presupposing that they have been transformed into socially accepted discursive validity claims. For that reason alone, it would be far easier for Honneth to start from the assumption that individual psychological experiences of suffering are the expression of distortions in forms of interaction and are therefore already intersubjectively structured: they are counterparts to normative failures that subjects can experience when participating in certain spheres of interaction. Reconstructing such a priori collective experiences would amount to disclosing immanent normative commitments that are derived not from individual psychological experiences (which are ultimately treated as epiphenomenal by such a theory) but directly from intersubjective normative experiences that are constitutive of the respective practices.[107]

These considerations suggest that Honneth's implicit model of immanent critique should, as far as possible, be understood not as an anthropological model but as a practice-theoretic model. In fact, Honneth repeatedly explicitly refers to a model of social practice when he takes up the idea of immanent critique as part of the tradition of critical theory:

> The different models of practice that Horkheimer, Marcuse, and Habermas offer, then, are all only representatives of that one thought, according to which the socialization of human beings can only be successful under conditions of cooperative freedom. However the particulars of the anthropological ideas may be sorted out, they ultimately stand for an ethical idea that places the utmost value on a form of common practice in which subjects can achieve cooperative self-actualization.[108]

This reference to a form of social practice suggests that the anthropological discussions – as central as they appear in Honneth – can ultimately only be understood as a clarification of the preconditions for the development of a model of social practices. This is also what Honneth identifies in *The Struggle for Recognition* as Hegel's achievement: in contrast to the atomistic premises of mainstream modern social philosophy, Hegel sees the normative foundations of modern societies – which means, above all, the actualization of individual autonomy – as anchored not in the demands of individual subjects but in the *ethically (sittlich) rooted intersubjective attitudes and practices* of members of communities. This highlights the extent to which the relevant norms of social critique must be located in such forms of 'ethical life' (*Sittlichkeit*), social practice or institutional organization, but not in the claims of individual subjects, atomistically understood.

In his argument against Nancy Fraser's 'perspective dualism' (which assumes that demands for recognition of one's identity and demands for distributive equality are two distinct sources of justified social claims), Honneth finally explicitly avows his 'moral-theoretical monism',[109] which at least suggests that he must likewise hold a corresponding social theoretically monist position. If he wants to remain faithful to critical theory's commitment to the notion that its normative claims are rooted in social practices, it must therefore be assumed that his moral monism entails an equally monist view of the social practices underlying moral demands, according to which *all* normative claims that become thematic in social struggles are grounded in social practices, understood in such a general sense that they can make both redistributive and recognitive struggles intelligible.

At this point, however, there is a revealing gap between this theoretical assumption and Honneth's concrete analyses of different types of recognition and their pathologies: on the one hand, Honneth claims that a reconstructive theory should take the implicit embeddedness of normative demands in intersubjective interactions in the most general sense as its starting point; on the other hand, he seems to use a similarly general idea of practices as the foundation of his model of immanent critique. Nevertheless, he never spells out the connection that would be necessary to develop a theory of social practices that is complex enough to explain how the different kinds of claims for recognition can emerge from this general foundation. Such a theory could lay the foundation for an interaction-theoretic model of recognition as a practice-based model of immanent critique.

(c) The practice-theoretic alternative. In 'Democracy as Reflexive Cooperation',[110] Honneth spells out the connection between political and social integration in full detail for the first time, by means of Dewey's theory of democracy. Honneth discovers in Dewey's late work an understanding of politics to which he would like to broadly adhere: politics, according to this model, always emerges from processes of social cooperation that initially only involve a few members. However, as soon as it becomes apparent that others are also affected by the consequences of the social cooperation at issue in potentially problematic ways, both groups must enter into a reflexive problem-solving process in which rules and solutions are sought in rational ways, and in which the members of the society are at the same time assured of both their individual freedom and their social membership.

This model of multistage cooperation is attractive as a general basis for recognition theory. On the one hand, the model of politics as problem solving allows for a plausible picture of a normatively regulated social practice (in which problems of misrecognition are negotiated) that is resistant to discourse-theoretic idealization;[111] on the other hand, it is abstract enough to incorporate the various forms of practice that underlie more particular forms of recognition. Unlike what Honneth's talk of 'experiences of disrespect' may suggest, Honneth must have a model of immanent critique in mind that reconstructs norms the fulfilment of which is not only expected contingently by individual subjects. The normative expectations whose violation can be disclosed in the context of an analysis of social struggles must rather be expectations that individuals have in virtue of their membership in a form of practice that is constituted by these norms. Immanent critique would therefore be based on the reconstruction of the immanent norms of a cooperative practice.

There is a tension, however, between Dewey's pragmatist idea of 'problem solving', which is best illustrated in the context of overcoming common practical problems, and the idea that in political metapractices – and therefore in practices that serve to organize such problem-solving practices – a form of informal rationality can emerge that is not limited to instrumental reason. A full integration of Dewey's model into recognition theory would therefore require that Dewey's instrumentalist conception of action be dropped, or at least broadened into a *general* model of social practices that also includes expressive and normative judgements as independent sources of normative attitudes that are integrated in corresponding forms of practice. The forms of practice that underlie the political sphere – for example, practices in families, culture and the state – cannot all be equally understood as pure cases of goal-oriented cooperation. Furthermore, not all arguments advanced even in the political context relate to the satisfaction of interests. Quite the opposite: a paradigmatic example of political struggle concerns whether a field of practices should be governed by individual freedom as its standard, or whether instrumental or normative and cultural considerations ought to regulate it (for example, in questions of medicine, environmentalism, cultural politics and immigration).

A suitably expanded concept of social cooperation would therefore understand the underlying general form of social practice as the sum of all those activities in which the members of a society follow norms or realize values in an essentially communal way. On such a model, the discursive sphere of politics could then be understood as a necessary but not exhaustive component of this cooperation, and at the same time a necessary condition of the freedom of its members.

In his 2001 interpretation of Hegel's *Philosophy of Right*, Honneth finally attempts to spell out this practice-theoretic foundation. He assumes on the one hand that Hegel specifies *communicative freedom* as the fundamental good of human existence and on the other hand that Hegel assumes that 'communicative relations fall under the class of goods that can be created and preserved only through concerted effort'.[112] Consequently, in contrast to *The Struggle for Recognition*, Honneth derives Hegel's tripartite division of ethical spheres not from the formal-anthropological conditions of successful individual self-relation but rather from a comprehensive analysis of social practices. *Sittlichkeit* – that is, the totality of those freedom-directed practices that are normatively relevant to members of modern societies – is analysed by Honneth throughout in a practice vocabulary as a 'pattern'[113] or 'network',[114] as an ensemble of practices, 'spheres of communication characterized by specific forms of intersubjective action',[115] or even as 'language games'.[116] Hegel's work, however, is not well suited to this combination of a general practice-theoretical, social ontological analysis and Honneth's analysis of social struggles as motivated by prepolitical experiences of injustice. It is certainly true that Hegel supplied the idea of a 'struggle for recognition' that is central to Honneth's moral-theoretical understanding of social struggles, but Hegel's analysis of politics – which is ultimately too strongly based on already institutionalized demands – cannot provide a meaningful model of social change. Honneth further suggests that this more general social ontological analysis – as is laid out in *Suffering from Indeterminacy* – must ultimately correspond more or less to Habermas's model, supplemented by a more sophisticated model of socialization. This is shown by the fact that he always refers to genuinely normative ethical phenomena as *communicative relations*.[117] There is therefore still a tension between the demand that normativity be understood as immanently institutionalized *in social practices in the most general sense* and the lack of an elaborated social ontological theory that would allow for an explicit grasp of this normativity.[118]

Even if the adoption of pragmatist elements could offer clues as to what a recognition-theoretic immanent critique of social practices might look like, the social ontological foundation of the epistemology of disrespect remains unclear, such that the question of which facts the justification of such a critique rests on must remain open.

4.2.4 Immanent Critique and Normative Progress

(a) Recognition and social change. Honneth's theory aims to reconstruct the 'normative grammar' of social struggles from a philosophically substantive analysis of these struggles. For this reason, it aims to offer a theory of social change alongside a normative analysis – namely, a theory of struggles for recognition. It is not Honneth's intention to treat any and every kind of social struggle as a struggle for recognition in the relevant sense. Struggles motivated by the pure needs of survival, or by material interests in a broader sense, are not to be thought of as morally structured struggles in a narrow sense, as no reference to normative attitudes is necessary to explain why people engage in them.[119] Only in the experience of disrespect – which can refer either to a situation in which people desire to have their identity recognized in a more extended sense than hitherto possible or to a violation of norms embedded in social practices – can one find potentials that can unify whole groups in normative dissatisfaction and thereby provide the basis for social protests. If these protests lead to the subjects' becoming clear about their demands, and if they are not ideologically forced back into private life,[120] they can find political expression, as Honneth illustrates by means of various modern social movements.

In addition to an empirically plausible analysis of social change, a theory of immanent critique must also provide criteria that allow *specific* forms of change to qualify as normative progress. It was not long before Honneth's theory was confronted with the objection that recognition – which is primarily regarded positively in his theory and appears to lead to pathologies only by virtue of being absent – can also have an ideological and oppressive character.[121] Recognition can establish the identities of subjects in a way that ultimately disadvantages them;[122] likewise, not all demands that arise as demands for recognition are justified.[123] Here we see the problem that Honneth's theory tends to run together the *origin of normative claims as such* (namely, the idea that recognitive expectations that are incorporated into our social practices *ground* immanent normativity) with the *origin of the normative justification* of valid claims (the idea that the critic must consider all such normative expectations as normatively significant). Therefore, additional arguments must be introduced to distinguish between progress and regress when it comes to changes in relationships of recognition. Honneth has two options here. On the one hand, he can settle on a thick anthropologically based concept of recognition that applies positive criteria derived from *external* sources (i.e., philosophical anthropology). On the other hand, there is the option of applying standards that are *internal* to practices of recognition, which they generate from themselves and which are sufficient for the distinction between ideological and nonideological recognition.

Honneth attempts to find a middle way between these two strategies; on the one hand, he opts for a 'moderate value realism'[124] that grounds the normative force of legitimate demands for recognition in a cognitive ability that he takes us to possess as part of our 'second nature', gained through socialization. At the same time, he adopts a formal criterion that describes as *ideological* those forms of recognition that do not allow for the cultivation of new forms of perceiving recognitively relevant properties, and that thereby block the development of our second nature. This strategy, which counts *any* advances in our moral sensibility as progress, threatens to founder, however, when one considers that the 'second nature' that is formed in socialization is precisely formed through social practices of recognition, and that therefore ideological forms of recognition can also lead to the development of new 'moral perceptual abilities'. To give an example, the traditional ideological, sexist ideal of 'womanhood' has undergone many modifications over the years, in the course of which ever-new attributes have been identified as belonging to this ideal; women have been attributed with these characteristics as a source of social status without this ideal being any less ideological.

If we further assume that adopting an external standard is incompatible with recognition theory, it seems clear that we need to identify criteria for 'correct' recognition by means of the *formal properties* of the social processes by which new claims for recognition emerge. This means that we must identify normative criteria for judging the reflexive practices through which social communities determine when and how to expand those claims for recognition that they accept and that are internal to these practices.

As Dewey's theory suggests, the sphere of politics offers itself as a paradigmatic case: if Honneth understands politics as a struggle for inclusion and consideration of interests, and if one combines with this the criterion of a continuous expansion of relations of recognition, this can only mean that we should regard as ideological those forms of recognition that prevent the participation of social groups not in just any practice whatsoever, but in those *practices that define criteria* for the distribution of recognition. As long as normative conflicts in a community are deprived of the possibility of becoming reflexively accessible through the ideological exclusion of certain groups from participation in the negotiation of normative practices, these normative conflicts cannot become explicit but remain under the political threshold of perception as 'a system of daily violations of norms and rules'.[125] Consequently, not so much (or not only) individual social suffering, but forms of deviance, sabotage, aggression and criminality would be the practical indicators of such pathological states, as in Hegel.

Developing such a formal, recognition-internal account of the structural characteristics of progressive developments in struggles for recognition would have the further advantage of bypassing the well-known metaethical problems of moral realism. However, to be able to integrate the political reflexivity of normative practices (as in Dewey's theory) into a recognition theory, Honneth needs to develop an explicitly political theory of struggles for recognition.[126] That means that his theory of the normative grammar of social struggles must be supplemented at least by a theory of the logic of political action. The building blocks of such a theory are not difficult to imagine. In line with the idea of the fundamentally antagonistic constitution of the social world, a political theory of recognition would be *a conflict-based theory of politics*:[127] political action driven not so much by cooperation based on transcendentally backed-up claims about justification but rather by the expression of conflicting claims grounded in social practices. Politics would be seen as a form of conflict that always plays out between already socially recognized recognition claims and suppressed demands for justice. A logic of politics would have to explain how the experiences of injustice that do not initially occur as normative validity claims can be made explicit *as* such claims, while transforming the inferential structure of the normative discourses in new, initially unacceptable directions. If politics is in fact 'reflexive cooperation', then it consists not only in the solution of new social problems in reflexive ways but also, above all, in the question – which admits of no final answer – of how and with what right new normative claims may be introduced into the recognitive order, and thereby what it means to be a recognized subject.

(b) Recognition theory and immanent critique. The question of the form and constitution of social normativity is also bound together in Honneth's theory with the question of understanding social changes as progress, and thereby with the justification of critique: 'Basically, what I am concerned with is the attempt to use the concept of recognition to develop the normative foundations on the basis of which social criticism can be justified.'[128] Honneth thereby commits himself to two premises that can only be made compatible in the context of a complex theory: On the one hand, he would like to derive standards of critique from the social relations themselves and rejects both independently derived standards and a strong transcendentalism, dedicating himself explicitly to reconstructive critique. On the other hand, he in no way shares the 'communitarian' thesis that normative standards can only be determined from within a particular cultural and historical context and that different societies may endorse thoroughly incompatible and nonetheless justified norms.[129] He instead advocates a universalistic perspective that entails an idea of normativity that does not vary with the cultural context.

How can Honneth bring these two perspectives together? Initially, two alternatives appear to be open. On the one hand, he could again take recourse to the anthropological thesis and understand social struggles and experiences of suffering primarily as the frustration of deep anthropological needs, the satisfaction of which every society must be committed to and which can therefore serve as a basis for critique. On the other hand, if one can always analyse the sequence of struggles for recognition in different societies in such a way that it proceeds by means of a particular line of development – for example, a continuous expansion of claims for recognition – then a criterion of progress can be established that is independent of any anthropological assumptions but is nevertheless universal, and that can therefore serve as a normative ideal.

Both in *The Struggle for Recognition* and in his debate with Fraser, *increased individualization* – which can be achieved through the recognition of newer aspects of one's own individuality – and the *egalitarian inclusion* of more groups in the recognitive processes of a community serve as criteria for marking progress.[130] Both criteria can be characterized as normatively central, to the effect that they are necessary for and instrumental to the formation of human autonomy.[131] If this is the model of progress, then it allows for immanent critique of social practices to be understood as a combination of immanent and external criteria. Critique must then – if it reconstructs violations of normative expectations by means of the social struggles of a society – always privilege those interpretations of these expectations that make it possible to conceive of these struggles as struggles for inclusion and individualization. In so doing it is able to apply a criterion that is already known to be relevant a priori.

Both this model of progress and – as already discussed – the anthropological model suffer from many problems. Just as it is unclear why a particular component of human nature should serve as a normative criterion, the idea that inclusion, individuality and autonomy are demands that always *precede* the respective struggles for recognition and practices is dubious. The meaning of these concepts cannot be determined independently of the properties that are seen as grounds for recognition in each given case. This critique can also be formulated more directly: inclusion, for example, is only a normatively relevant criterion within those *specific* practices of recognition that constitutively push for the recognition of all participants; individualization only pertains to the previously normatively recognized aspects of the individual personality of the recognized.[132] Consequently, these seemingly external criteria for the determination of progress are always already internally linked to an understanding of the properties that are regarded as worthy of recognition and with concrete, particular practices of recognition, such that it is difficult to explain how they can function as criteria for the *evaluation* of social practices in general – and therefore potentially for the evaluation of practices that are not characterized by these internal norms.[133]

Honneth attempts to avoid this dilemma by understanding the practice of elaborating these criteria – that is, the practice of critique itself – as a social activity, which exists at the same level as the evaluated practices: judgements about the progressiveness of a social change are always made from the perspective of the members of a society and the values they already recognize.[134] In particular, the realization of social progress is essentially a *learning process*[135] – the realization of progress is dependent on the fact that members of a society can orient themselves in their tradition in a certain way, which means that they can take a standpoint from which a new form of social progress appears as progress against previous forms. This fundamentally retrospective[136] position assumes that the criterion of rational social change consists in the fact that, from the standpoint of practical change, the social change in question must be judged to be justified. Through rational social development – that is, through embedding in rational social practices – members of society become able to reciprocally perceive each other as valuable under an always more comprehensive perspective and to develop corresponding demands. The corresponding abilities – even if they are based on human needs – are then ultimately justified by the fact that they are modified through a learning process, which we can describe as rational on the basis of its internal dynamics.

This model puts Honneth in a position to provide a formal definition of the criteria for progress – one that certainly does not ignore the historical embeddedness of argumentation but is less abstract than the purely hermeneutic perspective of Taylor and MacIntyre. New relationships of recognition are understood as progress if they are convincing in the context of established values and practices; make a motivating form of self-esteem possible for a person; apply an appropriately contrastive vocabulary about their practices; serve to express a hitherto unrecognized value; and are compatible with their material realization in new, modified practices.[137] These criteria may still be to some extent dependent on embedding in particular narratives and forms of argumentation, but they refer above all to formal properties of the respective practice contexts, which are not only 'understood' in everyday life but can also be taken into view social scientifically, or at least proto–social scientifically. Thus, it is at least conceivable that a model of social practices could be used to develop criteria for determining how a concrete practice can help to provide its participants with new moral perceptual abilities in appropriate ways. These possibilities lead both to a conception of progress and to a conception of normative epistemology beyond the relatively undetermined hermeneutic models.

According to the account of Honneth's model proposed here – as a theory of social practices characterized by a dialectic between reciprocal recognition, the practical intersubjective constitution of norms and moral perceptual faculties – there are substantial advantages to such a theory. The strength of Honneth's proposal lies in the fact that he envisages a normative epistemology that allows socially constituted claims to be found immanently in social reality and to be understood as having the potential to transcend this reality. Therefore, one can – on the basis of this model – develop an account of immanent critique that determines the form of existence of immanent normativity in such a way that all social practices are characterized by reciprocal normative expectations, which on the one hand are so essential for the self-relation of their participants that their violation leads to conflicts, and which on the other hand are not coextensive with the explicitly accepted norms of a community.

Despite these advantages, however, this program remains relatively abstract, as long as it remains unclear which model of social practices – and above all, of the social constitution of norms – underlies Honneth's proposal. Unlike Habermas, he appears to understand the norms that are relevant to critique as immanently institutionalized in practices in such a way that not only communicative practices but cooperative practices in a broader sense, and then, in a narrower sense, those practices in which people can reciprocally experience certain aspects of their identity as worthy of social recognition, form the basis of critique. However, it remains unclear (a) how we should understand the claim that recognitive demands are always already implicit in any given social practice and (b) through which concrete forms of relationship the reciprocal obligations on which critique is based arise.

4.3 CONTEMPORARY CRITICAL THEORY AND IMMANENT CRITIQUE

Habermas's and Honneth's answers to the fundamental problem of immanent critique reveal two things. *First*, it is clear that the most important difference between their approaches consists in how they answer the question of which potentials various everyday practices of social cooperation carry in themselves. Their approaches do not share the optimism of Hegelian Marxism or that of hermeneutic theories. They acknowledge that the idea that social criticism can or should always reconstruct an *already socially shared* background understanding has been shown to be implausible by social scientific insights regarding the degree to which the cultural sphere can be shaped by domination, insights that Western Marxism, Gramsci and not least the early Frankfurt School made a commonplace of critical social theory. Similarly, the main competitor of the hermeneutic account of immanent norms, that is, the Marxist claim that the basis of immanent critique is to be found not in the internally reconstructible meaning of cultural practices but in the objectively characterizable features of practices of *production*, is also doubted by both approaches. While it had been assumed by many (following Marx) that practices of (or 'relations of') production yielded the potential for a liberated society in the form of the proletariat, Habermas aims to discover critical potentials not in the mode of production but in the mode of communicative rationality. Honneth also disburdens the practice of production of its claim to generate the relevant norms from itself. For him, it is the claims that subjects bring to the totality of intersubjective relationships, grounded in the conditions of their identity formation, that form the normative basis for critique.

There are undoubtedly both political and philosophical reasons that speak in favour of rejecting the production paradigm, but the analysis laid out here has also shown that turning away from the paradigm of production is all the more problematic the more it prompts us to turn away from a more comprehensive idea of social practice. In Habermas, the theory of communicative action remains bound to actual communicative practice.[138] The way in which Habermas separates communicative action from noncommunicative action, however, as well as the resulting focus on the formal-pragmatic reconstruction of validity claims, loses track of the deeper question of how the norms that are constitutive of this specific practice are institutionalized in social practices in a more general sense. In Honneth, finally, the idea that there are normative demands that can be found in particular forms of interaction remains closely linked to the problem of subjective identity formation. Both models minimize the idea of the practical immanence of norms in general in favour of more particular forms of reconstruction.

This raises the question whether a general model of immanent critique can be derived from their proposals. Immanent critique – according to the basic idea of this book – must be guided by norms that are immanent in the social practices to which it refers and must critically apply these norms directly to these practices. At this point, Habermas's theory appears too narrow as it is unclear why the norms that arise from the formal features of the practice of communication should regulate not only the practice of communication but social practice *generally*. Similarly, Honneth's model faces the question of whether the successful realization of one's self-relation can readily be proven to be the relevant viewpoint for all social practices, or whether we should rather understand the establishment of successful recognition relations as the internal demands of a particular form of cooperative action.

Both models assume not only that communication and recognition are social ontologically basic (as they are preconditions for the normative structure of *further* practices) but that the normative structures that they identify allow for an exhaustive analysis of the normative potential of these practices. Nevertheless, neither Honneth's model of interaction nor Habermas's conception of the lifeworld is sufficiently social ontologically comprehensive to show that the resulting principles can really be understood as immanent principles *of social practices in general*. In order to formulate the general theory of interaction that is at least implicitly presupposed by both approaches, we must determine the more general sense in which normative potentials are inherent in forms of interaction that can serve as a basis for immanent critique.

4.4 SOCIAL ONTOLOGICAL QUESTIONS CONCERNING THEORIES OF IMMANENT CRITIQUE

4.4.1 Normativity, Progress and Epistemology

The most general presupposition that a theory of immanent critique must make is the assumption that there are norms that can be found in the social practices of a society which at least potentially stand in contradiction to those practices. The existence of such 'immanent content' is insufficiently understood to allow for a full model of immanent critique, however, if one assumes – as in the hermeneutic models – that this content can be made accessible solely by interpretative reference to the shared values and norms of a community. A convincing approach must spell out the kinds of social practices that shared meanings can be immanent in, and it must do so in a way that goes beyond a participant's subjective belief that a specific understanding of this content is correct. The practice-based models that approach the issue more from a social scientific perspective at least take this question seriously. In their existing form, however, they are unable to make the *form of the existence* of the implicit normative content of social practices intelligible.

A plausible model of immanent critique in the general sense must also fulfil two further demands that have proven relevant in the discussion of the models previously presented. It must explain how the relevant agents can gain cognitive access to the norms on which they can draw in the process of critique (the problem of normative epistemology), and it must explain how the changes in practice that result from the appeal to these norms can be understood as progress, and why the immanent norms provide good reason to change a social practice (the problem of progress).[139]

The hermeneutic models answer the epistemological question by analysing our capacity to refer to fundamental, practical norms as a capacity to engage in a *process of interpretation* that takes place concurrently with the process of critique, such that explication and critique of the fundamental self-understanding of a community coincide. The norms to which critique refers can only be disclosed by the hermeneutic reconstruction of the normative self-understandings that they then can serve to correct.

The hermeneutic models answer the progress question by introducing the assumption that there is a surplus of meaning in those self-understandings (which are constitutively interwoven with social practices) that is not exhausted by the corresponding explicitly formulated self-understanding of the group at issue.

These forms of hermeneutic critique consequently remain bound to the norms that can be found in the *self-understandings* in which a practice articulates itself. Accordingly, the concept of progress in these models is unclear: when it comes to the interpretation of common norms that are never exhausted by this interpretation, the object of this interpretation never fully determines which interpretation is correct – that is, which of the strong evaluations of a practice should be given priority.

The practice-based models of immanent critique of Habermas and Honneth offer an alternative that refers to a source of immanent norms beyond the actual self-understandings of a community. Their models identify fundamental normative commitments as the reference point of immanent critique that can be reconstructed from the formal conditions of communication or of recognitive practices. With regard to the fundamental question of the basis of immanent critique, these models answer that it is always in the *structure of the practice under examination itself* that normative claims are found on which an immanent critique can draw.

Habermas and Honneth acknowledge that the reconstruction of these claims must take the given self-understanding of a community as a starting point (in the form of the hermeneutically reconstructible content of the lifeworld, in Habermas, or in the form of the prepolitical consciousness of injustice in Honneth). But they also assume that immanent critique always requires, as a corrective, a social-scientific analysis of normative structures that do not coincide with this self-understanding (the pragmatic preconditions of communicative actions in Habermas, or the historically institutionalized conditions of the development of a successful self-relation in Honneth).

In these models, the reconstruction of immanent norms is therefore reliant *both* on the hermeneutic understanding of demands emerging from the lifeworld *and* on a theoretically guided analysis of those formal structures that 'underlie' these demands. Only through the reconstruction of this foundation can pathological cases be identified that arise when the norms that are actually institutionalized in a practice violate the normative commitments immanent in these formal structures. The normative epistemology in these models consequently emerges from the interplay between fundamental social theoretical assumptions and the diagnosis of pathologies, which at the same time informs their conception of progress.

In such practice-based models of critique, three components can be distinguished: First, such a model requires the components of a *formal reconstruction* of the fundamental 'critical' norms N_1 in which the relevant practices are anchored. These norms, on which a critique that goes beyond interpretation must rely, are part of the *formal structure* of the practices of communication or recognition. The task of the reconstruction of these norms is undertaken in Habermas by universal pragmatics, and in Honneth by the anthropologically or practice-theoretically led analysis of the conditions of the development of a successful self-relation.

Second, practice-based models also include a *hermeneutic component* that concretizes these formal norms. Honneth and Habermas assume that formal analysis can always only abstractly reconstruct the preconditions for successful communication or successful self-relation. The formal normative commitments that such a formal analysis reconstructs only exist in the form of demands that have always already received a more or less concrete articulation in the self-understanding of the agents in the lifeworld. Therefore, the formal analysis must be supplemented by a hermeneutic reconstruction of the claims that actually exist in the lifeworld, which can fill the initially abstract norms with historically concretized content.

Third, there is a component of *social scientific explanation*, which must fulfil three tasks: (a) it must show that the formal requirements of communication or identity-constituting practices (the norms N_1) actually have an effect on self-understandings in the lifeworld; (b) it must analyse the actually accepted norms N_2 that determine the practice that is to be criticized and which at least potentially stand in contradiction to N_1; and (c) it must prove that the normative force of the basic norms N_1, which contradict the practice actually regulated by N_2, is a *necessary part* of this practice.

A model of critique only results from this last component if it is shown that the (discursive or recognitive) norms that are uncovered by formal analysis arise from a structure that is not optional for the social practices of the community at issue. In the case of the preconditions of communication and identity formation, the force of the critical demands that are derived from them only emerges from the *necessity* of these preconditions for the reproduction of *social practices in general*. However, it remains unclear in both Habermas and Honneth whether this necessity only holds as a matter of contingent fact or whether it is to be understood in the sense of a constitutive relation – whether any normative practice can only count as a normative practice if it also respects these norms. In other words, it remains an open question whether they privilege a specific set of normative considerations without fully justifying why they should serve as the standard for an immanent critique of social practices in general.

4.4.2 Which Model of Normative Social Practice Does Immanent Critique Need?

We cannot solve the fundamental problems of immanent critique and these specific problems without saying more about the fundamental structure of social reality. The possibility of immanent critique depends on the fact that there are *actually* certain forms of normativity in society for which the following holds: they must be appropriate objects of interpretation, but not exhausted by interpretations; they must be broadly independent of the conscious practical orientations of individuals; and they must be appropriate grounds for normative critique.

Claims about the existence of such immanent social norms, on whose justification the possibility of immanent critique always depends, are not trivial. The claim that norms are immanent in 'lived practices' requires explanation – that is, social ontological analysis. This explanation can be replaced neither by methodological stipulations nor by empirical evidence from the social sciences, because it concerns the structure of society itself. Only if it can be shown that social practices are determined not only by people's explicit beliefs and their actual behaviour, but also by immanent norms, can a model of practices serve as a basis for immanent critique. In order to show this, the domain of social critique must be temporarily abandoned, and the discussion needs to move towards formal deliberations on the structure and form of the existence of social practices. This is the focus of the chapters to follow: ours is now the task of developing a model of social practices that can answer the social ontological question of immanent normativity.

Chapter Five

Collective Intentionality

5.1 THE SOCIAL ONTOLOGICAL PRECONDITIONS OF IMMANENT CRITIQUE

In the first two chapters, I identified the existence of immanent norms as one of the fundamental theoretical presuppositions of immanent critique. Put briefly, this concerns the question of *which premises* we must accept in order to justify claims about the *content of immanent norms*. Such premises refer to normative content that exists – in a yet to be established sense – 'in' the practices of a community and that is not identical to the content of the explicitly accepted self-understanding of its members. Claims about such immanent normative content are first and foremost *social ontological* claims. They emerge in the context of certain explanations that presuppose specific kinds of facts and entities.[1] In the following chapters, this social ontological premise – that it is legitimate and sensible to introduce such facts and entities into explanations – will be examined and defended. The argument will proceed in two steps. I will first develop a model of collectively shared attitudes, which will be extended in a second step into a model of normative social practices. Before both arguments can be developed in detail, I will sketch an overview of the general strategy I will pursue.

(a) The first step: shared normative attitudes. Both varieties of immanent critique – the hermeneutic model and practice-based approaches – assume that members of social communities *share* beliefs, attitudes and norms in a strong sense. The hermeneutic models draw on the claim that the self-understandings, strong evaluations, traditions and practices they examine are not idiosyncratic ideas that are merely contingently shared by individuals; rather, the self-understandings of the members of the communities at issue are collective self-understandings in a stronger sense and therefore connect and

oblige their members in a specific way. MacIntyre's 'traditions', or the 'normative vocabularies' in which, according to Taylor, our self-understanding is articulated, are not only shared in a weak sense but are objects of joint, collective orientations.[2] For the practice-based models of Habermas and Honneth, it is also not sufficient to see the normative standards of the societies they analyse as merely existing in the form of individual 'inner' beliefs, or to see them as only a matter of externally institutionalized rules. At least in cases where violations of norms produce resistance, these models assume that the respective social groups rely on these norms as 'their' *joint, shared* norms, which they collectively deem to be binding for themselves.

The evaluations, norms and standards to which we feel bound as members of a social community are therefore, from the point of view of both models, not only 'our' values in the sense that they are accepted by each individual individually but are in a stronger sense *our common* values insofar as they are (a) constitutive of the respective interaction forms and of a community of actual and potential interaction partners and (b) a common object of reference for this community (or at least they can be). The normative force attached to the critical interpretation of these values put forward by social critics is also only explicable by the fact that we do not merely recognize these values individually – such that we could simply renounce them in response to critique; rather, they determine our common life, and we feel committed to them as collectively accepted values. When examining the attitudes by which we adopt such values as 'ours', the leading idea must be that *joint attitudes* – in contrast to individual attitudes – establish *specific kinds of obligations*.

In order to better understand this idea, the first section of the following chapter will temporarily leave the terrain of social critique and instead focus on a discussion that has taken place in the more analytically oriented currents of philosophy in the last twenty years. This is the discussion of the concepts of *collective action* and *collective intentionality*.

In the last decades, scholars – especially in continental philosophy – have argued, against the so-called 'intentionalist paradigm', that joint commitments should never be thought of as states of collective intentionality. Talk of 'states of collective intentionality' is – according to a widely shared assumption – taken to be a remnant of an outdated form of Cartesian or idealistic 'philosophy of consciousness'. Proponents of this view argue that such intentional language should be replaced with analyses of interactions, linguistic rules, practices or 'dispositifs'. However, I am of the opinion that a model of critique that employs the concept of social practices as a foundation for a theory of society cannot do without a strong concept of action or a conception of collective attitudes (or states of collective intentionality in the widest sense).

In what follows, I will discuss an approach that does not regard collective intentional states as an illegitimate idea. I will argue that all approaches that seek to redescribe collectively intentional states in an individualistic way as the intentional states of individual subjects (or that seek to explicitly exclude such collective attitudes) disregard the possibility of an unproblematic analysis of collective attitudes, which is essential to the question discussed here. This argument will allow me to make sense of the idea that a community can be the subject of a collective attitude and that, in the interpretation of that attitude, the group members must refer to it as an attitude they share as a group, not merely as an attitude shared by individuals.

(b) The second step: the normative content of social practices. The analysis of collective attitudes and beliefs that I will propose is not yet sufficient on its own to justify a model of immanent critique. First, the discussion of the practice-based models of immanent critique has shown that these models refer directly to practically institutionalized norms without applying the language of shared beliefs or values. Secondly, the proposed analysis of collectively shared intentional states will rely on the possibility of socially institutionalized obligations. This possibility requires explanation. It is therefore necessary to supplement the analysis of collective attitudes through an analysis of *practically shared norms and commitments* – and to thereby directly thematize the fundamental question of immanent critique: how can norms 'exist in' practices?

In that discussion, I will assume that such norms are always at least in part *implicit* norms. Hermeneutic approaches to immanent critique, as discussed in chapter 3, assume that the normative obligations that arise from people's self-understanding are never exhausted by any given interpretation of that self-understanding. They therefore presuppose a social ontology in which there must be a place for further elements that form the critical standard by which such interpretations can be measured. Similarly, the theories of society developed by Habermas and Honneth rely on the possibility of implicit social norms of which individuals need not necessarily be conscious, but which arise from either the quasi-transcendental conditions of communicative action or the requirements for the intersubjective achievement of successful self-relations. If such theories want to abstain from overly strong assumptions about the structure of human subjectivity, they will have to locate these norms in the structures of practices themselves, as is the case with regard to the strongly practice-theoretical model of immanent critique proposed at the end of the last chapter.

In order to answer this question about implicit norms in social practices, it is appropriate to rely on a theoretical tradition that, at first glance, is not directly connected to the project of social critique. The reception of the work of Ludwig Wittgenstein triggered a turn in both sociology and philosophy which led to the emergence of theories that no longer took features or states of the subject to be the decisive element for the existence of implicit normativity, but rather social practices. Under the force of Wittgenstein's argument, it is widely accepted that explicit laws or explicit rules cannot be the most fundamental normative phenomena. Wittgenstein's arguments suggest, rather, that the practical embedding of norms in shared contexts of action must be seen as an indispensable precondition of normativity.[3] According to Wittgenstein, we can only make sense of the notion that people follow rules if we acknowledge that the need to refer to common, shared practices decides which rules a person actually follows (and not only believes they follow). In the second step of the argument, I will therefore argue that we can only understand normativity in general on the basis of an analysis of social practices that describes such practices as being structured by immanent norms. In particular, I will argue that a specific kind of intersubjective attribution of authority, which I will call 'recognition', is an essential element of any kind of normative practice and thus allows us to make sense of the notion of immanent norms.

As I will show, the ideas of shared attitudes and immanent norms are not only complementary – as they are seen as two necessary components of the social ontological foundation of immanent critique – but also internally linked: we can neither understand the idea of shared attitudes without the idea of a social practice nor explain what it means to be practically bound by a rule if we do not understand what it means to take a collective attitude towards an action. This means that the importance of examining these two debates together will only become apparent at the end of the entire discussion. Therefore, rather than aiming to arrive at an answer to the problem of immanent norms quickly, my analysis will initially follow the internal logic of the issues under discussion.

5.2 COLLECTIVE ATTITUDES

What are we referring to when we refer to the shared beliefs, values or norms of a group in order to assess and critique their behaviour? A statement about the shared beliefs of a group could initially be understood in such a way that it merely describes the fact that all members of the group have these beliefs *individually*. This is insufficient in many cases, however – in central and important cases, people's beliefs, convictions, norms and intentions are shared in a 'strong' way, which goes beyond the convergence of individual beliefs or the individual acceptance of norms.

This difference between 'weakly' and 'strongly' shared beliefs can easily be illustrated: if the sun is shining in Frankfurt, I can form a belief about the weather by looking out the window. Perhaps I also have the true and justified belief that most other people whom I see on the street share this belief. I 'share' this belief with these people, however, only in the same way that I share a certain hair colour or the feeling of being hungry with many of these people – through factors that are fully independent of any relationship between us, we have simultaneously acquired certain beliefs that still exist if we are not standing in any relationship to each other. In particular, the fact that I believe that the weather is beautiful does not depend on the beliefs of other people. The fact that we 'weakly' share this belief is therefore a superficial feature of that belief that does not affect its essential properties in any way.

It is different if I meet a colleague in the corridor and we talk about the weather's being beautiful today. Through this interaction, the weather's being beautiful becomes an object of an attitude that we now hold *jointly*, as we have now *agreed* – notwithstanding the trivial nature of the case under discussion – through our discussion that this is a correct statement about the weather. We can therefore refer to the corresponding belief in the future as 'our' belief. This also changes the character of our individual beliefs: in addition to our individually attained beliefs about the beautiful weather, we can now understand ourselves as *parties* to a *joint* belief to which we can refer, for example, when it comes to justifying statements about the beautiful weather or when we speak about appropriate clothing. Finally, this joint belief also constitutes us as a group of a certain kind, namely, one that can ascribe to itself a belief in the first-person plural: 'We believe that the weather is beautiful.'

There is, consequently, a difference between the statement that several people *collectively or jointly* believe a proposition or intend to perform an action and the statement that all individuals in this group display this attitude *by themselves*. We acknowledge this difference in everyday life whenever we are confronted with the difficulty of deciding whether we feel justified in making use of the pronoun 'we' for such a statement. The mere fact that I know that someone, for example, shares a political opinion with me does not appear to justify my turning to third parties and saying 'We believe such-and-such'. This could be perceived as an unjustified attempt to create a joint position that does not actually exist.[4]

In less trivial cases, this difference is even more apparent: it is certainly the case that I share a belief about some policy question with many unknown people. But as soon as we form a group – a party, for example – that rejects or endorses a particular policy as a joint position, then the way we share this belief changes.[5] In such cases, we can jointly *commit* to a particular belief, thereby collectively *binding* ourselves to it. This commitment can then rationally inform our decisions about how to act collectively. Collective attitudes in this strong sense are therefore not independent of the relationships that exist between people and are therefore not to be located 'in' individuals independently of each other.

5.2.1 Strong Collective Attitudes as an Object of Social Critique

Strongly shared beliefs are usually those that interest us when examining joint beliefs. When we enquire into joint beliefs, we are typically interested not in those beliefs that people share as a matter of coincidence and without mutual knowledge – for example, personal preferences or values – but the beliefs they share *as a group*. The difference between merely distributively shared and strongly shared beliefs is especially important when conflicts occur: strongly shared beliefs and individual beliefs need not always coincide for every person. We can, for example, imagine a community in which a particular moral ideology is commonly shared and publicly recognized, and whose members collectively commit themselves to it as their common conviction, while at the same time the majority of members accept different, competing personal values.

Only strongly shared social values and beliefs are an appropriate point of reference for immanent social critique in the sense discussed here. Admittedly, we can in principle measure the practice of a community against the norms that are individually accepted by its members. But then a critique that follows from such an evaluation addresses these people *as individuals*. It would then involve claiming that these individuals should affirm the values they individually recognize as the values of their community. This would not constitute a form of immanent *social* critique, however; it only becomes so if it addresses people as members of a social practice.

But this is not the only reason why we must distinguish weakly distributively shared beliefs, norms and values from strongly collectively shared phenomena. Collectively shared joint commitments – in the full sense – play a specific and irreplaceable role in the lives of people and groups. If, for example, I have an unspoken or explicitly acknowledged wish to discuss an article with my colleague, no *obligation* for us to do so follows from this for us, even if my colleague happens to have the same desire. This is true even if we know this about each other – for example, if a third person told each of us confidentially about the desires of the other. However, this changes immediately once we *agree* that this is what we wish to do. Then it is not only sensible but in some sense even *obligatory* for us to form a joint intention to act accordingly, as through this joint desire we now stand – unlike with merely distributively shared desires – in a specific relationship to each other: through the joint commitment to this joint desire, we are in the normatively significant relationship of being participants in a *joint project*.

If *joint beliefs* and *joint projects exist in the strong sense*, this changes the relationship between people: they become members of a common group and together adopt the relationship between participants in a joint project or a joint belief, who have reason to accept the reciprocal particular obligations that accompany this role. This means they will be in a position to make *joint social commitments* that can be referred to by others when they criticize their social practices.

Forms of social critique that refer to collective beliefs and collective normative commitments must therefore look at people not only as individuals but *as members of communities*. The beliefs to which these forms of social critique relate are above all not the beliefs of individuals (even if individual beliefs can also play a role in social critique) but the beliefs that have normative force in a group, which this group jointly exhibits, and which are understood to be generally accepted. The same is likewise true of the institutions, practices and customs on which social theoretical models of immanent critique are based: these phenomena also do not exist as a part of the natural environment but only through the joint practices of human beings. An institution is only a real social force when particular procedures are treated by a group with certain normative expectations, which in turn are not the expectations of individuals but the joint expectations of the group.

5.2.2 Social Ontological Questions Concerning a Theory of Strong Collective Attitudes

Accordingly, I will take the question regarding the existence of collective attitudes and beliefs as a starting point for my analysis.[6] These phenomena are very important on both the micro and the macro level for our understanding of the social: we are accustomed to speaking of the fact that parties, organizations, the government or even states and the United Nations have a particular intention, advocate a particular belief or act in a certain way, even if we know that these organizations comprise thousands of people who naturally all have their own intentions and beliefs, not all of which contribute in the exact same way or even at all to the actions of their organization. These statements are therefore in need of explanation, even if we can assume that we will usually use them with a meaning that is relatively obvious.

A further problem is that we often encounter common positions and intentions of groups and institutions that are not coextensive with the individual intentions of their members: the position of a company need not be shared by all of its employees, and a party leadership's eulogy at the funeral of a prominent party member may indeed be perceived by all members as legitimate without this entailing that each (or any) party member actually feels the expressed grief as their actual emotional state.

This is even more relevant in contexts of social critique: if we draw people's attention to their collective commitments, we do not merely demand in a banal way that people do what they already want to do as individuals, but we refer to something that can constitute a reason for people to develop new individual intentions or beliefs. Therefore, it cannot already be identical or coextensive with them from the outset. The ascription of collective attitudes in critical contexts will therefore always be controversial and require justification.

Finally, it is most important to note that it is unclear which normative claims and obligations follow from the fact that we have joint beliefs and intentions. The simple fact that a random coincidence of opinions exists, for example, creates no obligation for anybody to change their opinion. But what of a case in which an intention shared between several people leads them to begin a joint project? Here there appear to be thoroughly normative consequences that impose themselves all the more strongly in cases in which a community has strong joint normative convictions – as becomes obvious if one thinks, for example, of political parties, religious communities or associations with morally relevant goals.

5.2.3 Individualistic and Collectivistic Options

This raises the question of the constitution of shared intentional states, which will be investigated below. After some introductory clarifications, I will first compare the fundamental assumptions of individualistic and nonindividualistic solutions to the problem of collective intentionality and advance arguments to the effect that a nonindividualistic and norm-focused approach can offer a superior solution. By means of Margaret Gilbert's theory – which I hold to be the most plausible formulation of such an approach – I will show, however, that even the best theories of this kind remain unable to solve certain central problems. These problems will prove to be solvable, however, if one introduces the social ontologically fundamental relationship of recognition into the theory.

Accordingly, I will proceed in the following way. I start with two individualistic claims: that the vocabulary of collective intentional states *need not* be applied as we can manage without it, and that it *should not* be used, as it is metaphysically questionable. I reject both of these claims. I will first show that we are *entitled* to use this vocabulary, and indeed *must* use it (section 5.3). In a second step, it can then be shown that the allegation that one has to endorse a questionable metaphysics to make sense of this vocabulary only has force if one models the ascription of collective intentional states too closely on the ascription of individual intentional states – which is neither necessary nor plausible. As an alternative to such a theory, I therefore propose a normative analysis of ascriptions of collective intentional states (section 5.4).

Once these general questions are answered, I will show that all individualistically inspired attempts to clarify collective intentionality fail at a single, central point: they cannot explain the normative aspects of collective attitudes (section 5.5).

I will therefore argue that an intentionalist theory that grasps collective intentionality exclusively by means of its nonnormative aspects must be inferior to an explicitly normative theory. For this reason, I turn to an alternative, which I find in the work of Margaret Gilbert (section 5.6). This alternative focuses on the normative aspects of collective phenomena. This argument is still limited insofar as it leaves central aspects of these phenomena unexplained. Therefore, it must be supplemented by a plausible explanation of the origin of the normativity of collective phenomena. I locate this origin in the irreducible recognitive attitudes through which subjects must relate to each other in order to be able to form collective intentional states (section 5.7).

5.3 THE NECESSITY OF COLLECTIVE INTENTIONAL STATES

The question of *whether* one may assume that there are collective commitments[7] – as immanent critique presupposes – appears wrongheaded, as the attribution of such states is part of everyday life and the way we speak and think about social reality. It therefore seems nonsensical to adduce arguments for the existence of something that everyone believes exists, so long as no persuasive doubts can be raised about its existence.

Such doubts, however, do in fact exist. They are not limited to academic philosophical debates; their echo can be found in society's self-descriptions. Even if most people use phrases like 'The government believes in the importance of human rights' without hesitation, the suspicion can easily be roused that such phrases represent an oversimplification: 'The government' is ultimately – one can easily object – not a subject who can 'believe' anything in the narrow sense.

Is the ascription of collective attitudes therefore an abbreviation of a more complicated statement about individuals? Is it ultimately an 'inauthentic' way of speaking, which is always open to the danger of ideological misuse, especially against the rights of individuals? Consider, for instance, Margaret Thatcher's – famous argument: 'And, you know, there is no such thing as society. There are individual men and women, and there are families. And no government can do anything except through people, and people must look to themselves first.'[8] The scepticism expressed by Thatcher – that talk of groups and societies obscures the real object of discussion – is cogent as far as it should lead us to respond to statements about 'collective interests', especially concerning the alleged importance of such interests, with a healthy amount of scepticism. We must therefore propose an argument if we want to defend our everyday way of speaking against this scepticism.[9] Even if this challenge must be taken seriously, however, I believe that it can be answered. An argument for the assumption that there are irreducibly collective beliefs and intentions can be advanced in three steps.

First, we can refer to the *phenomenology of our everyday actions*. Here we find numerous examples that cannot be described other than via the attribution of joint attitudes and actions. So, for example, the joint upbringing of a child by its parents can only be understood as the combination of the individual actions of two people with great difficulty. Likewise, political projects and movements, sport teams, and even short-lived and smaller groups – for example, a couple eating together in a restaurant – determine their intuitive self-understanding according to the fact that if they are to act together in the way they desire they cannot do so without having actually joint – and not merely matching – intentions, beliefs and attitudes in a strong sense. Of course, referring to our intuitions is not sufficient by itself to reject analyses that reduce such joint projects to individually attributable attitudes, as these intuitions might be shaped and distorted by traditional (but revisable) preconceptions.

Secondly, one can argue in favour of our everyday intuitions that there are many *theoretical problems* in the theory of social action that are only satisfactorily reconstructible if we assume that there are collective attitudes. Robert Sugden, for example, has argued that both the actually observed patterns of altruistic action in prisoner's dilemma–style situations (and also the possibility of their rational solution) depend on the fact that we do not always understand each other as individual utility maximizers but rather as members of 'teams' who are in a position to form collective attitudes.[10] A similar, persuasive argument for the necessity of a concept of collective action can be found in Philip Pettit's work: Pettit shows that 'discursive dilemmas' can emerge in groups – namely, situations in which rational inferences must proceed differently at the level of the group than at the level of the individual.[11] Such situations typically emerge when both the premises and the conclusion of a logical argument are potentially the result of a (majority) decision in a group. A group, Pettit shows, can jointly accept, by majority vote, several premises that are all individually necessary and together sufficient for a conclusion but still jointly reject that conclusion, without the individual rejection of the conclusion by each member being irrational. Pettit draws from this the conclusion that groups that want to pursue collective purposes in a rational way cannot tolerate such inconsistencies. In groups that want to act consistently, reason must be *collectivized*. This means, however, that we can, with good reason, attribute collective beliefs and intentions to groups – at least in the normative sense of a commitment to the conclusion of such inferences – which are no longer straightforwardly dependent on the beliefs and intentions of their members. The possibility and necessity of such ascriptions represents a prima facie argument against a reductionist-individualistic theory of shared attitudes.[12]

Finally, a heuristic strategy can be developed from the clarification of our everyday intuitions and a theoretically informed examination of which social ontological commitments are consistent: if we grant at least provisional validity to our intuitions, and then examine which individualistic attempts at explanation are brought forward for the seemingly collectivistic content of these intuitions, this might prove that there is no individualistic solution that both captures our intuitions and is also theoretically consistent and comprehensive. This strategy of the reciprocal correction of intuition and theory will be pursued in the following sections.

5.4 ON THE STATUS OF COLLECTIVE ATTITUDES

5.4.1 The Normative Role of Attributions of Collective Intentionality

The widespread idea that collective intentionality is ultimately reducible to individual intentionality derives its plausibility not only from the implicit belief that we do *not need* the vocabulary of collective attitudes but also from the fact that the implicit metaphysical strangeness of such a vocabulary implies that we *should not use* such a vocabulary, even if we apparently need it. Even if we cannot manage without the assumption of collectively intentional states, it still has not been shown that this assumption itself refers to something that can be integrated into our ordinary ontology in a plausible way. It is therefore above all the *metaphysical status* of collective intentional states and collective commitments to values and norms that causes them to appear puzzling.

Clearly, groups can only act if the individuals of which they are composed act. But if there are only individual agents, then must not every statement about collective intentional phenomena be reduced to statements about individuals?

Such a conclusion is only compelling within a philosophical project that attempts to describe collective action in the already established vocabulary of the theory of individual action. But this is not a relevant reference point for a critical social theory. In this chapter, the much more productive strategy of exploring the debate about collective intentional states conducted in analytic philosophy will be used to explain the concept of collective commitment, in order to examine how it is capable of reconstructing the *use* people make of the concept of collective commitment.

The ascription of individual intentional states already allows more than merely one use. We can identify, roughly, three kinds of use of the attribution of individual intentional states: there is first a predominantly *descriptive* use. It is without doubt interesting to know whether a person believes that they are being persecuted by the KGB or by aliens. This also applies if this belief has scant direct practical consequences. We are therefore often interested in the truth of particular accounts of people's intentional 'household'. Likewise, such attributions can serve *expressive* functions – above all, the self-attribution of intentional states. One need only think about how important it is to people – often beyond all practical consequence – that they express the fact that they have certain beliefs and communicate this to others.

These descriptive and expressive uses of the ascription of intentional states seem to chime well with a picture of the mind that presents the mind as something 'in' which mental 'content' exists, which can be truthfully described and authentically expressed. Accordingly, we often implicitly assume that the descriptive truth and the expressive authenticity of the description of my own intentional condition depends, above all, on the fact that I have certain *mental states*, or at least exhibit dispositions to form such states, at some time. However, there is a further way of using the ascription of intentional states – namely, a *normative use*. Our beliefs and intentions – among other things – determine which actions are *rationally required* (or irrational): my intention to write a lecture tomorrow morning already makes a certain behaviour rational for me and thereby binding, namely, to refrain from spending the whole night with my friends in the pub. This normative use of attributing intentions accordingly helps us to evaluate our own behaviour. Far more important, however, is the fact that through the attribution of intentional states we can also give *meaning* to the behaviour of others. Accordingly, the *understanding* of social actions – as Weber[13] analyses it – is bound to the fact that we can adopt accounts of the intentions and beliefs of other agents which let their actions become rationally intelligible.[14] Through the ascription of intentional states, we integrate people's behaviour into a normative space, within which we can *evaluate* subsequent acts as rational or irrational and can *understand* them via an assumption of their rationality. In this context, we are not so much interested in people's mental setup as in finding out which plans or actions they have committed themselves to in a certain way.

Ascribing intentional states to others in this normative sense often, but not always, goes along with forming beliefs about their mental states or dispositions. We can employ intentionalist explanations of the behaviour of others without necessarily needing to believe that they have corresponding mental states or dispositions. With regard to individual agents, we are usually inclined to believe that their intentional states supervene on certain mental states or dispositions, even if we can in principle remain agnostic about whether that is the case.

The thesis I will explore in what follows is that our attributions of collective intentional states are *only analogous to the attribution of individual intentional states in a normative sense – and do not involve such attributions in the descriptive or expressive senses*. This means that individual intentional states are, according to this thesis, normally sufficient for the attribution of mental states in the broadest sense, but that the same relationship does not hold for collective intentional states.[15] If this thesis holds, then it becomes obvious that a theory that uses the attribution of collective attitudes in its explanations is by no means committed to any questionable metaphysics about 'group minds'. Of course, this still leaves open the question of what the correct understanding of such attitudes is, but at least the main reason for the alleged inadmissibility of such attributions will thereby be removed.

5.4.2 What Obligations Follow from Collective Attitudes?

As already indicated, the ascription of collective attitudes – as in cases of individual intention – has consequences not only for which behaviour we can understand as rational or comprehensible but also insofar as collective attitudes always also imply new normative relationships: joint commitments and joint intentions in a strong sense always involve people implicitly or explicitly agreeing with others on a belief or goal and thereby normatively binding themselves to the attitude that accompanies such agreement, such that an *obligation* results.[16]

The answer to the question of whether collective attitudes necessarily come together with such obligations is not uncontroversial. But if collective phenomena are to be relevant for *social critique* – and therefore have a 'normative surplus' compared to individual attitudes – then only a theory of collective intentionality that takes this aspect of collective action seriously is worthwhile.

Hitherto, only a vague intuition has been presupposed, to the effect that the attribution of collective intentional states can always be understood as an attribution of normative obligations. To develop an adequate analysis, this intuition must be described more precisely. The role of the normative aspects can be best understood via an example:

> *The train ride*.[17] Let's suppose that Anna and Ben – who know each other – each take the same train from Frankfurt to Berlin without having planned this in advance and, at first, without each knowing about what the other was doing. They initially 'travel together' in a certain minimal sense – they are on the same train at the same time – but they are clearly acting not collectively but individually.
>
> Let us assume that Anna and Ben meet by chance in their compartment, recognize each other, and jointly decide to proceed on their journey together.

If we want to decide, in the case of Anna and Ben, whether their subsequent actions are guided by a collective intention, we must pay closer attention to all those circumstances that could serve to justify them in saying retrospectively to other people 'we have jointly decided to travel by train together'. What must Anna and Ben accept – beyond the already fulfilled condition of travelling in a shared compartment – in order to *jointly* intend to travel with each other? And, crucially: which normative consequences follow from the fact that we attribute to them (or they attribute to themselves) a corresponding collective intention?

We can use this example to make sense of the difference between merely *distributively shared* attitudes and *actually collective* attitudes: we can imagine, based on an analysis of their individual attitudes, that Anna and Ben each form certain intentional states individually – states that are related, only in terms of their *content*, to the other person. This obliges them to accept the normative consequences of their individually having these intentional states: they must each individually commit to the project thereby implied, individually aim at the success of the corresponding plan of their partner and so on. This remains a matter of individual, not collective, intention. Nothing about this circumstance has changed, even if they both know about their mutually interrelating intentions. To illustrate this, we can imagine the following discussion:[18]

> Anna could explicitly say to Ben something like: 'I intend to travel with you, in the sense that I would like you to be continually near me, on the condition that you have the corresponding intention towards me. In this case, I also intend to support your plans. Therefore, I will perform the actions that appear to me to be the most appropriate to bring about the fulfilment of all these intentions. I wanted only to call your attention to these facts.'

Ben could answer: 'What a coincidence – I have an exactly corresponding set of intentions!'

In such a situation, both participants have reciprocal knowledge about their conditional and mutually compatible – but still individual – intentions to perform an action that involves both of them. As already mentioned, such individual intentions do play a certain normative role. Through their individual intentions that are related to shared actions people commit themselves – as with all other individual intentions – to certain actions, such that they may be criticized as *irrational* if these are not performed. If, for example, the place next to Anna becomes free, she could justifiably say to Ben: 'Ben, as I know that you intended to stay near me, it would be rational for you to sit on this seat.' If Ben does not follow this advice, Anna would be justified in criticizing his behaviour as irrational. Ben, after all, goes against his own declared intentions. Should Ben act in this irrational way, Anna would even be justified in doubting the seriousness of his original speech act.

It is therefore uncontroversial that the conversation so described creates a social situation in which a particular, weak form of normative obligation exists, making a particular form of critique possible. The decisive question, however, is whether this is the form of reciprocal obligation that is typical of genuinely collective action. Let us continue the thought experiment:

Anna expresses the following critique concerning Ben's inappropriate action: 'As I know that you want to travel with me, your action is not very rational.' Or even, 'You are not acting in accordance with your stated intention – I no longer believe that you actually have this intention.'

Is this a critique that a member of a group engaged in joint action would express? This is not plausible. In a case of *genuinely* collective action, Anna would be justified not only in criticizing the *rationality* of Ben's *individual* action but in making a vastly stronger critique. She could say, for example, '*We* want to travel together – therefore *you* should actually do what is necessary.' This 'we' refers to a kind of community, which consists in more than mere mutual knowledge of shared goals or an individually accepted willingness to support mutual subplans. This stronger critique, which would seem normal to us in this case, would not merely refer to the fact that a person counteracted *their own* intention but would rather express disappointment or indignation about the fact that this person – by treating their *individual* intentions as decisive in the first place – *is no longer acting as a member* of the group and has perhaps already abandoned it in a certain way.

Although a discussion like the one described is rather contrived, philosophically and psychologically, it can serve as an example of the fact that strong collective intentions are distinguished from merely distributively shared intentions by the fact that they are accompanied by a specific relationship to a reciprocal obligation. In a situation in which the members explicitly or implicitly accept the attribution of a collective intention, project or plan, they usually thereby also accept an *obligation*. This is not only a self-directed obligation with respect to their own intentions and the reciprocally established individual plans, but an obligation towards the group or the 'we' of this collective intention. It follows from this that the mere cooperation of individuals that have interlocking *individual* intentional states is not yet a case of joint action.[19]

The normative role of collective intentionality is therefore not exhausted – as in the case of individual intentionality – by the fact that an observer's attribution of an intention to an agent allows their action to be classified or understood as rational or irrational. Rather, the 'external' attribution of collective intentionality is only justified when the participants in the collective intention can also treat *each other* as normatively bound in a certain way. The justification of an attribution of collective intentionality to a group is therefore dependent on whether the participants conceive of themselves as members of a group to which they ascribe a particular collective intention, and whether they ascribe a normatively meaningful participant status to themselves.

If Anna and Ben have openly agreed on a joint trip, but after some time Anna no longer wants to fulfil the obligations that result from this agreement, Ben is not only justified in wanting to know her reasons but also – if Anna cannot provide good reasons – in criticizing her for her behaviour. Through entering into a collective intention, a prima facie obligation to cooperate is acquired which cannot be rescinded unilaterally[20] – at least not without jeopardizing the collective intention and the existence of the group that is constituted by it.

The attribution of collective intentional states therefore does not primarily imply the attribution of a kind of obligation to individuals that can be reformulated as an obligation that would follow from the attributions of individual intentional states. Rather, it implies the ascription *of obligations of a new kind*. The obligation to cooperate, which participants in collective intentional states ascribe to each other, is stronger than a norm of rationality that individually obliges people to act in accordance with their own intentional commitments, as such an obligation – unlike those generated by individual commitments – cannot be rescinded unilaterally. It is, however, a conditional and contingent duty that is weaker than a moral duty.[21] It must therefore be a *sui generis* obligation.

Naturally, it could now be objected that this strong normative reading captures not all of our attributions of collective intentional states but only a limited subset of particularly strong cases. This is obviously right. But even if the properties described belong only to certain *strong* forms of collective intentionality, these strong forms – which shall be explored below – are in need of explanation and are exactly those forms of collective commitment that are important for a theory of immanent critique. Therefore, the full diversity of our attribution practices must be disregarded to the extent necessary to allow us to bring into focus the specific properties that are relevant to the purposes pursued here.

5.5. THEORIES OF COLLECTIVE INTENTIONALITY

If we assume that attributions of collective intentionality can best be analysed through the various aspects of the attributions of normative status they imply, instead of accepting that they are metaphysical statements about particular forms of mental state, this allows for a productive strategy for approaching current theories of collective intentionality. If we avoid 'psychologism' about intentions, we can evade from the outset the question whether groups have an equivalent to 'mental states' – a question that the dominant 'antipsychologism about social groups' mostly answers negatively anyway.[22] When discussing these theories, I will concentrate on whether they can correctly capture the *normative role* of the attribution of collective intentional states, independently of their broader metaphysical commitments. I will also focus on whether they can capture the normative difference between individual and collective actions, which also represents the decisive element for the critical application of such attributions.

In the current literature – besides Margaret Gilbert's work, which is discussed in section 5.6 – various strategies can be found, which I would like to discuss by means of their best-known representatives: with Michael Bratman, we can understand collective attitudes as the result of a certain relation between individual attitudes; with John R. Searle, by contrast, we can understand collective intentionality as an independent 'mode' of individual intentionality. Finally, Raimo Tuomela has proposed that we interpret a certain structure of intentional states as the obligatory 'ethos' of a group.

5.5.1 Relational Individualism

The first possible explanation of collective intentionality is to be found in theories of 'relational individualism'.[23] Such a theory assumes that collective intentional states exist when multiple individuals exhibit certain individual intentional states that are related to each other in a specific way in terms of their content.

A very simple form of a relational-individualistic explanation of collective attitudes can be found, for example, in theories of 'common knowledge'. The basic idea is that an intentional attitude A that is exhibited by individuals P_1 and P_2 is a joint attitude of them as a group if and only if P_1 and P_2 also know of each other that they have this attitude, if they *know about this knowledge*, and so on.[24]

Such a simple conception, however, turns out to be problematic. This is not only because it can be shown that it assumes an infinite number of at least potential beliefs on the part of the participants.[25] It is also because it cannot serve as an adequate description of the normative role of collective intentional states.[26] As shown in the discussion in section 5.4.2, collective intentional states, at least in their strong form, imply reciprocal normative obligations. It is far from clear, however, why we should acquire a special obligation to act in accordance with our own individual intentions merely because others know about them.

This problem can perhaps be avoided if we only count as constitutive of joint states those combinations of intentional states in which common knowledge about intentions is *added not merely to otherwise mutually independent* intentions but to attitudes in which the intentional states of the first order are also related, in terms of their *content*, to the states of the other person.

For example, Michael Bratman proposes that we understand the concept of *shared intention* such that the participants must not only individually aim to pursue a goal and mutually know that others have the same aim, but also individually intend (and mutually know of this intention) *that this goal be achieved by the group*, and indeed in a way that respects the individual participants' intentions to make a contribution of a particular kind to that shared pursuit.[27]

Bratman proposes a two-tier model to analyse this form of collective action. The minimal condition for collectivity is a *shared intention*. Simple shared intentions are necessary but not sufficient for *cooperative action* (which represents the second, more demanding stage), as they are compatible with cooperation's being compelled or unstable. Therefore, while shared intentions encompass a wide spectrum of collective phenomena, cooperative actions should only encompass people's joint activities in a narrow sense.

Shared intentions, in this stronger sense, are characterized by the following elements:

1. The participants must all individually intend that the group perform an action.[28]
2. The relevant intention should refer not only to the performance of the shared action itself but also to the fact that the shared action is performed

in such a way that the concrete plans of all participants with respect to their respective contributions ('subplans') are not frustrated.[29] Therefore, it is not necessary for all agents to be in agreement about the details of their collaboration. It is only necessary for their plans to 'mesh'. This criterion excludes – among other things – cases where intentions are only shared *de dicto* and not *de re*.
3. The fact that these criteria (and possibly further essential criteria of cooperative action) are fulfilled should be 'common knowledge'[30] – it should therefore be known to all participants that the criteria are fulfilled, and known that this is known to all participants, and so on. Bratman assumes 'common knowledge' as an intuitively plausible concept and foregoes a more precise analysis of it.

A Bratman-style account of shared intentions understands collective intentional states to be fully realized by individual intentional states. Such an account is not 'purely' individualistic, however, as both the criterion of common knowledge and the interlinkage of individual action plans in terms of their content presupposes relations between group members that can be characterized from the outside. Shared intentions are therefore not merely sums of the intentions of individuals but complexes that are built from individual intentional states.

Even if this is doubtless an adequate description of certain collective phenomena, it does not appear to grasp the essential element of strong collective intentions – namely, the obligations that they imply. The intentional states described in this way do not appear to constitute a strong collective intention as they do not entail a *normative* commitment to the realization of that intention, which members can reciprocally demand from each other.

Bratman is one of the few representatives of an individualistic conception of collective action who takes these problems seriously. He admits that collective intentions imply a certain normative obligation. Insofar as he takes shared intentions to be comprised of individual intentions, however, and insofar as individual intentions usually do not justify strong obligations to others, he can only explain the relevant obligations as generated through *additional* acts, such as promises and contracts.[31] As shared intentions do not necessarily presuppose such additional normative 'substructures', they cannot, as such, ground strong obligations.

In various articles, Bratman examines further sources of normativity: on the one hand, he is of the opinion that – while no special positive duty exists to help others to fulfil their respective subplans, which are parts of an interlocking shared plan – having an intention that forms part of a shared intention is incompatible with our accepting the needless frustration of the intentions of other participants. It follows that we must help other members of the same shared action if they need our help to realize their corresponding intentions, but only if we do not thereby endanger the realization of our *own intentions*.[32] Bratman calls this 'minimal cooperative stability'. In a later paper, he pursues a similar point,[33] drawing on an argument developed by Thomas M. Scanlon[34] to the effect that, on moral grounds, we may not needlessly frustrate the expectations of others once we have produced these expectations through our intentions. Both arguments, however, are characterized by the fact that they do not apply to all cases of shared intentions and systematically give priority to the realizations of one's own intentions.

Bratman's reference to moral reasons in explaining the obligation that is typical of collective intentionality shows that shared intentions themselves are not ascribed reason-generating power in this respect. Normative obligations are therefore not constitutive of their existence on Bratman's account. As a result, Bratman's model does not have the resources to explain the normative power of collective intentional states that immanent social critique must presuppose.

5.5.2 Collective Intentionality in the 'We-Mode'

John R. Searle's well-known theory represents an alternative to individualistic reductionist accounts of collective intentionality. According to Searle, collective intentional states are not reducible to individual intentional states[35] but are rather 'primitive' states[36] that are characterized by the fact that the *subject* of the state is *a group*.

This thesis appears more radical than it is, as Searle does not hold that an intentional state that has a group as a subject is also a *state of that group*. Rather, in his view, such states are mental states of individuals. This follows from Searle's internalist theory of mind:[37] According to Searle, the content of mental states is independent of all external conditions and is given solely through the internal state of a 'mind' that is realized through the neurophysiological states of individuals. Collective intentional states are therefore *necessarily* states of individuals that refer to a group (in terms of who is taken to be the subject of that state) but do not depend on the actual existence of that group, and therefore also do not presuppose corresponding intentional states in other people. Paradoxically, group intentions can exist without groups – as Searle explicitly argues, a (presumably solitary) 'brain in a vat' can have collective intentional states.[38]

Collective intentional states therefore differ from individual states not by virtue of the fact that only collectives can form them, but rather through the 'mode' in which these states are formed by individual subjects. Searle calls this mode the 'we-mode', understood as a co-original mode of intentionality. This idea of distinguishing between two modes of intentionality can only clarify the normative implications of attributing collective intentionality to a limited extent. This idea may be sufficient for explaining why, from the observer's perspective, we must assume that people who participate in a collective intention ought to have an additional *subjective belief* to the effect that they are obliged to other people. As soon as we know, however – which, according to Searle, must be possible – that a particular collective intention errs (insofar as a corresponding group does not exist), we can no longer claim that the relevant subject *is actually obliged*: we must rather assume that it would be rational for the person to no longer accept this obligation. With ascriptions of collective intentional states, therefore, a normative consequence of the necessary kind does not necessarily appear to be involved. Searle's theory cannot throw light on this aspect.[39]

5.5.3 Tuomela's Theory of the 'Group Ethos'

Neither Searle's nor Bratman's theory of collective intentionality can explain the normative aspect of the attribution of such intentionality, as they always start from a concept of intentionality that is so strongly oriented to the individual case that it cannot consider the differences involved in ascribing intentionality to collectives.

This unsatisfying analysis of the normative aspects of ascriptions of collective intentionality is recognized as a problem by some participants in the debate. Raimo Tuomela, for example, aims to make sense of these normative aspects through the introduction of the idea of a 'group ethos' and through a more complex analysis of the 'we-mode'. However, Tuomela also remains caught in a dilemma: on the one hand, he must describe collective intentional states as states that are ultimately held by individuals; on the other, he must assign independent normative force to the structure of these states.

According to Tuomela, the ascription of collective intentional states can constitute a basis for *reciprocal critique*, as members of the relevant groups obtain – through their collective commitment to a group ethos – the *authority* to normatively criticize each other. This can only be explained by the fact that this commitment constitutes a *social obligation* for them (that is – an obligation that is not attributable merely on the basis of individual intentions). As Tuomela writes:

> As to epistemic matters, there is a difference between the cases where there is mutual knowledge and where there is mere, possibly false, mutual belief about the existence of collective commitment. In the former case, the group members must somehow have made public their intentions and commitments toward the

ethos and what it covers. In the case of mutually believed collective commitment, the members might not *know* that the others participate in the collective commitment. Hence they cannot justifiably sanction each other.... If there is *mutually known* collective commitment, the group members will be publicly bound ... to maintain and satisfy the ethos and bear responsibility.... [W]ith *mutually believed* collective commitment we do get the right kind of collective maintenance and satisfaction behaviour, indeed group-binding action.[40]

The assumption that a *publicly known commitment* can give rise to a form of obligation that is typical of collective commitments in general suggests that publicity is a necessary condition for effective collective commitments. But this creates a dilemma: if a collective commitment is actually constituted by individuals' intentional states – as Tuomela, like Searle and Bratman, assumes – then such public knowledge about intentional states is either a matter of reciprocal knowledge about individual states (which Tuomela rejects, and which in any event would have no normative 'surplus value') or a matter of public knowledge about a collective commitment *on the part of the group*. This would be circular, however, as it would presume that the collective commitment exists before the publicity condition is met. Therefore, Tuomela introduces the idea that the relevant kind of normativity is to be explained by reference to certain obligations that are derived from *social norms* – that is, norms that are based on *social institutions*. He analyses the core of these institutional commitments as follows:

> Social commitment to others and to the group is the core of the reproachability feature involved in collective commitment: a publicly we-committed member who leaves the joint project or intentionally violates the ethos can be criticized by the others, whereas if he had been committed only 'to himself' he would in general have been less criticizable socially for letting the others down.[41]

Tuomela cannot analyse this institutional commitment further with his model of collective intention, however. If social institutions presuppose collective commitments,[42] and if collective commitments presuppose institutional commitments, the analysis becomes circular.

The theories proposed by Tuomela, Searle, and Bratman – even if they cannot be treated here with the detail they deserve – are three examples of 'intentionalist' theories of collective intentionality. These theories all presuppose the uniformity of attributions of intentions and must therefore attempt to understand the normative meanings of ascriptions of collective intentionality as a result of properties that ultimately only individual intentional states can bear. As a result, they cannot integrate those normative consequences of collective intentional states that do not follow from the ascription of individual intentional states.

5.6. A NORMATIVE THEORY OF COLLECTIVE ATTITUDES

5.6.1 Margaret Gilbert's Normative Theory

Margaret Gilbert's theory is the leading alternative to the theories analysed above that takes seriously the two normative dimensions of collective attitudes which were drawn from the examples we've considered.[43] I will forego presenting Gilbert's extensive and complex theory in all its detail. Instead, in examining its claims, I will attempt to concretize the core issues and to identify problems yet to be resolved.

Even if Gilbert does not consciously dismiss the vocabulary of individual intentionality in describing collective *commitments*, a nonintentionalist concept of 'obligation' forms the core of her analysis. In Gilbert's view, the crucial element that theories that explain collective intentionality through common knowledge lack consists in the fact that such theories cannot clarify how participants in a collective intention are committed to this intention in a different way than they would be to an individual intention.[44]

What Gilbert sets up as the main requirement for an adequate theory of collective intentionality is that it must be able to correctly characterize the particular kind of obligation that accompanies collective action intentions. To use one of Gilbert's favourite examples: if two people go for a walk together,[45] it is not sufficient for the strong meaning of the term 'together' that both participants individually intend to walk with the other person and that this is publicly known. To actually walk *together*, it is necessary that each recognizes a commitment to a joint project with respect to the other. As we've seen, this specific obligation cannot be explained through the existence of weakly shared intentions. It is rather a specific consequence of genuinely collective action.[46]

As we will see in this section, Gilbert's theory fulfils this requirement. However, it cannot fulfil another requirement, which represents an essential aspect of a successful theory of collective intentionality: an acceptable theory of collective intentionality must offer a plausible explanation of the 'dynamic' aspect of the attribution of collective intentional states. That is, it must offer a model that explains how the conditions for the attribution of such states can come into and pass out of being.

In particular, a plausible theory must be able to explain the relationship between a merely individual readiness to cooperate and the distinct form of responsibility that follows from participation in collective intentions. In order to clarify this, I must first explain Gilbert's analysis of collective attitudes in more detail, and we must then examine whether this analysis is able to fulfil some or all of the criteria we have enumerated.

Gilbert's best-known analysis of collective phenomena is the microsociological analysis of joint actions sustained by joint intentions.[47] The phenomenon of strong collective actions is understood in such a way that the weak sense of merely distributively shared actions which was identified in individualistic theories is excluded from the outset: Gilbert assumes that, alongside a *weak* sense of joint action, which only refers to the fact that several people do something in temporal or spatial proximity or with the same individual intentions, there is also a *strong* sense that we convey with the common expression 'doing something together'.

Gilbert illustrates joint action in this strong sense with the two – already mentioned – examples of walking together and travelling together on the train.[48] To employ the example of walking together yet again: we can distinguish between cases in which two people are *actually walking together* and cases in which they only happen to be *next to each other*: people who are walking together with another will wait if their partner falls behind or stops, they will not diverge from the path abruptly and so on. Each member of the walking community so constituted will therefore normally orient their contributing action to that of the other member. If we ascribe the intention of jointly walking together to two people, then we also ascribe to them a *commitment* – they jointly assume responsibility for the success of the group's project. To draw a contrast again to the individualistic view: it is not sufficient that two people perform the same action at the same time and in proximity, and nor is it sufficient (or necessary) that it is an action that can only be performed by several people in concert. Likewise, it is not sufficient to ascribe individual intentions to carry out this action in physical and temporal proximity and in a cooperative way with their partners to the participants, as one can easily illustrate with the case in which both partners have this intention but do not know of each other's intentions. To carry this further, the additional attribution of mutual knowledge of the mutual attribution of such individual intentions is also not yet sufficient, as even individual intentions in combination with mutual knowledge still do not establish the obligations typical of genuinely collective intentions.

Gilbert therefore describes the obligations and demands that arise from collective intentional states not as the result of the combination of individual commitments but as the result of a 'joint commitment'. A group of people is jointly committed to an intention if the readiness of the participants to jointly accept it is publicly known and if they form the 'plural' subject of this intention. This occurs when every single participant is willing to merge their individual will into a 'community of wills' and wishes to take part in a joint commitment. The members accept a goal 'as a body'.[49] Therefore, from any joint intention follows an obligation to do what is necessary in light of these joint goals and principles. According to Gilbert, the ascription of a collective intention therefore has consequences that go beyond the consequences of attributing individual intentions: collective intentions imply that the members acquire a special relation to one another, which normatively binds them together in a way that individual intentions are incapable of bringing about.

As the ascription of joint attitudes is an attribution of a contingent, context- and person-specific commitment, the people involved are subject not to universal but to particular norms that are bound to the context in which they were attributed. This intuition, which is still very much drawn from Gilbert, can be formulated in the following way:

Collective attitudes (1): The ascription of a strong collective attitude CA implies that the members of a group G ascribe to themselves a joint commitment to a collective project. From this follows the validity of a particular norm in G: that is, beyond the universal norms of concept use, of rationality and of morality, there are special obligations that follow from the fact that a collective attitude is ascribed to a group.

In other words: if a collective attitude CA is attributed to G, then the members of G are attributed with a commitment to a specific norm of action, which prescribes that they must act in the relevant contexts in a way that is compatible with the fact that G has the attitude CA.

This analysis is certainly circular with respect to the presumed concept of a 'collective attitude', as the participants in a collective action must already be able to understand it in a certain way. This circularity can be resolved, however: in order to attribute a collective attitude to a group, acceptance of the obligation to act in congruity with the collective attitude must be attributed to its members. However, this does not mean that they themselves must be able to apply the *concept* of a collective attitude in order to accept this obligation. Even those who do not know what a collective attitude is can know which obligations follow from a joint commitment to paint a house together with others, from the 'project' of walking together or from the plan to jointly overthrow the government, insofar as the practical consequences of such a commitment can be expressed in the form of a norm. This means that the acceptance of a project like walking together, for example, is not different from the acceptance of those norms that conventionally govern the practice of walking together, and which can be formulated without needing to explicitly refer to knowledge about the action type 'walking together'. There are norms that must be accepted, such as 'One must wait for others' or 'It is wrong to move on without appropriate communication with the group'.

What the acceptance of joint attitudes consists in is therefore a matter of norms and conventional definitions in social practices, which determine what is appropriate in such contexts. These social practices, definitions, conventions and customs do not depend on any complicated conceptual capacities. However, they need collective beliefs about what is appropriate, or at least – and this ends the regress – an acquired *disposition* that makes one type of participation appear correct.[50]

What is the significance of the fact that people need to accept a range of norms to participate in a collective attitude? For Gilbert, this is first and foremost practically significant: the acceptance of norms that bind the group together leads to the fact that the members of the group may legitimately *reprimand, criticize and correct* each other for violations of these norms. In contrast to the ascription of individual intentional states – which also makes possible critique and evaluation from the outside with respect to the rationality of actions – in the collective case this general, possibly external, normative perspective on group action becomes supplemented through an internal person-bound perspective established by the group members' attribution of authority to each other.

I would like to propose that the ascription of a strong form of collective intentionality, or of collective attitudes, is to be understood as necessarily implying that the members of a group possess a *special* authority to criticize each other, which other people do not have.[51]

> *Collective attitudes (2):* This applies for every member X of G: X is in the relevant, strong sense obligated only to the other members of the group. This means that only the members of the group are justified in reprimanding X if he fails to fulfil a specific norm N_A that arises from the collective attitude.

If, for example, a football player is a member of a team that has a collective intention to play an upcoming game and if that player refuses to carry out the consequences of this intention – for example, running across the field in the way their role requires – then two kinds of reaction are appropriate: *Everyone* is entitled to claim that the team as a whole has failed to carry out its intention. Similarly, everyone is entitled to question whether the player is still acting as a member of the team. But a random person is not entitled to a further critique.[52] The *members of their team* are, however, entitled to reprimand the player in a strong way, available only to members: the player in question has failed to do that which they are obligated to do as members of a group.[53] This possibility shows that collective intentional states imply a specific *group-internal* obligation.

5.6.2 The Nature of the Obligation Involved in Joint Commitments

One can reformulate Gilbert's proposal such that the group members' acceptance of a normative, reciprocal obligation to the consequences of a collective belief or intention is a *necessary and sufficient* condition for the legitimate ascription of a strong collective intentional state to that group. However, it must still be explained what, exactly, the obligation consists in, what grounds it rests on, and how it acquires its obligatory character. There are two interconnected problems: First, Gilbert must explain how individuals can accept obligations of the kind that are distinctive to collective intentions. Secondly, she must explain how joint commitments can develop normative force for individual actions.

(a) Where does the obligation come from? With respect to the first question, there is a *problem of constitution*. According to Gilbert, the subject of a joint commitment is the group. This subject, however, does not exist independently of this commitment but is rather constituted by collective attitudes.[54] This means, on the one hand, that groups, even if they can *subsequently* take on further commitments, do not *independently* exist as collective agents, and therefore also cannot collectively take on commitments, unless at least one of these commitments is already accepted. On the other hand, we cannot explain the emergence of collective agents through the fact that *individuals* accept joint commitments, as joint commitments are necessarily commitments of groups, not of individuals. But then how can groups or 'plural subjects' emerge at all?

Gilbert assumes that joint commitments emerge when there is reciprocal knowledge in a group that the members of the group have expressed their readiness to participate in a collective attitude.[55] Then, for each member of this group, 'in effect [he] volunteers his will for a pool of wills to be set up so that in certain circumstances, that pool will be dedicated to a certain end. His understanding is that just in case his so volunteering is matched by that of the relevant others, etc., the pool will be so set up.'[56] Or, even more clearly: 'The joint commitment comes into being when and only when it is common knowledge that both expressions have been made.'[57] The will to participate in a collective intention, made public by individuals, is obviously the will to carry out this collective action, together with others, and to be responsible for it. As they have acquired the collective intention by 'publicizing' their will, all participants are obliged to do their part.

But there is a conspicuous difficulty with this approach: clearly, it must be possible to describe the 'precollective' state in which the reciprocal readiness to participate in a collective attitude is 'out in the open' in terms of *individual intentionality*. It thus generates no obligation. I can publically acknowledge my individual readiness to put my will at the disposal of a group, even if there is no one who could accept this offer and without this individual readiness on my part establishing an obligation to others.

In addition, there must still be a difference between a mutual *readiness* to believe or intend something together and the *realization of this readiness*

– that is, the actual collective intentional state. The *fact that someone is ready to take up an attitude* must be able to be separated from the attitude *for which* he or she is ready. This raises the question of how the obligation deriving from the collective intention – which *cannot* be explained exclusively in relation to this individual readiness – comes about. If the individualistic readiness to participate in a collective intention or belief is not sufficient for a collective intentional state, then a further element must be added. But what is this further element?

(b) How can obligations that are relevant for individuals follow from collective intentional states? A second problem emerges when one takes the converse perspective: even if one assumes that Gilbert succeeds in describing a plausible theory of the emergence of the obligations involved in collective attitudes, such obligations are ascribed to the subject of the respective attitude – that is, to *the group*.

At least part of the practical significance of collective intentionality consists in the fact that a *mutual entitlement to criticize* between group members – that is, between individuals – follows from collective intentional states. But the ascription of a commitment *to a group* does not directly entail that the individual members of that group are entitled to criticize each other for their individual behaviour, or are obliged to accept corresponding criticism. Why should one subject, the individual, be responsible for the fulfilment of the obligations of *another*, plural subject – that is, the group? This raises the question as to why the individual members of a group can be made individually responsible for the obligations that the group has as an independent subject.

In order to answer this question, it must be explained how the ascription of obligations to collectives relates to the attribution of obligations to individuals. This is necessary in order to understand how the corresponding self-ascriptions in the actions of individuals can develop their normative power.

Gilbert first assumes that 'individual' commitments follow from joint commitments but distinguishes them from 'personal' commitments.[58] While personal commitments are commitments people can accept and reject at their own discretion, individual commitments that arise from joint commitments[59] are characterized by the fact that one *cannot* rescind them at one's own discretion – because they are not one's *own* commitments but the commitments of a group.

But if joint commitments are the commitments of a group, which can be distinguished from the personal commitments of individuals, then we must explain how individual obligations 'emerge' from these joint commitments; individuals appear to have no special reason to accept the commitments of another subject – namely, the group – as their own. Moreover, this makes it very difficult to understand how joint commitments, if they are *not* the commitments of the *corresponding individuals*, can nonetheless enable individuals to criticize each other for their individual actions.

Kenneth Shockley offers a related criticism of Gilbert: 'If there are obligations of joint commitment, then any theory accounting for these obligations must account for how individual persons might acquire them from a collective with which they, in some way, are associated.'[60] As Gilbert herself remarks, mere readiness to participate in a 'joint commitment' does not result in an obligation (even an *individual* obligation): 'No one will be individually committed to anything independently of the others'.[61] The conditions of the emergence of collective commitments are therefore not yet sufficient conditions for the ascription of individual commitments. But how can we explain, then, the fact that in our collective action we ultimately ascribe obligations to ourselves as individuals?

It appears that Gilbert's theory is unable to counter the objection that Shockley called the 'wrong sort of subject' argument.[62] According to this argument, joint commitments cannot play a role in individuals' deliberation about their actions because they are not the 'right sort of subject' to have such commitments. If this is the case, it cannot be demanded of individuals that they adhere to joint commitments, and consequently the obligations that follow from these commitments are without the practical relevance that Gilbert imputes to them.

There are several possible ways to circumvent this problem. As an initial attempt, *additional* (individual) commitments to conform with the intentions of the group could be attributed to the members of the group. This appears to directly lead back to the problems faced by the individualistic solutions, however, because it is questionable why people should be strongly bound by such individual commitments in the way at issue here.

Schockley offers a second solution. He proposes that the introduction of a 'principle of membership' explains why a derivative form of obligation *always* follows from membership in a group. Such a principle formally expresses that there is a (as yet undetermined) fact from which it follows that membership in a group entails certain obligations.[63] But what could this fact be? Here there are again two possible answers: on the one hand, such a principle could apply because the members of a group have a *reciprocal obligation*, and on the other hand it could apply because the members have an obligation *towards the group as a separate subject*.

Schockley argues that the first option is plausible but renders plural subjects unnecessary as it ultimately amounts to a contractualist solution. This option, then, explains all aspects of obligation in collective intentionality through the reciprocal acceptance of individual obligations by the group members. The second option must remain mysterious in Shockley's view, however, as it is still unclear how individuals could be obligated towards a separate plural subject.

This apparent dilemma can be solved. We can explain the extent to which collective intentional states are constitutively grounded in obligations between individuals and why talk of collective states is not unnecessary. To do so, we must distinguish between a commitment's *content* and its *force*.[64] Even if obligations between individuals are sufficient to explain the fact *that* these people are mutually obliged to each other (i.e., its force), this does not always suffice to answer the question of *what* they are obliged to. As Shockley rightly claims, it is plausible to think that the obligations that are relevant in collective intentionality draw their *force* from the reciprocal intersubjective relationships between the individual members of groups, and the reciprocal practice of holding one another responsible is therefore a practice that results from relations between individuals. But it does not by any means follow from this – as he seems to assume – that the *content* of the obligations relevant in this practice – that is, the norms that individual group members make each other responsible for complying with – can be explained without recourse to the group.

As one can see in the example of going for a walk, the mutual obligations of the individuals in such a practice are in no way identical to the obligations of the group as a whole. The joint commitment (of the group) to carry out the joint intention in many cases corresponds to *derivative* individual obligations (of the group members) that are *dissimilar in content* and cannot be analytically derived from the collective intention. What the *joint* intention implies for the individual participant depends on background rules that can generate extremely different individual obligations in different cultures or social contexts – what it *means* for individuals to walk together can vary according to these backgrounds. The content of these derivative individual obligations – even if their normative force is based on the mutual recognition of others' entitlement to critique one's behaviour – cannot be understood without reference to the joint intention: whoever walks together with others must be willing to accept criticism from members of the respective group if they walk off without special reason and without notice. Participation in a group walk is clearly distinguishable, however, from mere agreement between individuals not to move away from each other. The normative force of the derivative individual obligations rests on relationships between individuals, but *their content* can only be made explicable via their being connected in a determinate way to the joint commitments of the group. For this reason, this joint commitment is an indispensable element in the analysis of joint action.[65]

Collective Intentionality 147

The following proposal therefore offers a way out of Schockley's dilemma: the *commitments of plural subjects* are not reducible to *commitments of individual subjects (with the same content)* but supervene on relations between these subjects that are not reducible to the joint commitment (or vice versa). A member is obliged to perform a certain action *as* a member, so long as they acknowledge a *socially given principle of membership* as binding on them, which determines which individual obligations *follow* from the collective obligation. However, this must not be understood as an individual commitment to such a principle – that is, something the member can accept as an individual *independently of their relations*. Rather, a person ascribes membership to themselves through participating in a practical relationship with other group members, which then implies the validity of this principle of membership. Through (more or less voluntary) integration in a normative network of social membership, which must be understood as entailing the basic and irreducible adoption of a certain attitude, this principle of membership becomes binding for the person as a member.[66] Being a group member is therefore *not the result of an individual intention or belief* but of the acceptance of one's embeddedness in a network of status positions that objectively entail obligations. People are therefore obliged to act in the relevant ways as long as they wish to maintain their status as members. This obligation arises neither solely from the relationships between people as individuals and other individuals nor from their relationship to the group, but rather from their *status in the group*. The solution to the two problems outlined above therefore consists in understanding collective intentionality in such a way that it rests on relations of reciprocal obligation – that is, on normatively loaded dispositions to react to the actions of others and to accept such reactions – which are not to be understood other than through reference to a group's intentional state. The emergence of collective intentional states can thereby also be made comprehensible: a collective intentional state emerges precisely when individuals successfully enter into relationships with each other in which they mutually take on attitudes that imply both acceptance of the reactions of others and an expectation that your own reactions will meet with this acceptance.

5.7 COLLECTIVE INTENTIONS AND INTERSUBJECTIVE RECOGNITION

5.7.1 Collective Intentionality as a Group-Specific Normative Commitment

These considerations provide the key to an analysis of collective intentionality that can fulfil the requirements outlined previously. From the assumption that the power of collective commitments stems from the reciprocal relationships of the group members, it follows that we can understand collective intentionality as supervening on such relationships:

Collective intentionality: A strongly collective attitude (or a strongly collective intentional state) CA is shared by a group of people G if and only if every member X of G in the relevant action contexts:
  1. Is accepted by the other members of G as being obligated and accepts being obliged, in at least a minimal way, to respect the inferential consequences of the fact that G has the attitude CA.
  2. Is socially accepted as entitled to expect of every other member Y that Y will respect the inferential consequences of the fact that G has the attitude CA.

By the 'inferential consequences' of the fact that the group has a collective attitude I mean the *relationships of compatibility and incompatibility* that exist between this attitude and the actions of the group and group members – that is, which actions in which contexts are compatible with the claim that the group as a whole has the respective collective attitude. From these relationships emerges a group attitude towards the possible actions of the whole group and the actions of its members.

A group that intends to perform an action A is therefore committed, in virtue of general social norms regarding the ascription of intentions, to make arrangements leading to the execution of A, insofar as they are unproblematically possible. Certain additional beliefs can be ascribed to the group, such as the belief that A is a possible action. Both these collective attitudes and the corresponding collective beliefs play above all a normative role for the individual members of the group, insofar as they establish *derivative obligations*. These obligations, however, cannot be determined by the fact that the members have individual intentional states that correspond to the collective intentional states (i.e., that are identical in terms of their content). Rather, the possibility of any collective attitude presupposes a range of socially established norms that determine *the specific consequences of the collective attitude* for the individual members of the corresponding group. The normative preconditions of collective intentionality can only be understood in such a way that social rules determine the extent to which a collective attitude implies that individual member of a group must accept distinct individual obligations to comply with those norms which, according to these same rules, emerge from the fact that the group has this attitude.

But how can the realization of this network of obligations be explained in such a way that it avoids the emergence problem faced by Gilbert's theory? First, it can be held that according to this picture the *individual acceptance of an obligation* does not usher in the corresponding collective intentional state, but rather the collective intentional state consists in the socially shared *acceptance of the social consequences of a collective obligation*. But we have still not explained how this obligation comes to be. To answer this question, the idea of 'acceptance' must be cashed out further. Acceptance of the normative commitments of membership in a group can be understood as *acceptance of the obligations and entitlements* that members of a group have in relation to each other. The obligations of individuals as group members come along with – as should be made clear by the examples – an entitlement as members to expect from other members that they will respect the existence (and the normative consequences of the existence) of the joint collective intentional state.[67] Such a structure of entitlement and obligation concerns *specific*, especially strong, entitlements and obligations within a particular, limited group of people. They are consequently specific entitlements and obligations of particular people towards other particular agents, which cannot be presupposed a priori. Something further must be said about their emergence and the ground of their validity.

5.7.2 Collective Intentionality as a Group-Based Recognition of Authority

I would like to propose that the origin of those forms of obligation that are typical of collective intentionality can be located in a basic relationship of *recognition of authority* between group members. The authority in question involves the entitlement of group members to evaluate the actions of their interaction partners with respect to their compatibility with the group's position. This means that the obligation that accompanies collective intentionality is explained by the *form of relationship* that members of a group must enter into in order to be able to treat each other as obligated.[68]

People treat each other as mutually obligated by a norm if they accept that their own behaviour is measured by that norm and if they claim for themselves the right to evaluate the behaviour of others – by, for example, accepting sanctions and criticism of their own behaviour and by claiming a right to respond to the behaviour of others with sanctions and criticism.

In the next chapter, I will further clarify what this means. At this point, the practical attitude that is expressed in the readiness to mutually accept such forms of evaluation should be referred to as *recognition*. Recognition in the most fundamental sense should be understood as an indirect, implicit way of submitting to an obligation. One can recognize an obligation by conceding to another person in a particular context the right to evaluate one's own actions in relation to certain normative standards. The relevant context-specific standard is the norm that is derived from the collective intention.

Collective attitudes (3): The obligation that comes along with a strong collective attitude is grounded in the *mutual recognition* between the group members, who claim authority with regard to the relevant attitude and associated norms in a particular context. Therefore, a person X as a member of the group G shares in the collective attitude CA if and only if X recognizes the other group members by attributing to them the specific authority to judge X's behaviour in a particular context in terms of the norms implied by the group's having CA.

One can say that a group has a strong collective attitude only if its members judge their reciprocal attitudes towards each other's utterances, beliefs and reactions to be normatively relevant. This in turn means that *they reciprocally recognize each other*. I am jointly committed with other people to a particular collective attitude if and only if I accept their criticism and their agreement in terms of the obligations that follow for me from this attitude – that is, if I regard them as competent judges of whether an act is compatible with this attitude.[69]

This argument already goes some way to providing the missing explanation of normative obligation. For a full explanation, the concept of recognition – which here refers to a fundamental social relation – must be further cashed out:

Collective attitudes (4) – recognition: X recognizes Y as a member of group G with respect to the strong collective attitude CA (or in terms of the norms N_A which are constitutive of and implied by CA) if and only if:

1. X accepts the obligation to take seriously any evaluation (be it critique or agreement) of X's relevant behaviour by Y with respect to X's compliance with N_A in at least one context, without requiring further evidence than reference to X's membership in G to show that X is bound to N_A.

2. X claims to be entitled to serious consideration of his or her evaluations of Y's behaviour with respect to N_A in at least one context, without requiring more than reference to the group membership of Y in G as evidence that Y is bound to N_A.

Unlike individual intentional states, collective intentional states are characterized by the fact that the normative obligations that they imply do not merely depend on the intentions and beliefs of individuals, and they are therefore in a sense less optional. This means that, normally, a supplementary individual intention or belief, in addition to the collective intention of the group, is not necessary for the attribution of an obligation to an individual. And this in turn means that in cases where a collective attitude is present, the relationship between the group members must be understood such that one is not entitled – according to the norms of this relationship – to require, in addition to this collective intention, further reasons for why one is obligated by the respective norm.

Naturally, this does not mean that no further justification for the respective normative judgements (for example, with regard to their factual premises) can ever be required. Rather, it means only that for the normative justification of an ascription of a particular obligation *in the normal case*, no further justification is necessary *beyond the membership* of the relevant person in a group with a collective attitude. Group members – insofar as their mutual obligation does not exclusively depend on the existence of individual intentions – act under categorical, not hypothetical, imperatives insofar as they act as group members.[70]

It is helpful to compare this to noncontextual norms of rationality, which are essential to the attribution of *individual* intentional states: with regard to these norms, *everyone* is justified in judging my actions in light of my beliefs and intentions, insofar as I raise a claim to rationality. In the case of the norms that come along with collective attitudes, however, the obligation to follow a norm N does not mean that I am only obliged to act in a way that does not contradict my sharing in the collective attitude if I explicitly recognize that norm's bindingness. If I share in a collective attitude CA, this entails that I am committed to its normative consequences *by default*, rather than only on condition of my agreeing to that norm. The fact that I am a member of the corresponding group *simply means* that the evaluation of my behaviour by other group members in terms of the collective commitment is normatively binding. This normally needs no additional evidence (such as my giving an explicit affirmation of the fact that I am participating in CA). Being a group member therefore simply means that the other members of the group *may presuppose by default* that I must accept the normative obligations that accompany CA.

5.7.3 Recognition of Authority as Default Acceptance of Evaluations

How does recognition of the authority of other people differ from an individual intention – for example, the individual intention to observe a norm? In order to answer this question, I will again return to the question of what it means in the context of collective intentionality to accept the obligations that accompany participation in a collective attitude.[71]

(a) Recognition as acceptance of the appropriateness of normative reactions. Acceptance of an obligation is identical neither to a disposition to always act in conformity with this obligation – people can accept certain obligations but fail to fulfil them – nor to explicitly believing that one accepts an obligation. In order to decide whether a person accepts an obligation, neither their actual fulfilment of this obligation, nor their nonfulfilment of it, nor

their beliefs are relevant criteria. Whether someone accepts an obligation or not depends, rather, on which reactions to the nonfulfilment of the obligation they accept as appropriate.[72]

In the simplest case, the acceptance of an obligation means that the agent accepts sanctions in the widest sense if they violate the obligation – for example, penalties, reprimands or even strong criticism. One could say that a person accepts an obligation if and only if they accept that they are subject to sanctions in the case of their nonconformity with the rule to which they have committed themselves. The *acceptance of an obligation* can therefore be explained as the counterfactual *acceptance of a sanction* in case of violation of the relevant norm. This acceptance does not necessarily demand the existence of intentional states on the part of the accepting person.[73]

We can therefore assume that a group G has a collective attitude CA if and only if the members of this group *accept each other as mutually entitled* to *evaluate* and *sanction* each other concerning the conformity of their actions with the fact that G has the attitude CA. This is the case if and only if they mutually accept corresponding normative reactions (sanctions, for example).[74]

(b) The default acceptance of normative reactions. What does it mean to accept a normative reaction (for example, a sanction)? It would be too quick to say that a person only accepts an obligation – for example, the obligation to respect the existence of a particular collective attitude – if they endure without resistance the normative reactions of other group members and act in future in the manner necessary to avoid any further corresponding sanctions. Conversely, it is also not the case that a person who fails to endure a justified sanction does not therefore accept the obligation they violated. We can imagine cases in which a person *legitimately* rejects a sanction because they think that their breach of duty can be excused, for example.

A solution to this problem arises if one conceives of the authority to sanction not as an *absolute authority* but as a *default authority*. This means that a person accepts an obligation if and only if they either accept corresponding sanctions or, *if and when* they do not accept sanctions, they do so with reference to *overriding rules*, in respect of which they *again* accept *the authority of other people*. A sanction is thus accepted if and only if the sanctioned subject, in reaction to the sanctioning by members of a particular group in a particular context, *either* generally and regularly does not attempt to avoid or avert the sanction *or*, in rejecting the sanction, does so with reference to exonerating exemptions or overriding rules. Accepting a sanction means not turning against the sanction without relying on such exemptions or rules.[75] The members of a group accept each other as entitled in the necessary sense to evaluate the respective actions if they *by default* – that is, in the absence of exonerating reasons – accept the corresponding sanctions.

(c) Recognition as a default ascription of authority to others. The concept of recognition can accordingly be made more precise: recognition exists between two persons if and only if they accept the intersubjective obligations and entitlements that were just discussed. That means that they need to exhibit the practical attitude of readiness to act in the described way: that is, they generally and by default ascribe to each other the entitlement to sanction each other in the appropriate way. Behind this stands a readiness – specific to the relevant interaction partner – to accept the other's normative reactions. This means that the recognition of a normative reaction (which refers to a norm that is constitutive of a collective attitude) can only be counted as constitutive for that collective attitude if the agent generally,[76] in relation to a recognized person (or group of recognized people) and in relation to a particular action context, is unwilling to raise an appeal against any sanction in the absence of exonerating reasons. However, both the inferentially characterized content of collective intentionality – the relevant norms are norms that determine what follows from the relevant group's having the collective attitude at issue – and the possibility of exemptions cannot be described without reference to a more comprehensive normative structure in which normative attitudes build on each other. A collective attitude therefore cannot be broken down into individual dispositions to act. It must always be contextualized with regard to the norms that prevail in the social environment in which the corresponding group is embedded.

It is now easier to see how individual obligations can derive from collective commitments without having to attribute to the individual members an additional individual commitment to conform to collective commitments. A collective commitment supervenes on the reciprocal normative ascriptions of evaluative authority – which is in turn realized through a readiness to accept the corresponding obligations – in relation to a specific norm, to which none of the members need be personally or individually committed. The collective obligation does not derive from the individual relationships between the members but rather from the structure of the group as a whole.

As the evaluations and their acceptance are always related to a particular action context, it is also plausible that, through mutual recognition in relation to different norms, people can be members of various groups at the same time, which are based on different and even contradictory norms. As a party member, a person can be a member of a structure of recognition in which the institutionalized norm is that social equality is to be striven for; at the same time, as a member of a local board of trade, that same person can be a member of a structure of recognition in which the entrepreneurial norm of maximizing commercial freedom is institutionalized. In such cases, individuals will often be unable to live up to all their derivative, individual obligations at the same time, but so long as they accept the evaluations to which they are subject in their respective structures, they can still be members of their respective groups.

5.7.4 The Background of Collective Intentionality

The existence of norms – the recognition of which accounts for the existence of a collective intentional state – cannot be reduced to the fact that they are collectively accepted, as their normative character depends decisively on the possibility that the participants can fail to follow them: that a person is bound by a norm means not only that they *actually* accept the corresponding evaluations but also that they are *justified* in this acceptance, as these evaluations are *actually* bound to the corresponding norm. Which evaluations are justified, however, can only be decided against the *background of further norms*. Each individual obligation is embedded in a system of other, mutually supporting obligations. In every discussion of what our collective attitudes are, there is always an unquestioned but in no way unquestionable background of other collectively accepted norms and therefore other collective intentions and relations of recognition. Recognition therefore cannot simply be reduced to the de facto acceptance of normative evaluations. Rather, it must always be thought of as integrated into larger social structures of social judgement. By this I mean established models of group structuring and membership that are available as social resources to all people and that can be easily actualized and instantiated in every group. Because of these social resources, group membership does not have to be newly constructed afresh every time. As collective intentionality is therefore always dependent on the socially established validity of norms, a theory of collective commitment cannot carry the justificatory burden for a model of immanent critique alone. It leaves open how those standards of correctness that endow their specific attributions of authority with normative content are socially institutionalized.

5.8 SUMMARY OF THE ARGUMENT

In this chapter, an argument has been presented for the thesis that the attitude of recognition is a fundamental element of the strong collective attitudes that immanent critique presupposes in its description of the normative content of social reality. The proposal, accordingly, is to understand collective phenomena in such a way that they originate in the mutual recognition of people who ascribe specific authorities and thereby put a norm into effect in their group. The solution described in this chapter can satisfy the two criteria introduced at the beginning of this section and, at the same time, avoid the problems identified in Gilbert's theory (the problem of the origin of obligations and the problem of the obligation of individuals through collective commitments).

- The theory of recognition can explain the normative force of collective intentions and beliefs by describing them as constituted by mutual ascriptions of authority. This ascription of authority is sufficient to grasp the normative aspect of the respective intentional states, without justifying other possible uses of intentionalist vocabulary.
- Mutual recognition as a fundamental relation can explain how collective intentional states come to be. How relations of recognition emerge is not mysterious but both psychologically explicable and open to sociological analysis. Recognition as a social phenomenon is also sufficient to make normative structures understandable in their sui generis character.
- We can explain how individuals become motivated by joint commitments and how context- and group-specific quasi-individual obligations emerge from structures of mutual recognition if we take into account that the recognition of others is valued by individuals. This explanation does not reduce all obligations to obligations of individuals; it only explains how joint commitments can become motivationally effective for individuals. Social obligation is only conceivable in social relations of the kind described.

While collective attitudes were originally described as the object of a hermeneutic critique that – following Walzer and Taylor – focuses above all on the clarification of their content, the analysis provided here shows that this content is only established as an object of possible interpretation by a complex structure of concrete social relationships. The 'real' content of a particular, shared self-understanding is therefore not only the object of hermeneutic clarification but also possibly the object of a social scientific analysis of relations of recognition, in which fundamental collective attitudes and forms of authority derived from them are established in a certain group. In this sense, this analysis therefore allows for a hermeneutic form of critique to be combined with a more strongly social scientific form of immanent critique.

Chapter Six

Norms and Social Practices

The analysis of collective attitudes developed in the previous chapter already makes it somewhat clearer how we should account for the immanent normativity to which immanent social critique refers. But the analysis so far is not yet sufficient to fully comprehend the possibility of such norms: collective attitudes require that the members of the relevant groups are already able in some fashion to know which concrete obligations follow from their joint commitments. This presupposes the existence of already established social norms that determine what the fact that the group has the collective attitudes in question entails for the members of that group.

The ability of individuals to participate in collective attitudes therefore rests on their familiarity with *socially recognized norms* that define collective action types: on account of our socialization in our communities, we are all familiar with what it means to take a walk together, raise children, converse and act politically together. What these forms of collective action entail for their members is rarely settled by explicit beliefs or formal orders. Rather, in our society, *socially shared general models* exist for these action types; that is, disseminated, general action schemata that legitimate specific evaluations and are reproduced by them. I will call these general action schemata '*social practices*'. It is only the interlinkage of collective attitudes with such generally institutionalized normative models that makes them an appropriate point of reference for social critique. Social critique refers not to the one-off collective commitments of this or that concrete group but rather to temporally extended, generalized social practices and relationships in a community. At the same time, adopting a collective attitude means being involved in a social practice that essentially involves the possibility that one's own action, and the actions of the group in which one is a member, are criticized. This possibility of mutual criticism is a constitutive part of the normativity that social practices enable.¹ Immanent social critique therefore needs a *theory of social practices* as its foundation.

Accordingly, regardless of whether we reconstruct immanent norms from hermeneutically accessible joint commitments or directly from social practices, we need a theory of practices which – in order to provide an account of immanent normativity – must perform three specific tasks:

- *First*, a theory of normative practices must explain how the immanent norms of a social group can form a nonarbitrary critical standard, distinct from the explicit self-understanding of its members.
- *Secondly*, it must be possible to systematically grasp the activity of interpretation as a practice itself as well, if the mutual ascriptions of authority involved in that activity are understood as the negotiation and interpretation of common norms.
- *Thirdly*, the concept of a social practice that underlies the analysis of collective attitudes must be understood such that it satisfies the demand raised in our discussion of Honneth's and Habermas's social theoretical models: that is, it must clarify the social ontological foundations of the normative demands that underlie the practices that are constitutive of the possibility of critique.

The question of how we can accomplish these demands will not be answered directly in what follows. First, we must establish which criteria a theory of immanent norms must fulfil in order to be both philosophically and social-theoretically plausible. In order to develop these criteria, I will proceed from a philosophical debate in which this question – without being formulated in this way – has already been discussed for some time: namely, the debate on the problem of rule-following, as introduced to modern philosophy by Ludwig Wittgenstein.

I will take this approach for the following reason: If the only reason to speak of immanent normativity were that the assumption of such norms was a precondition for immanent critique, then it would not be clear why we should not simply reject the idea that this form of critique is possible. Immanent critique can only be given a firm foundation if it is shown that we are justified in assuming the existence of immanent normativity for reasons independent of our own preferences as social critics.

How must we understand a social practice with immanent norms? For the very reasons outlined above, this can be best explained by presenting a problem to which the assumption of immanent norms represents a solution. This problem can be found in the so-called 'rule-following debate': this debate proceeds from the question of what it means to say that an agent 'follows' a norm or rule. In the course of this debate, it quickly turns out that the problem of rule-following can only be solved through the assumption of *social practices* with *implicit rules*: in other words, through the very assumption that is fundamental to immanent critique.

This chapter is structured as follows: *First*, proceeding from the intuition that social practices are the substratum of implicit normativity, I will show how the concept of a social practice (section 6.1) and the idea that social practices establish social norms or rules (section 6.2) have recently moved into the centre of various debates in sociology and philosophy which – like the method of immanent critique – assume that implicit norms are institutionalized through social practices. In a *second* step, the discussion of rule-following will be explored in its connection to Wittgenstein (section 6.3). This will show that this discussion systematically leads to a model of implicit norms in social practices. It must then be clarified in detail which criteria for a theory of immanent normativity are established in this debate (section 6.4). The theory of practices and the rule-following debate are, *thirdly*, combined in the so-called 'social solutions' to the rule-following problem. These social solutions (section 6.5) form the background of the proposal I will present in the next chapter.

6.1 SOCIAL PRACTICES

A practice-theoretic model of immanent critique assumes that the immanent norms or rules to which immanent critique refers are institutionalized in *social practices*. If we are to investigate whether such immanent norms actually exist, it does not suffice to simply point out that the possibility of such an institutionalization is *desirable* for the theory of immanent critique. Independent reasons must be given for the assumption that it is also *plausible*. As already suggested, the rule-following debate in connection with Wittgenstein can be taken up in order to elucidate these reasons. In short – at least according to a popular reading – Wittgenstein's answer to his celebrated question of what it means to follow a rule suggests a solution: we can only explain our undeniable ability to follow a rule if we assume that implicit rules *are institutionalized in our practices and institutions*. The goal of the analysis that follows is to find out which reasons can be provided for this assumption. It is only when we know which independent reasons there are to accept immanent norms that we can determine what such norms and rules *are*, exactly. I do not claim that the concept of a practice that is developed in this debate is the only possible concept that can be used in analysing social practices, or that all social actions are characterized by immanent norms. My sole question is whether there are *some* social practices that have normative potentials such that it can be justifiably said that rules, norms or principles can be derived from them, on which immanent critique can rest.

The concept of a social practice is the object of a great number of philosophical and sociological theories. In what follows, these 'practice theories' (a) will be briefly characterized in order to (b) cash out their essential assumptions. In a third step, (c), the preconditions that a practice theory must fulfil in order to be able to serve as a basis of a model of immanent critique will be described.

(a) Practice theories. The idea that there are social norms whose validity rests not on the intentional states of individuals but on practical interactions among people is not uncontroversial: it is a paradigmatically modern idea that normative validity is not part of the objective 'external' world but results only from our subjective, individual attitudes towards external reality. Applied to the social sciences, this idea at least seemingly entails the claim that social reality must also be a meaningless space of objective facts. No norms in the proper sense follow from social facts – they can at best causally explain agents' normative beliefs.[2]

Objections have in recent times been raised against this conception of social facts: critics of a strong division between norms and facts – such as Charles Taylor, John McDowell and Robert Brandom – present arguments for a stronger connection between norms and reality with respect to both the allegedly value-free domains of objective reality and the allegedly not objectively describable domain of normative commitments. This allows for a connection to the tradition of critical theory, which, from its beginning and to this day, has presupposed such a connection between norms and reality. One of the central ideas that all generations of the Frankfurt School have advocated with equal emphasis is the critique of allegedly value-free social sciences. From Horkheimer's inaugural lecture, to Adorno's intervention in the positivism dispute, up to Habermas's *Knowledge and Human Interest*, one of the central elements of critical theory is the idea that the normative resources that are necessary for social critique are to be found in social conditions themselves – especially in the social practices that are constituted through the interactions of the members of a community.[3]

The fact that the idea of practices has again been revived in (post)analytic philosophy and modern sociology has also had a beneficial effect on the project of finding alternatives to a norm-free analysis of social facts. This revival makes it possible to overcome the limitations of the norm-free view, which is made clear not least in the admittedly diverse applications of the concept of practice by Charles Taylor, Hubert Dreyfus, Pierre Bourdieu and Anthony Giddens. At the end of the twentieth century, reference to social practices in philosophy finally became so pervasive that Stephen Turner could write in 1994 that 'practices, it would appear, are the vanishing point of twentieth-century philosophy'.[4]

(b) The central assumptions of practice theories. What is the central idea of theories of practice? The concept of a 'practice' involves the notion that, beyond subjective attitudes, conventions and actions on the one hand and causally effective environmental conditions, nonintentional structures and action-schemata on the other, another sphere of phenomena exists to which the social sciences can refer in their explanations: namely, those patterns of action that have a regular and routine habitual character. Such action patterns cannot be dissolved into a description of behaviour and a description of the intentions or mental states of subjects. The intentions that are relevant to social interactions can only be grasped in their full significance within the contexts and systems of practical distinctions that are constituted by practices. But practices are also not 'objective', meaningless patterns that can be described without reference to subjects. Practices are suprasubjective, objectified conjunctions of action patterns that are constituted through meaning in which subjects can relate to the objective and subjective conditions of their actions.

Practice theoretical approaches take practices to be more durable, more subject-independent and more intersubjective than individual actions or mental states. They are more strongly processual, changeable, subject-relative and reflexively structured than social structures, social orders or sign systems. They are not reducible to explicit intentions or mental states but characterized by implicit norms, and, unlike patterns of dispositions, they are characterized by the fact that they enable actions to be normatively evaluated: in a practice, there is always an internal distinction between correct and incorrect ways of acting.

Social practices, however, do not only govern forms of social behaviour that exist independently of these practices. They also make *new forms of behaviour* possible: practices – and this is a central hypothesis of all practice theories – always constitute practical options that are only comprehensible within these practices. As certain behaviours can only gain a normative status of a certain kind – that is, can only count as an action of a certain kind – within a practice, practices allocate new statuses to certain behaviours and thereby create new action options.

A social practice for a practice theory is consequently *an organized, enduring, reflexively structured pattern of actions that constitutes norms through the structure of the links between these actions, which allow for the distinction between right and wrong action and constitute new forms of social status.*

(c) Which properties must a practice with immanent norms have? What significance does this concept of a social practice have for the question of

immanent norms being pursued here? First, the concept of a social practice is necessary to complete the previously developed theory of collective attitudes. The presupposed standards that come together with collective action types and the very form of collective intentionality – that is, the presupposed normative relationships between collective attitudes and the individual actions of the participants – can only be explained through reference to practices.

As we saw, the possibility of collective attitudes presupposes that certain patterns of action – for example, in walking together – are determined by normative expectations that are characteristic of them. These expectations possess, at least in broad terms, a regular character and only exist insofar as they are actualized anew in any given token of the relevant action type by being accepted as practically guiding. That means that they either actually guide the behaviour of the participants by leading them to conform to each other's normative expectations or become effective in the form of normative reactions to violations of these expectations. If collective action forms are only sporadically carried out, it can also be the case that the mutual expectations are socially supported by a system of higher-order procedures. For example, extremely rare collective actions – say, certain exceptional legal or political actions – are determined in their normative patterns through being embedded in other, higher-order practices of legal interpretation or political discourse.

Practices must therefore have several central elements that distinguish them from mere regularities of behaviour. It has already been mentioned that the existence of practices implies that there are *rules* that determine the *correctness* and *incorrectness* of certain forms of behaviour in the context of these practices – the practice of walking together, for example, only becomes intelligible as a distinctive practice through the particular standards of correct and incorrect behaviour that it presupposes and that are applied within it. Of course, such standards are rarely explicit and are more often implicit in the sense of a shared understanding that is embodied in the unspoken but socially sanctioned normative expectations within such a practice.

Further, practices can assign a certain *status* to objects, actions or people through their rules. Practices that constitute new action types are generally termed 'institutional', even if they greatly overstep the bounds of classical institutional organizations.

A third distinctive characteristic of social practices consists in the fact that the rules that assign a new status to actions and people at the same time establish *rights and obligations* that come along with this status. Practices thereby constitute, distribute and regulate rights and power claims. Practices are therefore always at the same time an element of the organization of social power and control.

Fourth, the rules of a practice are not (or at least not always) imposed on agents 'from the outside'. Practices are always accompanied by a range of *motives, needs and goals* that count as legitimate or comprehensible within the practice, and accordingly with a corresponding set of irrelevant or inappropriate desires and goals. As can easily be seen in the examples of artistic practices or the practice of education, these appropriately understood motivational elements suggest which explanations of agents' actions in this practice are recognized as legitimate.[5]

These four elements are connected by the fact that they refer to a *normative* regulation of actions which is laid out in the action patterns of the practice. The normative expectations, obligations and claims that exist in the intuitions, customs and habits of a society have their foundations in the practical interactions of the subjects.

6.2 PRACTICES AND RULES

In determining the precise character of a practice theory, it is crucial to understand how, exactly, it cashes out the claim that social agents can orient themselves, through their actions, to *social norms or 'rules'*. For immanent critique, an especially significant question is how norms whose effectiveness is not based on the explicit, individual acceptance of agents can at the same time normatively regulate the behaviour of these agents, such that it can be justifiably claimed that they are *these agents' own norms*.

In order to answer this question, we must first clarify what it generally means to say that a norm or rule 'applies in' a social practice. This question divides individualistic, traditionally action-theoretically oriented social theories from nonindividualistic social theories. While individualistic theories explain the normative character of social reality with reference to the *intentional attitudes* of individuals, which are taken to account for the existence of shared rules as explicit or implicit agreements, nonindividualistic theories see *social relations* as constitutive of the existence of socially shared rules.[6]

The individualistic alternative initially appears to be the intuitively obvious choice: as the normative elements of reality cannot exist independently of uptake by subjects, so it appears that the normative force of all social rules has to trace back to the fact that the participants in the corresponding social practices have in some sense previously accepted them. Both the advocates of the individualistic view and their opponents agree that 'objective reality', in the sense of the domain of natural science, contains no normative facts. The norms in practices are created by humans and are dependent on their attitudes and actions. Nonetheless, unless more controversial premises are introduced, it is in no way clear that it is the features of human subjects *taken as individuals* that account for the existence of norms. Therefore, we must examine whether the idea that has been found to be central to the project of immanent critique – that norms can emerge *in social interactions* which cannot be reduced to the beliefs and desires of individuals – can be defended against the social ontological thesis of individualism. A social theory that could substantiate this idea – that is, a theory that does not attribute a merely derivative role in the constitution of normativity to social interaction relations but takes them to make a contribution that is independent of individual beliefs and intentions – is a vanishing point in the debate about social practices.

To clarify these questions, in the following I begin with the problem of 'rule-following', which will be examined in terms of its presuppositions. The question of whether one can speak of a social basis of rule-following in such a way that the normative elements of social reality are only explicable with recourse to this basis will be answered, as will the question of whether there are in fact norms that are grounded in social reality in such a way that immanent social critique can refer to them.

6.3 THE PROBLEM OF RULE-FOLLOWING

The classical reference point in debate about rules in contemporary philosophy is the discussion of rule-following in the late work of Ludwig Wittgenstein.[7] Wittgenstein's remarks on the concept of a rule are the starting point for many of those who see our capacity to follow rules as grounded in the social practices of a community. But while Wittgenstein made the idea that social practices must form the foundation for norms of all kinds popular, he had surprisingly little to contribute to a more precise definition or analysis of the concept of a social practice itself. His work rather exclusively focuses on the concepts of rules and rule-following, which is too narrow to answer this question. He is thus not an especially valuable interlocutor when investigating social ontology in a narrower sense.

Saul Kripke's influential essay *Wittgenstein on Rules and Private Language*, the publication of which led to the social foundations of rule-following becoming the centre of the debate, also initially had little impact on discussions in social philosophy. Therefore, a mere interpretation of Wittgenstein's or Kripke's arguments cannot take priority here. With that said, we must examine what broader significance they have for the question of the social foundation of normativity. This means that the presentation of these debates in what follows must be intentionally one-sided, and that all problems that are only interesting for the philosophy of language can be ignored. My discussion will rather be focused on the question of how agents create social institutions – to which social rules essentially belong – and how they can participate in them.

The most important argument for beginning with Wittgenstein consists ultimately in the affinity of his theory with a theory of implicit normativity. Wittgenstein deeply distrusts all strategies that would reduce the meaning of phenomena of human life like language, knowledge or the mind to fully explicable rules, or to the conscious mental states of individuals. Therefore, in nearly all of his late writings, we find in one form or another the claim that such phenomena are better understood if we consider them not in their transparent and explicit form, which is favoured by philosophical theory, but in terms of the implicit, only phenomenologically accessible, functions and everyday roles they play in human action.

This intuition in favour of privileging the everyday leads to a strategy that shall later become of central importance in our discussion – in order to understand the concept of a rule, Wittgenstein argues, we must focus on its *practical application*. Rather than examining abstract 'objects' of philosophical analysis, we must seek to understand what difference it makes in concrete, *practical contexts* to say that a person *follows a social rule* or to say that they *merely claim to do so*.

This focus on the pragmatic significance of ascriptions of rule-following provides a link to the theory of immanent critique. The significance of the concept of a rule for the problem of immanent critique consists in the fact that with this concept we refer to a certain aspect *of a practice of ascription and self-attribution* which we can reconstruct with it. That is, if we can determine which practical, normative conditions, behaviour patterns and relationships must exist in a community if its members are to count as being collectively oriented to a certain rule, then we know everything there is to know about the 'existence' of a rule in that community.

It has already been suggested in the discussion of collective attitudes that the practical aspects of social normativity can best be discussed when we direct our attention to the question of when we are entitled to ascribe a certain *status* to people – namely, the status of correctly following a rule or norm.[8] This idea will now be transferred to the debate on rule-following: the decisive question we must answer when we wish to determine whether a person or a group is following a rule is whether *we* are and *they themselves* are *socially justified* in attributing this status to themselves. The claim that another person or group is bound by a rule, as it is centrally at stake whenever we criticize others, is from this perspective therefore not merely one possible application of a theory that explains what social rules are. Rather, this question is the central question of a theory of rule-following. We can therefore grasp the essential properties of rule-following sufficiently precisely for our purposes if we know the conditions under which we are *justified in ascribing the status* of following a rule to a person. This does not mean that the question of what rules are and how they are constituted is meaningless, but this question is posed from a certain perspective – namely, the pragmatic perspective of an interest in what justifies intersubjective attribution.[9]

6.3.1 What Is the Problem with Rules?

What function do rules and the attribution of rule-following[10] have in our everyday practices? In the simplest form of a *prescriptive rule* ('You must always close the door behind you!'), a rule describes a standard for action that serves as a criterion for deciding whether the rule is fulfilled. Even rules that are not prescriptively aimed at specific people, that is to say 'standards' in a narrower sense, serve to allocate a normative status to actions or states in this way. According to the rule 'The door must always remain closed', a state of affairs in which the door is closed counts as correct, while an open door counts as an incorrect, 'wrong' state of affairs.[11]

The use of prescriptive rules in relation to actions, to stay with the simplest case, is at the same time closely linked to processes of normative judgement: we *justify, question or criticize* possible or actual actions with reference to corresponding rules: 'I have closed the door (action) because I must always keep this door closed (rule).' We further hold people *responsible* with reference to rules that apply to their actions or for their compliance or noncompliance with such rules.[12]

This practical use of attributions of rule-following presupposes certain abilities, which on closer inspection prove problematic. First, we assume that agents have the ability to *apply* a rule to an action. That is, they must be able to decide whether a given action conforms to a rule or not. We mostly imagine that decisions of this kind are determined by objective facts: a rule 'objectively' states that a class of actions or states are correct or incorrect. The question of whether a concrete action falls under this class is taken to be a matter of fact. Rules must therefore in some sense 'objectively' determine the correctness of actions and identify the relevant facts. To apply a rule, we must be able to recognize these facts and draw the right conclusions from them.

Secondly, attributions of rule-following also presuppose, on the side of those to whom such attributions apply, that they have the *ability to direct their behaviour* according to the rule, or *orient themselves* to it. Otherwise, it would be hard to understand how the normative status of an action (as either correct or incorrect, according to a rule) could also be legitimately 'transferred' to the agents (that is, how we could say of them that *they* act correctly or incorrectly). If we were unable to orient ourselves to rules, we could not hold each other responsible for doing (or failing to do) so.

Thirdly, the ability to orient ourselves to a rule must in principle be *fallible*: we can only practically make sense of rules in the way described if it is possible for people to both fulfil and violate rules. It would make no sense to say that someone orients themselves to a rule or is responsible for following it correctly if they were either unable to conform to it or unable to break it.[13] 'Orienting oneself to a rule' therefore cannot be a deterministic process, such that the rule ultimately – as in a law of nature – only *describes* what we do *anyway*. A rule must rather be something like an idealized description that behaviour *can* satisfy, but from which the agent can also intentionally or unintentionally *deviate*.

The fact that the claim that someone follows a rule implies that the person possesses these abilities is central to Wittgenstein's discussion of rule-following. Wittgenstein is mainly interested in rules because he is interested in our semantic abilities – that is, interested in our ability to use meaningful (linguistic or mathematical) expressions – but his remarks on rules are nonetheless of a more general nature.

What is the problem he is concerned with? According to Wittgenstein, we tend to conceive of these abilities in a way that leads us into a dilemma. The dilemma arises because, in order to understand how we use ascriptions of rule-following, we assume two aspects of rule-following that (at least under a certain interpretation) are incompatible: namely, the idea that a rule *definitively determines* which behaviour is correct in a certain situation, and the idea that following a rule is an activity that consists in the fact that we orient ourselves to a behavioural norm and that we can *justify* our behaviour through reference to this norm.

The dilemma is as follows. If a rule has an 'objective content' that is already determined before any application of it, then we must in some way have 'access' to this objective content in order to be oriented to the rule. But if we orient ourselves to a rule, then we can only (so it seems) orient ourselves to our *interpretation* of that rule. But every form of interpretation is itself an application of rules – therefore, every interpretation rests on our orientation to further interpretations. If rule-following is interpretation *all the way down*, however, then rules cannot guide people objectively, independently of their interpretations. We could therefore never orient ourselves to the *rule itself* but always only to interpretations or applications of the rule. It would therefore never be clear which rule we are oriented to, as our interpretations are necessarily fallible. As a result, our behaviour would never be guided by rules in any meaningful sense – any interpretation would ultimately be compatible with any rule. Then, however, 'the rule' could help us to orient our behaviour and consequently could never provide a justification for our actions.

Wittgenstein's remarks on this issue are – putting it mildly – opaque. Therefore, it is not useful to try to litigate between competing interpretations of Wittgenstein; instead, I will discuss the substantive problems Wittgenstein raises and examine their significance for the question of how social norms are constituted. Particularly interesting – as already mentioned – is the question of whether we can understand social norms as something that can be exhaustively explained by reference to the individual action orientations of agents or whether these norms are in need of an alternative explanation.

Saul Kripke doubtlessly presented the most provocative answer to the question of what consequences can be drawn from Wittgenstein's treatment of rule-following in his *Wittgenstein on Rules and Private Language*.[14] His argument thus seems to be an obvious starting point. Kripke's reconstruction of Wittgenstein's arguments rests on the following thought experiment:[15]

> For everyone who is capable of applying the rule of addition which is customarily referred to by the '+' symbol, there are – no matter how many additions they have performed in the past – pairs of numbers they have never added so far. Assume for the sake of simplicity that a person P has never added numbers larger than 56. Let us say that P, for the first time, correctly performs the addition '68+57' and arrives at 125 as the result. When asked why they arrive at this result, they justify their answer by referring to the rule governing additions that they follow and that they merely have applied to this case. For example, they might say: 'Proceeding as I did is just what I *mean* by "addition" and what I have always meant by that term'. In other words, they describe their action as another application of the same rule that they have followed in the past.

Justifying oneself by reference to a rule in this way is clearly a core function of such references, and for this reason it illustrates the function of ascriptions of rule-following.

Kripke now poses the question of whether a person who justifies themselves in this way can handle a certain *sceptical objection*. It could be doubted by a sceptic that P still follows the *same rule* they followed in previous applications of the '+' operator. The sceptic exploits the fact that it is unclear whether P, in their earlier additions, actually followed the *presently applied* (normal) addition rule ('plus') and not rather a different rule '$a \oplus b$' (an alternative 'plus' which Kripke calls 'quus') which is defined in the following way:

$$a \oplus b = \begin{cases} a+b & \text{if } a,b<57 \\ 5 & \text{if } a \geqslant 57 \text{ or } b \geqslant 57 \end{cases}$$

Kripke sees the following argument, which he attributes to Wittgenstein, as underpinning this sceptical objection. I will first present the argument in its entirety before discussing its individual steps:

1. If I claim to have produced certain actions in the past as a result of my following the same rule I now also follow, then I must be able to refer to facts[16] that justify this claim.
2. For every application of a rule, one can necessarily find cases that correspond to the example given above, in that there is no direct evidence in their past behaviour that shows that the rule they followed then prescribes the specific action they are performing now. There are therefore always 'new' situations in which a person applies a rule for the first time to a particular case.
3. My past behaviour is therefore not always sufficient to justify the claim that I am now following the same rule as before.
4. I could refer to the fact that in the past I followed an *explicitly defined rule* (an explicit algorithm). But even this is not evidence that I meant the *presently applied rule* with this definition. This is because I must again prove, for all terms of the definition, that I understood them in the past exactly as I do now.[17]
5. Similarly, it is insufficient for me to refer to a *disposition* to always interpret a rule in the same way and to claim that the same disposition guided me both in the earlier cases and now in its present application. A statement about a disposition (therefore a statement about what I *would have* done in the situation at issue at any given point in time) is no *justification* (says nothing about what I *should* do now according to the rule I have followed in the past).[18]
6. Reference to an immediately accessible 'special experience of meaning'[19] helps just as little.
7. Therefore, – Kripke's Wittgenstein claims – we should accept that there is *no* fact that determines that we followed any particular rule in the past.
8. The conclusion that there is no fact that shows that we followed a certain rule in the *past* immediately implies that there is also no fact that shows that we are following a certain rule *at present*.[20] This is because all the facts we could refer to regarding our present situation can also be found in the past, and vice versa.
9. A 'sceptical conclusion' follows from this: *there is no fact that determines the meaning of an expression.* But we obviously use expressions with meaning. A paradox thereby arises.
10. Kripke (or Kripke's Wittgenstein) then proposes a 'sceptical solution' to the paradox, which consists in relinquishing the notion that there are

truth conditions for what we mean with an expression (that we follow a certain rule) while defending the notion that there are *justification conditions* for these claims.

11. We can consider the statement that we mean something definite and continually the same with an expression (or that we continually follow the same rule) as justified if, in our application, we frequently – and above all in simple cases – agree with other members of our linguistic community.

Today, many view the above as both an implausible exegesis of Wittgenstein[21] and an unconvincing independent argument.[22] Without wishing to decide these questions here, it is worth first pointing to the structure of the argument: Kripke's approach consists in examining whether a range of possible 'candidates' identify a fact that can be used as evidence for past rule-following. But all proposed candidates fail the test, as it can be shown for every one of them that they are not sufficient to justify the claim that somebody has followed a specific rule (including oneself).[23] To this extent, even if the argument as a whole does not establish the conclusion adopted by Kripke, its individual components can still help us to better understand aspects of the concept of a rule, and thereby to prepare the ground for a social philosophical theory of immanent normativity. In particular, it is helpful to examine which conditions must be satisfied such that a normative commitment can be attributed to somebody in order to find out whether this can also be the case for social groups, in the way assumed by the idea of immanent critique.

6.3.2 Rules and Justification

(a) Kripke and immanent critique. Kripke explicitly emphasizes that he is not proposing an *epistemological* argument but a *constitutive* argument[24] – that is, he wants to present a sceptical argument that claims that there *are no facts* concerning a person which would be sufficient to attribute to that person the status of having followed a certain rule (and that there *cannot be* such facts). The importance of Kripke's discussion for a theory of immanent critique rests on this constitutive argument: if we want to attribute to a social community a commitment to norms that do not correspond to the explicitly accepted norms, then we must explain why we accept as justified the claim that this community has this normative commitment.

Accordingly, for immanent critique, the *ontological-constitutive* question must be distinguished from the *epistemological* question in quite the same way. Classical theories of immanent critique often engage exclusively with the epistemological question of how we can arrive at justified *beliefs* about which (immanent) norms a group has committed itself to in their practices.

With Kripke, however, it can be shown that before answering this epistemic question, the constitutive – or, in the case of collective norms, social ontological – question must first be answered: the question is whether there are any facts that make it true that a group is immanently committed to a norm. This constitutive question is, at least initially, independent of the question of whether and how these facts can be recognized by a critic.

Naturally, Kripke does not refer to the social norms that immanent critique attempts to understand but proceeds from the apparently unproblematic case of an individual's orientation to norms: Kripke's sceptic grants us optimal conditions to justify the claim that there are facts that constitute 'rule-following'. In particular, his example does not restrict the range of facts we may cite (we may also refer to mental episodes or similar phenomena with regard to which it may be epistemologically problematic to claim knowledge). Nonetheless, we will not succeed – such is the sceptic's assumption – in justifying our claim that we know what we previously meant by an expression.

If this sceptical argument succeeds, it will turn out that a theory that would like to give an answer to the individual rule-following problem will be in the situation in which critique that draws on collective norms has *always* found itself: namely, in the situation that *reasons* must be found to *justify* a specific practice's reference to norms. In the case of collective commitments, there is indeed also the intuition that a community has privileged access to the norms that regulate its own practice. Unlike in the individual case, however, the possibility of *conflicts about ascriptions* – which destroys the illusion of the pure transparency of this access – is easier to understand. With even greater justification than Kripke's sceptic, the immanent critic can therefore reject the claim that *we* (in a collective sense) *know best* which normative commitments we have made or are currently making and can claim that our self-descriptions are not incorrigible.

Unlike Kripke's sceptic, however, a theory of immanent critique should not assume that the *corrigibility* of self-ascriptions leads to their being *baseless*. The immanent critic agrees with Kripke's sceptic that there is no privileged access to one's own normative commitments but nonetheless assumes that one can rightly speak of such commitments. The immanent critic therefore at least partially accepts Kripke's premises but contests the conclusion: we can – such is the claim of every theory of immanent critique – justify the ascription of normative commitments 'from the outside'. But how?

(b) Scepticism and justification. The hypothetical situation that Kripke constructs is interesting above all in one respect: it is focused on how subjects who attribute the status of following a rule to themselves or to each other can justify these ascriptions against a sceptic. Kripke's examples draw our attention to the fact that reference to rules in our linguistic practice serves primarily to *justify* or *criticize* a certain behaviour.

Citing a rule that someone follows is a meaningful speech act when, for example, a reason is requested as to *why* a person has carried out an action in a context where naming a cause would not be sufficient.[25] If a person asks me why I stop at a red traffic light, then usually their question would be answered when I name a specific rule that prescribes it and explain that I follow this rule. It is then perhaps not yet clear whether I also have good reasons overall to act in this way. But at least my answer makes clear that my reason for action consists in the fact that an accepted rule prescribes this behaviour. The reference to a rule that I hold to be valid and to a context to which this rule applies is consequently an important type of justification. The paradigmatic context in which questions of whether someone follows a rule arise is therefore the context of social interaction, and especially the context of the justification of social actions.[26]

Therefore, the rule-following argument can be disconnected from the specific problems of the philosophy of language – with which it is usually linked in the analytic debate – and related to the broader context of all those actions that are able to be practically justified.

(c) Conflict as the pragmatic context of the ascription of rule-following. In order to take this perspective, it is first necessary to diverge from an understanding of the word 'rule' that only recognizes explicit linguistic representations of norms as rules. Rather, behaviour must also be counted as rule-following behaviour if it is at least oriented to a nonexplicit normative standard in such a way that it is in principle *capable of being justified*.

Secondly, the concept of justification has its home within a particular *pragmatic context* in which orientation to norms plays a role. Justifications usually become relevant when a person's behaviour is either *brought into question with regard to its intelligibility* or criticized with regard to *its conformity with norms*. Contexts in which justifications are relevant are therefore typically contexts of difficulties in understanding, of disintegration in social orders or of conflict.[27] A theory of social normativity must therefore be judged – among other things – on how well it is able to illuminate the actual behaviour of people in such conflict-laden situations. This way of approaching the issue goes against the idea that social norms are social entities that have an uncanny, objective and context-independent existence behind and beside people's behaviour. A pragmatist understanding of norms that avoids such errors locates norms in contexts of human interaction.

It turns out, therefore, that references to rules have a specific everyday use that should not be neglected in the analysis of rule-following. Unlike what the concept of the rule derived from philosophy of language suggests (a suggestion that is further reinforced by the widespread focus on linguistic rules), knowledge of the use of a rule as an *instrument of justification* is often not explicit knowledge that can be easily cited in discourses but rather a *practical competence to practically gain the status of justification* in normatively structured social interactions.[28]

The concept of justification is also – unlike the concept of competence, or knowledge, for example – a relational concept: one is always justified with respect to other specific people. That is, the status of justification cannot be assigned to a person or action in isolation, but only to the person in a specific relation to others. The relations in which a person is considered justified under reference to a rule thereby constitute the environment in which their actions can achieve the status of conforming to rules. Rule-following is not an independent property but a *normative status* grounded in social reality.

(d) Justification and orientation as central components of an analysis of the status of following a rule. A plausible theory of normativity that operates with the concept of a rule must satisfy two conditions: It must on the one hand be able to explain the phenomenologically immediately evident fact that we are able to *orient* our behaviour by rules. That is, it must be able to explain how normative orientations that are neither coextensive with causal determination nor fully subject to the agent's arbitrary decisions can play a role in the agency of subjects. On the other hand, such a theory must also grasp the fact not only that we encounter this orientation in the phenomenology of individual action but also that its normative significance lies in the possibility of (intersubjective and subjective) justification. It must therefore explain which resources subjects have at hand in order to be able to describe their actions as rule-following and thereby to justify them, and to offer criteria for answering the question of whether these resources are actually sufficient justifications.

Both functions – *orientation* and *justification* – are involved in Kripke's dilemma, and both share the same difficulty: it is unclear which objective facts are capable of fulfilling these functions. The reason for this lies in the apparent or actual incongruence of the two requirements: On the one hand, to provide a normative orientation, rules should fix, for *an in principle unlimited number of cases*, what the correct behaviour is – one can call this the *problem of infinity*. On the other hand, they should do so in a normative way; that is, they should not causally determine our behaviour but rather only oblige us – one can call this the *problem of normativity*. These two aspects – as I will explain in the course of this chapter – can only be harmonized with difficulty, at least for the case of individual orientation to rules.

Therefore, I will first, like Kripke, explain these two aspects and functions of rules. The difficulties that thereby emerge offer a reason to argue, in the following section, that the functions of orientation and justification must be detached from each other.

6.4 CRITERIA OF ADEQUACY FOR A THEORY OF RULE-FOLLOWING

If immanent critique wants to draw on norms in social practices, then it must justify the assumption that these norms *exist* in a specific sense. If, as Kripke's sceptic claims, rules can only guide behaviour at all if they can fulfil certain functions, however, and if it is unclear which facts would establish conditions under which a rule (in whatever sense) exists that fulfils these functions, then this justification depends on the availability of a theory that explains that there are such facts and under which circumstances they obtain. In order to explain what this means, exactly, it is worth further considering the case of Kripke's sceptic, at least briefly, in order to better understand the dilemma that it attempts to explain.

(a) Infinity. As already mentioned, two aspects of rule-following are especially interesting: what can be termed the *infinity* and *normativity* of rules. A rule, in the normal or at least in the paradigmatic case of linguistic or legal rules, determines how one must act for an *entire class* of situations. This means that a rule must be able to guide and evaluate people's behaviour in a range of cases and situations that has no a priori limit.[29] That also means, however, that orientation to a rule in a certain sense *must anticipate an unlimited number of situations of application*. This means that a fact that is constitutive of a person's following a rule must apparently be a fact of the kind that can both orient and in a sense *ground* the justification of corresponding behaviour *for all possible situations of application*.

This entails, first, that for any general rule it is always possible to present a case in which that rule has never been applied. The example used by Kripke can therefore assume that no addition has ever been carried out on the basis of which one could determine whether the person in question previously applied the 'genuine' addition rule or the deviant 'quus' rule. For the same reason, the agent's past behaviour (which necessarily forms a finite sequence) cannot determine sufficiently precisely which rule they have followed such that a particular action is singled out as a correct application of the same rule for new situations in the future.[30]

The rule that a person follows is not only underdetermined by their previous behaviour. Their orientation to a rule also cannot consist in the fact that they accept the rule in a form that represents all possible applications in advance as an exhaustively *enumerated set*. The facts that are constitutive of someone's following a rule cannot consist in a mental representation of all possible situations of application – as limited agents cannot represent an infinite number of situations in the form of a mental list.

The suggestion that an intention to follow a rule, which involves an *extensional representation* of an infinite number of situations, is constitutive of orientation to a rule would not be convincing in any case. When we follow a rule, we are not guided by an intention that explicitly addresses every kind of possible situation of application. Rather, when we follow a rule, our intention to do so 'contains' our future behaviour in the sense,[31] one might think, that we are either following *explicit rule-principles* – that is, *general formulations* of a rule that are then applied to the situations in question – or, as an alternative, we are guided by *dispositions or habits* that allow us to recognize the right action in every situation more or less automatically.

(b) The regress argument. As it turns out, however, the idea that our rule-following becomes rule-following by virtue of the fact that we *intend* to observe a rule that we represent in the form of an explicit, general rule-principle (in Robert Brandom's terms, the idea of 'regulism')[32] is not tenable either. If we must apply such a general rule to a particular situation in order to determine what we must do to obey that rule, this 'application' is again an activity that we can carry out correctly or incorrectly. Consequently, this activity itself *must be guided by a rule*. As every general rule that we mentally represent does not already contain its application and can be interpreted in various ways, we must, in order to apply it *correctly*, introduce a further rule that determines how the original rule is applied correctly.

Wittgenstein refers to this problem in a classic passage:

> It can be seen that there is misunderstanding here from the mere fact that in the course of our argument we give one interpretation after another; as if each one contended us at least for a moment, until we thought of yet another standing behind it. What this shews is that there is a way of grasping a rule which is *not an interpretation*, but which is exhibited in what we call 'obeying the rule' and 'going against it' in actual cases.[33]

If we assume that there are no other forms of rule-following than those in which an abstract general rule is applied, then we must present every application of a rule (in the sense of the orientation to a rule) as an infinite series of rule applications, as every rule requires another rule of application. It is generally accepted that such a regress would be fatal.[34]

This problem is also central to the *justification function* of rules that Kripke has in mind. Even if a person cites their *intention* to follow a particular general rule principle as evidence for the claim that they have thus far followed a specific rule, the sceptic can always argue that it is unclear why any given application of this explicit principle should count as an application of the *same* rule, as long as we cannot additionally show that we applied the *same rule of application or rule of interpretation* in each case.[35] Rule-following therefore cannot always be understood as interpretation of an explicit rule. However, this establishes a claim that is decisive for the project of immanent critique: practices can only be normative practices at all if there are *nonexplicit forms of rule-following*, and thereby also nonexplicit modes of the existence of rules – and, this means, if there are rules to which immanent critique can refer.

(c) Normativity. If the fact that a person follows a rule cannot be explained merely through reference to their intentional observance of an explicit rule principle, then there must be a way rules can be followed without interpretation.

But how can a person follow a rule without interpreting it? Several answers to this question have been proposed in the literature, which differ above all with regard to the extent to which they conceive of orientation to a rule as a mental phenomenon. The strongest 'mentalistic' alternative, which is explicitly discussed by Kripke, is the idea that *grasping* a rule is 'an irreducible experience, with its own special *quale*, known directly to each of us by introspection'.[36] This proposal involves a specific formulation of a more general position, which can be termed 'rule Platonism'[37] and which consists in understanding rules as abstract objects that can be *accessed by us without interpretation* in one way or another. The proposal that rules can be accessed by us through sui generis mental experiences is unconvincing, due solely to the fact that it is not clear what solution it can offer for the rule-following problem – besides its implication that there is no such problem.[38]

A more precise analysis of all the arguments Wittgenstein himself brings to bear against this position shows, however, that the failure of this solution points to a further adequacy condition for theories of rule-following: rule-following must be understood as an essentially *fallible* activity. Because a rule *prescribes* how behaviour *should* be and does not merely *describe* how behaviour *is*, any attempt to follow a rule must always exhibit the possibility of failing and *breaking* the rule. The breaking of a rule must thereby be understood as a deficient form of rule-following – breaking a rule involves more than simply failing to observe it. This insight into the normativity of rules, which always leaves open the possibility of failure, is suitable to refute not only Platonist but also – as will be shown below – dispositional theories.

As far as Platonist theories are concerned, according to Wittgenstein's famous 'private language argument', the crucial way in which normativity comes into play is by the fact that there must be a distinction between *believing that one is following a rule* and *actually following it*. If believing that one is correctly following a rule were the same as actually correctly following it, then someone who believed they were correctly following a rule could not fail to do so, as this person could in no way be wrong about the truth of their belief.[39] The belief would thereby be infallible. Rule Platonism therefore fails because it potentially allows any attempt to follow a rule to count as successful. What the rule prescribes thus becomes identical to the totality of its actual applications, and the rule can no longer be applied as a standard for the distinction between correct and false applications.

If we apply to the theory of rule-following the criterion that such a theory must understand orientation to a rule as a fallible, normatively guided activity that is not guaranteed to be successful, then it turns out that there are other theories, besides Platonism, that cannot fulfil this criterion: those attempts to solve the rule-following problem which make do without beliefs or mental events and seek instead to explain the fact that people can follow rules with reference to *dispositions*, to *acquired abilities* or to *acquired normative viewpoints*, fail at precisely this point: if the question of whether a person follows a rule is decided by the fact that we refer to their dispositions, it is likewise unclear in what sense this disposition represents something that could be 'violated' or 'failed'.[40]

This is ultimately an expanded version of a general argument against the identification of rule-following behaviour with merely *regular* behaviour: for Kripke, a description of a person's previous, rule-conforming behaviour – that is, any descriptively graspable *regularity* – is not sufficient to make sense of their *orientation* to a rule. This is not only due to the fact that we can describe any finite sequence of behaviours as instantiations of infinitely many, sufficiently complex rules. An identification of the rule with a regularity that only *describes* a sequence of behaviours cannot explain what it means to *violate* that rule. The fact that an agent's behaviour is consistent with a descriptive regularity does nothing to explain how they can be oriented to rules and simultaneously be fallible in their conformity to them, as conformity to a regularity is precisely defined in terms of an absence of deviation. We cannot determine the rule by which behaviour is guided through reference to the regularities that that behaviour fulfils – as then it would not be possible to break the rule.

This objection concerns not only the analysis of rule orientation as rule conformity (in Brandom's words, the strategy of 'regularism')[41] but also, as already mentioned, those theories that refer to dispositions and abilities.

A dispositional theory is a theory that assumes that a person P follows a rule if and only if they possess a *disposition* to behave in conformity with that rule. A disposition to do X – ignoring the obscurities bound up with this notion[42] – can initially be defined such that P always does X if certain descriptively specifiable conditions C obtain. The identification of rule-following with a disposition initially appears to have the advantage that P can indeed 'break' the rule – namely, if they do not conform to the rule because the conditions C do not obtain. A dispositional theory can additionally explain the sense in which all future applications are already 'contained' in the rule, without needing to introduce metaphysical strangeness. Such an analysis is also attractive because it avoids an overly intellectualistic picture of rule-following and promises to be able to link individual and social rule-following via the formation of corresponding dispositions through socialization.

Kripke attempts to show that a dispositional theory ultimately can fulfil neither the infinity criterion nor the normativity criterion.[43] However, one need only prove a second, less contested claim in order to reject dispositional theories:[44] If the fact that a person follows a rule could be explained by the fact that this person always carries out a certain behaviour sequence under certain conditions, then the claim that they follow a rule would be a purely descriptive statement. This means, however, that this theory cannot explain a violation of a rule as a violation: the fact that I *would have* acted in such and such a way under hypothetical conditions does not show that my *actual* behaviour under the *empirically given* conditions violates any rule that I *'follow' in those empirically given conditions*. Or in other words: which rule I follow is determined not by some set of facts that fix how I *would act* under *ideal* conditions but by something that fixes how I *should* act under *all* conditions. A description of any set of facts that determine my hypothetical actions under ideal conditions, however, does not identify any such normative 'should'.[45]

(d) Implicit rules? The criteria of infinity and normativity allow Kripke (or Kripke's Wittgenstein) to reject all proposals concerning facts that are taken to be constitutive of a person's following a rule. However, the dilemma that emerges from the *finiteness of explicit rules* and the *lack of normativity of direct mental access, dispositions and merely regular behaviour* is only a real dilemma if one assumes that these are the only candidates.

Wittgenstein obviously assumes that there is an alternative, which he terms 'practices', 'institutions' or 'customs'.[46] His remarks, however, hardly go beyond suggestions,[47] and it is often unclear whether he wants to clarify the *preconditions* for the kind of justification that is typical of contexts in which ascriptions of rule-following are thematic or whether he would like to offer us an *explanation* of what such a justification could refer to. For this reason, it is necessary to go beyond Wittgenstein's theory and to investigate which reasons could speak in favour of assuming something like *'implicit rules' in social practices*, to which we can refer if we want to clarify what it means to follow a rule, and to which methods of immanent critique could also refer.

About such proposals, Karin Glüer rightly remarks:

> One of the problems of any such strategy consists without doubt in the difficulty of making sufficiently clear what implicit rule-following is in the first place.

The difficulty consists less in drawing a line between explicit and implicit rule-following, but rather in showing that the behaviour in question is an instance of rule-following at all, that is, in distinguishing it from merely regular behaviour.[48]

Therefore, the proposal that 'implicit rule-following' could be a solution for Kripke's dilemma cannot be judged abstractly. Rather, a concrete version of this proposal must be examined and analysed. It is also at this point that the chances of success for a model of immanent critique that assumes other normative resources beyond the explicit self-ascriptions of rules will ultimately be determined. In what follows, the focus of the investigation will be above all on those attempts that seek to answer this question by reference to social models of the existence of implicit rules. The justified objections against individualistic solutions, which arise from the two criteria of infinity and normativity, will in turn be applied in judging these social solutions.

6.5 SOCIAL SOLUTIONS TO THE RULE-FOLLOWING PROBLEM

The rule-following problem is relevant to the theory of immanent critique as it can only be solved if we assume that there is an immanent form of normativity. The assumption that there must be *implicit orientations* to rules arises from the failure of models of explicit rule-following in connection with the criteria of normativity and infinity.

The thought suggests itself that these approaches fail because the justification of an action with regard to a rule is always a *justification to others*, which cannot be explained by a theory that only draws on the individual. Therefore – so we might suspect — an analysis of this kind of justification must always deal with the relations of individuals to a community. This is the fundamental idea of social solutions to the problem of rule-following.

In order to understand the surplus value that the discussion of social solutions has for the theory of immanent critique, it is helpful once again to bring to mind the status that the problem of rule-following has for the question of this book – that is, for the question of whether there are social forms of normativity that could represent a sufficient basis for the method of immanent critique.

While the classical rule-following problem asks about the status of rules *in general* and problematizes it, the question of the general conditions of immanent social normativity is more modest: in order to make the concept of social normativity fruitful in the way proposed here, it is only necessary to assume that there are *some* norms that are socially institutionalized. In addition, there is the hope that a social ontological model can be found to account for how this social institutionalization can provide critical theory with previously undeveloped resources for critique.

In this sense, the previous discussion of the rule-following problem was necessarily one-sided, as it was motivated only by the interest in finding criteria of adequacy for the social forms of institutionalization discussed below: the paradoxes in which intuitive assumptions about rule-following are tangled are only relevant for a theory of immanent critique insofar as they point out that social institutionalization of a certain type is a necessary precondition of these assumptions.

I will therefore forego undertaking an exhaustive evaluation of individualistic attempts to solve the rule-following problem. Rather, what has been said should point to a fundamental property of all rules that even a social approach – be it comprehensive or not – must fulfil in order to count as a genuine solution to this problem.

Accordingly, I will now leave the terrain of a general discussion of the rule-following problem. In the following, only those theories that are relevant to the question pursued here – namely, the question of the normative content of social practices relevant to critical theory – should be discussed: that is, only theories of the social institutionalization of implicit or immanent normativity.

It will initially be shown (by means of examining an argument by David Bloor) that the aspects of orientation and justification are not reducible to features of a single social fact but that social interaction plays a different role in each respect (6.5.1). This argument forms the background for an examination of two social models of rule-following. First, I will discuss John Haugeland's conformism (6.5.2). I will attempt to show that his model must fail on the normative criterion since it cannot show how the conditions of the justification of the actual behaviour of group members can form a meaningful standard (6.5.3). The second model is the social model of Robert Brandom, which avoids these problems but still remains unclear at important points (6.5.4).

6.5.1 Social Practices as a Solution

Kripke's account of the rule-following problem conflates various questions: first, Kripke is committed to a certain picture of what facts could, in principle, be used to justify rule-following to a sceptic. His starting point is – as David Bloor rightly remarks[49] – individualistic: Kripke's sceptical argument only shows that no fact about an individual and their behaviour – considered in isolation – can justify saying that this individual follows a rule. Second, Kripke appears to assume – together with many participants in the rule-following debate – that the explanation of how we *orient* ourselves to a rule and the analysis of the way the reference to rules can serve to *justify* refer to the *same class of facts*. That is, Kripke assumes that there must be *one kind of fact* that simultaneously determines what we *orient* ourselves by in the application of a rule in a new case *and* normatively determines which action-option we *should* choose in any given case.

As has been shown, however, the idea that subjective orientation to rules requires direct access to the rule as a normative 'object' is highly deceptive – as with all other approaches that assume that rule-following behaviour must in some way be brought about directly by the subject's grasp of 'the rule itself'. Such approaches assume that the idea that 'the rule' determines its application, which appears plausible to us in a *normative* respect, can be transferred to the *explanation* of action orientation without loss.

There must rather be a distinction between two aspects: the normative standard that a rule provides is decisive for the question of justification – that is, for whether a person should and can be granted the *status* of someone who counts as following a certain rule. The distinct question of how we become capable of *subjectively orienting* ourselves to this status cannot, however, be answered by the fact that we 'directly' grasp such a norm. Rule-following should therefore be better understood as a phenomenon with two components. The component of *normative justification* concerns the possible justifications that a person can cite for their behaviour under a certain rule and the normative status of being justified in one's actions by some rule. This normative status cannot in principle be explained by reference to nonnormative statements about facts concerning individuals. By contrast, the question of how to explain the second component – that is, the component of *practical orientation* as the exercise of an ability to follow a rule in an underdetermined situation – as part of the everyday behaviour of subjects is not – as the regress argument has shown – to be answered *directly* in terms of a grasp of normative standards. An explanation of the ability to orient oneself by rules cannot refrain from considering the explanatory power of dispositions, mental states and similar components.[50]

This argument is based on David Bloor's idea of understanding rule-following as a 'dual' social phenomenon: 'The duality involves, on the one hand, the presence of a certain tendency to act, which will be found, in one form or another, within each individual. On the other hand, alongside this aggregate of dispositions, there will be a shared currency of verbal responses for their evaluation. Both sides of this story capture indispensable features of rule-following.'[51] If rule-following – and thereby rule-following practices – is understood to have this dual structure, this allows for a *decoupling* of the question of how to account for the normativity of standards from the question of how to explain people's ability to orient themselves to rules. As will be shown, such a decoupling is indispensable for a solution to the paradoxes of the rule-following problem.

The element of justification is explicable from such a perspective by the fact that agents are integrated into a common practice in which the social authority to ascribe the normative status of rule-following is distributed according to certain standards. The orientation function, however, can only be understood if we assume that the members of such a practice are endowed with certain abilities and dispositions that are sufficiently sensitive to the norms of this practice but that nonetheless determine neither these norms nor the status of rule-following.[52]

Put differently: to be *justified* in performing an action because one thereby follows a rule is a social status that can only be assigned within the normative practices of a community. The *orientation* of an action to a rule, which is a necessary precondition for an action's being a candidate for this social status, can only be explained by the fact that the agent possesses abilities and dispositions that reflect some familiarity with the criteria for following the rule. Individuals *acquire* these abilities or dispositions through being socialized and through participating in practices that determine the corresponding status – but these abilities and dispositions are not directly constitutive of the normative status.

This also explains certain aspects of the fallible character of rule-following: the ability to orient oneself according to a socially institutionalized rule (acquired through socialization) is never infallible. As a result, even if an individual is successfully socialized in a community and possesses a sufficient capacity to orient themselves towards rules whose content is ultimately determined by the practices of that community, this does not guarantee that their actions are in fact ascribed the status they implicitly aim at – it is always possible that their individual dispositions will misfire and do not conform to what the community takes to be the rule. That we are still justified in saying that it is the 'same' rule that both *orients* and (potentially) *justifies* their actions, however, reflects the fact that successful learning processes form the dispositions of individuals in such a way that their normative orientations are coupled in reliable ways with their community's practices through which the status of 'conforming to the rule' is distributed. It does not entail, however, that this normative status is constituted by or can be reduced to individual dispositions.

If orientation and normative justification are disentangled, it becomes obvious that the second aspect should also be understood as socially constituted in terms of its *content*. The normative justification of claims to the effect that one follows a rule can only be understood in the context of social interactions: a person follows a rule (in a normative sense) if and only if their behaviour proves acceptable to others in their mutual interactions.

This promises an elegant way to sidestep the seeming contradiction between the normativity criterion and the criterion of interpretation independence established by the regress problem. If the reactions and actions of other people provide the criterion for the correctness of a person's behaviour, one can always fail to conform to a rule – behaving so as to win the approval of others is, after all, an extremely fallible orientation. The approval of others therefore seems to constitute a genuinely normative standard. At the same time, the question of whether others approve or reject behaviour as being in line with a shared rule is also in sufficient measure a matter of facts that do not require further interpretation.

Finally, if justification is seen as a matter of social interactions, this not only explains the normativity aspect of rule-following but also covers the infinity aspect: if rule-following is described as a social status, there is no reason to think that the interactions of a community could not have a structure that determines an allocation of statuses to a series of cases that is not limited in advance.

The fundamental thesis of a social solution is thus as follows. All norms that justify social practices are ultimately grounded in the mutual interaction and orientation of individuals to each other or to each other's behaviour: they are contained in the *social practices* of a community – that is, in shared patterns of action. This means not only that social rules are always actually *shared* rules but also that the fact *that* they are shared has ontological significance: 'The very ontology of rules is social and grounded in patterns of interaction.'[53]

6.5.2 Conformism

In order to better understand this idea, it must be explained *which* interaction structures can be sufficient for a person in a community to possess the status of being someone who follows a rule. In order to clarify this question, we should now look at one of the most interesting formulations that the social theory of rule-following has received, under the name of 'conformism'. This formulation is, as it were, only secondhand: John Haugeland deserves the credit for describing it in its ideal form,[54] which he derives from the work of Martin Heidegger, Wilfrid Sellars and Robert Brandom.[55]

Haugeland explains the model of 'conformism' – which he himself does not necessarily hold to be a solution to the rule-following problem – by means of an imaginary community of individuals about whom he only makes two minimal assumptions: they are led in their actions first by a tendency towards the imitation of others' behaviour and secondly by a tendency to censure deviant behaviour.

> Imagine a community of versatile and interactive creatures, not otherwise specified except that they are conformists. Conformism here means not just

imitativeness (monkey see, monkey do), but also censoriousness – that is, a positive tendency to see that one's neighbors do likewise, and to suppress variation. This is to be thought of as a complicated second-order disposition, which the creatures have by nature ('wired in').[56]

These two tendencies can remain relatively unspecified regarding their realization in concrete traits of agents. To explain these tendencies, neither intentional states such as preferences nor other cognitive states, and consequently no linguistic abilities, are necessary. The individuals only need the ability to react differentially to the environment and the ability to adapt their own behaviour in response to the reactions of others.[57]

The conformist disposition is designed to guarantee not only that the community members will orient *themselves* to the behaviour of others but also that they will be inclined to *evaluate* others' behaviour with sanctions, according to the degree of accordance of that behaviour with their own. The sanctioning disposition is assumed to operate not only on the first level but on all levels: they are disposed to punish not only those who act differently from them, but also those who punish differently from them.[58]

The result of such a conformist dispositional structure's being continually effective in a community is – according to Haugeland – that from every initial position a 'gravitational centre' of common behaviour will necessarily be formed, towards which individuals condition each other through systematic group pressure. The disposition to sanction and the tendency to respond to such sanctions leads to clusters of similar behaviour. Which behaviour ultimately emerges as 'normal' in a certain situation is a matter of accident and depends on both the natural endowment of individuals with other complementary dispositions and the environmental conditions of the situations and problems these individuals encounter.

These 'gravitational centres' do not represent a merely descriptive regularity in behaviour, however. Rather, such a clustering – as soon as one exists – is at the same time *itself* a standard that the conformist disposition takes up and is guided by whenever the question of sanctioning arises.[59] Therefore, this analysis fulfils one of the conditions set out above: it explains – without relying on normative concepts – how individuals can be practically oriented to a rule. Their capacity to select actions as 'conforming to the rule' emerges directly from the previous behaviour of all community members, in combination with their second-order dispositions.

The idea of a sanction makes possible a pragmatist analysis of those attitudes of community members that are constitutive of *norms*: normativity is actively institutionalized by the individual members who practically classify the actions of other members through their reactions.[60] The criteria for the application of the concepts 'correct' and 'incorrect', with which actions can be described on this model, depend only on the factual practices that determine how behaviour is to be evaluated.[61] For this reason, this theory also appears to ground real normativity with respect to the justification aspect: 'The community-wide classes of similar dispositions that coalesce under the force of conformism can be called "norms" – and not just collections or kinds – because they themselves set the standard for that very censoriousness by which they are generated and maintained.'[62] A peculiarity of the second-order dispositions Haugeland describes is that they are not related to specific rules that apply in a community – that is, a disposition to follow the rule x or y – but are dispositions about how behaviour is normatively handled *in general*. This is what Haugeland means by 'second-order dispositions'. His conformist analysis therefore appears to be able to also avoid the problems of a dispositional theory.

Such a social pragmatist theory already comes very close to the goal of this investigation, namely, to provide an analysis of norms that are implicit in practices: according to such a theory, it can indeed be the case that members of a community not only individually systematically violate the collective dispositions of the community because of unfavourable environmental conditions but also systematically misunderstand them.

Nonetheless, this conformist solution is not satisfactory. It turns out that it (a) insufficiently grasps the normative dimension of rule-following and has an individualistic prejudice, (b) entails an unacceptable conformist consequence and (c) cannot sufficiently recognize the reflexive character of social normativity.

(a) The normativity problem and conformism's individualistic prejudice. The most important critique of this theory – Robert Brandom's – raises the question of whether this model can avoid the normativity problem of dispositional analyses. Even the conformist model – Brandom argues – is still committed to a reductionist approach, similar to the individualist dispositional theories discussed previously. Even if not on the primary level, the explanation of norms through dispositions leads, at the level of second-order attitudes, to the normative content's being again reduced to merely descriptively graspable regularities in action, namely, to the dispositions to sanction.[63]

As Brandom argues:

> This is a way of failing to take sufficiently seriously Kant's distinction between acting according to a rule and according to a conception of a rule. Sanctions theories fund this crucial distinction by means of the distinction between producing a performance and assessing it. But assessing, sanctioning, is itself something that can be done correctly or incorrectly. If the normative status of being incorrect is to be understood in terms of the normative attitude of treating as incorrect by punishing, it seems that the identification required is not with

the status of actually being punished but with that of deserving punishment, that is, being correctly punished. Of course sanctioners can be sanctioned in turn for their sanctioning, which is thereby treated as itself correctly or incorrectly done. Nonetheless, if actual reinforcement of dispositional regularities is all that is available to appeal to in making sense of this regress, it might still be claimed that what is instituted by this hierarchy of regularities of responses to regularities of responses ought not to count as genuinely normative.[64]

At first glance, one might think that one can easily respond to this objection[65] by acknowledging that the conformist disposition that Haugeland describes is not a second-order disposition in a substantive sense, that is, a disposition to sanction certain specific actions (or sanctions). It must rather be understood as a formal disposition that operates at *each* of the normative levels of evaluation: the conformist disposition determines on no specific level (neither actions, dispositions to sanction, dispositions regarding the sanctioning of sanctions and so on) in advance how behaviour must be evaluated. Rather, at each of these levels it only determines that the evaluations of others themselves are measured against the agent's own dispositions ('You should judge like me!') – and similarly for the case of evaluations of evaluations, and so on.[66] Consequently, what the norm is never coincides with any concrete disposition. The disposition that Haugeland refers to is rather *a disposition to form dispositions at the relevant level*.

Nonetheless, the conformist theory described by Haugeland has a problem with the normative dimension of rule-following: the conformist practice relies on the actual dispositional capacities of empirical individuals. But can an empirical disposition to form certain dispositions constitute an ability to orient oneself to a norm – that is, to form the *correct* dispositions? In other words, is the sense in which these dispositions establish a 'norm' strong enough to make sense of the fallible character of rule-following?

This question can be better understood if one considers that the reactions that Haugeland refers to are still the *reactions of individuals*: something like collectively shared norms arises only through the conformist tendency towards synchronized dispositions – which are shaped by mutual sanctions. Rather than being rooted in a shared understanding of what ought to be done, however, these collectively shared norms are the result of mutual *behavioural conditioning*.

The problematic character of this individualist model can easily be seen if one looks at those situations in which the corresponding dispositions come into conflict: if an individual A perceives a deviant behaviour of another individual B, then A can *either* correctively sanction B *or* adapt their own disposition. Put differently: when dispositions diverge, an individual can always choose between practically classifying either their own disposition as incorrect or that of the other individual. But it is unclear which resources are available to make the correct decision in a case like this. One could first assume that A always sanctions deviant behaviour. If A and B have exactly congruent dispositions, this would mean that B, in turn, must also sanction A for having a deviant disposition to sanction – and so on. Naturally, this chain would break eventually in any empirical instance, but the theory described by Haugeland cannot show that 'the conformist disposition' itself plays any *orienting* role by selecting any particular scenario in which this plays out as the correct one.

A further problem arises from the lack of normativity of dispositions: we can retrospectively classify the actual cluster of behaviour in a community that arises in this way as conformist because we can describe a certain regularity in the behavioural sequences from the observer's perspective. But this assumption does not help us to understand how the behaviour of any agent is actually guided by that regularity. A's corrective sanctioning of B's behaviour is only the application of a specific rule if A's (sanctioning) disposition is the *correct* continuation of this rule (or the correct application of the conformist tendency). That is, the metadisposition must – if we want to understand the conformist community as being 'led' by the conformist disposition in their respective behaviour orientations – be understood as a disposition to choose conformist behaviour *in the correct sense*. But what 'correct' means here is no longer graspable in the vocabulary of a nonnormative concept of a disposition.

From these objections we can draw the conclusion that a disposition towards agreement between individuals cannot establish a rule that has normative content with reference to which the possibility of genuinely normative sanctions (which refer to a prior failure to satisfy some standard) becomes intelligible.[67]

(b) The conformist prejudice. A second problem concerns the possibility of normative change and normative fallibility. The particular way norms are 'immanent' in the actual reactions and dispositions of members according to Haugeland's theory leads to the problem that no distinction between norms and collective behaviour can be drawn and that his model cannot make sense of the fallibility of rule-following. This is true even if one introduces the conformist disposition only as a regulative element. Such a theory cannot – as Haugeland in a later paper explicitly points out[68] – explain how an objection against a unanimous evaluation by all other members could be justified and is thereby committed to the unacceptable conformist thesis that *any* interpretation of a norm that the community *as a whole endorses* – whether we understand 'community' in a summative way like Haugeland or, as yet to be clarified, as the subject of an independent commitment – must be accepted and determines the content of the norm.

But this violates the normativity criterion. *Any* social practice of interpreting a rule that a community actually exhibits would then be a *correct* practice. The behaviour of the community as a whole could no longer be critically assessed with a view to the norms that apply in that practice.

(c) The reflexive character of rule-following. Finally, there is a third problem: we cannot conceive of social norms such that their meaning is exhausted by interactions between individuals. Social norms are not merely a sum of all expectations people have regarding each other's individual actions but go beyond that. As H. L. A. Hart remarks, enduring social norms differ from mere orientations of individuals towards the possible sanctions of others (for example, in the example of a bank robbery, the cashier's orientation to the bank robber's threat).[69] The interactions in which social norms are expressed are not merely based on individual demands to *now* act according to *my* will but *refer internally to a shared social norm* and require people's evaluations of one another to be *oriented* to such a norm.

This means that we can only fully understand the role of individual normative sanctions or reactions if we assume not that they are prior to the norm but that they always *refer* to an *already existing* norm. Because the actions and reactions that account for the social existence of the norm must always be understood as internally oriented to a norm, norm following is necessarily *reflexive*. Haugeland assumes in his conformist model that we can only speak of norms if there are 'gravitational centres' – that is, if individual reactions are causally directed by the average behaviour patterns. But this 'guidance' is diagnosed from the observer's perspective and does not play a role from the perspective of participants.

6.5.3 A Collectivistic Normativity Problem

The most important of these arguments against such a strong collectivistic theory is the objection that it cannot sufficiently distinguish between the *actual* interpretations of a norm by a community and the interpretation that is *required* by the content of that norm. This is the mistake I described in the last section as a 'conformist prejudice' and that Paul Boghossian calls 'communitarianism':

> Communitarianism is a response to the perceived inability to define a distinction, at the level of the individual, between correct and incorrect dispositions. The suggestion that correctness consists in agreement with the dispositions of one's community is designed to meet this need. The proposal will not serve its purpose, however, if the problem at the level of the individual is now merely to be replayed at the level of the community. A communitarian does not want

it to be a further question whether a given actual communal disposition is itself correct.[70]

From a conformist position, it seems to follow that whatever the relevant community evaluates *as correct is correct*. But this would – as in the case of individual interpretations – no longer make the correctness of the rule-following of the community as a whole a fallible achievement; instead, it would remove the distinction between what is correct and what only appears correct to the community.

John McDowell argues that Wittgenstein already rejected this idea:

> Taken as a whole, however, I think this reading gets Wittgenstein completely wrong. I can perhaps begin to explain my disbelief with this remark: it would have been fully in character for Wittgenstein to have written as follows: 'Could the justification of an action as fulfilment of an order run like this: You said "Bring me a yellow flower", upon which this one received approval from all the bystanders; this is why I have brought it? Wouldn't one have to reply "But I didn't set you to bring the flower which should receive approval from everyone else after what I said!"?'[71]

This renews the original normativity problem to which reductionist theories are exposed at the individual level. Even if it were granted that the normative aspect of rule-following could be 'outsourced' to a community, wouldn't the same objections apply that were previously raised against the theories that seek to explain rule-following by reference to the dispositions of individuals? Put differently: if the individual refers to the actual behaviour of the community in their justifications, to whom can this community in turn refer when their collective self-interpretation is brought into question? I will call this the *collectivistic normativity problem*.[72]

Any reference to the consensus of a community is – as in the cases of regularism and the dispositional theories – only a description of the community's actual behaviour, not a normative standard that also applies to that community. A genuinely normative rule, however, determines not only how an *individual* should act but also how their action should be *collectively evaluated*. This 'should' expresses a demand that the *actual evaluations* of the community have to meet. At least in principle, they must be able to violate the rule. Therefore, the idea that orientation to a rule can be identified with orientation to the consensus of a community is unsustainable.[73]

6.5.4 Brandom and Normative Phenomenalism

Orientation to a rule must be understood such that it is always in principle possible to distinguish between what an agent actually does and what the rule requires them to do. The 'conformism' described by Haugeland – like all those answers that would explain normativity by taking the behaviour or attitudes of the other members of a community to provide a normative standard – fails to address this problem. It cannot show how the aspect of normative justification that goes beyond individual or collective action can be rationally understood. Accordingly, in what follows I will discuss a second social model based on the work of Robert Brandom. To examine his strategy of 'normative phenomenalism', I will again (a) take up the argument from section 6.3.2, which shows that the ascription of the status of following a rule has a primarily *normative function*, namely, to justify and evaluate the behaviour of individuals. I will then (b) outline the basic features of his theory. On the basis of these arguments, I will sketch a model in the next chapter that can fulfil the conditions outlined above: a *recognition model* of social practices.

(a) Scepticism and normative phenomenalism. In order to be able to take the first step towards a convincing model of social practices, we must again look at the function that the ascription of the status of rule-following has in practical contexts: that of intersubjective justification.

The already mentioned social solutions to the rule-following problem cannot be convincing as they cannot make the status of this problem sufficiently clear. They all more or less agree with Kripke's idea that the ascription of rule-following has no truth conditions with regard to nonsocial facts 'in the world'. They therefore attempt to explain the conditions for justifiably ascribing the status of rule-following by reference to the *fact of intersubjective agreement* (which is ultimately also insufficient for explaining the normative character of a rule). Even if through this strategy they fail to properly account for the normative aspect of rule-following, the social models represent progress. Through reference to intersubjective agreement, they already bring into view an aspect of the *pragmatic function* of ascriptions of rule-following. One could say that what counts as a reference to a rule in social practices is always a constellation of behavioural patterns that can be *recognized* as such a practically successful reference. The criterion of agreement therefore displaces the focus from the 'objective properties' of the agents or individual actions to their *status* in relation to a community. But can a social solution that understands this status as constituted by the relation of an individual to a community solve the original problem of rule-following?

Wittgenstein connects the question of the facts that determine when someone follows a rule and the justificatory question of when one is entitled to say that one is following a rule in a strange way: time and again, it is about *self-ascription* and therefore about why, whether and how *we ourselves* can know or justifiably claim that we know how we should extend a rule. We can, Wittgenstein claims, only know that we are following a rule if the rule that we follow somehow goes 'beyond' our actual activity and if it allows us to 'in some way' anticipate future cases with which we are not already familiar. At the same time – such is the dilemma – there appears to be *nothing* that can 'guide' us in this mysterious way.

In Wittgenstein's spirit, it is therefore meaningful to ask *in which practical contexts* such a reference from a first-person perspective becomes practically relevant. The status of rule-following only plays a role in our life if a subject's assumption that they are following a rule is *brought into question* by others. Only then must they refer to 'something' that justifies this self-ascription. Unlike Kripke, Wittgenstein accepts the notion that such a self-ascription indeed has an 'objective' standard and that we therefore usually know what it means to follow a rule. For that reason, he criticizes the attitude to the problem of the extension of a rule that consists in wondering how, 'in a *queer* way, the use itself is in some sense present' in the action.[74] But he only criticizes the suggestion that there is something 'queer' about that presence of the rule – that is, something that can only be explained by a *special* ability or activity with which we grasp the extension. Rather, Wittgenstein argues, the extensions of rules are present in practices in a nonmysterious way.

With this critique of the notion that rule-following relies on unusual or mysterious abilities, Wittgenstein has a special version of the anticipation thesis in view. He rejects the idea that we have the rule as something like a formula 'before us', which we must newly interpret with every application. As the regress argument shows, not all rules can be understood in this way. There must be rules that do not require interpretation. Therefore, in Wittgenstein's deliberations, the question of how we can act according to a rule in its *practical execution without needing to interpret an abstract object* takes up a great deal of room.

Here, it is worth returning to Wittgenstein's claim that there is a way to grasp a rule that is *not an interpretation* but that is exhibited in what we call 'obeying the rule' and 'going against it' in actual cases.[75] But what does that mean? Wittgenstein's idea appears to be that we possess implicit standards *in our practical habits* that we no longer need to interpret. Reality appears to us – one could say – in a certain light, which allows a certain extension of our behaviour to appear natural.[76] By this Wittgenstein means an ability to see a situation in the light of its specific aspects. This ability to be aware of aspects should ultimately be the reason for the self-ascription of the status of rule-following. That we can refer to our possession of this ability *as an argument* in the aforementioned situations of intersubjective justification assumes, according to Wittgenstein, the contingent fact that the members of our communities in most cases simply *share with us* a way of accessing the world, a 'background' or an ability to see the same aspects in an unproblematic way.

This strategy of reference to an unproblematic 'background' neglects, however, the defining features of the social situations in which the vocabulary of ascriptions of rule-following is used. In order to see this, one must take into view the concrete processes of justification that are linked in concrete social practices with the statement that someone is following a rule: these are *situations of conflict or critique*, that is, situations in which neither unproblematic intersubjective unity in evaluation nor consensus concerning what justifies a certain statement can be presupposed.

This aspect will be obscured if one accepts Wittgenstein's picture of the normative 'bedrock' on which 'the spade is turned',[77] where no further reasons can be found but where *either* there is a shared perception of the normative significance of a situation *or* one's judgement cannot be further explained. The quietism suggested by this picture cannot sufficiently take into account the actual social relevance of scepticism – that is, the fact that others will regularly question whether we are indeed following one rule or another. Wittgenstein's reference to the everydayness and unproblematic character of ascriptions of rule orientation in our linguistic practice[78] strangely glosses over the problem of justification in situations of intersubjective doubt. Justification is always only necessary when the assumption that someone is following a rule, or this status, is problematized. However, it is exactly then that reference to an apparently unproblematic practice is no longer possible.[79]

(b) Brandom's social alternative to conformism. On the one hand, the question of which 'facts' are relevant to justification cannot be brushed aside as Wittgenstein does; on the other, however, we can only fully understand them if we understand the 'world' to which these facts belong not as static but rather as intersubjectively constituted in the context of normative facts negotiated in discourse.[80]

In *Making It Explicit*, Robert Brandom takes up and develops this idea. He does not merely propose a new approach to a social solution to the rule-following problem. He also transforms the question of the *facts* that could justify such an ascription into the question of the *practices* in which common access to an objective world is produced – that is, about those practices in which subjects can develop a corresponding ability to *ascribe* such a status to themselves and to others. From this, Brandom develops a strategy that he calls 'normative phenomenalism'. The fundamental idea of normative phenomenalism is that the concept of *normative status* is explained via the concept of a *normative attitude*.[81]

Brandom elaborates: 'On the broadly phenomenalist line about norms that will be defended here, norms are in an important sense in the eye of the beholder, so that one cannot address the question of what implicit norms are, independently of the question of what it is to acknowledge them in practice.'[82]

Forms of normative status are institutionalized by normative attitudes. That is, the question of what it means to follow a rule correctly is practically decided by the fact that certain people are ascribed an 'institutional' status by others. Rule conformity, according to this model, is itself a normative status that is created by normative attitudes. That someone has a normative attitude towards a given token behaviour here means merely that they treat it as correct or incorrect.

That someone has a normative status in a community is clearly not established by any particular person's attitude, but *only by those attitudes of others that can themselves count as justified in the light of the further practice itself.* An action on this picture therefore *objectively conforms to a rule* if one can *justifiably treat it as rule-conforming* in the context of a more general practice. The strategy that Brandom thereby proposes is a fundamental alternative to those strategies that underlie rule-following scepticism: as opposed to asking *which facts* in relation to our behaviour justify the claim that we are following a rule, we must begin by asking *which attitudes* make it possible for us to relate to each other in such a way that we become able to justify our actions such that we can grasp ourselves as bound by normative standards.

The phenomenalist strategy that Brandom proposes, and that will serve as the basis for the model I will propose, is not only developed by him into a model of practical normativity but also serves as the foundation for an inferential semantics. This complex argument cannot be examined here in full. Nonetheless, it is worth briefly describing the approach Brandom's theory would suggest with regard to the question I am dealing with, and the relationship between this theory and the proposal described in the next chapter.

Brandom proposes the following strategy for the rule-following problem: The normativity of *explicit rules* should be understood as resting on the normativity of *judgements implicit in practice*s – that is, of *treating* actions *as* correct or incorrect.[83] This level of practical evaluation in turn presupposes a naturalistically describable level of actual behavioural dispositions to which, however, the normative status of rule-following is not reducible.[84] Rather, we can only understand the criteria for assigning normative status from the perspective *we ourselves* take when we evaluate others, that is, when *we* consider the circumstances under which we *should* understand certain interactions as normatively justified.[85] We can only understand the normative status of rule-following by evaluating the correctness of specific judgements as members of a social practice who accept the evaluations of others as binding on our own self-evaluations.[86] For Brandom, the disposition to accept the evaluations of others only serves to explain what it means to say that there is a practice in which we can become oriented towards a rule. However, these dispositions do not fix the meaning of that rule. The meaning of any given rule is only explicable from the participant perspective. We must start with our individual representation or implicit understanding of what rule we are following together with others, but we do not take this understanding as the last word. Rather, we always defer to the judgements of others. Only from the perspective of a member of such a practice – that is, one who takes themselves to be committed to respecting the evaluations of others and as entitled to evaluate others (including the entire group of all others) – can we understand what it means to be subject to a socially shared norm that has a content that nonetheless goes beyond each individual and even the collective disposition to apply it in a certain way.[87]

In order to point out some objections to the way Brandom concretely works out this model,[88] it can be criticized that, in a certain way, it again turns away from social solutions. In contrast to Haugeland's conformism, Brandom's position grants no special significance to the community, that is, to collective evaluations. Brandom argues that the relevant evaluations for the normative status of an agent are not to be analysed as collective evaluations; rather, the normative interactions are to be understood from the internal perspective of an 'I-thou relationship' between individual subjects.[89] This means that we can only understand the normativity of social interactions if we take up the *attitude of an interpreter* towards those involved, that is, if we normatively treat them *as persons* to whom we ascribe a normative status of some form. This attitude constitutes the 'recognition' relation.[90]

With this emphasis on the individual participant's perspective, however, Brandom runs into the same individualistic problem faced by Haugeland: if the relationships between agents are understood such that they principally always allow for only symmetrical evaluations between individual agents,[91] then they can only explain with difficulty how, from this perspective, the evaluations of other *individuals* can have *normative authority* that surpasses the authority of our own implicit self-evaluations. Only if we relinquish this individualistic premise and proceed from the existence of collective attitudes, which are not exhausted in a purely formal relationship of recognition between two people but which are expressed in an *antecedent attitude of recognition* towards other people *as members of a group*, can we understand how these other people can possess context-specific forms of default authority. Brandom's individualistic, formal concept of recognition – which ultimately only expresses the idea that people generally treat each other as normatively significant – is too *weak* to ground the normativity on which a meaningful form of immanent critique could rest.[92] It is also unable to explain how norms can be shared by a group in a strong sense.

These deficiencies in Brandom's model, from the perspective of the project of immanent critique, of course arise above all from the fact that he does not anticipate a social-philosophical application of his theory.[93] For the justification of a general theory of semantics, representation and intention, he must rather seek a form of normativity that does not apply to specific groups but whose 'we' encompasses all rational beings.[94] This explains a further drawback to his approach from the perspective of immanent critique: as Brandom above all pursues the goal of explaining the implicit basis of explicit norms, it remains unclear whether his model is able to plausibly reconstruct contradictions between these implicit and explicit norms.[95] Therefore, Brandom's model should indeed be accepted with regard to its fundamental phenomenalist and pragmatist strategies. It must be corrected, however, with regard to the role of collective attitudes and the conception of recognition and at least be supplemented and concretized with regard to the role of implicit norms and the idea of collectively shared standards. This is the task of the following chapter. There, I will start with Brandom's idea that the normativity of socially institutionalized rules is sustained by the attitude of reciprocal recognition, but I will develop a model of the constitution of this normativity independently of Brandom's theory.

6.5.5 Summary

The social solutions to the rule-following problem locate the source of the normativity of rule-following in the attitudes or practices of a community. The question of whether a person is following a rule is therefore answered by these solutions in an attempt to measure individual behaviour against a standard that arises in some way from the social interactions of the community. Therefore, on a simple conformist model, it turns out that neither conformity of behaviour nor interactions controlled by a second-order disposition can plausibly be understood as the foundation of such a standard. Brandom's model represents an improvement on these approaches, as the simple comparison of individual behaviour with the behaviour of others no longer serves as the standard but rather the intersubjectively constituted status of a person. But insofar as this status is again resolved into an individual ascription, it remains unclear where the authority that must come along with social ascriptions of rule-following should stem from in order to make it possible for individuals to orient themselves to rules.

Chapter Seven

The Immanent Norms of Social Practices

In the previous chapter, I examined a number of arguments for the idea that the capacity of human beings to follow explicit rules depends on there being implicit rules instituted in their social practices which are not to be identified with, and can always diverge from, any individual practice member's representation of what the rules of the practice are *and* from any collectively shared belief about these rules. These arguments defend stronger claims than those needed to justify a theory of immanent critique. According to these arguments, the existence of immanent norms is necessary for an explanation of many of our conceptual abilities and social institutions. By contrast, to justify a theory of immanent critique we only need to be able to show that it is possible for such norms to exist.

The examination of these arguments yielded two important results for the theory of immanent critique: first, the observation that we cannot fully explain the existence of immanent norms on the basis of individuals' features or abilities but only if we consider them to be rooted in the patterns of interaction of a community; second, the observation that there are two distinct problems that must be solved by a social model by providing two separate, independent arguments. The first is the problem of explaining how it is possible for individual agents to orient themselves in their action to a rule that is not identical to either their actual patterns of behaviour or any representation of the rule. This problem can be solved by a theory that understands this capacity as a disposition to defer (all other things equal) to evaluations by others. The second is the problem of how to explain the idea that a genuinely normative standard or rule 'exists' within the patterns of interaction in a community such that it is still possible for that community to be 'mistaken' about what the rule requires. That is, a successful theory must not eliminate the possibility that both the patterns of action exhibited by that community and the patterns of mutual evaluation in that community are mistaken. It is this second requirement in particular that has not sufficiently been addressed by the social theories of rule-following that I discussed in the last chapter.

The fundamental thesis of this chapter can be spelled out as follows: the ability to follow rules rests on the fact that implicit norms are institutionalized in communities by virtue of the fundamental relation of recognition (section 7.1). The term 'recognition' is used in this context to denote a defeasible attribution of authority to others who are thereby acknowledged as representatives of a group with a collectively shared attitude. On the one hand, the 'default-and-challenge' structure of this social relation entails that neither any individual evaluation of behaviour nor the sum of all evaluations between members of a community determines the content of the norms immanent in their social practice. On the other hand, as the relation of membership in a group with a collectively shared attitude requires agents to accept the evaluations of others in the default case, the model can explain how that relation is capable of providing guidance to agents. A general model of social practices can then be developed from this proposal (section 7.2), which is able to clarify the social ontological background assumptions that a theory of immanent critique must make.[1]

7.1 A RECOGNITION THEORY OF SOCIAL NORMATIVITY

The question of rule-following is relevant to the discussion of immanent critique insofar as it involves the question of *how a community as a whole can bind itself to a norm*. Based on the discussion in the previous chapter, I will assume, following Brandom, that the immanent normativity of such a collective commitment is to be explained through prediscursive *ascriptions of status* and that, consequently, the status of a community as following a rule can be explained by referring to the way a community *practically treats* a given standard *as binding on itself*. Such a social pragmatist theory, however – to recap the previous discussion – has the following three problems:

1. It cannot explain how individual, mutual evaluations of behaviour can add up to a genuinely *shared* standard. This problem follows from the individualistic prejudice of any theory of Haugeland's type.[2] It is therefore necessary to explain how genuinely *collective* normative commitments can be integrated into a social theory of rule-following.
2. It cannot explain how it can avoid the individualistic prejudice without ending up with a form of strong collectivism, which in turn cannot solve the *normativity problem at the collective level*. This is the danger of *conformism*.[3]

3. A social theory on the model described by Haugeland ultimately cannot take into account the *reflexivity* of social practices, as it cannot explain how individuals can reflexively *refer back* to rules in their evaluations.[4]

In what follows, I will attempt to outline a model that can avoid these difficulties. From the conformist approach, I will take the insight that *individuals and their attitudes alone cannot* be the source of norms, and not just because attributing a normative attitude or a practical normative reaction to an individual understood in abstraction from their relationships to others makes no sense. Even models that – like Brandom's – focus on relationships between individuals cannot explain how the evaluations of other individuals can become *normatively authoritative* for an agent, or at least not in such a way that they exceed the normative authority of the agent's own reflexive self-evaluation. A normative standard of the relevant kind can only emerge from the interactions of a community. Such a standard, however, cannot be understood as an aggregate attitude of others, and particularly not as the attitude of 'the community' in the sense of a supra-individual subject. Such a standard must rather be understood as a structural, irreducible property of the intersubjective relationships that are constituted by practical interactions.

If we want to understand the authority of the social relations to which individuals must be able to orient themselves if they are to be able to follow a rule, then we must conceive of this authority as resting on intersubjective relationships, but without reducing the normative standard that is established by them to a mere description of what these relationships empirically consist in. The fundamental idea of this proposal is that this authority arises from the fact that people *recognize* others as authorities with regard to certain rules; that this recognition is justified insofar as the recognized person is recognized as a *representative of a community* through which the content of these rules is socially determined; and that, however, there is still a difference between what this community de facto determines as the content of a given rule and what this community *should* determine as its content. As soon as people stand in relationships to each other in which they reciprocally recognize each other in this way – so it is argued below – they jointly follow, and ascribe to themselves the status of being bound by, a rule.

Such a recognition theory of social norms assumes with Brandom that the central building block of normativity arises from the fact that subjects recognize each other as normatively significant. This derives from the following thought: both the practical relevance of *conflicts about justification* (the only context in which reference to the truth or justification of an ascription of rule-following is meaningful) and also the practical relevance of *scepticism about rule-following* (the denial of the general possibility of justifying such an ascription) always assume that we are subject to an intersubjective *pressure to justify ourselves*. This pressure, however, cannot be explained by our commitment to a further rule but must be explained by reference to a basic acceptance of the normative significance of others – the basic acceptance of the fact that our actions may at least sometimes be legitimately evaluated by others.

A recognition theory further claims not only that recognition is a *necessary* condition for social normativity but that by means of relationships of recognition, all the elements that are necessary for the existence of immanent social norms can be explained. Recognition relationships are therefore also *sufficient* for the emergence of this form of normativity.

A recognition theory of social normativity therefore comprises two interlinked theses:

Social norms: In a group G, there is a norm N if and only if the members of G reciprocally recognize each other in relation to the collective acceptance of N (that is, if they ascribe a default authority to each other to determine whether actions are in conformity with N).

Rule-following: A person P follows a rule R if and only if

(a) they are a member of a group G in which a social norm N applies which determines what counts as correct action under R;
(b) they stand in specific recognitive relationships with other members of G that imply that any of P's actions that are covered by N may be legitimately evaluated by reference to R.

The fundamental idea of this recognition theory is, first, that we can use the concept of recognition to make sense of how, within a social group, a normative standard can be established, and second, that we can then enquire how according to this normative standard the *status of rule-following* will be distributed among the members of this group.

My argument for this model encompasses – presented schematically – the following steps:

1. The question of whether a person is following a rule – as far as it is about the justificatory aspect of rule-following – is not only secondarily but primarily a question of *practical, intersubjective justification*.
2. Intersubjective justification is – as became clear through the analysis of the problems of social theories – ultimately only possible if an agent can refer to *collectively shared standards* from which it follows that an action

may legitimately be recognized as being an instance of following a rule by other people and *should* be so recognized.[5]
3. Consequently, a *joint commitment* to a *shared rule* must exist in a group, which (as the analysis in chapter 5 has shown) is at least partly constituted by the fact that the people *ascribe an entitlement to each other* to mutually judge their behaviour.
4. The *actual* practical evaluation of behaviour by others is, however, not the ultimate arbiter of the normative status of an action (as in conformist theories), but the practice of evaluating one another in this way is itself regulated by norms that can be made explicit in cases of conflict (and thus, any given instantiation of that practice can turn out to be mistaken or defective).
5. These *further* norms are constituted through the same form of reciprocal recognition. This entails that any conflict about whether a given ascription of status is justified must ultimately be solved with recourse to a *joint commitment* that is unproblematic in the context at issue.
6. Reciprocal recognition is therefore not only a matter of agents recognizing each other as competent authorities in relation to rules but also of the ascription of a *default authority*. That is, it is a matter of a mutual acceptance of each other's evaluations as expressions of a context-specific consensus that are taken to be legitimate *by default* without needing any further support from a rule.
7. Both the orienting function of rules and the emergence of actual agreement can in many cases be explained with recourse to a dispositionally constituted ability to successfully navigate empirical practices. This dispositional element is systematically bound up with normative practices by processes of socialization. But it is not constitutive of the normative *content* of these practices.
8. The normative force of the (dispositionally anchored) orientation towards collective ascriptions is based on the authority of a community which is, in turn, based on reciprocal recognition and which, even though it allows for particular disagreement, does not stand in question as a whole.[6]
9. The recognitive attitudes that underlie the ascriptions of status through which an action can be recognized as correct, and through which a person can be recognized as entitled to evaluate others in specific ways, are attitudes that must ultimately precede any discourse. They must be understood as *constituted through practical forms of interaction*.

Before this recognition theory can be spelled out in more detail, it is necessary to briefly point to a possible misunderstanding which could be suggested by the concept of recognition, which I use in a different sense than other accounts in contemporary social philosophy. The concept of recognition that I use in this chapter is neither a concept that belongs to ethics in the broadest sense nor based on anthropological assumptions. In contrast to those concepts of recognition that are used by theories that make such assumptions, the concept of recognition in what follows is a very formal one: recognition means nothing more than an attitude by which one can ascribe normative authority to another person which is not justified by any further norm and normally does not even allow for any such justification, and which is tied to a specific social and normative context – that is, a context that is governed by a socially institutionalized rule.

After a brief description of the relationship between recognitive relations and recognitive expectations (7.1.1), I will clarify which role collective attitudes play in my account of rule-following (7.1.2 and 7.1.3), before discussing the relationship between authority and recognition (7.1.4). After a formal analysis of the concept of recognition (7.1.5), the reflexive nature of a normative practice (7.1.6) can finally be explained.

7.1.1 Recognitive Expectations

Individual elements of the theory outlined here are already present in various social-theoretically informed theories of normativity. Habermas, for example, reconstructs a Wittgensteinian social theory of rule-following by reference the idea that such a theory explains the intersubjectivity of a rule by reference to the fact that the participating agents are determined by each other through *reciprocal expectations*.

> If we analyze the intersubjective validity of a rule in this way, we come across two different types of expectations: (a) [B's] expectation that it is [A's] intention to carry out an action in applying a rule, and (b) [A's] expectation that [B] will recognize or admit his action as satisfying a rule.[7]

The *recognitive expectation* that A has towards B when A implicitly or explicitly makes the demand that B must recognize a rule-conforming action as such is, however, only a meaningful attitude towards B if A implicitly and practically recognizes that A's action is not yet *socially established* as rule-conforming merely through A's recognitive *expectation* but accepts that this action receives the *status of being socially counted as rule-conforming* through B's actual (justified) recognition. The reverse is not true, however. A's action does not have to count as improper just because B does not (currently) recognize it as rule-conforming: in this case, the recognitive expectation remains in place, and the status of A's action depends on whether B's denial of recognition itself can and must be recognized as correct in the wider network of interactions in the respective community.

This assumes that B's recognition has the power to confer a normative status to which A's recognitive expectation must refer, and that B's recognitive attitude itself is subject to evaluations by others according to rules to which A's expectation implicitly refers. That assumption is only satisfied if A also *ascribes normative authority to B* to confer (or withhold) the normative status of rule conformity by means of their recognition. That means that it is only fulfilled if B is recognized by A *in advance*.

The concept of recognition should therefore designate a *normative attitude* towards another person which consists in the fact that this person is ascribed the necessary *authority* (in a specific context of actions) to legitimately judge actions that belong to this context[8] and that their judgements are treated as justified at least by default.[9]

If it is to ground the existence of a socially shared rule, the attitude of recognition must be a *reflexive* one. This is because a rule will only emerge from relations of recognition through which potential evaluators are recognized as competent evaluators of *some specific rule*. It must therefore always be presumed that the subjects recognize each other with reference to some specific rule. Accordingly, the authority conferred by such recognition is a *rule-bound authority*: I follow a rule R if I orient myself to the collective attitude such that it follows that the other members of a community are normatively justified to evaluate my action with respect to its conformity to *that particular* rule. For this to be so, I must be situated in intersubjective relationships in which subjects grant each other the authority to evaluate whether the behaviour of their interaction partner is correct or incorrect with regard to a specific rule in a specific context.

7.1.2 The Position of the Community

The attitude of recognition (which, according to this account, is fundamental to the normative force of social rules) is internally linked with collective attitudes and therefore cannot be understood as a mere relation between individuals. This is made particularly clear by the central problem confronted by models like Haugeland's conformism. As discussed earlier,[10] this problem consists in the fact that we cannot explain, on the basis of individual dispositions, how individuals can be justified as *correct* in choosing one of several controversial options in situations of social conflict.

A conformist model which explains the normativity of social rules by imputing to all participants individual preferences for (or dispositions towards) the conformity of their own behaviour with that of their interaction partners cannot explain how the agents can *justifiably* choose between the adaptation of their own behaviour or the sanctioning of the behaviour of their counterpart.

A normative reaction that expresses a normative claim must have some *authority*. This authority must be explained in such a way that it does not lead to a regress of appeal to further rules. That the interpretations of *others* should have such authority (and not the original interpretation of the acting individual), however, can only be justified without regress if the other is not some random individual without especial significance but a fellow member of a *community* that is itself recognized as having authority:[11] if the respective normative sanction is not merely the individual reaction of an individual partner but an *expression of an attitude held by the community as a whole* towards the evaluated behaviour, then the symmetrical relation between two individuals that Haugeland describes is changed into an asymmetrical relation between an individual and their community. Here the community can be ascribed a *default* (although not irrefutable) authority. This is not because the evaluations of communities are 'more valuable' in some way but because only an agreement within a community can serve as a background, and thereby provide guidance, for the reciprocal evaluation of rule-following behaviour.

Brandom also describes this 'collectivistic' option as attractive: such a model assumes that what confers authority on any evaluation of the behaviour of others as correct or incorrect is comparison to a presupposed collective judgement of what it is correct to do. That means that the 'correctness' of any given token behaviour would be a matter not of the reciprocal evaluation of behaviour by individuals but of the evaluation of individual behaviour by the *community as a whole*.[12] Brandom presents this option in the following way:

> As a response to this concern [i.e., the collectivistic normativity problem], the leading idea of this sort of the construal of norms as implicit in social practices is that of *communal assessment*. On this approach, the key to the importance of the social is taken to lie in the possibility that the performances individual community members produce are assessed, responded to, or treated in practice as appropriate or inappropriate by the community to which the individual belongs.[13]

Brandom, however, ultimately rejects this idea of collective assessment. He assumes that introducing the notion of a collective evaluation of an action is problematic from a social ontological perspective. 'First, the idea of communal performances, assessments, or verdicts on which it relies is a fiction. Second, the approach smuggles normative notions illicitly into what purports to be a reductive, nonnormative regularity theory.'[14]

The second of these objections can be rebutted immediately: the search for a reductive, regularist theory must be abandoned (even in Brandom's view) if one wishes to construct a plausible social theoretic model of immanent normativity. Only a reconstructive model oriented to intersubjective practice can explain how interaction partners normatively determine, from case to case, who follows which rules.[15] The first objection, however – that collective evaluations are purely fictional – deserves a response. The claim that some evaluations express *attitudes of the community* must be justified. This question of how collective evaluations can be described such that they are not 'fictions', finally, provides a link to the account of collective intentionality discussed in section 5.7. There, I argued that the assumption of collective normative attitudes does not depend on social-ontologically questionable premises. Rather, I attempted to make the possibility of such collective intentional states plausible by means of a recognition model. That theory's approach also makes it possible to explain why the position of the community can claim default authority, even when it is expressed through evaluations of interaction partners who are not necessarily endowed with greater authority.

The *relation of intersubjective recognition as it is operative in joint commitments* is therefore the desired element that can serve to explain how people can be genuinely normatively committed to rules without entering into an infinite regress of appealing to further rules. As will be explained shortly, this does not mean that a recognition order is not further normatively regulated. The attitude of recognition is internally structured, however, in such a way that it does not require further elements external to itself in order to generate genuine obligations.

7.1.3 The Institutionalization of Social Rules through Collective Attitudes

The combination of a social answer to the rule-following problem with a theory of collective intentionality can contribute to integrating the theory of collective phenomena into a comprehensive model of social theory.[16] In particular, it can further clarify the connection between social rules and collective actions. While I've already discussed why the possibility of collective attitudes depends on the institutionalization of collectively shared rules,[17] in the context of the discussion of the binding force of social rules it turned out that this binding force is dependent, in turn, on collective phenomena – that is, both social forms of normativity are internally linked to one another.

The most important reason for this claim lies in the fact that both the stability of the intersubjective institutionalization of a social rule through reciprocal evaluations and its normatively obligating force are dependent on the fact that in *cases of conflict*, the reference to a communal interpretation establishes an *asymmetric situation* – that is, an evaluation that refers to a communal norm against a deviant individual interpretation has at least a prima facie superordinate authority which, in the absence of further contextual reasons, conclusively answers the question of the normative status of the respective action. This will later be explained by means of a recognition model of rule-following which understands recognition as the ascription of default authority.[18] Accordingly, the force of social rules can only be explained by the fact that the members of a community jointly commit themselves to accepting the *consequences* of their collective acceptance of this rule through their reciprocal recognition as being entitled to apply certain standards of critique. The resulting possibility of *communal evaluation* is only conceivable against the background of the possibility of collective commitments. Collective commitments are therefore a specific configuration of social normativity but also underlie the very possibility of social normativity itself.

Due to this complex connection, it is necessary to clarify the way collective attitudes and social norms serve to explain each other: the force of a social norm is dependent on the fact that all particular cases of evaluations are backed up by collective attitudes that are themselves to be explained by reference to socially shared rules: a norm only applies in a community when one can react to an act that falls under a norm with a corresponding evaluation. Member Y's evaluation E of an action A by member X as correct or incorrect only counts as justified and has normative authority, however, if a collective commitment on the part of the respective community exists to the effect that an action of that type demands an evaluation like E. According to the analysis of collective attitudes developed in chapter 5, this means that all members of the relevant group must be ready to accept criticism of their behaviour if they do not evaluate others accordingly.

Put differently, if a norm N_1 is socially institutionalized in a community according to which an action A is correct or incorrect, then this means that there must be a collective commitment to a norm N_2 in that community which marks out a certain interpretation of this norm in social interactions – that is, certain evaluations of actions – as required. That the group has this collective commitment in turn has consequences for its individual members. The norm N_2 that justifies the collective evaluation to the effect that A is correct or incorrect is therefore not identical to N_1, although N_1 is what *accounts for* A's being correct or incorrect; N_2 is the *norm of social evaluation and interpretation* that demands that all members of the relevant community should act on the collectively shared belief that A is correct or incorrect.

This analysis of the constitution of social norms by collective commitments should not be understood as claiming that communities always enter into a collective process of negotiating their common standpoint regarding all of their members' actions. In most cases in which actions are intersubjectively evaluated, it is improbable that all members of the respective normative community know of this action in the first place. Rather, the existence of background norms is decisive here: justified by their own understanding of the shared norms, every individual member who judges the performance of another must always *presuppose* a collective commitment, which only exists implicitly at that moment, and – if they have been successfully socialized into the communal norms – they can normally trust that their own evaluation will be a correct actualization of that commitment.

The existence of a social norm in a community is thus explained by reference to a complex structure of collective and individual commitments, which ultimately rests on the attitude of reciprocal recognition. Therefore, the existence of social norms can be described – even if simplistically – such that the members of a community mutually recognize each other's default authority with respect to a norm, which requires them to evaluate each other's behaviour according to whether it is compatible with their collective acceptance of another norm according to the inferential rules that are valid in this context.

On this basis, we can attempt to grasp the idea of an immanent commitment to social norms more precisely. We must begin with the *symmetric* case – that is, the case in which all members of a community possess the same authority to evaluate. The analysis of the existence of social norms[19] given above can, accordingly, be made more precise in the following way:

Immanent norm (grounded in symmetric recognition): In the practices of a community G, there is an immanent social norm N that is grounded in symmetric recognition if and only if

1. in the context of further practices of recognition in G, every member X of G is practically recognized as a matter of the group's joint commitment to N, such that X possesses a *default authority* to evaluate the actions of every other member Y. That means that Y must recognize X as entitled to evaluate Y's actions with respect to their compatibility with the group's collective acceptance of N, based on a shared interpretation of what N entails. It therefore counts as correct for Y (ceteris paribus), in the context of social practices in G, to accept those of X's evaluations that explicitly or implicitly refer to the group's collective acceptance of N.

2. in the context of further practices of recognition in G, every member X of G is obligated as a matter of the group's joint commitment to N to recognize the default authority of every other member Y. That means that X must recognize Y as entitled to evaluate X's actions with respect to their compatibility with the group's collective acceptance of N, based on a shared interpretation of what N entails. It therefore counts as correct for X (ceteris paribus), in the context of

the social practices in G, to accept those of Y's evaluations that explicitly or implicitly refer to the group's collective acceptance of N.

Consequently, the more complex case of an *asymmetric* institutionalization of social norms can be explained by this recognition model as well. In an asymmetric case, the existence of a norm is grounded in the fact that *specific members of a community are recognized as entitled in a special way to* evaluate the behaviour of other members. Ascribing and recognizing such a *special authority* is itself a case of a rule-following practice. This means that the norm that certain members have special authority can only be institutionalized in a broader social practice that is governed by symmetrical relationships of recognition. The question of who possesses special authority can only be answered in the context of a broader practice that does not already presuppose this authority. The following therefore holds:

> *The necessity of recognition for immanent social norms:* If there is an immanent norm N in a community G, then all members of G must mutually recognize each other with respect to the collective acceptance of N (or – in an asymmetric case – with respect to a norm of authority distribution, from which the validity of N follows) as being endowed with default authority.[20]

If we put these pieces together, the analysis of rule-following changes slightly:

> *Rule-following:* A person P follows a (social) rule R if and only if:
> (a) they are a member of a group G in which a complex structure of social norms N applies that determines which actions are to be collectively accepted as correct, and therefore
> (b) they stand in specific relations of recognition with other members of G which imply that P's action may be legitimately evaluated under reference to R according to N.

These conclusions are conditioned by two acceptable restrictions. First, this analysis does not provide for a *reduction* of statements about social normativity to a description in a different vocabulary, but it attempts to explain the practices in which social norms are constituted only as far as is necessary in order to secure the possibility of empirical and social scientific access to them. That is, it must describe the pragmatically sufficient conditions for understanding which processes are necessary for social norms to exist in a community. Second, the analysis of any individual practice already presupposes a normative social context of practices that is necessary in order to give content to the concepts 'sanction', 'recognition' and 'obligation'.

With these limitations in mind, an analysis of the existence of immanent social norms in terms of a theory of social practice can be defended. Such a practice analysis can fulfil all previously presented requirements for an analysis of immanent normativity. It can explain how rules can serve to *justify* behaviour by providing an analysis of *justification as a social process*, which describes what it means for people to assign a social status to each other's behaviour without allowing the meaning of that status to be explicated in terms of nonnormative conditions; it allows us to understand how rules can serve to orient behaviour through the idea that people can acquire dispositions through socialization that help them to anticipate the results of social processes of evaluation; and it helps us to understand the 'infinity' aspect of rule-following by acknowledging that social interactions are *principally open and can play out in an unlimited number of ways*.

7.1.4 Recognition and Default Authority

An essential difference between the theory defended here and Haugeland's conformist model is that the status of rule-following cannot be reduced to an exercise of a *disposition towards conformity* with actual evaluations but depends on the recognition of the default (but not absolute) authority of others. I follow the rule 'Everyone must greet the chief when they see him' if I recognize others' authority to assess my behaviour according to this rule. If I recognize the authority of others, then I must (explicitly or implicitly) accept criticism for failing to greet the chief. However, I must only accept this criticism if it is *justified* – that is, if according to other further relevant norms I must accept the statement that I failed to do so.

If, however, recognition means accepting people's evaluations *insofar as they are justified*, then the concept of justification seems not to be *explained* by the recognition model but rather *presupposed* by it. Can the recognition theory claim that it really provides an explanation of rule-following, then? After all, it does not reduce an intricate phenomenon to more simple or unproblematic phenomena or unknown processes to known modes of action. It appears, rather, to 'explain' simple cases of rule-following through describing a complex interplay of actions oriented towards more numerous and intricate rules.

The objection that this explanation cannot satisfy the original project of a (reductive) analysis of rule-following is justified.[21] Adopting the strategy of normative phenomenalism rather leads to a shifting of the explanatory goal. The basic idea behind the strategy of normative phenomenalism is to explicate what it means to be justified *in saying that someone is following a rule* by saying what it means to be justified *in evaluating someone as being correct in treating another person's behaviour as a case of rule-following*.

In order to correctly evaluate someone else's evaluation, however, one does not always need to refer to another level of higher-order standards (that is, one does not need to cite standards for the evaluation of evaluations of evaluations, and so on). Rather, in any normative social practice, people must treat each other – and this is the fundamental idea behind the concept of recognition that I introduced above – as having a *default authority*: a normative reaction by another agent that is antecedently recognized can *only* be rejected if the individual who is subject to the reaction (or, perhaps under certain conditions, a third party) can appeal to *further* normative resources beyond the normative commitments to which the reaction refers and, in so doing, can justify rejecting the original assessment. Thus, in order for the default authority of another agent's evaluation to be contested, a justified rejection of that evaluation (that is, a rejection that is justified by 'higher order' rules) must be brought forward – a mere refusal to accept it is not enough.[22]

We can therefore assume that an action's normative status is typically determined by the actual reactions of others but nonetheless avoid the normativity problem if we only award a default authority to these reactions. This avoids the objection levied against the classical conformist theory regarding a lack of genuine normativity, but it also avoids the danger of infinite regress, as this default authority is able to stop a regress in the application of rules without treating any particular, actual application of a rule as being justified a priori.[23]

Unlike Haugeland's conformist model, this amounts to neither a reductive nor a constitutive analysis of normativity but rather an elucidation of it:[24] the question of whether the normative force presupposed by a certain form of critique actually rests on 'ultimately' or 'objectively' legitimate norms can only be answered by reference to yet further norms. However, this does not apply to the question of whether the critique must be taken seriously, given the normative commitments of a community. This question is answerable against the background of the common forms of institutionalized normativity.

7.1.5 The Formal Structure of Recognition

The concept of recognition was introduced in chapter 5 in the context of a discussion of collective intentional states.[25] The provisional analysis provided there can now be assessed by means of a developed theory of social practices.

A normative practice can – as already discussed – be understood as a practice in which individuals can acquire various forms of normative status, whereby the status that an individual possesses primarily relies on the conformity of their behaviour to a rule. Whether their behaviour conforms to the rule, however, cannot be understood as determined by the objective qualities of their behaviour or by their mental states. Describing their behaviour as conforming to the rule is rather an expression of the fact that it may be *practically treated* by others as rule-conforming in relationships within which these others can legitimately ascribe this status to them – that is, in relationships where the participants reciprocally recognize each other.

If we accept this argument, it turns out that people who stand in a relationship of recognition to one another must also always recognize each other as competent evaluators of higher-order norms.[26] This is because, in order to be able to understand themselves as participants in the same shared practice even when they diverge in their interpretation of first-order rules, they have to be able to at least recognize each other as having the capacity to apply a shared rule that specifies how to react to such divergence.

The primary and social-ontologically fundamental form of recognition is therefore symmetric, reciprocal recognition between two people who treat each other as competent evaluators.

Building on this, the concept of recognition can be defined as follows:

Recognition: If N is a social norm that represents a shared rule or standard that belongs to a practice P, then X *recognizes* Y as a participant in P with respect to N if and only if

1. X accepts the obligation to accept any evaluation of X's relevant behaviour by Y (whether critical or affirming) with regard to the agreement of this behaviour with N by default, without requiring further justification beyond reference to the common practice P to show that X is bound by N.

2. X takes themselves to be entitled to a serious consideration of their evaluation of Y's relevant behaviour (and its agreement with N) by default, without X's needing to provide further justification beyond reference to the common practice P to show that Y is bound by N.

3. X accepts the obligations, and claims for himself the entitlements, that arise from the fact that X and Y are mutually obliged and entitled to invoke higher-order rules in order to justify their rejection of an evaluation whenever they do not accept one such default obligation or entitlement.

4. X accepts that the totality of the obligations that arise from this structure for X and Y are counted as fulfilled for X or Y if the corresponding norms are habitually followed in the normal case or when further practices exist in the relevant community in which these entitlements and obligations are institutionally secured.

It could be argued that the concept of 'obligation' leads us into a circle. If the concept of recognition is used to explain rule-following, and this concept is in turn explained by reference to the 'acceptance of obligations', which can plausibly be understood as the *following of a rule*, then is the concept of rule-following not already presupposed? As already mentioned,[27] however, the shift in the object of analysis from the 'objective' status of behaviour to the social status of mutual acts of evaluation comes along with a shift in the criterion of success for the theory: what the theory aims to explain is no longer *primarily correctness of behaviour* but rather the *legitimacy of evaluations*. In order to judge the legitimacy of evaluations, it is not necessary to find an ultimate foundation that answers the question of this legitimacy from an observer's perspective. In social practices, the legitimacy of evaluations that are de facto accepted against the background of an observance of the general standards of discourse in a community is rather *the standard case*.

Whether an evaluation (and, consequently, critique) is *actually* legitimate is indeed a question to which a final answer can only be given if we ask for every level of evaluation (and evaluations of evaluations, and so on) whether it is justified in light of the social norms that govern the next level up. But this infinite regress does not emerge when we ask whether a specific, concrete evaluation *ought to be accepted*. This question can be answered if one knows whether those involved can rely on reasons that are recognized de facto and that relieve them of the standard obligation to accept evaluations. If this is not the case, then we know that, in virtue of their membership, they ought to accept the evaluation as authoritative. That is, the regress does not disappear, but it is shown that the members of such a practice are justified, under certain conditions, in stopping it by claiming an authority for their evaluation that is no longer dependent on further rules or interpretations.

In the context of such a model, reciprocal recognition is the basis that allows individuals to gain the authority necessary for their evaluations to become constitutive of the social existence of norms. A recognition model is a social pragmatist model of the explanation of the justificatory function of our reliance on rules in actual social practices, which can explain how reference to such rules (beyond a reference to actual behaviour or explicit beliefs) can play a critical practical role. This model – if one properly elaborates its reflexive structure and its aspects that relate to collective attitudes – is able to make sense of the two features that are essential to the project pursued here. First, it allows us to reformulate the problem of rule-following such that it can be understood as a problem that is internal to *practices of critique* and, consequently, to present a plausible model of how this problem can be solved. Secondly, it can make the concept of 'immanent norms' sufficiently comprehensible that it becomes clear how people can refer to such norms when engaging in a critique of social practices. Proceeding from such a model of immanent normativity – which has thus far for the sake of simplicity only been discussed with regard to the relationship between actions and rules – we can now broaden our perspective again, in order to clarify what it means to say that norms are immanent in social practices, as structured contexts of social normativity.

7.1.6 The Reflexive Nature of Norms

But can this model also explain *reflexive orientation to norms*? This requirement was justified by the observation that an action can only count as following a rule if it conforms to that rule not 'accidentally' but rather because the rule-following agent has *oriented* themselves to the rule in their action and the aim to conform to the rule has at least implicitly played a motivating role in their action.[28]

Clearly, we must avoid a simple solution that explains this orientation as a matter of individual *intentional states* (for example, claiming that the only action that counts as rule-following is one that is motivated by the explicit intention to follow this or that rule) and thereby falls back into the problems of individualistic theories. By the same token, however, a solution that offers a dispositional or structuralist theory (both of which systematically neglect the reflexivity of rule-following in favour of purely causal accounts, or non-intentional conformity with rules) can scarcely be convincing either. This raises the question whether the pragmatist analysis of collective attitudes allows for the necessary reflexivity of rule-following. The normative force of recognitive relations – which, according to this analysis, provides the foundation for collective attitudes – remains mostly implicit in such attitudes, as participants in social practices usually do not intentionally orient themselves to the recognition of others but act on the basis of dispositions that are only indirectly connected to the collective standards. Therefore, we cannot explain this aspect of reflexivity by assuming that agents *actually* refer to the rule in every instance of a rule-following action. Rather, this aspect of reflexivity must be explained on the basis of the assumption that such a reference is always, *counterfactually*, at their disposal if there is a social conflict about whether their action is an instance of rule-following.

This kind of reference is only possible, however, if norms are not only *actually enforced through sanctions* in the case of normative conflicts but also *thematized as norms*. The idea that agents negatively sanction behaviour because it deviates from their own is ambiguous in this respect insofar as this can be understood both in the sense that such deviance *causes* them to sanction and in the sense that it *justifies* their sanctions. In a normative practice, not only must transgressive behaviour empirically lead to sanctions, but those sanctions must be such that members can understand them *as justified by the irregularity of the sanctioned behaviour*. Members' reactions to each other's behaviour may not be analysed as a self-contained standard. Rather, normative reactions must always be understood by the members as also expressing a commitment to normative claims that precede these reactions.[29] Only if the reciprocal evaluation of behaviour can be understood as an expression of a normative judgement that is oriented to standards that go beyond the act of evaluation at issue does it become clear how agents can be oriented not only towards avoiding de facto sanctions but to 'the rule' itself. This reflexive structure must be reflected in the internal structure of rule-following.

Therefore, a person can only follow a rule if they at least implicitly refer to the rule in their action. Bloor writes: 'To think you are M-ing is to be able to account your actions in terms of the institution of M-ing where that institution itself is constituted by those very accounting practices along with, of course, the accountable patterns of behavior themselves.'[30] However, one must distinguish two possible claims: Bloor may be taken to suggest that a social practice presumes that the individuals can always *describe* their own actions in terms of a certain, explicitly formulated rule. This does not follow from the demand that the individual must be able to *orient* themselves to a rule: an individual's ability to understand their normative reactions as part of a normative practice only presupposes that they understand themselves in a minimal sense as following some (perhaps unspecified) rule or another and that they are able to apply this rule in practice in the normal case such that they can understand the reactions of the other participants to their behaviour as guided by the same rule (whatever it is). However, it does not follow from this criterion of reflexivity that an agent must have a certain *belief* to the effect that they follow a *specific* rule. Such an assumption would be counterintuitive, as many social institutions – for example, standing in a queue[31] – are meaningfully comprehensible as involving an understanding on the side of the participants to the effect that they are participants in a rule-governed practice, without the participants' necessarily having any beliefs in any sense about which specific rules they follow.

It must therefore only be shown how the reciprocal commitment that is involved in relations of recognition can be reflexive to such a degree that agents can understand their actions as always already oriented to a rule, and such that they are thereby in some sense willing and sufficiently reliably able to differentiate between cases that fall under this rule and those that do not. This understanding of one's actions can be described as *practical competence*: a capacity to follow a shared rule and, in cases of uncertainty, to give explicit justifications. However, this does not usually require any antecedent representation (mental or otherwise) of an explicit rule.

One could now object that it would be very unsatisfactory if we were to attempt to avoid the regress problem by assuming that agents can reflexively intend to follow a rule, while at the same time claiming that this is possible without their knowing *what it means* to follow that rule. If that were the answer, the sense in which there is a reflexive relation to the rule at issue would remain unclear.

An extension of this model is therefore necessary: the dispositional basis of rule-following must be given sufficient space so that it can be recognized that the practical implementation of social practices can in large part be based on purely dispositionally governed behaviour that requires no reflexivity. The practices made possible by that capacity must, however, be *institutionally reflexive* such that the corresponding actions are always accompanied by a specific kind of commitment to a norm.[32] Such a commitment does not require that the agents involved be able to make explicit which rule they are following on the spot. The relevant kind of commitment is rather constituted by their practical ability and willingness to move towards a practice of giving reasons for their behaviour when (and only when) the correctness of that behaviour is questioned – that is, *in their ability and willingness to participate in further practices of (explicit) justification*. This will ultimately often involve developing an explicit understanding of what rule they take themselves to have been following all along. For this to be possible, it must at least be the case that when their reasons for action are called into question, the agents are disposed to understand themselves as following a norm, and that they therefore can and will carry out social processes of negotiation that, in cases of conflict, allow the *content of this norm to be determined* – not that they must already have *in advance* a belief about *which* specific norm they are following.[33]

The dispositional reactions of individuals are therefore always to be understood only as an element of overarching, multilevelled, normatively regulated, social practices. Every individual norm already presupposes a whole network of other social norms that together constitute a social practice with ascriptions of social status, with normative responsibility and with sanctions and critique. These elements explain each other without being reducible to each other. Such a social pragmatist, holistic theory is the only plausible option that neither eliminates the normativity of rules, as in regularism, nor reifies the normativity of rules as not further explicable, as in Platonic regulism.

Furthermore, if we take seriously the idea of the *duality of social practice*,[34] we can explain the function of behavioural orientation – which answers the question 'How can we orient ourselves to rules as natural beings?' – by a limited introduction of a dispositional theory, without thereby already answering the further question of justification: people can orient themselves to a collective standard by forming a certain disposition that counts as the internalization of this standard and that is also accompanied by certain minimal reflexive dispositions.

7.2 SOCIAL PRACTICES

As has been shown in the context of the discussion of the recognition model of social normativity, we can never individuate social norms such that it can be meaningfully said that a single norm is institutionalized in a given practice. Both with respect to the default authority established by recognition – which is characterized by rules governing exemptions and rules establishing specific obligations to give reasons – and with respect to the common background of collective intentions, it has become clear that any institutionalization of 'a' social norm is only possible within a network of further normative expectations. Following Wittgenstein and contemporary sociological theories, one can call such a network, which serves as a background for any individual ascription of an action's being oriented to a rule, *a social practice*. The norms immanent in a community are therefore always institutionalized in social practices. A recognition model of social practices is a model that also explains how the standards of justification that are *constitutive* of certain social practices are practically institutionalized by the establishment of certain collective attitudes that are themselves grounded in relations of recognition. The consequences of the adoption of such a model for a *critical theory of social practices* can now be examined with respect to its social ontological significance (section 7.2.1). In an excursus (section 7.2.2) – in anticipation of the transition to a theory of immanent critique – we can describe the respects in which such practices might take on a pathological form.

7.2.1 The Social Ontological Constitution of Social Practices

I propose that we understand social practices as those patterns of action that are normatively of significance to members of a community and in which they grant each other the authority to criticize each other by reference to a shared standard.

In the following, I would like to emphasize certain properties of social practice that concern their social ontological structure. As already mentioned,[35] the assumption is that the members of a community must understand those of their actions that are part of the practice *as* part of that practice, and that they must recognize in cases of conflict that their actions have an implicit reference to a standard of correctness. From this it follows that such social practices must be *reflexive* and therefore, in a weak sense, *social institutions*. The constitutive function of rules that is crucial in this context can now finally be analysed (a). Subsequently, I will summarize which elements must come together such that collective intentionality can actually be constitutive of a social practices (b) and what role recognition plays (c).

(a) Constitutive and regulative functions of implicit rules. As already shown,[36] we can only speak of orientation to an implicit rule in a practice if we assume that the rule-following behaviour not only contingently conforms to a normative standard but is *reflexively oriented* to this standard in some sense. But to what, exactly, is rule-following behaviour oriented? One could say that rule-following behaviour is oriented to the possible *status* of the resulting action of being rule-conforming. This status is an *institutional status* that is made possible by the social practice of rule-following.

In order to better understand the institutional status of actions, one could attempt to translate the model of the constitutive role of social practices proposed here into Searle's terminology. Searle assumes that institutional facts are facts that arise because certain persons, actions or objects are conferred a certain institutional status through collective acts of assignment. Money – Searle's standard example – is money because it is collectively accepted that certain pieces of paper (or electronic traces) *count as* money – that is, because they play a certain role in a network of institutions determined by further rules. More formally, one could say that according to Searle, institutional reality exists through the fact that a *constitutive rule* of the form 'X counts as Y in context C' is collectively accepted, where Y is a normatively institutionally embedded term and where 'collective acceptance' – as already shown in section 5.5 – must be understood as designating an intentional state of some kind.

If we try to understand this phenomenon from the viewpoint of the model of social practices presented here, we can say that rule-following behaviour is oriented by the (possible) rule-conforming status of a behaviour, which in turn is assigned to this behaviour by collective intentionality. The recognition model reconceptualizes Searle's idea of collective intentionality in terms of *interactions*. This means that collective intentionality is not understood as a mental state but emerges from the interactions in which people grant each other default authority.

The *institutional character* of a social practice must consequently be understood such that the collective acceptance of a constitutive rule is always expressed in the interactions that make up the practice, which grant possible actions a quasi-institutional status. This means that people accept, through their readiness to accept each other's evaluations, a rule of the following form:

Actions to which the criteria $X_1 \ldots X_N$ apply count as *correct* or *incorrect* in view of the norm N in the context of the practice in question.

One could say that the acceptance of such a constitutive rule creates the standard to which the participants of the practice can orient themselves, even if not necessarily explicitly. This analogy cannot fully be cashed out, however: Searle emphasizes that the allocation of status functions by the acceptance of constitutive rules ('X counts as Y in context C') always results in a *new* social status, which is only comprehensible from within the practice of the respective institution.[37] But 'correct' and 'incorrect' are not forms of social status that take on a fully new meaning for any social practice; rather, they serve to evaluate actions in a way that can always be presupposed as comprehensible. The acceptance of implicit rules thus appears to institutionalize only *regulative* standards.

However, it should be remembered that the distinction between constitutive and regulative rules only has a heuristic value:[38] constitutive rules always also have regulative functions insofar as the acceptance of constitutive rules has repercussions that normally consist in the fact that the conferral of an institutional status onto an object or an action makes certain other actions appropriate or inappropriate.[39] This means that a combination of constitutive rules can always be understood as a combination of specific regulative rules that determine which actions in which contexts may and must be carried out.

The difference between constitutive and regulative rules is therefore not absolute. Rather, it consists in the fact that regulative rules signify those rules in a practice that, in even a systematic failure of compliance, do *not* license *exclusion* from the praxis in question, while constitutive rules determine which behaviours count as parts of a practice *at all*. As such, we can distinguish in every practice between rules that allow for the distinction between correct and incorrect behaviour in a practice (and in some circumstances attach sanctions) and rules the violation of which leads to one's no longer participating in the practice at all (and thus licenses one's being excluded from the practice). One may think, for example, of practices like art, jurisprudence or the writing of scientific monographs, in which we can distinguish – even if not precisely – between cases in which the norms of the practice are broken and cases in which people no longer fulfil the minimal conditions in order for their actions to be seen as part of such a practice at all.

Constitutive rules therefore have a close connection to the recognition of actions as part of a practice, while regulative rules stand in connection with the recognition of a certain behavioural quality, the attribution of which already presupposes that the action is part of the relevant practice. For this reason,[40] the difference between constitutive and regulative rules can be understood as a difference in the social function of norms in a practice. Social practices are institutionalized by the collective acceptance of certain constitutive rules, which in turn are to be understood as the rules that regulate membership in these practices.

As far as one of the functions of regulative rules is concerned, however, they are also constitutive of a given practice. Insofar as *orientation to* and (at least occasional) *compliance with* regulative rules is a condition of membership in any given practice, only actions with that orientation can count as part of the practice and as attempts to follow its rules, whereupon further regulative rules can be applied to such actions. The corresponding collective attitudes of acceptance of this criterion of membership are constitutive of the practice and, at the same time, ground the normative force of the rules to which the individual participants in this practice can reflexively refer in their rule-following.

(b) The elements of social practices. However, collective attitudes can only serve this constitutive function – that is, can only establish those normative differences that are essential to the nature of a social practice – if they serve as the basis for self-stabilizing patterns of social interaction, in which the participants express the acceptance of certain norms through the reciprocal recognition of each other's default authority. These norms are at the same time constituted as 'social facts' by this recognition – that is, by collective attitudes. This assumes that the *causal effectiveness* of social practices is anchored in dispositional behaviour schemata; their *normative content*, by contrast, arises from the irreducible normative structures of default recognition, which only become empirically accessible in cases of conflict and whose content cannot be determined in a noncontextual fashion. The justification of the claim that immanent norms exist therefore refers to a complex structure of social facts, which only jointly amount to the existence of a social practice that institutes these norms.

This leads to the following definition of the concept of a social practice:

Social practice: A more or less schematizable sequence of actions or a combination of several such sequences SA is a social practice in a community C if and only if

1. SA or the action sequences that belong to SA reliably recur under certain conditions;

2. the social facts on which this reliable recurrence depends reproduce themselves reliably under normal conditions, given the other practices in C;

3. the fact that SA is carried out under certain conditions is normatively relevant to C – that is, if the fact that SA is carried out or not is suitable to elicit normative reactions in the members of C (for example, criticism, punishment, justification);

4. SA is either dispositionally anchored in agents or is produced with the aid of dispositionally anchored behaviour schemata;

5. SA in C is in a weak sense a source of relevant, institutional status forms – that is, SA is (at least as far as possible) reflexive; this is the case if the critique and justification of actions (or omissions of actions) that belong to SA, under the

correct circumstances, regularly takes place with reference to the believed (or the implicit presumption of the) existence of a shared social practice;[41]

6. in the context of reciprocal evaluation, members of C (at least implicitly) treat as collectively accepted the norm that what count as correct extensions of the shared practice of performing SA are those actions that are either collectively accepted as reflexively correct by C (the standard case) or are deviations from collectively accepted action sequences that the respective agent can (reflexively) justify with respect to actually shared, higher-order norms of C, or with respect to norms justifiably imputed to an idealized and extended community.

Properties 1 and 2 result directly from the requirement that social practices must be enduring and stable elements of social reality, as a one-off successful interaction can hardly be counted as a practice. Rather, a pattern of action must exist or be expected by a community for at least a certain time span in order to count as a social practice (and as a result of the agents' orientation to a norm).

While properties 3, 5 and 6 arise from the analysis of the necessary conditions for the existence of social norms presented in this chapter, the fourth property is not a direct consequence of this analysis. The idea of default justification[42] is only a plausible solution to the regress problem if it is assumed that in a sufficient number of cases there is *at some level* an empirical agreement among interaction partners that does not require further justification. Thus, there have to be some shared dispositions in order for social practices to exist. Further, the assumption of dispositional anchoring offers a plausible model of the empirical-causal internalization of social normativity that is also compatible with the relevant sociological theories.

Finally, the concept of 'reflexive correctness' must be explained, which means nothing other than that the standard of correctness is tied to a specific description of the corresponding action, under which it is at least implicitly performed. An action is part of the practice of child rearing, for example, if it is collectively *accepted as part of this practice*. One should therefore not be tempted to understand 'correctness' as a strong normative standard, such that an action only counts as an instance of child rearing if it is collectively recognized as *good* child rearing, for example. The requirement of 'reflexive correctness' only signifies that any action that is part of a social practice is collectively accepted as an exercise (whether more or less good) of a certain *type* of action.

As has already been shown by means of the distinction between constitutive and regulative rules, many practices have standards of *excellence* beyond the rules that merely regulate what is part of the practice. One can make this clear with the simple example of language: to speak a language correctly and to use a language in an especially excellent (that is, in a beautiful, expressive, persuasive) way is a matter of two different standards. The basic case is the minimally correct use – that is, the minimal conditions one must fulfil in order to take part in the practice at all. Criteria of excellence beyond the constitutive rules of participation in the practice can be institutionalized in the practice through *other* forms of critique and praise, which must be distinguished from the more fundamental form.

This means that, in addition to the rules whose acceptance is essential for participation in a practice,[43] there are also always further rules whose nonfulfilment does not elicit the kind of critique that amounts to an exclusion from the practice, but whose acceptance as an evaluative standard nonetheless can be more or less constitutive of the practice. These evaluative criteria are in most practices associated with a set of motivations and a set of affective relations to the activity and to its objects and objectives that are accepted as appropriate, which Schatzki calls its 'teleo-affective structure'.[44] The resulting complex structure of norms and motives is of significance for social ontology only insofar as they are themselves governed by the fundamental norms of the practice. Their further role – which is crucial for the *sociological* analysis of practices – can initially be neglected.

(c) The central role of recognition. The analysis of this chapter regarding the central role of recognition can be summarized in the following way: an action can only be collectively accepted as correct (and thereby gain the corresponding status of *being* correct) if the participants in the practice reciprocally practically and implicitly award to each other the authority to judge their respective reactions by means of a standard they collectively accept. Both an agent's orientation to a rule and their conformity or nonconformity to such a rule are only socially possible as *normative positions* in a context of socially ascribed types of status; that is, they are only possible if those involved confront each other in the mode of reciprocal recognition and treat each other as possible sources of normative reasons. The role of recognition is therefore decisive both for understanding the constitution of those collective attitudes that establish a normative standard and for explaining the relationship of agents *to* this standard, which must be rooted in recognition in order to establish genuine normative commitment and not mere conformity.

The fact that social practices must be analysed phenomenally by investigating the form in which social interactions proceed through time follows from the fact that recognition is a relationship that is expressed in concrete interactions of reciprocal evaluation. The constitutive role of this relationship for the existence of social practices, and the constitutive role of social practices for all genuinely social-normative phenomena, necessitates this phenomenal analysis. This is the case, in particular, because normative relations between individuals are never to be observed independently of the corresponding interactions in which they are normatively meaningful and are treated as such. Accordingly, the phenomenal existence of social facts has a fundamentally procedural and public character.

Social practices can never realize their character as practices in isolation: they always require *further* practices for the possibility of criticism and practical argument. This is because what a collective attitude entails in a particular context can only be determined under the assumption of further rules.[45] All particular practices are therefore necessarily integrated in systems of other practices. More specific forms of recognition must always be accompanied by unspecific, general, higher-order forms of recognition, which can only be practically realized in specific forms. This leads to the fact – to address a final problem – that the individuation of practices must itself be part of the argument about practices and cannot be achieved at the level of social ontological analysis. Where one practice begins and another ends only becomes relevant when we question which particular demands for recognition may be introduced in a given conflict and which higher-order norms can be appealed to. Therefore, this question is always a part of the conflict itself.[46]

7.2.2 Excursus: Pathologies of Social Normativity

The constitutive elements of social normativity have thus far been described by reference to ideal types – that is, by assuming conditions that are not normally given. In all normative communities, relations of mutual recognition are at least in part replaced by power and violence, by the prohibition of criticism or by the suppression of dissent. The appearance of normative unity is manufactured in such cases by other ('illegitimate') means. Moreover, no normative practice is ever free from the suspicion that conflicts that arise in the future will reveal such elements.

Therefore, it is worth examining the *changes and pathologies* to which systems of social normativity will be exposed if the idealized conditions of the validity of social norms are violated. For this purpose, I will introduce arguments from H. L. A. Hart's theory of law. Hart's model of social norms, which primarily aims to explain the possibility of positive law, consists in two elements – on the one hand, the rules that are *adhered to* in the everyday actions of the citizens of a state, and on the other hand, the rules that are *explicitly recognized* as rules in official actions concerned with rule enforcement. A pathology[47] occurs in such a system when the rules in both areas diverge beyond a certain extent – that is, when people consistently act in everyday life in a way that differs from what is legally recognized as required by the official codes, or conversely, if rules other than those norms that citizens observe are officially recognized as law. Such a divergence can be caused both by a change in the practice and also by a change in the official norms, and it can arise spontaneously (for example, with the collapse of a weak state) or be consciously brought about (from civil disobedience to revolution).

The present model of social practices, which does not primarily aim to explain the validity of legal norms, can take up this definition of a pathology and apply it at a deeper level: there can be pathologies in Hart's sense even in the context of social norms constituted by reciprocal recognition. We can, for example, imagine a community that *explicitly recognizes* certain norms by virtue of the fact that these norms are regularly described as the norms of a community, are cited in practical conflicts as justifications and so on. This would allow us to say that, in the normative actions of the community, reference to this norm constitutes the reflexive moment. A pathological situation (in the sense in which Hart applies the term 'pathology') would arise in such a community if this explicit, normative framework no longer cohered with the collective attitudes constituted by recognition. This would then be the case if people who violated these norms no longer, or only begrudgingly, accepted criticism of their behaviour which referred to these norms, if they no longer recognized the collectively expressed critique in the name of these norms as a correct interpretation of their own normative reference points, and if they were increasingly less disposed to ascribe to other members the authority to practice critique under reference to the explicit collective attitudes.

Such a pathological situation will have two consequences. It will first – at least temporarily – *weaken* the *reflexivity* of social action: in the long run, those who no longer practically recognize certain norms as an appropriate standard for critiquing their actions can also no longer maintain the explicit belief that they are orienting themselves to this norm. Secondly, in the corresponding area of social interactions, the readiness to recognize the criticism or evaluations of others will have a tendency to decline in general, as the difference between explicit and implicit norms leads to a situation in which the implicit recognition relations can no longer find expression and thereby forfeit their normative force *altogether*. As long as no alternative standard that competes with the explicitly accepted norm is formed within the practice of mutual evaluation in such a way that it can at least potentially be made explicit as an alternative, the standards for reciprocal recognition will be imprecise, vague and uncontrollable and thus will not appear to create any obligations. A pathology of specific social norms will therefore always also have the effect of weakening the binding force of social normativity as a whole.

It is clear at this point how this formal concept of pathology is connected to how the sociological tradition employed this term, in particular to

Durkheim's theory of anomie.[48] Durkheim also assumes that in social crises, the communal commitment to communal rules wanes in force and thereby clears the way for anomic phenomena. In this sense, every social situation that involves a weakening of the practical force of the explicitly accepted norms would then be a pathology.

However, as soon as implicit and explicit norms are distinguished from each other, it is easy to see that a pathology in Hart's sense need not always lead to such an anomic weakening. Incongruity between explicit and implicit norms can develop in various forms: in addition to the possibility of the *collapse* of the power of explicit norms, there is always the possibility that *competing interpretations* of the common norms will emerge, or even that the idea that the communal practice demands new norms will be accepted. In these cases, everything depends on how the recognition relations are constituted. If these relations allow for the possibility of explicitly raising the question of the proper criteria according to which the interpretations (or normative assumptions) of individual agents are to be collectively recognized at the level of explicit norms, then the social pathology can be dealt with as an explicit conflict.

Therefore, labelling *all* conflicts between explicit and implicit norms pathologies appears too hasty. Such conflicts are only a sign that certain implicit norms cannot yet be recognized and that, consequently, social change is probable. A social pathology deserving of the name emerges only when the dynamic that arises from the incongruence between explicit and implicit norms cannot be dealt with as an *explicit conflict about norms* for systematic reasons. Such a pathology only exists when it is not only impossible in the framework of a practice to explicitly recognize the thus far implicit norms, but the *rules of the practice already* obstruct *recognition of the fact* that the practical commitments of the agents have normative significance. In this situation, the practical, implicit commitments of whole groups, or indeed of all members of society, cannot come up for consideration for structural reasons. One could call this a 'structural reflexivity deficit' or a 'second-order pathology'.[49]

Such *second-order pathologies* emerge when the normative structure of a community is constituted such that it is impossible to criticize those parts of its structure that do not properly reflect normative change that has already happened at the level of the implicit norms, or if such criticism is not accepted as a legitimate part of the practice at issue. Such pathologies are caused by the fact that the criteria for deciding which interpretations to recognize are themselves considered not to have been socially instituted (and therefore changeable) but *given in advance*. A community where it is impossible to question the criteria according to which those forms of social status are ascribed that ground the authority to evaluate other people's interpretations of communal norms can only react to social pathologies with the suppression of conflict, with struggles that are not normatively regulated or with its own dissolution.[50]

These two forms of social pathology correspond to two forms of social critique. In those situations in which divergences between the explicit (in Hart's case, legal) order and the immanent recognition relations can become thematic within the given normative order, in which this conflict can thus develop into an explicit conflict about the legitimacy of the normative commitments, the task of social critique is of a primarily *expressive* nature: the social scientific examination of the claims that are implicitly contained in the normative reactions and needs of the members can prepare the way for making these claims explicit, which is necessary if they are to become an explicit alternative to the dominant order and to become perceivable and justifiable (and possibly also rejectable)[51] as an explicit alternative. In the second case, the genuinely pathological situation of a social reflexivity deficit, in which such a thematization in the framework of a meta-order of recognition is not possible, the task of social critique is a more important one. Here, the fact that the higher-order rules of the normative order at issue obstruct the corresponding recognition claims from becoming explicit needs to be subjected to critique.

7.3 SUMMARY OF THE ARGUMENT

This chapter and the previous one provide an answer to the question of how we can understand the thesis that immanent norms can be located in social practices. The discussion of the rule-following problem has shown that the statement that a person or a group is following a rule is only comprehensible if we understand it as a claim to the effect that the action of the respective agent has a certain status to which they can refer for their justification. This status – such is the basic idea of a social theory of rule-following – is a social status, that is, a status that individuals gain through their participation in a community. The orientation to a collective practice or a collective evaluation, however, can only be understood as both normative and fallible if we imagine it as part of an overall practice in which people attribute authority to each other through their reciprocal recognition. On the basis of this conception, I developed a model of practices of recognition, which can serve as the basis for an answer to the question of immanent normativity. According to such a model, explicit normative beliefs are not necessary for a community to commit itself to a norm in such a practice.

For immanent critique – that is, independently of the more general discussion of rule-following – it is of decisive importance that the model proposed here can grasp s*ocial conflicts* as essential moments of social practices. Every social action necessarily involves the risk of a divergence between individual and collective attitudes, which can always potentially lead to normative conflict. There is therefore a source of both normative conflict and normative progress in the nature of social action itself, as every action is always at the same time an interpretation of a shared normative framework. As such an interpretation, it can be subjected to critique.

What exactly does it then mean to say that immanent norms exist in a practice? The claim of this chapter is that, insofar as members of a community mutually ascribe a default evaluative authority to each other, there exist immanent, collectively accepted norms that in principle can deviate from the norms with respect to which those people are disposed to explicitly accept them.

It could be objected that the explicit collective acceptance of norms was already explained through recognition relations and that it therefore appears that a community can *never* collectively accept norms in an explicit form without to some degree also accepting them implicitly at the level of the practice. This is true, but only in a specific sense: in any case in which a community collectively accepts certain norms, it must also be the case that the members of the community mutually ascribe a default evaluative authority to norms that regulate which consequences follow from this collective acceptance. But this does not answer the question of *which* pragmatic consequences the respective community ascribes to the collective, explicit acceptance of any given norm. We can imagine a community in which certain norms are explicitly collectively accepted, and in which it only follows from this collective acceptance that the members ascribe a default authority to each other exclusively with respect to their discursive behaviour, but not with respect to the practical implementation of these norms. In such a community, the members would treat one another as obligated only to *say* they are committed to the norm, not to act in any specific way. It would not be incorrect to say that in such a community the respective norms are collectively accepted, but only in an insincere way.

The collective acceptance of *explicit* norms must consequently be understood such that it is about the reciprocal ascription of a default evaluative authority regarding the discursive behaviour of the members of the respective community. The acceptance of explicit norms is therefore expressed above all in the fact that the members commit themselves to certain norms, which they are obliged *to discursively affirm* together. The *implicit* acceptance of *immanent* norms is constituted such that it consists in the reciprocal ascription of a default authority, which is primarily expressed not through evaluations of the discursive behaviour of other members but through evaluations of nondiscursive evaluations, and through nondiscursive evaluations of the nondiscursive behaviour of others.

We can therefore conceive not only of cases in which the discursively explicit acceptance of norms has practically no consequence, but also of cases in which norms are accepted in a way that limits their practical significance to the discursive. Such a situation in which a community only pays lip service to a range of norms can emerge when its members do not hold each other responsible for the practical consequences of their commitments. But it can also be a consequence of a situation in which it is too unclear which practical consequences follow from a particular norm, or in which the participants are simply not motivated to develop a practice of sanctioning each other. Conversely, in our everyday lives, we can find practices governed by norms of honour, shame and other reactions in many areas that are not discursively explicit and that remain largely implicit. Such immanent norms always exist when people treat each other as justified in acting as representatives of collectively shared norms, without thereby making it explicit which norms they take themselves to be bound by.

If immanent norms compete with explicit commitments in a community, then a new possibility emerges for social critique: it can criticize the explicitly accepted norms and the behavioural regularities at the same time by referring to the immanent norms that are constituted by a readiness to accept collective evaluations. For a theory of social critique, analysis of this possibility primarily contributes to clarifying the claim that there are immanent norms. The question of which consequences for the methodology of social theory are to be drawn from the arguments presented here, and whether they allow us to justify even stronger forms of critique, still remains open.

Chapter Eight

The Possibility of Immanent Critique

We now have an answer to the question of which social ontological presuppositions a theory of immanent critique must accept: The norms to which immanent critique refers are realized in social practices. They are institutionalized in these practices in the form of a specific kind of ascription of context-specific, reciprocal default evaluative authority, which I have called 'recognition'. An agent recognizes an interaction partner as a member of such a practice if they treat their partner as a legitimate member of a community that is constituted through a collective attitude such that the community may evaluate actions that belong to that practice. This community's evaluations are themselves contestable with reference to other, higher-order norms.

What follows from this for a theory of immanent critique? Immanent social critique – if one accepts this description – refers to norms that are practically institutionalized in relations of recognition. As these norms are only indirectly articulations of a 'self-understanding', immanent critique goes beyond mere interpretation. It can, however, integrate aspects of the hermeneutic model of critique: as soon as it is accepted that interpretively and narratively constituted self-understandings are constituted by normative commitments within a *specific* type of human practice – namely, practices of discursive, interpretative investigation of one's own identity – which is systematically linked to other practices, then it becomes clear how the norms connected to such self-understandings are practically *institutionalized*, on the one hand, and where their *normative force* and the dynamic of their internal conflicts come from, on the other: from the never-ending struggles for recognition.

This model of critique also goes beyond Habermas's and Honneth's more sophisticated social theoretical models: critique, according to this model, draws on practical norms that are not limited to the preconditions of communicative action or to normative claims that are necessary for the development of undamaged identities. Rather, the model discussed here proceeds from a question that is not sufficiently answered by either Habermas or Honneth: the question of how norms can be socially institutionalized such that conflicts regarding them can be recognized as *social* conflicts (in distinction to other pathologies).

What is immanent critique, then, when we understand immanent normativity in this way? *Immanent critique (a) criticizes the actual behaviour of participants in a practice, their explicit normative convictions or both components at the same time, (b) on the basis of the immanent norms of the practice, (c) in order to make reasons that speak in favour of changing the practice available to those participants.*

Even if one clearly cannot prematurely distil a political theory out of this model of social practices, this abstract definition of immanent critique can still be supplemented by a more detailed argument that examines how immanent critique can actually proceed in relevant social situations, what kinds of arguments can be offered in these situations and what reasons members can give for their respective actions.

The argument of this chapter will proceed by identifying a number of typical instances of immanent critique (8.1) in order to then analyse the various forms of social conflict from which immanent critique can emerge in such situations (8.2). This will allow me to discuss the questions of the epistemology and practice of critique (section 8.3), as well as the problem of progress (section 8.4). Finally, the idea of 'constitutive contradictions' will be discussed, which represents a key part of the classical model of immanent critique (section 8.5).

8.1 SITUATIONS OF IMMANENT CRITIQUE

Situations in which immanent critique can emerge are characterized by the fact that there are immanent norms that are implicit in the relations of recognition that make up a practice. But immanent critique is only a meaningful possibility in such situations if these immanent norms are not in agreement with the explicitly recognized norms – if all immanent norms are also explicitly available, then immanent critique is unnecessary, as there is nothing to reconstruct. The situations in which immanent critique can occur are therefore precisely those situations that, with Hart, we can call *pathologies of a social practice*,[1] but which can be better described as a specific form of social conflict. In such situations, the explicitly and practically recognized social norms deviate from each other.

To understand the possibility of this kind of conflict, it is necessary to distinguish three kinds of norms in social practices. In addition to the norms that a group of people explicitly and discursively accept, and the norms that immanently apply to this group because their members ascribe a default evaluative authority to each other with respect to them, there are also 'norms' in the sense of de facto regularities that the behaviour of these members exhibit. A group can explicitly recognize a specific set of norms, its members can grant themselves evaluative authority in relation to another set and they can nonetheless act according to neither set of norms.

We can therefore distinguish three levels in a practice:

1. The level of explicitly accepted norms
2. The level at which the members of the practice reciprocally accept each other as entitled to evaluate their behaviour in the name of a collective attitude
3. The level of regularities in actual behaviour

Immanent critique relies on the norms of the second level and can therefore criticize *both* the actual practice *and* the explicitly accepted norms. This form of critique is possible even if both of these levels are consistent with each other – that is, if the explicitly accepted norms are also actually adhered to.

We can assume that immanent critique is relevant only in those situations in which the explicitly accepted norms and the regularities of the actual practice agree, that is, situations in which *internal* critique is not possible. In all other cases, one might think, critics can refer to the contradiction between explicit norms and actual behaviour even without engaging in immanent critique. However, such agreement between the explicit and the actual will only occur in exceptional cases. This is because, on the one hand, social groups almost never fully observe their explicitly accepted norms, and, on the other, all three components are subject to continual changes in most social situations, such that the assumption of an 'agreement' between two levels can only refer to a momentary occurrence in any case.

Is immanent critique therefore merely a rare and peripheral form of critique? Even if this appears prima facie to be the case, the answer must be no. We can first imagine a case of a group that comes close to acting in accordance with the norms its members explicitly accept. In such a case, internal critique – that points out remaining minor inconsistencies between explicitly accepted norms and actual behaviour – is possible. It would not, however, be especially insightful. In such a case, immanent critique makes possible a more extensive set of objections to the respective practice. Secondly, it is still the case that even if internal critique is possible and meaningful, the question of *which direction* resolution of the contradiction between norm and reality should take – that is, whether the norms or the behaviour must be changed

– remains open. Immanent critique can play a decisive role in such situations through its reference to immanent norms and their relevance for the practice.

8.2 SOCIAL NORMS AND SOCIAL CONFLICT

Immanent norms are established in social practices by the fact that those involved mutually ascribe a default entitlement to reciprocally evaluate their behaviour. Up to now, the critique of the *individual behaviour* of social agents has been described as the paradigmatic form of such evaluation. This kind of critique – which is not yet social critique – therefore always already exists as a possible 'move' in normative social practices *as such*.

Such criticism *of individual actions*, which is always made possible by the normative framework of any given practice, must not, however, be equated with a critique *of the practice*. Nevertheless, it is worth first taking a brief look at the critique of individuals' actions *in* practices in order to understand how social critique in the narrow sense – that is, critique *of* practices – can develop from it. In this section, I will therefore develop an account of the general role of conflicts in practices (8.2.1), the necessary reflexivity of immanent critique (8.2.2) and the transition from social conflict to social critique (8.2.3). Finally (8.2.4), I will distinguish two forms of social practice with respect to their handling of critique.

8.2.1 Conflicts in Social Practices

Within social practices, conflicts always take place when a specific form of behaviour is under consideration and is negatively evaluated (and therefore 'criticized' in the widest sense). Whenever a certain kind of behaviour is criticized, we can take this to mean that the behaviour does not conform to the rules that are constitutive of the practice and that it is therefore 'outside' the practice. Conversely, the absence of critique would at least tend to signal that the rules of the practice are adhered to. Criticism would therefore always be an indication that a social practice is not functioning well in the full sense.

This would be a misunderstanding, however. In contrast to a conformist understanding of social practices, which understands membership as the simple *agreement* of behaviour with a collectively accepted regularity, the model presented here understands membership in a practice not in terms of the *conformity* of one's own behaviour with that of others but as a *normative commitment to the authority of the community*. As the normativity argument concerning rule-following shows, normative commitment to a rule must always be understood as fallible – one can follow a rule even if one violates it. Therefore, the fact that an individual's behaviour is subjected to critique is not a sign that it stands 'outside' the practice. Rather, the readiness of the members of a practice both to accept criticism of their rule-violating behaviour and to criticize the behaviour of others shows that they are committed to the rule *especially* in situations of nonconformity.

The same argument also applies to reactions to critique: it is not the actual, 'conformist' acceptance of critique that is constitutive of individuals' commitment to a rule but rather their normative readiness, in principle, to accept further criticism of their reactions to criticism. It is therefore never actual behaviour but always *readiness* to participate in *further* practical processes of negotiation, if they become necessary, that integrates an individual into a practice. Put differently: conflicts about the reciprocal evaluation of actions are not pathologies or dangers to the cohesion of a practice but rather the genuine mode of existence of social normativity.

8.2.2 The Reflexivity of Immanent Critique

When differences in the application of norms arise, those involved are usually forced to make explicit, in a minimal sense, the rules that they previously perhaps only followed immanently.[2] In order for a token of behaviour to be understood as a sanction at all, its relationship to a rule must be intelligible in a minimal sense to those involved. Individuals need not necessarily understand *which* rule forms the basis of their being sanctioned. A sanction must, however, be comprehensible as something that sanctions failure to conform to *some* – in the borderline case, unspecified – rule and therefore at least in some sense convey the message 'One does not do that'.

In contrast to mere sanctioning, *critique* goes beyond this minimal reflexivity: it is precisely when there is no longer agreement about which behaviour in a certain context is correct that reference to an abstract rule on the model of 'What we do in this situation is this' is no longer sufficient. In the critique of behaviour that is collectively evaluated as false, it must be made explicit *which* rule was violated, and an interpretation must be brought forwards that makes the norm governing the ascription of a practical standard of correctness explicit, in the form of a rule. The articulation of *reasons for sanctions* thus has an *expressive* function: it should express a rule to which the community may be assumed to have committed itself (by means of its members forming corresponding recognitive expectations) but which, through deviant behaviour, now stands in question. As soon as such a sanction is in turn contested, and as soon as a deviating individual insists on their expectation of recognition, they can only sustain this expectation of recognition by articulating a *critique* of the prevailing understanding of the practice, as expressed in its explicit rules. In this case, the explicitly accepted rules not only become thematic through the explicit interpretation that is offered but can be called into question. Therefore, it is always a central moment of social conflicts when agents attempt to make explicit parts of the *previously implicit totality of normative reaction and recognitive expectations*.

Those who rebel against a previously hegemonic interpretation of a norm must therefore first develop an alternative set of norms that – they can then attempt to argue – better agrees with the totality of the practice's governing recognitive expectations than the norms that presently explicitly legitimate the behaviour of other agents.[3] In the simplest case, immanent critique justifies an alternative by reference to its greater consistency with the immanent norms, and in more complicated cases such an attempt will lead to the emergence of other normative systems to which critique can then refer.

8.2.3 From Critique in Practices to Critique of Practices

Even this form of critique initially remains only an *individual critique* of the behaviour of *individuals*, as long as the criticized normative reaction is understood only as an individual misinterpretation of a rule and not as an expression of collective attitudes. A connection between the critique of individual behaviour and social critique only becomes apparent when we consider cases in which an agent's recognitive expectations are frustrated by an evaluation that they must understand as a *collective* evaluation. In this case, they can dispute the default authority of the collective reaction to their own attitude either with reasons relating to their own particular case – for example, by proposing an argument that justifies an exception – or by invoking facts of which the community was previously unaware. They can also, however, bring forward reasons to think that the collective reaction is *unjustified in general* – that the explicit norms of a community are false against the background of immanent norms.[4]

The repudiation of normative reactions in social conflicts can therefore deploy three kinds of reasons: it can dispute that the evaluated behaviour is a case that *falls under* the recognized norm, it can dispute that those who undertake the evaluation are *entitled* to do so or it can deny that the *correct norm* is being applied in the right way. The third objection in particular is prototypical of the move to social critique. Social critique in a narrow sense, however, is not about norms that only concern individual action but rather about norms that concern socially constituted practices.

Immanent social critique is therefore a possible action in social conflicts which consists in the possibility of criticizing a social practice of socially institutionalized, explicit normative evaluations by making reference to its immanent norms, with the aim of making them explicit and showing that they require that the explicitly accepted norms must be rejected.

8.2.4 Excursus: Liberal and Conservative Practices

The role of conflicts in social practices must be emphasized so strongly because without this pointed emphasis it would seem that the insight that the normative force of critique is strongly dependent on social foundations necessarily leads us to a conservative position. In particular, the idea that the validity of social norms is always bound to the recognition of the authority of a community could be understood in such a way that a conformist-integrative position follows: if the normative content of a position is ultimately only constituted by the justifications that can be brought forward for this position from within the practices of a given community, it appears that, in the end, the community's practices will always prevail against critique. Sabina Lovibond therefore rightly questions whether it is not paradoxical to try to build the idea of a social critique on a radical social theory of normativity:

> On that view [which is committed to a social theory of norms], our competence with moral language ... arises organically out of our personal experience in the relevant social practices. ... How, then, could we ever find ourselves in a position to pass a negative verdict on the rationality of the commitment brought to light by philosophical self-scrutiny? How could there be such a thing as a reasoned rejection of those commitments? For it is precisely our personal history of participation in language-games which, according to the present line of thought, equips us to reason about anything at all.[5]

This doubt is taken up by conservative conceptions of social practices, which dispute the possibility of radical critique: as each of our reasons receives its force only from our participation in a social practice – such is the conservative argument – only a local critique of certain aspects of a normative practice is conceivable. However, the constitutive role which the network of institutions and practices plays as a whole must remain superior against the critical interventions of individuals. Individuals ultimately have no other choice than to recognize the norms of the dominant practice, if they do not want to abandon their membership in the community altogether.

Lovibond justifiably rejects the conservative argument that an individual's rejection of a central norm of a practice necessarily entails that they are no longer taking part in that practice. This presupposition is not self-evidently true. The fact that a fundamental consensus on the interpretation of the rules is a precondition for critical judgements means only that a person can no longer make critical judgements regarding a practice if they no longer agree to *any* shared interpretation of *any* common rule. However, whether a critic ends up adopting such a radically antagonistic stance depends not only on the critic but also on the other members of the relevant community: a local critique only leads to a global rejection of a normative order if there is a consensus among the other members of the relevant community that the diverging interpretation of the norm is not only *false* in light of all the other common norms but *cannot count as an interpretation of the relevant norms at all*. This means that the deviating member is not only characterized as rejecting a specific collectively shared interpretation of a norm but also classified as a person who is not bound to the constitutive norms of the practice in such a way that their interpretation of norms can count as an interpretation of the same norms that the other members accept.

This exclusion of a deviant judgement and its authors from the relevant community is not automatic, however, but only *one* possible result of a practical, rule-governed decision about how to handle criticism and about the question of when a reaction counts as withdrawal from the common commitment to a norm and when it should only be counted as a diverging interpretation of a norm that is still substantially shared. If one understands the question of whether people are referring to the 'same' or 'different' rules not as a metaphysical question but as a question about social justification, then we can understand different ways of treating radical critique as the result of a collective decision about the criteria that govern the distribution of a certain form of social status. That is, we can understand these ways of treating critique as resulting from a *political* decision. Lovibond distinguishes between two strategies, which she calls 'liberal' and 'conservative':

> The adherents of these different positions should, I believe, be seen as advocates of different policies towards deviant or *unsittlich* behaviour. The liberal commends a policy of toleration – of keeping an open mind as to whether the anomalous way of acting can be brought into connection with established social practices; the conservative, by contrast, calls for a strict policing of *Sittlichkeit* and demands positive disciplinary measures against the author of any anomaly. The relevant discipline consists in a withdrawal of the recognition previously extended to that person as a serious participant in the language-game.[6]

The contrast between both positions is less clear than Lovibond assumes, however. First, the two strategies of liberalism and conservatism, as described, are only limiting cases. Neither an unlimited liberalism (which allows any combination of behaviours to count as an interpretation of common norms) nor an unlimited conservatism (which classifies every deviation as a sufficient reason for the retraction of membership status) is practically conceivable. At most, communities can adopt these strategies in relation to certain classes of problems and certain classes of deviations. Secondly, even for a conservative community, there is more than one way to deal with deviant interpretations: besides exclusion, the option of sanctioning behaviour is always available. All the same, the difference that Lovibond identifies is of fundamental importance: the question of whether a person's actions should count as a failed attempt to satisfy a norm or rather as evidence that they are bound to a completely different norm, or no norm at all, is identified as an eminently political question, which is not answerable through recourse to theoretical reflections alone.

8.3 EPISTEMOLOGY AND THE PRACTICE OF IMMANENT CRITIQUE

Immanent critique as a form of social critique takes place when the members of a community in everyday situations criticize *both* their explicit norms *and* their actual practices with reference to implicit normative obligations – obligations to which they take themselves to be committed and which they presuppose (rightly or wrongly) to be collectively binding. With respect to this form of critique, the question of normative epistemology almost solves itself: the search for the correct social norms is above all not to be conceived as a process of *gaining knowledge of an independently given fact* but as a search for the correct *expression* of the commitments held in common – that is, as a process in which a position is taken in the social conflicts on the correct self-understanding of a community.

Therefore, the ability to 'recognize' the norms immanent in situations of social conflict must fulfil two functions: First, those who have reason to engage in critique – that is, the members of groups which have been oppressed or unjustly treated in some sense – must be able to develop an alternative to the explicitly recognized rules of their community. Secondly, they must be able to *justify* the claim that these new, alternative norms deserve recognition as a better expression of the immanent norms of the practice than the norms that are currently accepted.

The first requirement cannot be easily captured by theory because it is only met whenever agents develop a new understanding of their practice that makes a new description of it available to them. To a certain degree, they must distance themselves from the currently accepted understanding of the practice and independently develop a new one. As soon as this creative achievement is completed, however, the theory of immanent critique can make the second requirement comprehensible: the *justification of normative interpretations*. It is not difficult to find examples of such justifications:

many explicit rules – for example, laws, regulations or even the explicit self-conceptions of groups, communities or whole states – are regularly criticized by the members of these social groups for contradicting their implicit self-conception: 'This is not who we want to be!'

However, a theory of immanent critique must go beyond the mere *identification* of this everyday normative strategy. Without postulating an epistemic break in a narrow sense, one can assume that models of critique – as found in critical social theories – are not only reconstructions of the everyday activity of criticism but can claim to clarify the methodological preconditions of social critique.[7] The model I have developed thus far suggests that the first stage of such a methodological clarification of immanent critique consists in considering which normative features participants in social conflicts can refer to in social conflicts (not only from case to case, but *systematically*) to justify their alternative interpretations of the norms of the social practices of the community.

I will first discuss the epistemic aspects of arriving at such a justification (8.3.1). I will then examine the question of how the reference to the immanent norms developed in this way in a practice can acquire rational force. This relates to the practice of critique (8.3.2).

8.3.1 Epistemology

The question of epistemology – which here will only be examined in its second, 'justificatory' aspect – can initially be clarified by means of examining the possible evidence that a person might produce for the claim that a particular community is bound by a particular immanent norm. It is useful to consider once more the discussion of rule-following which proceeded from Kripke's provocative argument that there can be no such evidence in a narrow sense since no 'facts' are sufficient to justify the assumption that a person (or a group) is following a rule. In analysing that argument, however, it turned out that such 'facts' are not even necessary, when one considers that producing evidence for ascriptions of rule-following can only play a role in the context of normative conflicts. Just as people in everyday situations can produce evidence for the claim that they are following a rule, so can critics regarding immanent norms.

As I have argued in the case of individual rule-following, a person is entitled to claim that they are following a rule in the normal case not only if their behaviour generally conforms to the collectively shared understanding of what it means to follow that rule but if they are also willing (and have been willing in the past) to accept the default authority of other members in cases where deviation from the rule is alleged. This argument can now be applied to the question of when a community can justifiably be said to be following a rule, a question that is at the core of the epistemology of immanent critique. A critic, then, can justifiably claim that a community is immanently committed to a specific norm if they can produce evidence that a certain standard exists in the normative interactions of that community, in light of which those who interact reciprocally ascribe default authority to each other's evaluations.

The persuasiveness of such a description of the interactions within a community assumes – as hermeneutic theories rightly recognize – a shared *horizon of understanding* concerning the question of what counts as evidence for such a description. Hermeneutic theories in Taylor's sense also correctly emphasize that it is only through the articulation of a norm in a specific normative vocabulary that the unarticulated and habitual normative practical attitudes that are institutionalized in the interactions of a community can be given a clearer, and thereby discursively negotiable, content: The expressive vocabulary that people employ when referring to implicit attitudes in order to justify their normative positions does not leave those attitudes untouched. Rather, interpreters give these attitudes a definite form and a new meaning by describing them in such a vocabulary, which in turn shapes the actual behaviour in these social practices.

All the same, the practice of articulating immanent norms goes beyond the aspects reconstructed by the hermeneutic models, as a reconstruction of immanent norms is not properly understood as an articulation of already existing, semantically rich 'self-understandings' or 'identities' but as an articulation that must be measured against the practice of a community, which can contradict the explicit self-understanding of the community in question and which can only be reinterpreted to a limited extent. An articulation can only count as an informative interpretation of the practice if the actual normative interactions on the various levels can be explained through it in such a way that they can be broadly understood as rational with respect to the articulated principle, or at least can be explained in their inconsistency. Further, any articulation of an immanent norm must pass the test that comes along with the ascription of a collective attitude of acceptance of that norm: it can only count as a good articulation if present and future practical normative conflicts are comprehensible via reference to the proposed norm.

The communally shared horizon of normative preconceptions therefore only acts as a *precondition* in this process. Evidence that is presented as part of immanent critique for the correctness of a proposed articulation of the norms at issue goes beyond a mere suggestion regarding how one could understand a shared practice better or differently. Rather, such evidence consists in empirically backed ascriptions of implicit norms, which must always be evaluated with respect to actual normative behaviour.

How might this epistemological model apply in the practice of immanent critique? One must assume that immanent critique seeks to show that the practices of reciprocal normative evaluation in a community – correctly understood – refer to norms that the participants did not previously explicitly recognize.

One cannot simply muster all the observable behaviour of members of a practice as evidence for such norms – at least some parts of their behaviour should not be reconstructed by critique but *changed* by it. However, it is also hardly sufficient to take the entirety of the actual, normatively laden *reactions* to behaviour as a foundation for critique. Even if we may normally assume that the normative reactions that can be observed in a community may be understood as an expression of their commitment to immanent norms, a mere description of these normative reactions cannot be sufficient. Obviously, every community's practices will contain some normative interactions that do not conform to its immanently recognized norms. For example, the fact that some members do not accept certain normative reactions but rather explicitly treat them as false may spark a conflict in a community about what their implicit norms are. It is thus always an open question which reactions are implicitly recognized as correct. Therefore, critique must focus on the *higher-order* reactions – that is, reactions *to normative reactions*.[8] This is because reacting normatively to the expression of a collective attitude means taking a stance on the question of which standards one takes oneself to be collectively bound by. Examples of such reactions are reactions to public sanctions, to the rebuke of others and to official and unofficial evaluations of the behaviour of others conducted by those in whom the normative authority of the group is invested. For example, it is only the *reactions* of family members *to other family members' reactions* that show which norms apply in a family. That a family is committed to antiauthoritarian norms, for example, is not simply a matter of the parents never punishing their children. Rather, whether this is so depends on how family members collectively react if such punishment occurs or is attempted: if the children react with indignation, if the other parent expresses criticism and if the parent who engaged in the behaviour is ashamed, we can assume that, practically speaking, this family *treats itself* as a family that is committed to antiauthoritarian norms.

Such reactions do not constitute behaviour that can be identified without paying attention to the normative context. Whether a certain behaviour on the part of a community is actually an instance of a normative evaluation, and whether certain evaluations are sufficient evidence for the existence of collective attitudes, cannot be clarified independently of the question of which further general rules that community follows. The claim that a specific immanent norm is laid out in the practice of a group can only be meaningfully justified against the background of a presupposed agreement among the participants on what the relevant normative behaviour is.

The epistemology of immanent normativity therefore contains, in addition to the already mentioned empirical evidence, another irreducibly hermeneutic moment that can only be understood from a participant's perspective. All the same, the process of identifying the relevant norms is not to be equated with a process of pure 'interpretation', as described by the hermeneutic models. The normative reactions to collective evaluations to which immanent critique refers are, in their normative content, *precisely not* constitutively dependent on the first-order self-interpretations that agents bring to this practice. Put simply: the answer to the question of which norms are immanently accepted through such reactions is not dependent on how the agent in question understands their *own* action. Rather, the content of normative reactions is constituted by the self-understanding of the agents in a different, indirect sense. By treating certain reactions *as normative reactions* and integrating them into their social practice, they *create* the material from which immanent critique can reconstruct normative standards without recourse to explicit normative beliefs.

It must therefore 'only' be assumed that there is a consensus that serves as an epistemological background that determines which behaviour counts as evidence for the acceptance of norms. Insofar as this background is given, the critic can emend the self-ascriptions of the members on the basis of empirical evidence – which can be interpreted against this background. Under these conditions, the claim that a group recognizes and is following a norm is no longer a claim that depends on the agreement or consensus of the group itself. For example, if it can be proven of a particular community that their collective evaluations express a shared readiness to accept critique of certain behaviours in certain contexts, together with a readiness to collectively regulate these evaluations themselves, then that community is no longer free to simply reject the conclusion that they are in fact following a norm in their practice the explicit formulation of which can indeed be controversial but which is largely determined by the objective normative structure of that practice.

8.3.2 The Practice of Immanent Critique

(a) Two forms of contradiction. As was already shown at the beginning of this chapter,[9] immanent critique – unlike internal critique, which contrasts actual practice and explicitly accepted norms to each other – has to do with three components that are in principle independent of each other: first, regularities of behaviour; second, the explicitly accepted norms that relate to this behaviour; and third, the norms that are implicitly institutionalized in the normative

reactions to such behaviour. The interesting case for immanent critique is therefore that in which the regularity of the practice *and* its explicit norms harmonize with each other but contradict its immanent norms. There are two possible forms that such a contradiction can take. The first arises when, although certain explicit norms and rules are collectively recognized as binding and implemented in a social practice, the participants show a readiness to accept collective evaluations of actions – and to participate in collective evaluations of actions – that are inconsistent with these explicitly accepted norms. In such cases, critics are justified in mobilizing 'sociological' knowledge about the practice in order to point out inconsistencies between the implicit and the explicit norms. Resistance to 'official' evaluations is evidence for the hypothesis that other norms have evolved at the level of intersubjective recognition – norms that cannot be articulated at the level of the 'official' norms. The fact that such an inconsistency can develop in the first place – that is, that a social group systematically accepts norms that contradict official social norms in an inarticulate way – demands at least an explanation. Similarly, if we claim that there are implicit norms that are never articulated on the level of explicitly accepted rules, this claim will rightly be met with scepticism as long as it cannot be shown why the expected articulation of these initially implicit norms *fails* to occur. It is nonetheless often possible to correctly identify such reasons: for example, an adequate explanation of the emergence of contradictions between explicit and immanent norms can be found in the systematic exclusion of certain positions and norms from official discourse, in the existence of inadequacies in conceptual competence and discursive self-consciousness caused by deficient education, in structural discursive pathologies, in taboos and so on. If critics are able to identify causes of the divergence of the two levels of explicit and implicit norms, then they are justified in ascribing to the members of the corresponding groups acceptance of the immanent institutionalized norms. Many actual examples of social critique function like this: hardly any attempt to criticize a society's actual or alleged violations of its own immanently accepted norms can be justified without an explanation that attempts to show why many members of the society do not recognize or affirm this critique. If these explanations are successful – that is, if they actually show that, for example, the exclusion of dissent from public discourse, or systematic disinformation by the media, explains the ongoing acceptance of certain explicit norms – the claim that certain norms are immanently accepted cannot merely be defended as being potentially true but rather supported by argument, as manipulations of this sort are only necessary if they prevent the acceptance of norms that would be accepted in their absence.

Such a simple contradiction between sets of explicit and immanent norms is hardly the standard case, however. As a rule, it is not a simple a matter of reconstructing *one* consistent and unproblematic normative structure from actual practices and from a readiness to recognize evaluations, which then needs 'only' to be shown to contradict the explicit norms. In actual communities, it is usually the case that a web of competing practices is institutionalized, where each practice is structured by competing immanent *and* explicitly accepted norms. Resistance to 'official', explicitly formulated and enforced norms therefore does not usually rely on a consistent system of rules on the side of actual evaluations and officially recognized commitments that are confronted by another consistent system of normative attitudes. Rather, we would usually expect that conflicting patterns of reaction will compete with each other in practices, each of which more or less corresponds to a set of explicit rules.[10]

In this situation, the task is not simply one of reconstructing 'the' unified set of practical norms from observable interactions. Making the attempt to ascribe a consistent system of rules to actual social practices commits the mistake of already taking sides in social conflicts through one-sidedly interpreting the practical reactions found in that practice. Accordingly, a more complicated procedure is required in cases of complex practices. In this context, we can distinguish between two cases:

1. The problem of epistemic access is relatively simple to solve if the competition between various practical attitudes is also expressed *explicitly* in competing interpretations of one and the same norm, or even in competing norms. Examples are cases of political protest in which the various attitudes to one and the same practice are reflected in the form of fundamentally different political programmes or collective beliefs. In these cases, the self-understandings of the agents can be taken seriously: this is a genuine conflict about which norms are correct, which cannot be decided by social theory but only by the critic arguing for their own position in the context of the broader commitments of the community.
2. The more complex and interesting case for immanent critique is one in which one set of competing practically institutionalized norms *monopolizes* the level of explicitly acknowledged normative validity for itself. In this case, one set of norms, which corresponds to a part of the practical commitments of the community, is represented as the whole of the normative commitments of that community at the level of explicitly accepted norms and excludes the expression of competing practical attitudes as illegitimate.[11]

Frank Parkin argues for this understanding of the competition between 'official' and 'suppressed' value systems in his *Class Inequality and Political*

Order: 'It could be hypothesized that in situations where purely abstract evaluations are called for, the dominant value system will provide the moral frame of reference; but in concrete social situations involving choice and action the . . . subordinate value system . . . will provide the moral framework.'[12] Empirical evidence for the existence of such suppressed normative attitudes can be found above all in the *absence of readiness* to *sanction* the official norms. In practical reactions, the discursively affirmed values are shown not to be collectively binding. The reconstruction of such suppressed practical norms, however, is always only possible with a caveat: because the practical attitudes of the participating agents have not been transformed into consistent systems under the pressure of explicit discourse, any reconstruction of a single rule for their normative action is necessarily a counterfactual assumption, for which only hints and prima facie support (but not evidence in the strong sense) can be submitted. As previously explored, such empirical support will consist above all in showing that it is only through assuming practical acceptance of a certain norm, and through showing that this assumption is repeatedly confirmed in new situations, that the normative reactions of participants can be rationally understood.

Members' explicit agreement to the critic's reconstruction of their implicit norms (or of contradictions between such norms) therefore cannot serve as a touchstone for the reconstruction of their implicit attitudes, if these attitudes are ideologically delegitimized and their open acceptance carries social costs. It may only be possible to form hypotheses about which attitudes are constitutive of the normative practice under observation and about which norms the members of that practice *would* recognize if some of their evaluative intuitions were not systematically suppressed. The provisional character of such assumptions makes their justification at least partially dependent on the further course that normative conflicts take. Accordingly, in addition to a direct 'use' of these norms in substantive critique, the possibility of a shift to a meta level should not be neglected. Such a shift would ask how the social conditions that hinder agents from realizing certain norms and making them explicit are in turn systematically rooted in the practical attitudes of the members. Even if an explicit, social scientific emphasis on these conditions is not usually a part of everyday forms of critical discourse, we are nonetheless able, in nonscientific contexts, to heuristically determine whether people's failure to agree with the normative allegations we make against them is an expression of the fact that we have misunderstood them or an expression of the fact that certain conditions hinder them from gaining unimpaired access to the norms they already immanently accept. It is beyond doubt, of course, that this latter claim always stands in need of justification.

(b) The normative force of immanent critique. In adumbrating the situations to which immanent critique applies, the question of what makes the

norms recovered from practices *reasons* remains open. I will first discuss this question with respect to why (i) collective attitudes can be said to represent practical reasons in order to then (ii) propose a possible extension of the model that combines both reconstructive and transcendent aspects. The resulting model of critique is (iii) limited by the constant possibility of normative collapse, against which there is no conceptual guarantee.

(i) Actual normative attitudes as reasons. It has so far been taken as the standard case of immanent critique that participants in a practice thematize immanent norms in their normative discourses with the aim of justifying their own deviating normative reactions towards others by stipulating that there is another normative order laid out not in the explicit normative statements of other participants but in their practice, that is, in their actual behaviour.

This is an assertion that must be justified against the background of shared beliefs about how the community comprehends its own practice. This means that immanent critique itself is a normatively regulated activity that builds on an assumed consensus about which references to which practical behaviour should have a persuasive effect on interaction partners and should therefore be effective.

In order for a reference to immanent norms to count as a reason for those to whom it is addressed, there must be *norms* in the overarching social practice of a community that *qualify that reference as a reason*. The rational force of immanent critique is not transcendentally guaranteed but rather socially institutionalized. Immanent critique only has force when there is a readiness to count references to implicit institutional norms as arguments *at all*, and when there is consensus about *what kind of normative dispositions* one can refer to as an objection to certain norms. There must therefore be at least one implicitly (or explicitly) recognized metanorm that establishes that if one acknowledges that there are certain normative attitudes that are part of a practice, this represents a reason to also recognize the corresponding norms explicitly. The fact that the acceptance of such a metanorm is *not inevitable* does not mean, however, that it is *not rational* to accept it: it is imperative that rational agents ascribe at least a default justification to their own normative attitudes – because it is only when agents accept reference to their de facto normative attitudes in the past as prima facie reasons to act that they can ascribe an ongoing practical identity to themselves.[13]

(ii) Extensions of the model. However, it is not only the *existing* normative attitudes that can be introduced into normative conflicts as reasons. Parties to a conflict often also attempt to apply *counterfactual* normative reactions as reasons. In everyday life, people often try to make us consider how we would react to certain hypothetical situations to activate our normative imagination and to convince us that we should actually be sympathetic to behaviour that

we currently condemn and sanction as false in accordance with our explicitly advocated norms. In doing so, they attempt to convince us that we should not sanction it, as in essential aspects it resembles behaviour that we usually judge positively.

Such attempts are not limited to mobilizing *individual* dispositions: in disagreement over contested norms, for example, it is often the case that reference to the overarching community is of central importance. If one's own normative attitude is rejected by reference to a collective commitment, one can, for example, attempt to justify an objection against this evaluation by extending the relevant community: in this way, one can attempt to represent the contemporary or local dominance of an interpretation as a deviation from a temporally and spatially more extended practice.

As Thompson points out with regard to the English social revolts of the eighteenth century, normative reactions to certain material injustices that are initially expressed in spontaneous revolts can become reflexive protests if they are understood as expressions of rights that have belonged to the citizens of the country 'since forever'.[14] Even if the traditions or communities conjured up in such reflexive protests are often broadly fictitious and their 'recovery' equates to the establishment of new norms, it is nonetheless not the case that this is merely an ideological dressing up of self-interest. The reference to a temporally and locally extended community – which can contain the future as well as the past – must always rest on the potentials in the actually existing community. The power of the idea that 'future generations' will condemn a certain practice is ultimately dependent on the fact that it is accepted that although a future community is indeed freed of some 'disruptive' influence, in essence it still has the *same* normative commitments as the contemporary community.[15] That means that even the idea of counterfactual norm acceptance draws its normative power from the fact that it can justify, according to the accepted rules, a claim to make certain potentials explicit which are in a minimal sense already 'in' the 'existing' practice.

(iii) Critique without metaphysical guarantee. It can now be objected that the previously developed model of critique does not explain why those who are addressed by a critique *must accept it*. It is always possible that they will reject the interpretations of the common ascriptions of authority, or that they will reject the background hermeneutic principles adopted – that is, that they will not agree with the picture drawn of the recognitive structure on which the particular claims of immanent critique are based.

How we answer this objection depends on how we understand the 'must' in the idea that they 'must accept' the critique addressed to them. If this means that they *cannot do otherwise* than accept the critique, then this standard is certainly too high. Social norms are not fixed 'rails to infinity'[16] – they do not have the power of coercion. The normative necessity of socially institutionalized norms is not causal but social necessity.[17] If critics demand that the subjects of their critique accept a certain demand, then they are claiming only that the overarching social norms that the critic and the criticized share require the acceptance of this critique. There is no guarantee that these social norms will always have the last word. The power of normative commitments is not logically guaranteed but socially institutionalized, as it is supported by relationships that come along with the recognition of authorities. Such relationships can always break down. If it turns out that certain posited immanent norms are not actually institutionalized as obligatory relations of recognition, then immanent critique becomes useless. There can be no philosophical safeguard against this outcome.

8.4 IMMANENT CRITIQUE AND NORMATIVE PROGRESS

A final question concerns the idea of *progress* – that is, the question of how immanent critique can justify concrete change to normative practices as the best available option.

To begin with, it is constitutive of the possibility of immanent critique that there are norms in the practices of a community that prescribe that contradictions between implicit practice and explicit norms must be resolved. Our ability to use the immanent norms of a practice as reasons requires not only that members of that practice accept them as reasons but also that immanent collective attitudes can become an issue in the practice at all. The practice in question must therefore be reflexive to a certain extent – that is, it must be a practice in which the norms that govern it are at one's disposal to some degree. Only then does the reference to normative attitudes amount to a justified objection. In addition, the immanent, reactively institutionalized attitudes must be able to be transformed by the critic into explicit norms that can achieve acceptance as expressions of an implicit self-understanding.

Correlatively, it is only if a certain practice is generally understood as a normatively regulated sphere of interaction – and not merely as a sequence of contingent episodes, or as fully determined by necessity – that it makes sense to refer to its norms at all. By the same token, it is only the institutional possibility of the thematization of norms that creates a basis for critique. Ultimately, participants in a social practice must understand their behaviour as subject to a possible range of normative reactions. Only if all of these institutional preconditions obtain is it possible to thematize explicit norms, on the one hand, and to understand one's own behaviour as oriented to immanent norms that can find expression in the form of competing normative conceptions, on the other.

We must therefore presuppose the existence of institutional norms of the relevant kind. It can easily be shown, however, that this assumption is usually justified: the function of norms, of practices of justification and of evaluations, usually consists at least partly in regulating and controlling behaviour, or, put differently, in enabling decisions about what may and should be done in certain cases. If a community is composed in such a way that it accepts mutually incompatible norms in its explicit attitudes and in its implicit reactive readiness, then this function is endangered, at least prima facie. There may be practices in which the internally inconsistent fundamental reactive dispositions can only be preserved if they are not explicitly thematized, but such practices are necessarily *practically unstable*, as they are exposed to a risk that reflexive practices need not bear.

From this general justification of demands for normative consistency, it does not follow that either the *implicit* or the *explicit* norms should always be realized. Whether one normative system is 'better' than another can only be decided against the background of *further practices* of justification. The practices of intersubjective justification that form the context of any explicit norm therefore have absolute priority.

A community, therefore, is in no way *forced* to take evidence to the effect that there is an immanently institutionalized counternorm in its practice as a reason to adjust the practice to this norm. We might equally draw the conclusion that, given a context of further norms and other practices, the immanent norm, which perhaps previously was *incompatible* with other norms, now – having been made explicit – stands in *contradiction* to them and therefore should be abandoned together with its corresponding practice.

We can, for example, imagine a practice that is characterized by the explicit acceptance of a prohibition against discrimination but in which the members nonetheless implicitly accept racist or sexist norms. Not only does their behaviour contradict their explicitly accepted norms, but they mutually accept corresponding reactions to their own behaviour. This acceptance often expresses itself in a coded form, or in the form of subliminal sanctions of violations of the 'boundaries' of one's group. In such cases, naturally, a justified critique ought not to demand that the immanent, discriminatory norms should be realized. As this example shows, we should not assume that critique always ought to demand the realization of the immanent norms of a practice. In some cases, it must restrict itself to criticizing a social practice in which there is a contradiction between its immanent and explicit norms *as a whole*.

This limitation only applies, however, if, from the critic's perspective, it is taken for granted that the realization of the immanent norms would be normatively unacceptable. The force of immanent norms can only be overridden by other, more important, norms that rule out their application. A criterion of progress can therefore be formulated in the following way:

> If a practice P exists in which immanent social norms and explicit normative convictions stand in a relationship of mutual incompatibility, then a practice P' represents an advance over P if and only if
> (1) in P', a set of explicit norms N are accepted which are not subverted by incompatible immanent norms, and if either
> (2a) N integrates the previously immanent reactive attitudes, if these are acceptable in the context of the unproblematic normative standards of the community in question, or
> (2b) where the previously immanent reactive attitudes are not reflexively acceptable, the institutionalization of N in P' eliminates the causes that previously led in P to the development of the objectionable reactive attitudes.

The immanently institutionalized norms of a community must consequently be considered sources of reasons to revise its explicit norms at least *by default*. In the absence of overruling normative objections, everything speaks in favour of the fact that the norms that a community practically accepts should also be explicitly recognized and adopted, as they are constitutive of this community.

The fact that the members of a normative practice are bound by their normative reactions does not mean, however, that this commitment always has *the last word*. For us as individuals, our own normative judgements represent reasons to follow those judgements and to explicitly accept them, but these reasons can be countermanded, as we can form second-order judgements that qualify our reactions on the first level as prejudiced, irrational or false in other ways, thus allowing us to distance ourselves from them. In just the same way, a community can distance itself from its own immanent attitudes if it develops rational second-order attitudes.

This argument can also be connected to the idea that the interpretive critique of norms must be understood with reference to the concept of 'tradition'. The term 'tradition' denotes in this context a historically extended process of the interpretation and revision of self-understandings, which includes its own criteria for the appropriateness of such interpretations.[18] The basic idea of tradition models is that interpretations are valid if they can raise a claim to being a solution of previously open problems in the context of the previous revisions in the history of the tradition, and if they can make the previous developmental history of the tradition, including its problems, rationally reconstructible. In such a process, critique – according to the idea developed by means of MacIntyre's model – involves putting forward an opposing interpretation against the explicitly accepted norms of a community, which is justified by reference to the claim that this opposing interpretation is better justified in the context of the reconstruction of a rational tradition. However, it remains unclear on this model whether conflicts in traditions have a systematic source, which in turn generates a dynamic of progress. Secondly, the social basis for critique within traditions remains vague. Even if the model of norms immanent in social practices goes beyond a hermeneutic model in a narrow sense, it can also serve to clarify the preconditions that underlie the processes of interpretation that are distinctive of traditions. We must see traditions as developing on the basis of very specific, discursive normative practices. The model of social practice proposed here understands the implicit conflicts in practical interactions as the fundamental form of dispute. On the basis of this model, the question of the source of social conflicts in traditions can be posed in a new way, for as long as the *explicit, discursive* self-description of a tradition was seen as the primary arena of normative dispute, the source of conflicts could always only be located in the contingent 'environmental conditions' of discourses. If normative conflicts are understood as disputes about the *evaluation of behaviour in interactions*, however (whereby the concept of tradition becomes newly understood in terms of a history of practical disputes about forms of interaction), it seems obvious to describe these sources differently: in any instance of a normative evaluation of interactions, the enforcement of claims to recognition and authority is always at stake. This systematic opening of areas of conflict can be understood as the source of the dynamic of traditions. Traditions must ensure that they either become capable of integrating their internal conflicts, and solutions can be anchored in unproblematic forms of recognition, or they must conservatively break off their own learning processes by excluding deviant interpretations.

It is not only that an account of traditions can be concretized and improved by a model of social practice. The theory of social practices can be supplemented by the insights of the theories that operate with the concept of tradition. The idea that we never encounter context-free normative questions – that they are always presented in a context constituted by the preceding normative conflicts of a community and by the history of the solution to these conflicts – has the following consequences for the model of immanent critique. When rationally reconstructing norms that are immanent in the relations of recognition of a practice, we are never able to come to a conclusion by referring exclusively to the *contemporary* practices of a community. In order to justify a certain interpretation about which norms people in a practice have always already committed themselves to, reference to previous normative conflicts can play a role, especially since a certain configuration of practices often can only be fully understood if we know how the problems of previous practice configurations were solved through its emergence (meaning, through the institutionalization of its constitutive relations of recognition). This obviously applies in the same way to the judgements at stake in the practice: participation in a discursively reflexive practice always also implies that previous judgements – and thus also the authority of those who have made these judgements – must be accepted as relevant to the present situation.[19]

The fact that individual judgements are bound to a history of progress should be understood neither so weakly – following Taylor and MacIntyre – that the integration of a new normative commitment in a tradition is always only retrospectively rational nor so strongly that – as some interpretations of Hegel suggest – it is about the 'unfolding' of something that is always already pregiven.[20] As the discussion of the rule-following problem showed, a normative commitment is not an automatic mechanism that determines agents to exhibit the right behaviour in every situation. All the same, the idea that future, correct normative commitments are 'in some way' already contained in the current form of a tradition is not without some justification: the current normative commitments of a community are ultimately the only reasons we can appeal to in order to justify our future commitments. However, the process of justification under these conditions does not merely unfold the pregiven but rather justifies a certain extension of a norm with reference to the past.

8.5 EXCURSUS: THE CRITIQUE OF PRACTICALLY MEDIATED CONTRADICTIONS

The questions about the ontological status of immanent norms, about the epistemology of critique and about the model of progress are equally relevant to all forms of immanent critique. However, as was mentioned in the first part of this work,[21] besides these general questions there are also problems that only concern those theories of immanent critique that orient themselves to the 'classical model' – which assumes the existence not only of immanent norms but also of *constitutive contradictions*. In my discussion of Marx and Hegel, I referred to the corresponding model as being based on the idea of 'practically mediated contradictions'. A practice is subject to a practically mediated contradiction when its constitutive rules demand that the participants be orientated to a certain norm or value and when these normative orientations are systematically frustrated by the practice constituted by those very rules.[22]

A *practically mediated contradiction* accordingly exists in a practice if and only if

- it is constitutive of the practice that it is performed according to a set of rules or norms N_1;

- the existence of the practice (and thereby the fulfilment of N_1) is simultaneously constitutively dependent on the fact that the participants in the practice *orient* their actions (implicitly or explicitly) to a set of norms N_2 (put differently: the fulfilment of N_1 consists at least partially in the orientation of behaviour to N_2); and
- the actual practice (and thereby the actual fulfilment of N_1) necessarily violates the fulfilment of N_2.

This account must be cashed out further in two respects. On the one hand, it must be clarified (a) whether it is meaningful at all to say that a practice can be 'constitutively' contradictory – whether constitutive rules can in fact be violated. On the other hand, it must be shown (b) that it is possible to imagine such a practice at all.

(a) Can constitutive rules be violated? If we describe the structure of a practice as exhibiting a constitutive contradiction, this could be understood to mean that the rules *that are constitutive of it* are violated. What arises immediately is the problem that it is very unclear whether a constitutive rule – that is, a rule that determines what a practice *is* – can be violated. Such a rule appears not to be prescriptive in the sense presupposed by talk of violations of rules but rather to describe an exclusively ontological aspect. If we say that a rule R constitutes a practice P, then we are merely saying that if R is unfulfilled, P ceases to exist. Strictly understood, a practice that violates this rule is actually *another* practice – to which the rules of P no longer apply. Therefore, these rules cannot be violated.

But we need not abandon the talk of constitutive contradictions if we grasp the concept of a constitutive rule more precisely:[23] The constitutive rules of a practice are – such is the initial idea – those rules that determine what receives which normative *status* in this practice, this normative status only being comprehensible in the context of that practice. Constitutive rules consequently determine not only what kinds of behaviour must exist in a community but which institutionalized behavioural *relations* must exist, such that it counts as a community possessing this practice at all. The rules of chess can serve as an example: whoever does not accept that certain chess moves count as something specific – as *checkmate*, for example – is not playing chess incorrectly but rather not playing chess at all. Not only can constitutive rules in this sense – that is, rules of the form 'The figure with this form counts as a king' – not be violated, but it is not at all clear what it would mean to violate such a rule.

The talk of 'violations' of constitutive rules can, however, be understood as a meaningful description if one considers that constitutive rules do not emerge in isolation. The 'creation' of institutional facts by such rules – for example, the institutional fact of 'checkmate' – consists in making *new* behaviour possible. This new behaviour is always accompanied by certain norms. This means that the purpose of the introduction of a status like 'checkmate' consists in allowing the formulation of new *regulatory rules*.

The role of a piece of wood in functioning as a king in chess has the function, for example, of allowing for the establishment of certain regulative rules that determine which moves one may make with a king. *Outside* of these regulative rules, the new institutional fact has no 'use'. A constitutive rule of the form 'X counts as Y in context C' is therefore always in connection with normative statements of the form 'For X in context C, the regulative rules R_1, R_2 and so on apply'. These rules determine what it *means* to be a Y at all.[24]

The acceptance of constitutive rules is therefore never an end in itself. Conversely, any regulative rule is always (in a certain sense) constitutive as it always creates a new normative status, namely, the status of an action as correct or incorrect according to the correlating regulative rule.[25] These new forms of status are only relevant insofar as they serve as a basis for those further regulative rules that determine which reactions to actions of one type or another are legitimate. Therefore, it is not helpful to distinguish between constitutive and regulative rules solely by means of their form. It is more useful to place the focus on the *pragmatic role* that this distinction identifies: talk of constitutive rules picks out the fact that certain people, objects and actions, to which certain criteria apply, are integrated into a network of practices through social acceptance as new institutional objects, and that certain commandments and prohibitions apply to actions that concern them. Regulative rules, by contrast, are rules whose validity can in principle be understood independently of this integrative function – and thereby ultimately also independently of their reference to a certain practice. Put differently: constitutive rules express the role of norms in securing the boundaries of and membership in a practice, while regulative rules serve to evaluate individual behaviour, even if mostly under the presuppositions of the context of a practice.

This means that, for example, the rules of chess initially consist in a range of constitutive assignments of certain institutional terms ('king', 'queen' and so on), which are not accidentally but necessarily accompanied by various commandments and prohibitions. The constitutive aspect of these rules (which can be formulated as both constitutive and regulative rules) consists in the fact that they are suitable for determining the *conditions of participation in the practice*. Whoever executes prohibited moves under certain circumstances – for example, openly in the sight of others and without being willing to accept the incorrectness of these moves – can be said not to be playing chess at all. In other contexts, however, one will declare him an inattentive or fraudulent chess player. In contrast to these applications, we can distinguish a use of rules that have no constitutive contexts of application, for example, rules that determine what counts as especially shrewd or elegant play. Finally, there is the limiting case of what Theodore R. Schatzki calls the 'teleo-affective' structure of a practice.[26] These are the intentional and pre-intentional action orientations that are constitutive of a practice. It is obviously the case that even a player who loses has played chess – but it is essential to the practice of playing chess to at least *aim* at winning.[27]

The following consequence emerges from these considerations: as long as people follow an immanent norm that is structured such that the fulfilment of certain criteria has normative consequences for the status of certain objects, people or actions, we can say that this norm is based on a constitutive rule.

Suppose, for example, that in a community a person who fulfils certain criteria occupies a certain position of authority Y. There is therefore, as Searle says, a constitutive rule of the form 'X counts as Y (for example, as a king) in context C'. The status Y can also be explained through a network of behaviours that are normatively regulated through reference to this status. We can now imagine a situation in which the members of the aforementioned community are kept from observing these normative rules by third parties: they are, for example, coerced to express their defiance of X and thus to violate the normative consequences of the constitutive rule that they accept. All the same, we could still say that the constitutive rule – in the form of the prescriptive rules that are intrinsically bound up with it – still 'applies' (that is, is followed) so long as the members of that practice *accept* that they may be *criticized* in the appropriate way for failure to observe the rule and that they are responsible for such failures. So long as they either accept sanctions for their violations or provide reasons to be excused, the rule is still in effect. Constitutive rules can therefore be in operation in a community even if the regulative rules that derive from them are systematically violated, so long as the members of the community reciprocally treat each other as bound by these prescriptive rules.

By means of this analysis, we can understand the concept of the practically mediated contradiction at least in respect to the first of its two aspects: we can imagine a practice that is constituted through certain rules and that exists *as a practice* for those who belong to it by virtue of the fact that it allocates to certain entities a normative status that is at the same time constituted in such a way that the normative consequences of these allocations are systematically disrespected. Such a practice 'contradicts', in a specific sense, its own constitutive norms.

(b) Constitutive, practically mediated contradictions. However, how can we, in order to understand the second aspect of this idea of practically mediated contractions, imagine a practice that makes (in the sense just described) the fulfilment of its 'own' constitutive rules *impossible*? Here an example may also serve as an explanation.

We can initially imagine a community in which certain people count as members by means of the following constitutive rule:

R_1: People who meet criteria $C_1 \ldots C_N$ count as members of community G in context C.

Assume further that the membership status comes along with normative consequences. Members have a right to be gifted diamonds by other members at regular intervals, for example. In addition, members have a right, when one has given a gift, to receive a gift of the same value after a certain time. This practice therefore establishes, through its constitutive rules, the demand that members orient themselves to the fulfilment of these norms. These norms do not have a fundamental character, as they refer to a further institution, namely, the institution of gifting. 'Gifting' – we might imagine – is determined by the following constitutive rule:

R_2: In the context of interactions in G, the passing of diamonds from one person to another only counts as giving a gift if the gift giver does all they can to conceal their identity from the recipient.

By incorporating this additional constitutive rule into the definition of membership status, it becomes a constitutive component of the practice.[28] As is easy to see, however, such a practice will systematically produce situations in which reciprocity is violated, as the members will simply be *unable* to follow the rules and reciprocate their gifts, as they will not know who has given them. A problem obviously arises: even if these norms are not *logically* inconsistent – every member stands under the norm of giving a gift of equal value for every gift they receive – they are *practically contradictory.*[29] The normative orientation must *be systematically frustrated* by the constitutive rule that defines the conditions of its successful realization, as it is never known who gave what to whom. Therefore, the individuals are asked to internalize the goal of giving gifts in return but cannot reliably achieve it. In the chosen example, it is even the case that the practice remains viable so long as only a few interactions occur but becomes all the more self-contradictory the more frequently and effectively the 'correct' activity is performed.

Usually, in real-world communities, such situations are resolved through the creation of alternative solutions. We can, however, imagine an ensemble of rules that closes off each of these alternatives. The realization of the normative orientations that are constitutive of such a practice is (if its rules are observed) systematically obstructed. Such a practice fails to function in a very obvious way. However, it is not dysfunctional because people *do not follow the rules*. The people described follow all the rules to the best of their ability. If we criticize this practice, this will not be a case of internal critique that simply compares norms and practice. If the given norms are presupposed, there can indeed be no 'better' version of such a practice. It could only function in a 'better' way if it altered its constitutive norms – that is, if the understanding of what 'functioning' meant changed. However, one need not appeal to 'external' norms to demand a change of practices and rules of this kind. Still less are 'external' criteria necessary to understand why this practice is dysfunctional.[30]

Marx's reference to the idea of constitutive contradictions in relation to the character of the capitalist economy, which was described in the first part of this book, shows that a model of practically mediated contradictions can also serve to describe actual social crises. Independently of whether one shares the premises of his argument, Marx's model appears to be based on exactly such a model of contradiction:

> The contradiction between the purpose and goodwill of the administration, on the one hand, and its means and possibilities, on the other hand, cannot be abolished by the state without the latter abolishing itself, for it is based on this contradiction.[31]

This means that the constitutive form of the state consists, inter alia, in the fact that its officials are led by certain normative orientations (by 'purpose' and 'goodwill') and that the institutional means of realizing these orientations (the 'means and possibilities') systematically frustrate these orientations.

Not every form of immanent critique concerns such practically constituted contradictions. All the same, these are more than an interesting special case or an obsession of the Hegelian–Marxist tradition. The case of practically mediated contradictions reveals the advantage that immanent critique has over other forms of critique: only immanent critique can capture the objectivity of a contradiction that is constitutive of a practice.

Chapter Nine

The Critique of Reification

Alongside immanent critique, one further form of critique that plays an important role in the tradition of critical theory can be reconstructed with the aid of the practice-theoretical model. This is the critique of reification.

9.1 CRITIQUE AND METACRITIQUE

In order to clarify the relationship between immanent critique and the critique of reification it is worth turning, briefly once again, back to the central problem of this work: how can the idea that there are normative claims and commitments that are immanent in practices help to develop a model of social critique?

To start, a limitation of the theory that I have presented so far must be stated: from the perspective of this theory of the immanent norms of a social community, no particular critical claims follow. The theory of social practices only explains and describes what role social norms play in interactions. The theory of immanent norms presented here does not offer a justification of any particular first-level normative claims. If, for example, social scientific inquiry shows that there are particular attitudes or patterns of interaction, this does not make available *completely new* sources of reasons for accepting certain norms to those involved in the practice. The theory of social practices cannot independently *justify* immanent normative claims but can only analyse them, help us to understand them and, in doing so, possibly enlighten people about their own normative commitments.

But if the theory of social normativity does not provide social critique with reasons that the community in question has not, at least implicitly, previously accepted, what benefit can social critique draw from being informed about itself?

I contend that there are two levels on which the aforementioned theory has consequences for the practical activity of social critique. *First*, it can clarify what, precisely, a specific form of critique is appealing to: the form of critique that criticizes the explicitly recognized norms of a community with reference to the implicit norms of that community that are immanent in a social practice. The legitimacy of this form of criticism is necessarily contentious since the justification of the normative criteria it uses is not obvious. Therefore, those who do not wish to accept a criticism of this kind rightly demand that arguments be put forward showing that these criteria not only arise out of the fancy or wishful thinking of the critic, but that they actually have validity in social reality.

Alongside this 'core business' of the theory of immanent critique there is, I will argue, another respect in which the insights of a plausible theory of social normativity can have an effect. *Secondly*, this model helps us to make sense of a traditional line of argument in critical theory that considers possible a form of critique that concerns not the *content* of the intersubjectively constituted norms on the first level but the *form of their constitution*. Such a *metacritique* thematizes not the specific practices of a community but the structure of these practices as a whole. It is concerned with the way not only this or that specific norm but *normativity in general* is institutionalized in a practice through relations of recognition.

Such a critique is only possible because most complex practices have a reflexive character.[1] That means that the explicit rules of many practices reflect the participants' understanding of *what kind of* practice they are participating in. The rules of democracy, of science, as well as many games, forms of communication and the like are so constituted that, in addition to containing rules that fix how their members are to act, they include commitments as to how the *norms of those practices themselves* are constituted and which forms of justifications apply to them. Such reflexively constituted practices always institutionalize, through their norms, new types of action that allow their members to influence the norms of the practice, to change them or to establish new norms. In this way, such practices make it possible for their members to perceive the practice as a part of social reality constituted by recognition. In such reflexive practices, not only the concrete arrangement of first-order relationships of recognition but also the constitution of the practice can come under criticism. With regard to such practices, we can criticize not only the rules according to which their members attribute normative authority to each other and the rules they follow in doing so, but also the *mode* in which this is done.

In the history of critical theory, there are different conceptions of second-order critique of this kind.² Examples include ideology critique,³ the critique of systematically distorted relationships of communication, the critique of technocracy, the critique of instrumental rationality and many more. These forms of critique do not so much thematize the violation of particular norms as evaluate practices in terms of how they function *as practices*. That is to say, they assess whether these practices institutionalize their norms in a transparent way, compatible with the autonomy of their members, or whether they include self-conceptions that systematically misrepresent the form of their own normativity.

Most of these forms of critique determine what counts as a wrong form of institutionalization of normativity in a practice based either on external normative criteria, the history of their origin or their consequences for the subject. By contrast, the *critique of reification* – as I will try to show in what follows – takes into view the constitution of social practices as such. It is, or so I will argue, a form of *immanent metacritique*. It takes the insight into the reflexivity of practices itself as its starting point and takes place when a practice is criticized not only for being guided by the wrong norms but for having a basic constitution that cannot become an object of action to the extent that the self-understanding of the practice requires.

The critique of reification, as I will reconstruct it, assumes that there are social practices that are essentially characterized by the fact that particular norms are immanently institutionalized as norms in them and that they are constituted such that those social relationships that institutionalize their norms *cannot be reflexively questioned*. The critique of reification thus switches to the meta level of immanent critique. Unlike ordinary immanent critique, it does not investigate first-order contradictions between immanent and explicit norms. Rather, it investigates contradictions between claims that are immanent in the more general practice of intersubjective norm constitution and the form that this practice acquires in a specific social situation.

9.2 WHAT IS THE CRITIQUE OF REIFICATION?

The critique of reification, in the most general sense, is any criticism of the fact that people take themselves, others, social relationships or processes as 'mere things', that is, as something that confronts them as a static, external object. This kind of criticism is most straightforwardly understood in the case of social relationships. Anyone who treats or perceives social institutions or rules as if they had a purely objective unchangeable character commits a category mistake and denies themselves the chance to change or to improve these social relations.

In this sense, the critique of reification is not a modern phenomenon. At all times, critics of one or the other norm or institution have rejected the idea that these phenomena are a reflection of a natural or divine order. In this sense, the critique of reification always aims at a form of enlightenment that points out that certain norms are not given to human beings from the *outside* but are *socially constructed*. If it is successful, this form of critique changes the *form* of the practices in question. Because the critique of reification opens up space for the questioning or changing of norms, understood as self-made, it allows these practices – possibly for the first time – to become *reflexive*. The idea that the social order of our practices is our own product can only become practically effective if it is accepted that it is generally legitimate to criticize social practices, not only with reference to externally given norms, of religious or philosophical origin, but with reference to norms constituted in and through these practices themselves.

This relatively universal form of critique, which discloses the social constitution of practices to their participants, is, however, only one of its possible manifestations of the critique of reification. The critique of reification is also present in practices that have already become reflexive. The fundamental diagnosis of a specifically modern form of critique of reification is the observation that the mode or form in which particular social practices are institutionalized has the consequence that these practices structure the relationship that people have to their surrounding reality in a specifically 'reifying' way. This form of reification critique asserts that reification consists in people relating to other persons, to processes, to their own character and to the meaningful things that surround them as though they were 'mere things,' as though they were a part of nature.

Examples of such a critique of reification can be found in many everyday situations. We criticize other people on the basis that they treat social relations as if they were without alternative, unable to summon up the power to imagine that they could be otherwise. People also protest against being viewed by others as mere consumers or producers, as mere factors in a balance sheet, without playing a role as subjects. Finally, people criticize one another for treating their own emotions as strategic resources and for regarding their natural and cultural surroundings from the point of view of instrumental disposal. In all of these cases, the criticism relates to the fact that things, persons and norms are, in a particular way, treated as things. They are only included in the practical deliberations of the subject as external factors devoid of meaning.

The critique of reification can also go beyond individual phenomena. A generalized diagnosis of an all-pervading objectified and ossified relationship to one's self and to the external world can be described as one of the most important forms of modern cultural and social criticism. The experience of encountering social relations and the norms and practices of our social environment as external barriers to our individual wills, as purely objective relations that remain foreign to us, unchangeable and unquestionable, has been thematized since the nineteenth century by a variety of critics and can be referred to as an almost canonical form of everyday, artistic and philosophical criticism of modernity. A true explosion of philosophical and cultural critical attempts to conceptualize these experiences took place particularly in the first two decades of the twentieth century. Max Weber and George Simmel can, together with Martin Heidegger and conservative forms of cultural criticism, be mentioned in this context. The underlying idea of a critique of reification was prepared by Hegel and Marx, on the one side, and by the romantics Schiller and Nietzsche, on the other.[4] However, it was only through the work of Georg Lukács – who understood how to bring these strands together in a unique way – that the concept of reification came to characterize the core of the theoretical paradigm of critical theory up to today.[5] The reference to Lukács plays a central role not only in Adorno's thought but also for Habermas and Honneth. Because Lukács, as I would like to show, builds his theory on a model of human practices that today's theories reject, for good reason, later attempts at renewing his theory are only partial reconstructions that discard essential parts of his model.

In the following, I will show that Lukács's particular achievement consists in the fact that he sketches a *comprehensive* explanation of the phenomenon of reification. This explanation is, however, based on implausible philosophical theories of the subject and of totality. If the theory of reification is to be systematically reconstructed, it must find an alternative foundation. A practice-theoretical reformulation of the theory of reification can achieve this and gain new access to the concept of reification.[6] First, however, we must clarify which problems the critique of reification aims to describe and how the two classical attempts by Marx and Lukács attempt to deal with them.

9.3 THE NORMATIVE CONTENT OF THE CRITIQUE OF REIFICATION

'Reification' is not a concept that philosophical analysis can take up from ordinary language. It is rather a category in which everyday experience and theoretical assumptions flow together. In order to understand how this concept got its specific content, one must therefore understand the theoretical context from which the critique of reification emerged. The critique of reification experienced its greatest popularity in the period between the end of the nineteenth century and the beginning of the twentieth. First and foremost, Lukács and Simmel grasped the historical situation in which they developed their theory as having been shaped by the rise of a particular type of experience. According to their diagnosis, in the society of their times, a certain mode of reference to the world – or, as Lukács formulated it in neo-Kantian terms, a 'form of objectivity' (*Gegenständlichkeitsform*)[7] – had become dominant. People experienced their environment, other people and social institutions to an ever-increasing extent as things. This means that they perceived their everyday lives as a collection of objective phenomena that were detached from one another, neither intrinsically meaningful nor capable of being influenced by the subject. This likely typical description of a specifically modern dimension of experience, which can be found not only in social theory but also in literature, links the concept of a 'thing' to a specific form of objectivity that is distinguished through a detachment of objects from the attitudes of the subject, from meaning and from everyday purposes and associations.

The rather general cultural-critical and sociological analyses of the phenomena of reification that accumulated at the beginning of the twentieth century and worked with this vocabulary gain their plausibility not least from the fact that they summarize a range of everyday experiences which, in turn, mobilize intuitions derived from a variety of contexts. These intuitions can be found in numerous everyday discourses about when we are justified to treat something as a 'mere thing' and when it is a mistake to treat phenomena as one would a thing. Kant's prohibition of instrumentalization is certainly the most well-known philosophical formulation of these intuitions. Going beyond moral judgements in a narrower sense, at least four forms of reification critique can be distinguished, each containing intuitions on which an analysis of the concept of reification must reflect:

- First, critique of the reification of our relation to social reality. This form criticizes attitudes toward institutions and practices that make them appear to be relationships between objects, as natural or unchangeable phenomena.
- Second, critique of the reification of our relation to other people. Such a critique focuses above all on phenomena related to instrumentalization, depersonalization and treating others as mere things, and considers these phenomena in light of the effects they have on intersubjective relations.
- Third, critique of the reification of our relation to our own subjectivity. This critique concerns all of those behaviours in which we take an objectifying stance on ourselves and treat our capabilities as mere instruments or resources.

The Critique of Reification 263

- Finally, critique of the reification of our relation to objects: whether these objects are the product of our own work, natural objects or everyday things, forms of critique can be found that criticize our relation to such objects if we perceive them to be without meaning, 'mere' things, as immediately given objects. These critics maintain that in so doing we miss a crucial dimension of reality.[8]

9.3.1 Reification as an Epistemic Pathology

In all of these forms of critique, the mistake involved in the criticized relationships can be characterized as our falsely *perceiving* a particular dimension, an aspect or even the essential constitution of the object area in question. For example, for the criticism of the reification of social relations, the central idea is that agents take institutional forms of society and social norms as immediately given, perceiving them as a piece of objective reality that is independent of them and their constitutive concerns. In these cases, we lose track of the fact that social institutions and norms but also communicatively institutionalized forms of reference to the lifeworld are dependent on subjects, that they are, as Searle would say, 'ontologically subjective'.[9] Consequently, the insight into their dependence on the subject can no longer become effective in the relationship that the agents have to them because they are not recognized as such. This seemingly abstract phenomenon of losing sight of the connection between social reality and one's practical concerns becomes practically relevant if, as a consequence, the collective or individual conduct of people becomes irrational, false or bad – if they, through this attitude, no longer perceive alternatives in their decisions to act. This is the case, in particular, when the assumption that certain conditions exist 'naturally' or 'objectively' makes certain behaviour appear as though it is 'without alternative' when, in fact, there are alternatives.

At the very least, the critique of this form of reification is always about the epistemic availability of alternative courses of action. Only if actors realize and recognize their own constitutive role in the existence of a social institution, for example, can the availability of particular action options become practically accessible. The epistemic availability of these options enables individuals to act rationally because it enables their autonomy. So understood, the mistake of a reified reference to reality consists in the fact that a deficient epistemic stance is taken by a subject. This leads not only to the subject's falsely grasping reality, but also to its treating reality in a way that endangers its autonomy.[10]

This epistemic interpretation, central to many interpretations of the critique of reification that conceptualize reification as a false belief, cannot grasp every relevant aspect of the phenomenon of reification, however. An understanding of reification as a phenomenon that is brought about purely by false beliefs locates the ground of reification more or less in subjective features of consciousness. However, this is to a large extent implausible. The experiences associated with the critique of reification are not primarily distinguished from nonpathological cases by the fact that people in 'unobjectified' contexts have special insights or cognitive competencies. Participants in social interactions normally do not have, in any significant sense, a belief to the effect that they are a coproducer of social reality. This is so if only because in everyday discourses the vocabulary for forming such a belief is not generally available. But it is not only for this reason that an epistemic analysis of the process of reification appears unsuitable. Regarded phenomenologically, reification is closer to a habitualized practical disposition than to an epistemic relation. The feeling of being confronted with a social reality that is like an 'iron cage', the feeling of being confronted by a nature devoid of meaning, is not so much the reflection of the epistemic inaccessibility of the respective objects. This feeling results much more from the failure of specific forms of practical appropriation of the world. The modern criticism of formal bureaucracy is not only fed by experiences of the relevant processes as cognitively incomprehensible. Rather, it reflects the experience of being helpless in the face of these processes, that is, of being unable to achieve certain practical aims.

This practical helplessness only becomes thematic in specific contexts. The modern boom of the concept of reification can hardly be explained by the fact that individuals were better able to understand or influence their fate in premodern societies and that this ability was lost in the transition to modernity. On the contrary, in modern societies, the right to determine one's own actions and one's own social position is often institutionalized to a much greater extent.

For this reason, reification is a phenomenon that is bound to specific social contexts in a way that is difficult to illustrate from a purely epistemological perspective. If a person, for example, treats social role expectations as a piece of objective reality, then this 'mistake' is understandable independent of the practical situation they find themselves in. However, if we want to decide whether a corresponding practical attitude – for example, a strategic adaption to such expectations – can be designated as pathological, it is important to know whether these role expectations form the background of everyday actions that are not experienced as problematic and that the subject takes for granted while solving other problems, or whether they form the subject of political conflicts or social scientific discourses. Whereas in the first case it is not obviously pathological if the actors do not refer to the subjective constitution of role expectations, practical neglect of the fact of this objectification in the second case would be problematic.

That the experience of reification in this way is connected to the features of the practical contexts in which it occurs makes it plausible to assume that we should not understand it primarily as an epistemic error but rather as a result of a violation of the constitutive rules of those particular practical contexts.

9.3.2 Reification as a Practical Pathology

Compared to the epistemic view, the critique of reification as formulated by Marx and Lukács raises claims that are more strongly related to social practice. Their critique is not only concerned with epistemic errors but rather always also with the constitution of the objective side, and thus with a particular condition of social reality that is the object of reifying attitudes. In addition, Lukács in particular broadens the subject area of reification critique from the critique of a lack of epistemic insight into the social construction of social relations – which is still central for Marx – to three further dimensions: subjects' relations to objects, to other subjects and to their own subjectivity. For Lukács, we reify not only things that can be recognized as human made (e.g., social institutions) but also the internal and external world itself.

This approach to the problem appears to be more appropriate to the experiences that the critique of reification takes up from everyday life. In everyday life, our criticism is not limited to cases where people treat social facts as though they were determined by nature – this may even be the least common form of everyday criticism. To a greater degree, we are intuitively inclined to say that the worst form of treating something as a thing, or as a mere piece of objectivity, concerns other people. In these cases, we rarely deal with false beliefs – someone who instrumentalizes other people, or treats them as mere objects, typically has no false beliefs but rather commits a moral or practical mistake. We can even describe physical objects as 'reified' when they lose their meaning and become mere objects. This is the case when, for example, in modern factory work, the worker is cut off from their products, or when nature in modernity becomes a domain of pure causality, devoid of meaning.[11] But this criticism likewise pertains not to false beliefs but to a practical relation.

From this perspective, even true beliefs can belong to a pathological practice. In modern societies, the individual's belief that they are but a cog in a machine – the experience of the emptying of social relations and the 'iron cage' of institutions – is not a mere illusion. Society is in fact constituted such that this attitude is (at least partially) epistemically correct. The ontological dependence of institutions on the individual is in many situations a purely theoretical insight without practical relevance. In order to reconstruct the concept of reification, we must therefore clarify the extent to which an epistemically correct attitude can nevertheless be an expression of a practical failure. Moreover, the normative foundations of the critique of reification – which are normally nothing more than intuitions that always run the risk of succumbing to a romanticized contrast between modernity and allegedly unalienated, unmediated conditions – must be specified.[12]

9.4 REIFICATION ACCORDING TO MARX AND LUKÁCS

The problematic relation between perception and practice that is disclosed by the concept of reification, as well as the variety of phenomena that this concept aims to capture, can best be understood through a reading of the two theorists who introduced the critique of reification into the discourse of the critical theory of society, that is, Marx and Lukács.

In his early critique of alienation, Marx incorporates arguments that are critical of reification. In the 'Paris Manuscripts', he describes 'alienation' as a process through which the products created by the worker confront them as something foreign,[13] with the consequence that the work itself becomes 'alien' and 'hostile',[14] eventually becoming a coercive system that the worker can no longer understand as an expression of their own intentions. On the basis of this inaccessibility of the workers' own products, Marx explains the emergence of a relationship between self and world that he describes as the alienation of the human being from their self, from their 'species being' and from their fellow humans.[15] The thesis that alienation is the result of a loss of contact with one's own creative work relates to those activities in which a material product is created, in which work is invested and thus, as Marx says, 'externalized' (*entäußert*). In the process, he revises his initial epistemological model of objectification, relying not on the theoretical but rather on the practical abstractions that such externalization entails. The model of practice on which he bases this revision is highly problematic, however. He takes up Hegel's idea that the relevant form of 'externalization' is found in productive practice. The externalization of the essential powers of the worker in a product that can be distinguished from them becomes characterized negatively, that is, as a loss. This assessment clearly relies on an analysis of a specific form of externalization of individual plans and purposes in the sphere of the intentional production of a product of labour, without making a distinction between the general aspect of externalization (*Entäußerung*) of internal intentions that is part of every kind of action and the alienating dimension of the inaccessibility of this externalization. It is only the latter that can be linked to the experience in which the products of labour (mediated by market relations) lose their connection to their producers.

Marx justifiably criticizes Hegel for his fixation on the cognitive forms through which alienation is supposedly overcome. But this criticism does not go beyond formulating more or less strong intuitions about nonalienated labour, referring primarily to – already disappearing – forms of handicraft and artistic production that are characterized by a low division of labour. Alongside the ambiguity of the model of nonalienated labour, Marx's model is also problematic because it privileges a specific form of practice. It is concerned with the productive transformation of nature that Marx, in a way still strongly orientated by Hegel's discussion in the *Phenomenology of Spirit*, understands as the externalization of something inward. This is, however, a conception of labour that is not only difficult to reconstruct without inconsistencies but also receives all of its plausibility from a specific organizational model of labour bound up with specific historical conditions.[16] In particular, this idea does not help us to understand the mistake we commit when we reify social relationships if we do not wish to represent the constitution of social institutions, implausibly, in analogy to the production process as a form of intentional transformation of external reality. In order to understand what it means to say that the societal world is constituted by the activity of subjects, one must rely on a conception of action that not only breaks away from a conception of the subject in which the productive capacities in labour are central but is also suitable for comprehending social practices beyond production.[17]

By contrast, the central reference for the now classic Marxian theory of reification is, without doubt, the famous chapter on the 'Fetishism of the Commodity' in *Capital*. There, Marx develops the thesis that the social institutionalization of the free exchange of commodities establishes the value form (*Wertform*) which is a shared property of all commodities. That commodities take on this form makes their comparison according to value and a 'just' exchange possible in the first place, regardless of the specific qualitative properties of these commodities and the specific needs of the actors. The value form acquires objective reality, and even becomes the dominant form of objectivity of commodities, through the process of the institutionalization of the market. Once this process is complete, the commodity ultimately only has the function of acting as a bearer of this value property. According to Marx, the natural properties of things recede in favour of a 'supra-natural'[18] – that is, social – property. The institution of money ultimately takes over the function of converting this form of value into 'objective fixedness and general social validity'.[19]

In capitalism, the value form becomes the dominant medium for the regulation of the relationships between humans and nature and among humans.

It thus becomes an ineluctable part of social reality. The fact that the value form appears as a property of things conceals the fact that the apparently static property of having value is, in reality, a property of a social relationship, namely, the relationship between the producers of the commodities in question, whose average necessary expenditure of labour power in its proportion constitutes the value of commodities.[20] Reification as generated by the value form is therefore not a false belief that is grounded in the structure of human consciousness. It is not a mental epiphenomenon that is merely added to objective relations. Rather, reification is an objective feature of capitalism: social labour is conducted in isolation and mediated only through the exchange of commodities. Therefore, from the perspective of the individual producer, social relations are indeed bound up with things.[21] This also means that it cannot suffice to solely criticize the *perception* of value as a natural property of things. This epistemic critique of political economy, which assumes the existence of value as unproblematic, is not yet sufficient to attack the authority of the corresponding beliefs.[22] Rather, reification and its resulting manifestations are an objective consequence of the specific form of the practice of production and exchange that capitalism involves. Marx therefore localizes the fundamental cause of reification and commodity fetishism not in the domain of perception but rather in that of action:

> Men do not therefore bring the products of their labour into relation with each other as values because they see these objects merely as the material integuments of homogeneous human labour. The reverse is true: by equating their different products to each other in exchange as values, they equate their different kinds of labour as human labour. They do this without being aware of it.[23]

The problem of reification is thus evidently grounded in a deficient form of human activity. However, the 'mistake' lies not in the subjective presuppositions of this activity – for example, in false beliefs – but in the way in which this activity – insofar as it does not just happen accidentally and occasionally but is instead organized as a social practice – becomes determined through structural features of the surrounding society. Here, the focus shifts from the fundamental character of work to the *structure of the organization* of this form of activity; subsequently, in *Capital*, psychological vocabulary tends to become less significant.

It is no longer the product of the worker that becomes inaccessible but rather the features of social relationships attached to the products. However, it turns out that the narrow production-orientated conception of work found in *Capital*, in contrast to the richer conception in the 'Paris Manuscripts', is even more narrowly tailored to industrial production and cannot bear the burden that Marx wishes to place on it. That is, it is precisely the structural aspects of social organization that are determined and generated through forms of practical behaviour that cannot themselves be understood as the production of material goods.[24]

In his classic essay on 'Reification and the Consciousness of the Proletariat', Lukács not only takes up the Marxian concept of the reifying structural conditions of production but transforms it into the basis of a comprehensive critique of modern practices. He succeeds in combining Marx's critique of the value form with the Weberian theory of rationalization, such that the resulting theory subjects the modern form of life in its entirety to a critique of reification. This means that he takes the reification of social relations and of commodities, which constitute the paradigm cases for Marx's theory, and makes them the foundation of a more comprehensive theory that can explain all four abovementioned phenomena systematically, as forms of one pathology. Furthermore – and here Lukács's theory clearly had its greatest impact – he attempts, with recourse to Hegel's dialectic, to analyse the philosophical and scientific forms of self-reflection of modernity as having been shaped by reification, thereby merging ideology critique and social critique.

Lukács takes up the Marxian analysis of the value form and distinguishes – not unlike Marx – between the mediation of human cooperation through things and the ideological hypostatization of this situation, which ascribes value properties to things themselves. He stresses, much more strongly than Marx, that objects already acquire a new form of objectivity whenever they are socially treated as being determined by their function in the process of social mediation. Through the quantitative nature of value, an 'equal exchange of qualitatively different objects'[25] that presupposes a 'break with the organic, irrational and qualitatively determined unity of the product' is made possible.[26] The effect of reification on the structure of the objectivity of things corresponds to a parallel effect on the subject: the mechanization and temporal quantification of human labour that tends to be brought about through the market-based mediation of labour in capitalism – which no longer takes place in situations of original cooperation determined by the quality of labour but rather in the value-mediated division of labour – leads to a loss of the qualitative differences in the course of human activities, to a 'fragmentation of the subject' and, finally, to what Lukács calls the 'contemplative stance'.[27] This concept refers to the listless attitude of a subject who can no longer grasp themselves as a producer of the surrounding reality and who, in the sphere of this practice, assumes a subjective stance that is entirely appropriate to this practice but is ultimately alienated from it. In Lukács, subjective and objective aspects are combined in the concept of reification: objectively, reification becomes effective when the social rules that adhere to things develop objectively into self-steering laws that can only be recognized but no longer practically overhauled. Subjectively, the abstraction of labour transforms the actual conditions of the labour process, which virtually enforces a particular subjective attitude.[28] Ultimately, Lukács completes his diagnosis of reification by arguing that the encroachment of reification on the forms of objectivity and on the subject lays the basis for a development through which the process of reification can detach itself 'from [its] economic bases' and 'must embrace every manifestation of the life of society'.[29] Modern law and, in particular, modern bureaucracy become fellow players in the process of making things calculable and in the process of rationalization described by Weber. According to Lukács, this process is made possible by economic reification on the one hand and consolidates its results on the other. While the extent to which our practices increasingly escape our control was originally restricted to the economic sphere, it has gradually become a universal feature of our form of life.[30]

With the assumption of a universalizing tendency towards reification, Lukács ultimately goes beyond the Marxian schema and takes up the insights that Weber's rationalization theory, on the one hand, and Simmel's *Philosophy of Money*, on the other, contribute to our understanding of the consequences of capitalist rationalization. According to these theorists, the form of social relations begins to develop a pattern of individualization, differentiation and loss of qualitative differences in all domains of society, such that a new form of social integration comes into being.

Three consequences follow from this. First, what results from this process is the already mentioned reification of the self that is established as the 'unified structure of consciousness'[31] in capitalism:

> The specialised 'virtuoso', the vendor of his objectified and reified faculties does not just become the [passive] observer of society; he also lapses into a contemplative attitude vis-à-vis the workings of his own objectified and reified faculties. . . . This phenomenon can be seen at its most grotesque in journalism. Here it is precisely subjectivity itself, knowledge, temperament and powers of expression that are reduced to an abstract mechanism.[32]

Second – and here is where the relationship between Lukács's critique of reification and the classic project of immanent critique becomes apparent – the resulting structure of social organization and of reference to reality, which are both characterized by the dominance of formal rationalization, is in a very specific way self-contradictory. This is because reified action can no longer grasp the qualitative particularity of its objects. These particularities can only emerge as disturbances, as irrationalities, which ultimately lead society into crisis.[33] Third, reified consciousness's inability to grasp qualitative differences also makes it impossible to systematically understand the whole of society, the 'totality' of social relationships. The 'concrete whole' that this expression denotes cannot be grasped under conditions characterized by the form of reality generated by capitalism and leads bourgeois thought into antinomies which Lukács demonstrates in an impressive reconstruction of the problems of classical philosophy.

According to his account, only Hegel succeeds in correctly grasping the problem of totality. This is because only Hegel seeks to grasp seemingly alien objectivity as a whole as the product of a subject that is not separate from it. Admittedly, according to Lukács, this subject is only conceived by Hegel mythologically as the world spirit. The actual subject of totality is, according to Lukács's understanding, not a history-transcending collective subject but rather an actual historical collective, namely, the proletariat. The proletariat is, in principle, subject to reification in the same way as the bourgeoisie.[34] Unlike the bourgeoisie, however, the proletariat is totally determined by reification, without room for subjective illusions. As a result, the proletariat knows no form of liberation other than revolutionary emancipation and can only aim at a complete reorganization of society. In the practical appropriation of its role as a collective producer, the proletariat can, as a class, seize the sociohistorical totality and thus abolish reification. The proletariat's potential knowledge of totality, which it can acquire as the 'subject-object' of history,[35] is at the same time understood as a revelation of the objective structure of the world.[36] All societal facts then turn out to be historically mediated, as moments of the societal process of which the proletariat is the subject.

In this conception of the proletariat as the revolutionary subject, the problems with the Lukácsian model of reification are clear. Lukács can only represent the abolition of reification as a reappropriation of reality that is to be understood as analogous, in principle, to the reappropriation of the products of labour by the labouring subject. Even if – contrary to what many interpretations suggest – he in no way imagines that the proletariat, as a suprasubject, could ever fully carry out this appropriation,[37] he is compelled to introduce an idea of subjectivity that not only burdens itself with all the problems of the idealistic conception of subjectivity, but even exaggerates it in that the constitution of that subject is not a mere precondition for insight into the social totality but also a philosophically graspable process that can be conceptualized in advance. Furthermore, the thought that the problem of reification is, above all else, ultimately a problem of the 'opacity of totality' leads Lukács to describe the problem of reification, at least in relation to its overcoming, in primarily epistemological terms. This leads to the fact that he does not attribute any power of resistance against reification to the proletariat; it is only the theoretical reflection of philosophy that sets in motion a process of becoming aware – one that culminates in revolution by means of which the proletariat comes to be the subject of history.[38]

9.5 THE CRITICISM OF LUKÁCS'S CONCEPT OF REIFICATION

From the beginning, the Lukácsian conception was sharply criticized for these theoretical commitments. This was above all the case for the problematic notion of totality, to which the equally problematic subject model of the proletariat corresponds. In addition, however, those of Lukács's claims that are social theoretical in the broadest possible sense have become subject to objections that ultimately endanger the theory of reification as a whole.

With good reason, Jürgen Habermas has objected that the idea that philosophical theory can anticipate the apprehension of totality in the theory of class consciousness itself is tantamount to an attempt to endow philosophical theory with a power that exceeds even that of Hegelian metaphysics.[39] The exaggerated claims in the self-description of the theory do not form the only objection against Lukács's concept of totality, however. The implications of this concept from a theoretical perspective are even more troubling. In Lukács's diagnosis of a disunited totality of practice, he merges ideology critique and social theory with the Hegelian model of the appropriation of the products of labour through the subject. As a consequence, it appears that the 'mistake' involved in reification ultimately always lies in a failure to appropriate a product of a subject's activity. At the same time, this appropriation is always understood in the vocabulary of 'consciousness', allowing for an easy transition to the theory of class consciousness. Not only can the well-known objections against the philosophy of consciousness[40] be raised against this commitment, but Lukács himself – albeit under external pressure – later recognized the idealist and subjectivist implications of this theory as a problem.[41]

An even stronger criticism is formulated by Adorno, who accuses Lukács of understanding reification as a mere form of consciousness and thus neglecting the insight into the role of reification as the possibility of constituting a determinate form of objectivity. Since Lukács assumes that the end of reification is only reached when the irrationality of the material is uncovered as an illusion by the 'identical subject-object', every form of objectivity that does not allow for such transparency must count as the residue of a state of affairs that ought to be overcome:

> If a man looks upon thingness as radical evil, if he would like to dynamize all entity into pure actuality, he tends to be hostile to otherness, to the alien thing that has lent its name to alienation, and not in vain. He tends to that nonidentity which would be the deliverance, not of consciousness alone, but of reconciled

mankind. Absolute dynamics, on the other hand, would be that absolute action whose violent satisfaction lies in itself, the action in which nonidentity is abused as a mere occasion.[42]

This idea – that the critique of reification aims at complete transparency – is, from Adorno's perspective, itself a consequence of a reified viewpoint that considers the opposition between reification and accessibility from a perspective detached from concrete contexts and that ideologically privileges transparency.

At this point, Lukács loses insights that are at least laid out in Marx. Whilst Marx – as Lukács himself later admits – distinguishes between objectification and reification and in his discussions of work never loses sight of the fact that the accessibility of our practical activity finds its limit in the given natural substance,[43] Lukács treats the character of the social practices that he is concerned with in a purely formal manner. Without questioning, he adopts a model of the objectification of the subject in the product of labour that stems from a particular tradition of Hegel interpretation. He does not see that this model only makes sense in particular contexts, however. By committing himself to the idea of a completely transparent appropriation of social existence, he misses out on insights that had already been developed in the Marxist critique of Hegel. In addition, this leads him to adopt a model of the alternative to reification that is a static model of absolute unity in subjectivity: 'Here hostility to sociology, which he considered an inappropriate misuse of natural scientific methods, like psychology, had its costs. The result was a normative totality, a goal of complete constitutive subjectivity, that was little more than an abstract negation of a totally reified world.'[44] These problems suggest that Lukács's considerations can only plausibly be reconstructed if one abandons the subjective-epistemological implications of the concept of reification as well as the problematic category of 'totality'. As Axel Honneth remarks, it is then appropriate to locate the core of the Lukácsian idea not in an epistemic relation but rather in the practice of actors in capitalist societies.[45] To do this, Lukács's theory must contain criteria that allow for a distinction between 'right' and 'wrong' practices. Here, a second weakness becomes apparent: Lukács conceives of reification as a binary relation that ultimately only permits a type of evaluation of practices that either accepts or rejects them tout court, without drawing normative distinctions concerning their specific features.[46] The patterns of behaviour that Lukács denotes with the concept of reification are thus not understood in terms of any specific problems within the practices at issue. Instead, these practices are regarded as false without any context-sensitive assessment of their particular elements. It follows from this that Lukács opposes the complexity of the modern world, in which such patterns of behaviour always have their place, with an abstract utopia.

However, this criticism does not, as Habermas seems to assume, inevitably lead to surrendering the idea that a theory of reification could sensibly speak of human practices as such. We do not have to oppose Lukács's undifferentiated concept of reification with a differentiation into two fundamentally different types of practice, such that only in one of these types of practice is there room for the critique of reification. Rather, it is enough to demonstrate that social practices in and of themselves always bring with them different demands for transparency. In order to do this, it is necessary to clarify the type of normative claim made by the critique of reification.

A reconstruction of the concept of reification can only succeed if the concept is explained in terms of specific practical contexts and, above all, if reification is understood not as a static relationship between the subject and the world but rather as a practical breakdown of a subject's activities. That is, reification should be understood as a violation of normative claims that are practically institutionalized in some sense. Finally, we must clarify whether the ideal of social transparency can also be defended from such a practical-theoretical point of view without having to accept the problematic consequences of an idealist conception of totality.

9.6 A PRACTICE-THEORETICAL RECONSTRUCTION OF THE CONCEPT OF REIFICATION

On the one hand, the reconstruction of the critique of reification must be able to preserve the central normative intuitions of the Lukácsian model and its comprehensive character, that is, its explanatory power with regard to the abovementioned four forms of reification. On the other hand, it must avoid the problematic assumptions that Lukács makes concerning the concept of totality, the concept of action and the concept of nature. However, as soon as one relinquishes the conception of the subject that gives primacy to the labouring individual and replaces the epistemological formulation of the concept of reification with a conception which locates reification primarily in social interactions and in the practical forms of reference to the world, these problems can be solved.[47] If the model of social practices defended thus far is presupposed, then we must first clarify what the notion of different 'forms of objectivity,' which is so central to Lukács's description of the phenomena of reification, might mean. Objects, in both a narrow and a broader sense that includes persons, actions and processes, are characterized by the fact that they can have certain properties. However, this means nothing other than that people, within specific practical contexts, perceive actions, other persons and objects under particular aspects that are relevant to them in the context of these practices. One could say that in practices, depending on the aspects that become thematic, objects, persons and actions can be distinguished according to various criteria that in most cases cannot be understood independently of the aims and purposes of the practice in question. Distinctions, for example, between usefulness and uselessness, courage and cowardice, fairness and injustice, wisdom and mere cleverness, craftsmanship and amateurism, fine art and crafts, get their meaning from the overarching sense of the practices to which they are bound.[48]

The attribution of properties to objects is a normatively regulated form of action. Attributions can be correct or incorrect. If in a particular practice properties are attributed to such objects, then this presupposes that the participants of this practice are able to orient themselves towards a norm that regulates the ascriptions of such properties in the context of the aims and purposes of the practice. The attribution of such properties to objects therefore also presupposes a socially regulated ability to differentiate between relevant and irrelevant features of objects.

The *form* of a particular type of object, that is, the *way* an object is *determined* through its properties, can also in many respects be understood as bound up with the respective relevant practices on which the validity of the relevant norms is based. If a certain form of objectivity is supposed to be at the core of phenomena of reification, then this may have to do with the fact that these objects are constituted as the objects they are as part of a practice, which in turn has a certain reified form. The *form of objectivity* to which reification points has its counterpart in the *form of a practice*.

What might that mean? The answer I would like to propose is the following: the form of a practice is determined by its second-order rules, that is, the rules that determine how the practice is concretely institutionalized in its normative constitution through recognition.

Although every normative practice must fulfil certain conditions in order to count as such, these conditions can be satisfied in very different ways. In particular, the form in which these participants constitute these rules in their practical interaction, that is, in particular, the ways they can *reflexively refer* to the rules of a practice in their intersubjective interactions, can be extremely different. We can easily see that first-order rules – for example, the rules that determine the correct performance of a craft – can be institutionalized in very different ways through intersubjective practices of mutual recognition. The relationships of recognition that institutionalize these first-order rules will appear very different depending on whether these rules are subject to optimization in the context of a rationalized practice oriented towards efficiency, whether they are traditionally taught and passed on, whether they are understood as the result of virtuoso talent training, or whether they are ultimately dictated in an authoritarian manner. These different *modes of institutionalization* of social rules in practices can be distinguished by referring to different ways in which the mutual recognition that enables that institutionalization is subject to different rules that govern the question of which form of criticism is justified in which situation, and which form of authority can be claimed at various moments. Practices take on a different form depending on what opportunities their participants have to relate, practically and reflexively, to its basic rules in the mode of criticism or exercising authority. The form of a practice is therefore constituted through the rules that regulate the agents' legitimate relation to its norms. These are their *second-order rules*.

A reified form of practice – and through the distinctions it constitutes, a reified form of objectivity – arises when the form of a practice (i.e., the structure of its second-order rules) becomes pathological in a specific way. For example, we can imagine that a practice ascribes to its participants a constitutive orientation to the effect that they ought to appropriate and relate to the rules that are internal to a practice in a particular way. The only legitimate understanding could be one according to which these norms are seen as autonomously chosen, for instance. If the same practice is governed by second-order rules that prohibit the parties involved from intentionally changing its rules, criticizing them, thematizing them or questioning them, however, then this practice contains a constitutive contradiction, as discussed in section 8.5. Such a practice becomes inconsistent in a particular way.

What does this mean, concretely? We can easily imagine that particular practices that produce particular distinctions and particular 'forms of objectivity' develop through the establishment of relations of power and domination in a particularly pathological way.[49] In such cases, the ascription of standard authority – which constitutes the practice – becomes regulated by higher-order rules, such that the participants are implicitly forbidden from treating the rules of this practice as normatively institutionalized. For example, in a bureaucratically organized educational system, distinctions of 'talent' could be introduced that are based on particular rules for making distinctions between students. If the rules of a practice determine that 'talent' must be treated as something given and unchangeable, then a critical examination of the respective classifications with regard to the aims of the practice becomes not only illegitimate but impossible. Since critical reference to such internal distinctions is not envisaged, corresponding actions are not a legitimate part of the practice. It is precisely then, however, that internal distinctions lose their connection to the aims of the participating subjects: they, and the objects that are determined through them, become something that is 'merely given'.[50]

The 'reification' of objects should therefore similarly be seen neither as a (subjective) error, that is, a category mistake in a purely epistemic sense, nor as a state of affairs that can only be described from an objective standpoint. Reification should be understood as a practical failure within normatively guided social practices.[51] That this is the best strategy is made apparent by the fact that 'reification' actually designates the frustration of our demand for a particular kind of access to our practices. This demand is experienced as related to our practices – that is, as a practical, not epistemic, barrier – and is context relative. In order for us to speak of reification, not only must a practice be constituted such that it actually becomes inaccessible, but this inaccessibility must contradict particular internal claims of the practice.

With regard to the norms and rules of social practices, it has already been demonstrated that the idea of total transparency – that is, the idea that we can explicitly question all rules of a practice at the same time – is theoretically inconsistent. But this idea is also unnecessary since 'rules' generally only become practically relevant when conflicts of justification or action emerge. That is, we only need to refer to rules of practices when social reality becomes problematic in some way. The transparency of social contexts that Lukács seems to have had in mind would be better described as the context-specific possibility of appropriate *practical accessibility* of practices. This means that the image of a completely reified world[52] that Lukács paints must be rejected. This is because specific kind of failure that the concept of reification denotes is only intelligible with regard to practices in which demands for transparency are institutionalized that run counter to reification. More precisely: since reification must be understood by such a theory as the violation of immanent norms, it must be assumed that, in order to be reifiable at all, practices must institutionalize particular claims that can never be completely eliminated by reification.

Actions, persons and objects become reified if the form in which they are constituted becomes thematic for an actor who is taking up the internal demands of a practice and if, at the same time, the categories, forms and constitutive distinctions through which the respective practices are held together cannot be made sufficiently accessible – that is, accessible to the extent required by the actor's understanding of the agency that accompanies the practice. In this context, 'accessibility' means that the constitutive rules of the practice must allow self-referential actions to be recognized as part of the practice, that is, in particular, actions through which the relationships of recognition on which the practice is based *become thematic*. Usually, this concerns the possibility of explicitly thematizing the form, distribution and constitution of mutual recognition discursively. That the rules of a practice are practically accessible, however, can also be mean that nondiscursive forms of protest against the nonthematization of the 'rules of the game' are possible.

The question of what counts as 'sufficient' accessibility cannot be answered without reference to the norms of the respective practices. In fact, some practices are distinguished by the fact that they have institutionalized high standards for the possibility of problematization (for example, the modern legal system, democratic and scientific practices or forms of postconventional morality, in which we find explicit rules that allow their norms to be questioned). Others are so constructed that they only institutionalize entitlements of this form internally to a lower degree. For example, we may criticize premodern worldviews that are characterized by taboos which prevent the problematization of their normative distinctions. It would be inappropriate to describe these as forms of 'reification', however. This is because the inability to problematize a mystical practice, for example, cannot be understood according to its own rules as a failure of that practice. External criticism may be appropriate here, but in this case criticism of reification cannot be recognized as a form of practice-immanent critique.

It thus turns out that reification represents a special form of what was previously referred to as 'practically mediated contradiction': 'Reification' refers to a structural property: it occurs if, in a practice, specific orientations (regarding transparency, accessibility and the normative autonomy of the actors) are both *constitutively demanded* and *systematically frustrated*. Such an orientation, which is frustrated by reification, is not a normative orientation of the first order, however – that is, it does not relate to a concrete norm of action. Rather it is a meta-orientation towards a certain degree of accessibility when it comes to a practice, or, put differently, towards the possibility of consciously referring to the constitution of a social practice in one's own actions to the required extent.

Concretely, this means that reification occurs when the rules of a practice do not allow the actors in that practice to practically treat the rules of that practice as constituted through recognition. The problematic constitutive rules thus establish a situation in which the practice can only be treated as if it were part of nonsocial nature, although it could in principle be treated differently and should also be treated differently according to those orientations that are established as mandatory by the very same rules. In other words, such reifying rules exclude as illegitimate all actions that aim to renegotiate recognition claims, even though only such actions can realize the autonomy of the participants to the degree that is required by the practice itself.[53]

Marx and Lukács chose, not without reason, the system of market-mediated wage labour as an example of this phenomenon. On the one hand, the free exchange on the market is underpinned by the normative idea that individuals are autonomous, encounter one another through choices they make according to their own preferences and organize their social interactions in a self-determining manner, without thereby being subject to substantial heteronomous norms. This normative orientation towards autonomy, on whose existence the motivational power of the rules of the free market depends, is systematically frustrated by the fact that, through the mediation by commodities, social relationships in market contexts become disconnected from human agency. This makes the relevant interactions appear no longer as an autonomous realization of the participants' own will but rather as an exchange of goods that is determined by objective necessity.

From this perspective, the various aspects of the classical form of the critique of reification can be revaluated anew. The core of Lukács's critique can plausibly be reconstructed as soon as the idea of totality is replaced by a context-sensitive analysis of internal claims to accessibility and the epistemic suprasubject of the proletariat is replaced by the interacting subjects of social practices. The aspect of the inaccessibility of social interactions can be easily understood in such a model. Once the various social practices in a person's life context are no longer relatively independent of one another but integrated into one another to the extent that every single sphere of the practice presupposes the norms of all other spheres, and once this entire system of practices is structured such that it is impossible to bring into question the overall constitution of the system, then the claims to autonomy that the modern form of life prescribes to its members as a condition of the success of their social integration can no longer be realized. In this case, an individual finds themselves in a situation in which they must experience themselves as a mere spectator within a perfectly integrated, quasi-mechanically functioning context.

Equally unproblematically, it can be assumed that our relation to other people then loses its qualitatively determined aspects when the way these others encounter us as partners in recognition within social practices is no longer accessible to us as a normatively guided interaction but rather appears as mere facticity. Then we can no longer correctly engage with and perceive those relationships in which the other person encounters us as a person.

It could be objected that Lukács describes not only our *perception* of our social relationships and institutions but also a particular *quality* of these relationships (to subject, to activity, to objects) with the concept of reification. Furthermore, one could argue that the model of social practices employed here mistakenly privileges the epistemic perspective of access over the objective quality of a practice. The 'accessibility' of a practice does not, however, concern retrospective epistemic access to an object given independently of it. Rather, practical access to the constitutive conditions of a relationship is an essential component of the specific quality of that relationship. For the phenomenology of action, and even for the 'form of objectivity' according to which we perceive particular practically relevant objects, it is crucial which self-understanding we can make relevant in these practices, because in this self-understanding we give form to the distinctions that are constitutive of a particular practice.

Due to the inaccessibility of the distinctions and norms in reified practices, the subjects involved in these practices can no longer develop the necessary reflexivity that would allow them to understand themselves as normatively guided. As a result, the practices objectively tend to be perceived as a mere reaction to external circumstances. The objects, persons and even properties of their own subjectivity with which actors in these practices are confronted shift from being meaningful factors that can be understood as normatively relevant to being external, objectifiable entities that are only meaningful from a strategic point of view. The lack of accessibility of the normative basis of a practice has not only epistemological but also constitutive consequences for that practice. As long as we see this practice as being subject to normative demands, it will inevitably fail according it its own standards.

The most difficult aspect of the Lukácsian description of reification is the idea that in unreified practices we can experience a 'qualitative whole' of things and realize a 'unity of personality'. But, as soon as we keep in mind the classical idea – developed by Heidegger at the same time[54] – that things primordially become accessible to us in the context of their practical significance, the first aspect can be explained. When we engage with objects in a context of practices whose constitution and whose internal distinctions are inaccessible to us, the practical significance of those objects will remain inaccessible to us to the same extent, or only become abstractly accessible. Finally, with regard to the self-relation of subjects, a similar argument can be made concerning how we integrate the subjective potentials we experience in particular practices (our sense of which relies on their affirmation by others through recognition in those practices) both into the overall pattern of our personality and into the narrative structure of our lives. Here, too, it can be assumed that the objectification and dissociation of individual practices cannot persist without ramifications.

A practice-theoretical reconstruction of the critique of reification can therefore make sense of the different forms of reification that Lukács describes in such a way that they are treated as context-specific breakdowns of practices.

9.7 SUMMARY

The critique of reification, unlike first-order immanent critique, does not make internal 'moves' in social practices explicit. Nevertheless, we would be wrong to understand the critique of reification such that it relies on transcendent criteria that all social practices must satisfy. It is rather a form of critique that expresses a claim that pertains to forms of life as a whole, but which becomes relevant in a particular way in specific forms of life: namely, in the form of life of modern societies, in which norms are understood as an object of reflective discourse and therefore must be able to be thematized as such. This is expressed not least in the fact that these societies view their metanorms as the subject not only of political but even democratic decision-making processes. These decision-making processes are not procedures that remain external to the practice. Rather, democratic societies create an entitlement to the effect that the practices about which political decisions are made ought to be constituted such that they allow for practical reference to the political questions that arise in them. Even if the critique of reification is not a form of 'external' criticism, it must be acknowledged that it expresses different claims than immanent critique in the narrow sense, which mostly aims at only local revisions of practical norms. The critique of reification points out contradictions in a form of life as a whole and therefore has a transcendent moment – a reference to a better social order.

Chapter Ten

Conclusion
Social Conflict and Social Hope

A model of immanent critique, based on a theory of social practices, can meet the challenges set out at the beginning of this book. First, it can adequately capture the specific character of immanent critique as a form of social critique that confronts social practices with demands that are not external to them. Secondly, it can make sense of the ontological claim that immanent norms exist in specific social contexts. Thirdly, it can explain how we can justify claims about these norms. Finally, it can develop a model of progress, as it can show how legitimate demands for specific changes in the specific social practices it criticizes can be justified against the background of the broader social practices of a community.

The focus on the more technical, microlevel arguments that were necessary to explain this model should not obscure the central question of this work – namely, whether it is possible to reconstruct a form of immanent critique on the basis of the vocabulary of contemporary philosophy which allows us to criticize our contemporary society in such a way that we do not merely demand the realization of the norms we already accept but are also not compelled to completely ignore the perspective of the members of our society. Even if the *possibility* of such a critique has hopefully been demonstrated in this work, anyone who hoped not only for abstract arguments concerning theoretical possibilities and necessities but also to be shown the *concrete standards* of such a critique will perhaps be disappointed.

Of course, one might argue that the primary problem with contemporary approaches to social critique is not the fact that they are incompatible with current theories in analytic philosophy but that it is not clear which concrete standards social critique should employ. This objection is not entirely unjustified. The theory of social practices developed in this book is indeed not designed such that substantive statements follow. The claims defended here do not entail anything about what ought to be criticized in our current society or about the grounds on which it could be criticized. One might have hoped, for example, that the concept of 'recognition' could help to justify substantive normative demands. But that concept is applied in a fundamentally different way in this book than in the substantive recognition theories of social philosophy – Honneth's, for example – in which 'recognition' represents a normative ideal of human relationships that can be taken up and used as a guiding ideal by social critique. By contrast, the model proposed here assumes that the form of recognition that it analyses always already exists whenever there are social practices as the minimum standard that is necessary for the institutionalization of social normativity. Demands for *different* forms or *more extensive* relationships of basic recognition can only be derived by referring not to the constitutive role of relationships of recognition but to the specific norms that contingently exist in such practices. In comparison with substantive recognition theories, then, a certain amount of disappointment cannot be altogether avoided.

The prominence of the idea that philosophical theories ought to ground a normatively substantive critique of society is, however, in a certain respect, bound to a specific historical situation. At least on the surface, both Hegelian and Marxist theories reject (and not without reason) 'normative' theory, in the sense of a theory that claims that criteria external to our society can establish norms for its evaluation. In particular, Marx (and the twentieth-century revolutionary movements after him) had little use for a normative theory designed to provide guidance to social critique for two reasons: First, they always proceeded from already existing political movements that did not need theory to provide them with political standpoints since they already had them more or less explicitly available. Second, none of these theories assumed that political progress depended primarily on the antecedent development of a correct normative theory; rather, they took it to depend on the fact that *other forces* independently lent a normative direction to the social movements they aimed to inform.

The fact that the theory of social critique is currently confronted with different questions, and that the question of normative foundations has taken on such an urgent character, has to do with the erosion of the plausibility of both premises, but above all the erosion of the second presupposition: the idea that something like an objective historical development will equip social agents with progressive 'objective interests' in which we can positively trust has become foreign to us after the catastrophic experiences of the twentieth century. At the same time, we have become more sensitive to the fact that we must be able to give a principled justification of our already existing political commitments to everyone who would be affected by the changes that we advocate.

In such a situation, only two alternatives would seem to be open: either we must search for an objective, standpoint-independent truth behind the contingent practices of our society that can bear this justificatory burden, or we must adopt an 'ironic' position that allows us to relieve our normative convictions of the pressure of having to be understood as ultimate justifications for political projects in the form described above. However, both alternatives are limited in a strange way, in that they assume that whether any critique is justified is a claim about an objective feature of our present situation, the truth or falsity of which is therefore more or less epistemically accessible to us and only needs to be correctly conceptualized (or, as in the case of the ironic position, rejected). What is not taken into consideration is the possibility that whether any instance of social critique is justified is only tied to our present situation in a very weak sense: this might not mean more than that we *may now justifiably assume* that *we may be able to show in the future* that some particular demand is justified, because the social conditions are already in place today that will *then* justify our demanding recognition for our normative position.

The hermeneutic approaches to immanent social critique already go beyond the false alternative between asserting an 'objectively existing' justification of critique and an ironic 'as if' position, as they at least partially make use of the idea of a future consensus from which a specific normative change can be justified retrospectively. As it turns out, however, this is not sufficient to justify the demand for such changes in the here and now. A hypothetical future normative consensus that we can expect to emerge under certain, idealized circumstances cannot legitimately be used *in advance* as an argument for demanding the realization of these circumstances.

But perhaps the assumption that a correct perception of contemporary conditions alone must suffice to provide definitive guidance to people who struggle over the correct norms in social conflicts in the here and now is rendered unnecessary by these models, properly understood. If we assume that a process of social change will appear rational in retrospect, then perhaps we do not need conclusive reasons in advance to initiate such a process. In social conflicts, one might say, we often simply act without conclusive justification. Richard Rorty draws a radical conclusion from this argument, ultimately rejecting the idea of justifying social critique altogether. In his view, it is rather an 'unjustifiable hope'[1] that motivates the practice of social critique. At first glance, such a reference to the future could not be further removed from the model of immanent critique proposed here, which is fundamentally focused on the resources that people have at their disposal in their *present, actual* social conditions and that allow them to criticize these conditions.

But if we recall that norm-oriented action is not determined mechanically by a norm, but fundamentally consists in acting under a *recognitive expectation*, then this focus on the present is broken. The 'default authority' of participants in interaction – which is established through the relationship of mutual recognition and is always contestable – entails not only that (in the normal case) the actual recognition or nonrecognition of an action as correct by others is sufficient to qualify it as correct or incorrect but also that it is ultimately not the *actual* interpretations of what the relevant norm is but the *correct* interpretations that must form the ultimate standard for the correctness of actions. This conception of what counts as a 'correct interpretation of a norm' is bound up with a reference to the future: the correct interpretation of a norm, as already mentioned, is not normally determined by drawing on any kind of 'knowledge' of an unproblematically given fact that need only be grasped cognitively. Being orientated towards a rule is rather characterized by a *justified expectation* concerning others – that is, by an attitude towards others that *refers to the future*. This applies especially to the norms on which immanent critique relies: the justification of immanent critique consists not in the fact that a norm is already unproblematically given in a practice of a community and only needs to be awakened by a critic from its slumber, but rather in the fact that (under the presupposition of shared norms of interpretation) the critic can justifiably *expect* and *demand* approval and recognition of the norm they put forward, backed up by their interpretation of the actual behaviour of the community. This means that any critical norm is always developed with reference to a possible future recognition of that critique by those it addresses. When, for example, Rorty writes that 'the only point in contrasting the true with the merely justified is to contrast a possible future with the actual present',[2] it does not follow that the idea of truth has no justification in normative contexts but only that the meaning of this idea is not independent of the expectations people have concerning the recognition of their position. Truth and justification do not present alternatives in this context. Rather than referring to a possible future, the concept of normative truth (or correctness) is used in the expression of normative and political demands that we claim we are already entitled to put forward as legitimate and that we expect others to meet.

From this perspective, the immanent critique of society has two central functions. First, it seeks to show a possible way in which discontent with and opposition to false social conditions can be justified and to show that this justification entitles us to expect recognition of our position from others, thus giving us reason to hope. On the other hand, it has the more fundamental task of making visible previously undeveloped sources of recognitive expectations, thereby disclosing social hopes that were not previously intelligible *as* hopes.

The hope for positive change, and for recognition of the legitimate normative attitudes of whole groups, is indeed 'groundless' in this respect, as it cannot be derived from objective facts but only adopted, advocated and justified as a normative attitude. But it is not always *baseless*, as at least in favourable conditions one can rightly assume that resources are already inherent in the structures of social interaction which this hope can build on if it wants to justify itself to others.

In this sense, the model proposed here may satisfy the expectation that social critique should be supported by something more concrete than a mere abstract theory of normativity after all, for even if it does not discover a new source of substantive critical claims in the here and now beyond our contingent practices, it is still motivated by the idea that it can show that a correct understanding of social practices must always be accompanied by the knowledge that the present is not all there is. The structure of our practices is constituted such that the participants, with their contingent normative positions, are entitled to anticipate a better future – if they can assume that their social relationships already adumbrate a better future in the present. In this sense, engaging in immanent critique can always also be seen as an attempt to rekindle hope.

This careful optimistic reconstruction of the normative content of immanent critique is not an invalid revision of its original idea. In the letter to Ruge cited in the introduction to this book, Marx writes:

> It will then become evident that the world has long dreamed of possessing something of which it has only to be conscious in order to possess it in reality. It will become evident that it is not a question of drawing a great mental dividing line between past and future, but of realising the thoughts of the past. Lastly, it will become evident that mankind is not beginning a new work, but is consciously carrying into effect its old work.[3]

Notes

CHAPTER 1: INTRODUCTION

1. Karl Marx, 'Letter to Ruge, September 1843', in *Karl Marx/Friedrich Engels: March 1843–August 1844*, vol. 3, Marx & Engels: Collected Works (New York: International Publishers, 1975), 142.

2. Marx, 'Letter to Ruge', 142.

3. Raymond Geuss, *The Idea of a Critical Theory* (Cambridge: Cambridge University Press, 1981), 64–65; Axel Honneth, 'Reconstructive Social Critique with a Genealogical Reservation: On the Idea of Critique in the Frankfurt School', *Graduate Faculty Philosophy Journal* 22, no. 2 (2001): 7–8.

4. For the beginning of such an analysis, see Maeve Cooke, 'Avoiding Authoritarianism: On the Problem of Justification in Contemporary Critical Social Theory', *International Journal of Philosophical Studies* 13, no. 3 (2005): 379–404; James G. Finlayson, 'Morality and Critical Theory: On the Normative Problem of Frankfurt School Social Criticism', *Telos* 2009, no. 146 (2009): 7–41; and Rahel Jaeggi, 'Rethinking Ideology', in *New Waves in Political Philosophy*, ed. Boudewijn de Bruin and Christopher F. Zurn (London: Palgrave Macmillan, 2009), 75–79.

5. For example, Michael Walzer, *Interpretation and Social Criticism* (Cambridge, MA: Harvard University Press, 1987). Walzer's theory was soon debated in terms of its relation to current issues in critical theory and to the methodological problems in Rawls's theory. Richard Rorty's role in this debate should not be underestimated, even if he departs from very different premises than Walzer. See also Ian Shapiro, *Political Criticism* (Berkeley: University of California Press, 1990).

6. See Maeve Cooke, *Re-presenting the Good Society* (Cambridge, MA: MIT Press, 2006), 19–20.

7. Cooke, *Re-presenting the Good Society*, 39.

8. I use the term 'community' throughout the book to designate groups that either share certain normative commitments or are integrated through a normative practice without alluding to the traditional distinction between 'community' and 'society'.

CHAPTER 2: SOCIAL CRITIQUE

1. See James D. Wallace, *Norms and Practices* (Ithaca, NY: Cornell University Press, 2009), 76.

2. Of course, one could argue that engaging in such discussions is irrational or pointless. But they are nonetheless discussions in which social practices are compared to norms and can therefore hardly be described as anything other than social critique.

3. This is what Walzer implies in Walzer, *Interpretation and Social Criticism*, 35. As Brian Barry writes, 'criticism may convince those outside the society to support or undertake action to change things' (Brian Barry, 'Social Criticism and Political Philosophy', *Philosophy and Public Affairs* 19 [1990]: 368).

4. Social critique in the narrow sense – which Cooke calls 'left-hegelian critique' (Cooke, *Re-presenting the Good Society*, 38) – thus wants to convince its addressees to change their social practices. This does not mean that the group of addressees and the group of practice participants necessarily comprise the same people. The addressees are not necessarily those whose practices are described as bad but those who can change these practices.

5. As the distinction between a wide and a narrow sense already shows, this does not imply that there are no further rational, 'good' or commendable forms of social critique. Rather, this is merely a pragmatic limitation of the area of analysis discussed here.

6. These forms of critique may have practical intentions regarding their audience, but not necessarily regarding their object.

7. This also means that there are situations in which social critique in the narrow sense is not an option – situations in which there is no way to reach genuine intersubjective consensus because they are so distorted by violence, the breakdown of norms or structural pathologies that no agreement can be regarded as evidence for the rational acceptance of arguments.

8. As Walzer assumes in Walzer, *Interpretation and Social Criticism*.

9. 'Where an impersonal social structure, for example the capitalist market economy, has a lamentable effect, for example the immiseration of a class of workers, which arises due to the unforeseen consequences of the combined actions of a plurality of discrete agents, it is obvious why first order moral condemnation of this structure is not apt. Only actions (and omissions) for which agents can appropriately be held responsible are open to such criticism, and such criticism is thus properly directed only at responsible moral agents' (Finlayson, 'Morality and Critical Theory', 31).

10. See Cooke, 'Avoiding Authoritarianism'.

11. Of course, the language of reasons will not be appropriate to describe the link between critique and motivation in every case. The idea of 'disclosing' critique takes up this insight. But as far as that language is not appropriate, we are no longer dealing with the kind of social criticism at issue here.

12. See Honneth, 'Reconstructive Social Critique'; Mattias Iser, 'Gesellschaftskritik', in *Politische Theorie: 22 Umkämpfte Begriffe zur Einführung*, ed. Gerhard Göhler and Mattias Iser (Wiesbaden: VS, 2004), 155–72; Onora O'Neill, 'Starke und

schwache Gesellschaftskritik in einer globalisierten Welt', *Deutsche Zeitschrift für Philosophie* 48 (2000): 719–28.

13. Antti Kauppinen ('Reason, Recognition, and Internal Critique', *Inquiry* 45, no. 4 [2002]: 479–98) further distinguishes between 'ethnocentric' external criticism, which merely applies the standards of the critic without assuming that they are shared by those who are criticized, and universalist external critique.

14. Walzer, *Interpretation and Social Criticism*, 4.

15. O'Neill, 'Starke und schwache Gesellschaftskritik'.

16. Iser, 'Gesellschaftskritik', 169.

17. O'Neill, 'Starke und schwache Gesellschaftskritik', 725.

18. Constructivist-rationalist models of critique similarly depend on an idea of rationality that presupposes, even if a priori, that its addressees are interlocutors and thereby involves claims about what reasons they ought to accept.

19. This is not meant as a revision of the mainstream account but as a way of making it more precise. But this way of putting the issue still has consequences that lead to revisions of it, as an author like Michael Walzer – who is normally seen as an 'internal' critic – no longer counts as pursuing either external or internal critique.

20. This also aligns with the definition of 'simple internal critique' in Kauppinen, 'Reason, Recognition, and Internal Critique'.

21. This constitutes progress for the sole reason that Walzer, for instance, never describes himself as merely applying internal standards but locates himself between internal and external critique in a way that has yet to be explored.

22. See Wallace, *Norms and Practices*, 74.

23. *Manipulation* is a case in which the critic applies the reason-giving force of arguments in which he or she does not believe but hopes that the addressees see them (incorrectly, from his or her point of view) as good reasons. This should be distinguished from *influencing*, which is an attempt to change another person's position without relying on good reasons, the success of which does not depend on the other person's overlooking the fact that the considerations offered in favour are not genuine reasons.

24. This means that reasons are at issue that were not accessible as reasons to them beforehand, although one could say that, 'objectively speaking', they were already reasons but were simply not known or knowable by those involved.

25. It is precisely this property that makes it so difficult to find a form of exclusively external social critique. But this does not mean that it is a priori impossible for a form of external social critique to meet these conditions by showing, for instance, that there is a class of reasons that generate their own acceptance in every possible context.

26. See Martin Saar, *Genealogie als Kritik: Geschichte und Theorie des Subjekts nach Nietzsche und Foucault* (Frankfurt: Campus, 2007), 311.

27. See Richard Rorty, *Contingency, Irony and Solidarity* (Cambridge: Cambridge University Press, 1989), 9.

28. Kauppinen, 'Reason, Recognition, and Internal Critique' calls this 'internal reconstructive critique'. It seems unhelpful, however, to subsume immanent critique under the category of internal critique, even if these terms are used interchangeably

in much of the literature. If immanent critique is merely a form of internal critique, this seems to imply that it can draw on the same resources, that is, the explicitly recognized norms of a group. But this would prejudge the question of whether internal critique is the only form of nonexternal critique.

29. Honneth, 'Reconstructive Social Critique', 6. Raymond Geuss similarly describes this form of critique as follows: 'if the proponents of a critical theory wish to enlighten and emancipate a group of agents, they must find in the experience, form of consciousness and belief of *those* agents the means of emancipation and enlightenment' (Geuss, *Idea of a Critical Theory*, 65).

30. Compare the remark by Adorno (who confusingly uses the term 'immanent' for what I call internal criticism): 'The alternatives – either calling culture as a whole into question from outside under the general notion of ideology, or confronting it with the norms which it itself has crystallized – cannot be accepted by critical theory. To insist on the choice between immanence and transcendence is to revert to the traditional logic criticized in Hegel's polemic against Kant' (Theodor W. Adorno, *Prisms*, trans. Samuel Weber and Shierry Weber [Cambridge, MA: MIT Press, 1983], 30).

31. This passage was written in 2009.

32. In this sense, one can argue that 'connected' social criticism rests on 'disconnected' forms of normative analysis (Andrew Buchwalter, 'Hegel, Marx, and the Concept of Immanent Critique', *Journal of the History of Philosophy* 29, no. 2 [1991]: 279).

33. Georg Wilhelm Friedrich Hegel, *Elements of the Philosophy of Right*, trans. Allen W. C. Wood and H. B. Nisbet, Cambridge Texts in the History of Political Thought (Cambridge: Cambridge University Press, 1991), 20.

34. Pirmin Stekeler-Weithofer, *Hegels analytische Philosophie: Die Wissenschaft der Logik als kritische Theorie der Bedeutung* (Paderborn: Schöningh, 1992), 34–37. I am passing over the complex relationship between Hegel's social philosophy and his ontology more generally.

35. Georg Wilhelm Friedrich Hegel, *Encyclopedia of the Philosophical Sciences in Basic Outline*, trans. Klaus Brinkmann and Daniel O. Dahlstrohm (Cambridge: Cambridge University Press, 2010), 38.

36. Terry P. Pinkard, *Hegel's Phenomenology: The Sociality of Reason* (New York: Cambridge University Press, 1996), 8.

37. Pinkard, *Hegel's Phenomenology*, 9.

38. Robert B. Brandom, 'Sketch of a Program for a Critical Reading of Hegel: Comparing Empirical and Logical Concepts', *Internationales Jahrbuch des deutschen Idealismus* 3 (2005): 142.

39. Paul Redding, *Analytic Philosophy and the Return of Hegelian Thought* (Cambridge: Cambridge University Press, 2007), 213.

40. On the relation between critique and crisis, see Seyla Benhabib, *Critique, Norm, and Utopia: A Study of the Foundations of Critical Theory* (New York: Columbia University Press, 1986), 19. Benhabib also introduces the idea that a 'systemic crisis' becomes a 'lived crisis' as soon as its character becomes explicit (*Critique, Norm, and Utopia*, 226).

41. 'In that case we do not confront the world in a doctrinaire way with a new principle: Here is the truth, kneel down before it! We develop new principles for the world out of the world's own principles' (Marx, 'Letter to Ruge', 144).

42. This is the background of Marx's well-known claim that his critique – as on display, for example, in Capital – is at the same time an analysis of its object (see Karl Marx, 'Letter to Ferdinand Lassalle, 22 February 1858', in *Letters 1856–1859*, vol. 40, Marx & Engels: Collected Works [New York: International Publishers, 1983], 270). For the relation between a parallel method in Hegel's *Science of Logic* and the idea of immanent critique, see Michael Theunissen, *Sein und Schein: Die kritische Funktion der Hegelschen Logik* (Frankfurt: Suhrkamp, 1978).

43. Karl Marx, *Capital: A Critique of Political Economy*, ed. Ernest Mandel, trans. Ben Fowkes, vol. 1 (New York: Penguin, 1990), 103.

44. Marx writes: 'The contradiction between the purpose and goodwill of the administration, on the one hand, and its means and possibilities, on the other hand, cannot be abolished by the state without the latter abolishing itself, for it is based on this contradiction' (Karl Marx, 'Critical Marginal Notes on the Article "The King of Prussia and Social Reform. By a Prussian"', in *Karl Marx/Friedrich Engels: March 1843–August 1844*, vol. 3, Marx & Engels: Collected Works [New York: International Publishers, 1975], 401, emphasis in the original).

45. See Seyla Benhabib, 'Normative Voraussetzungen von Marx' Methode der Kritik', in *Ethik und Marx: Moralkritik und normative Grundlagen der Marxschen Theorie*, ed. Emil Angehrn and Georg Lohmann (Königstein im Taunus: Hain/ Athenäum, 1986), 86ff.

46. This also applies to the stronger form of reconstructive critique that Kauppinen assigns to critical theory in Kauppinen, 'Reason, Recognition, and Internal Critique'.

47. Karl Marx, 'Contribution to the Critique of Hegel's Philosophy of Law', in *Karl Marx/Friedrich Engels: March 1843–August 1844*, vol. 3, Marx & Engels: Collected Works (New York: International Publishers, 1975), 91.

48. Georg Lohmann, 'Gesellschaftskritik und Normativer Maßstab: Überlegungen zu Marx', in *Arbeit, Handlung, Normativität*, ed. Axel Honneth and Urs Jaeggi (Frankfurt: Suhrkamp, 1980), 248–49.

49. Marx puts this memorably: 'it is precisely the political state . . . that . . . everywhere becomes involved in the contradiction between its ideal function and its real prerequisites' (Marx, 'Letter to Ruge', 143).

50. I provide a more detailed analysis of the concept of a 'practically mediated contradiction' on pp. 251–52 section 8.5.

51. Seyla Benhabib, 'The Marxian Method of Critique: Normative Presuppositions', *PRAXIS International* 4, no. 3 (1984): 290.

CHAPTER 3: INTERPRETATION AND IMMANENT CRITIQUE

1. I cannot here systematically discuss the relation of this idea to hermeneutics as developed by Hans-Georg Gadamer and others. For the relation of this tradition to social critique, see Nicholas H. Smith, *Strong Hermeneutics: Contingency and Moral*

Identity (London: Routledge, 1997), and Michael Kelly, ed., *Hermeneutics and Critical Theory in Ethics and Politics* (Cambridge, MA: MIT Press, 1990).

2. Walzer, *Interpretation and Social Criticism*; Michael Walzer, *Spheres of Justice* (New York: Basic Books, 1983); Michael Walzer, *The Company of Critics: Social Criticism and Political Commitment in the Twentieth Century* (New York: Basic Books, 1988); Michael Walzer, *Thick and Thin: Moral Criticism at Home and Abroad* (Notre Dame, IN: University of Notre Dame Press, 1994).

3. Walzer suggests that only invention and discovery have thus far been philosophically recognized, which is why he wants to demand such recognition for interpretation as well. See Barry, 'Social Criticism and Political Philosophy', 365.

4. Walzer, *Interpretation and Social Criticism*, 5.

5. Walzer, *Interpretation and Social Criticism*, 7.

6. Walzer, *Interpretation and Social Criticism*, 10–18.

7. Walzer, *Interpretation and Social Criticism*, 14.

8. Walzer, *Interpretation and Social Criticism*, 21.

9. Walzer, *Interpretation and Social Criticism*, 37.

10. Intellectuals – who conceive of themselves as being the administrators of universal norms – are therefore not the only and not the best social critics, even if they try to exclude others from this category. See Walzer, *Company of Critics*, 6; for a critique, see Jonathan Allen, 'The Situated Critic or the Loyal Critic? Rorty and Walzer on Social Criticism', *Philosophy & Social Criticism* 24, no. 6 (1998): 25–46.

11. Walzer, *Interpretation and Social Criticism*, 42.

12. Walzer, *Interpretation and Social Criticism*, 46–47; Walzer, *Thick and Thin*, 42.

13. Walzer, *Company of Critics*, 3.

14. Walzer, *Interpretation and Social Criticism*, 6–7, 51.

15. Walzer, *Interpretation and Social Criticism*, 64. Walzer even connects this to imperialism (Michael Walzer, 'Nation and Universe', in *The Tanner Lectures on Human Values XI*, ed. Grethe B. Peterson [Salt Lake City: University of Utah Press, 1990], 541).

16. See Mattias Iser, *Empörung und Fortschritt: Grundlagen einer kritischen Theorie der Gesellschaft* (Frankfurt: Campus, 2008), 40–41. Forst objects that Walzer conflates these separate problems (see Rainer Forst, *Contexts of Justice: Political Philosophy beyond Liberalism and Communitarianism*, trans. John M. M. Farrell [Berkeley: University of California Press, 2002], 161).

17. Walzer, *Company of Critics*, 9; Michael Walzer, 'Mut, Mitleid und ein gutes Auge: Tugenden der Sozialkritik und der Nutzen der Gesellschaftstheorie', *Deutsche Zeitschrift für Philosophie* 48, no. 5 (2000): 709–18.

18. Forst, *Contexts of Justice*, 161.

19. Axel Honneth, 'Formen der Gesellschaftskritik', in *Desintegration: Bruchstücke einer soziologischen Zeitdiagnose* (Frankfurt: Fischer, 1994), 76. But Georgia Warnke ('Social Interpretation and Political Theory: Walzer and His Critics', in *Hermeneutics and Critical Theory in Ethics and Politics*, ed. Michael Kelly [Cambridge, MA: MIT Press, 1990], 204–26) rightly remarks that the existence of differences of opinion is not sufficient to show that there is no shared structure. Rather, a

difference of opinions points to a shared foundation, as it only makes sense if such a foundation exists.

20. See Joseph Raz, 'Morality as Interpretation', *Ethics* 101, no. 2 (1991): 349.

21. Walzer, *Interpretation and Social Criticism*, 47. See also Walzer, *Company of Critics*, 230; Walzer, *Thick and Thin*, 41–42.

22. Barry, 'Social Criticism and Political Philosophy', 364.

23. Walzer, *Company of Critics*, 5–6.

24. Walzer, *Interpretation and Social Criticism*, 41, 46.

25. Walzer, *Thick and Thin*, 47.

26. He writes, 'I want to deny that the critical enterprise is best understood with reference to its heroic moments' (Walzer, *Thick and Thin*, 51).

27. He quotes Gramsci, saying, 'What was previously secondary and sub-ordinate ... is now taken to be primary and becomes the nucleus of a new ideological and theoretical complex' (Walzer, *Interpretation and Social Criticism*, 42).

28. Walzer, *Company of Critics*, 17; Barry, 'Social Criticism and Political Philosophy', 369.

29. See also Ronald Dworkin, 'To Each His Own', *New York Review of Books* 30, no. 6 (1983): 4–6.

30. Walzer, *Spheres of Justice*; Michael Walzer, 'Objectivity and Social Meaning', in *The Quality of Life*, ed. Martha Nussbaum and Amartya Sen (Oxford: Oxford University Press, 1993), 165–77.

31. Joshua Cohen, 'Spheres of Justice by Michael Walzer', *Journal of Philosophy* 83, no. 8 (1986): 463–64.

32. Barry, 'Social Criticism and Political Philosophy', 370.

33. Shapiro, *Political Criticism*, 78.

34. Shapiro, *Political Criticism*, 76.

35. Cohen, 'Spheres of Justice by Michael Walzer', 461.

36. Barry argues that 'no modern society has a tradition waiting to be expounded by a social critic' (Barry, 'Social Criticism and Political Philosophy', 370). See also Raz, 'Morality as Interpretation', 394.

37. This is my own translation from Beate Rössler, 'Kommunitaristische Sehnsucht und liberale Rechte: Zu Michael Walzers Politischer Theorie der Gesellschaft', *Deutsche Zeitschrift für Philosophie* 41, no. 6 (1993): 1040. See also Cohen, 'Spheres of Justice by Michael Walzer', 465.

38. Michael Walzer and Ronald Dworkin, '"Spheres of Justice": An Exchange', *New York Review of Books* 30, no. 12 (1983); Warnke, 'Social Interpretation and Political Theory', 207–8.

39. It must be remarked, however, that Walzer also gives a distorted interpretation of Nagel's argument. Nagel defends the idea that we should engage in a step-by-step process of decentring our subjective perspective. This does not amount to the demand that we must completely retreat from society, as Walzer seems to argue (Walzer, *Interpretation and Social Criticism*, 6–7). For example, Nagel argues: 'Reasons for actions have to be reasons for individuals, and individual perspectives can be expected to retain their moral importance so long as diverse human individuals continue to exist' (Thomas Nagel, *The View from Nowhere* [Oxford: Oxford University

Press, 1986], 188). Similarly, the split in the self that Walzer attacks is not recommended by Nagel but described as a tragic feature of human life.

40. See again Barry, 'Social Criticism and Political Philosophy', 364. In more detail, see Iser, *Empörung und Fortschritt*, 589.

41. See Charles Taylor, 'Language and Human Nature', in *Human Agency and Language: Philosophical Papers 1* (Cambridge: Cambridge University Press, 1985), 215–47; Charles Taylor, 'Theories of Meaning', in *Human Agency and Language: Philosophical Papers 1* (Cambridge: Cambridge University Press, 1985), 270–92.

42. Charles Taylor, 'Interpretation and the Sciences of Man', in *Philosophy and the Human Sciences: Philosophical Papers 2* (Cambridge: Cambridge University Press, 1985), 26.

43. Charles Taylor, 'Self-Interpreting Animals', in *Human Agency and Language: Philosophical Papers 1* (Cambridge: Cambridge University Press, 1985), 64.

44. See Hartmut Rosa, 'Cultural Relativism and Social Criticism from a Taylorian Perspective', *Constellations* 3, no. 1 (1996): 44.

45. Charles Taylor, 'What Is Human Agency?', in *Human Agency and Language: Philosophical Papers 1* (Cambridge: Cambridge University Press, 1985), 15–44; Charles Taylor, *Sources of the Self: The Making of the Modern Identity* (Cambridge, MA: Harvard University Press, 1989), 14; Hartmut Rosa, *Identität und kulturelle Praxis: Politische Philosophie nach Charles Taylor* (Frankfurt: Campus, 1998), 98–126.

46. 'For what is important is that strong evaluation is concerned with the qualitative *worth* of different desires' (Taylor, 'What Is Human Agency?', 16).

47. Charles Taylor, 'Social Theory as Practice', in *Philosophy and the Human Sciences: Philosophical Papers 2* (Cambridge: Cambridge University Press, 1985), 101.

48. Taylor, 'Social Theory as Practice', 93.

49. Taylor, 'Social Theory as Practice', 97.

50. Taylor, 'Interpretation and the Sciences of Man', 35; see also Charles Taylor, 'Neutrality in Political Science', in *Philosophy and the Human Sciences: Philosophical Papers 2* (Cambridge: Cambridge University Press, 1985), 58–90.

51. Charles Taylor, 'Irreducibly Social Goods', in *Philosophical Arguments* (Cambridge, MA: Harvard University Press, 1995), 127–45.

52. Rosa, 'Cultural Relativism', 42–44.

53. Charles Taylor, 'Explanation and Practical Reason', in *The Quality of Life*, ed. Martha Nussbaum and Amartya Sen (Oxford: Oxford University Press, 1993), 215.

54. See Taylor, *Sources of the Self*, 72.

55. Taylor, 'Social Theory as Practice', 106.

56. Taylor, 'Social Theory as Practice', 106, 109.

57. Taylor, 'Interpretation and the Sciences of Man', 17–18.

58. Taylor, *Sources of the Self*, 71.

59. 'The proof of the validity of a theory can come in the changed quality of the practice it enables' (Taylor, 'Social Theory as Practice', 111); 'What makes a theory right is . . . that its adoption makes possible what is in some sense a more effective practice' (Taylor, 'Social Theory as Practice', 105).

60. Taylor, 'Social Theory as Practice', 109.

61. Taylor, 'Social Theory as Practice', 111.
62. Taylor, *Sources of the Self*, sections 4.1 and 4.2.
63. To resolve this dilemma, Löw-Beer proposes that we understand evaluative schemas not as transcendentally necessary but rather as 'existentially necessary', meaning that their absence is not inconceivable but practically unbearable for human beings (see Martin Löw-Beer, 'Living a Life and the Problem of Existential Impossibility', *Inquiry* 34, no. 2 [1991]: 225). Another solution is offered by Smith, who distinguishes between a strict, transcendental dialectics and an interpretive dialectics in Taylor, where the value of an articulated self-understanding is made intelligible through the latter (see Nicholas H. Smith, *Charles Taylor: Meaning, Morals and Modernity* [Cambridge: Polity, 2002], 60–64).
64. Smith, *Charles Taylor*, 125; Taylor, *Sources of the Self*, 85–90.
65. Taylor, 'Explanation and Practical Reason'.
66. Taylor, 'Explanation and Practical Reason', 219–20.
67. Taylor, 'Interpretation and the Sciences of Man', 53.
68. In particular, those addressed cannot know that they will understand more from their new position as long as they cannot understand that position itself.
69. Charles Taylor, 'Legitimation Crisis?', in *Philosophy and the Human Sciences: Philosophical Papers 2* (Cambridge: Cambridge University Press, 1985), 258. The idea here is that the premodern conception of a cosmic order is understood above all as an answer to the question of one's own role as an individual. But this seems to be an anachronism; see Taylor's own remarks in Charles Taylor, *A Secular Age* (Cambridge, MA: Belknap Press, 2007), 17.
70. Taylor, *Sources of the Self*, 57.
71. MacIntyre explains this with the example of Homer. Homer still describes a traditional, 'heroic' society (Alasdair C. MacIntyre, *After Virtue*, 3rd ed. [Notre Dame, IN: University of Notre Dame Press, 2007], 121–29) in which normative standards emerge immediately from the family structure, from an idea of cosmic order, and from traditional military values, but where they are not yet questioned as values. Homer himself, however, already reflects on these values from a different perspective than that of the agents he describes. He is already capable of questioning them (MacIntyre, *After Virtue*, 128). Therefore, he is a representative of the moral form of criticism that first develops at this stage of history.
72. MacIntyre, *After Virtue*, 188–90.
73. There is a difference 'between what any particular individual at any particular time takes to be good for him and what is really good for him as a man' (MacIntyre, *After Virtue*, 150).
74. They are 'not themselves immune from criticism' (MacIntyre, *After Virtue*, 191).
75. MacIntyre, *After Virtue*, 187.
76. MacIntyre, *After Virtue*, 187.
77. MacIntyre, *After Virtue*, 191.
78. MacIntyre, *After Virtue*, 191.
79. MacIntyre explains this with the example of chess: 'There are goods internal to the practice of chess which cannot be had in any way but by playing chess or some

other game of that specific kind. We call them internal for two reasons: first, as I have already suggested, because we can only specify them in terms of chess or some other game of that specific kind and by means of examples from such games . . . ; and secondly because they can only be identified and recognized by the experience of participating in the practice in question. Those who lack the relevant experience are incompetent thereby as judges of internal goods' (MacIntyre, *After Virtue*, 188–89).

80. 'That their achievement is a good for the whole community who participate in the practice' (MacIntyre, 190–91).

81. See David Miller, 'Virtues, Practices, and Justice', in *After MacIntyre*, ed. John Horton and Susan Mendus (Oxford: Polity, 1994), 248.

82. MacIntyre, *After Virtue*, 188.

83. MacIntyre, *After Virtue*, 190.

84. See Miller, 'Virtues, Practices, and Justice', 250.

85. At least if there are any external goods at all which are comprehensible without reference to the totality of practices in which they are embedded, then this seems also to be true for these goods.

86. See his critique of Aristotle in MacIntyre, *After Virtue*, 159.

87. A possible reason for this may be that MacIntyre thinks that external goods cannot ground more than a modern, individualist-subjectivist outlook. But this is only true as long as we assume that external goods are always only goods for individuals and never for groups. That this link between individualism and external good does not hold can also be seen from the fact that there are internal goods that are only comprehensible as goods for isolated individuals. The rich hedonist – one of the targets of MacIntyre's critique of modernity – can easily lead a life that involves many practices that do not have externally characterizable value.

88. MacIntyre, *After Virtue*, 200.

89. MacIntyre, *After Virtue*, 201–3.

90. MacIntyre, *After Virtue*, 6–11.

91. 'To enter into a practice is to enter into a relationship not only with its contemporary practitioners, but also with those who have preceded us in the practice' (MacIntyre, *After Virtue*, 194); for a discussion of these standards, see MacIntyre, *After Virtue*, 190.

92. MacIntyre, *After Virtue*, 153.

93. Alasdair C. MacIntyre, *Whose Justice? Which Rationality?* (Notre Dame, IN: University of Notre Dame Press, 1988); Alasdair C. MacIntyre, *Three Rival Versions of Moral Enquiry: Encyclopedia, Genealogy, and Tradition* (Notre Dame, IN: University of Notre Dame Press, 1990).

94. The Enlightenment encyclopaedists serve as a model for this mode even in earlier texts, however (see MacIntyre, *Whose Justice? Which Rationality?*, 6).

95. In this respect, the concept of a tradition is already in the background of the discussion of practices in *After Virtue*. The analysis of virtues as a shared understanding of social roles is introduced at the same time as referring to a shared understanding within a tradition (MacIntyre, *After Virtue*, 127). The reason for this is to be found in MacIntyre's theory of the meaning of actions, practices and shared properties,

which is internally linked to a claim about the narrative construction of sense. For his theory of action, see MacIntyre, *After Virtue*, 206–11.

96. MacIntyre, *After Virtue*, 222.

97. MacIntyre, *Whose Justice? Which Rationality?*, 374.

98. 'Continuities of conflict' (MacIntyre, *After Virtue*, 222; see also MacIntyre, *After Virtue*, 134, 147, 157; Alasdair C. MacIntyre, 'Epistemological Crises, Dramatic Narrative, and the Philosophy of Science', in *The Task of Philosophy: Selected Essays*, vol. 1 [Cambridge: Cambridge University Press, 2006], 11).

99. MacIntyre, *After Virtue*, 147.

100. The concept of a practice as 'systematic activity' is admittedly still employed in Whose Justice? Which Rationality but without that central position. See MacIntyre, *Whose Justice? Which Rationality?*, 30.

101. MacIntyre, *Whose Justice? Which Rationality?*, 56, 71, 77.

102. MacIntyre, *Whose Justice? Which Rationality?*, 71.

103. MacIntyre, *Whose Justice? Which Rationality?*, 71, 101.

104. MacIntyre, *Whose Justice? Which Rationality?*, 77.

105. MacIntyre, *Whose Justice? Which Rationality?*, 134.

106. MacIntyre, *Whose Justice? Which Rationality?*, 358.

107. 'Some other rival incompatible set of statements may also resist refutation with equal success' (MacIntyre, *Whose Justice? Which Rationality?*, 78).

108. MacIntyre, *Whose Justice? Which Rationality?*, 79–80.

109. MacIntyre, *Whose Justice? Which Rationality?*, 144.

110. MacIntyre, *Whose Justice? Which Rationality?*, 354.

111. MacIntyre, *Whose Justice? Which Rationality?*, 355.

112. MacIntyre, *Whose Justice? Which Rationality?*, 356.

113. MacIntyre, *Whose Justice? Which Rationality?*, 360.

114. MacIntyre, *Whose Justice? Which Rationality?*, 359.

115. MacIntyre, *Whose Justice? Which Rationality?*, 355–56.

116. MacIntyre, *Whose Justice? Which Rationality?*, 361–62.

117. MacIntyre, 'Epistemological Crises', 9.

118. MacIntyre, *Whose Justice? Which Rationality?*, 362.

119. MacIntyre, 'Epistemological Crises', 5.

120. That is, there is a competing tradition which they can characterize in their own vocabulary and regarding which they are capable of asking whether it has the expressive resources to plausibly describe the mistakes of their own tradition (MacIntyre, *Whose Justice? Which Rationality?*, 166).

121. MacIntyre, *Whose Justice? Which Rationality?*, 365.

122. MacIntyre, *Whose Justice? Which Rationality?*, 364.

123. MacIntyre, *Whose Justice? Which Rationality?*, 354–55.

124. MacIntyre, 'Epistemological Crises', 11.

125. MacIntyre, *Whose Justice? Which Rationality?*, 364ff.

126. See Rahel Jaeggi, *Critique of Forms of Life* (Cambridge, MA: Belknap Press, 2018), 290; Robert Stern, 'MacIntyre and Historicism', in *After MacIntyre*, edited by John Horton and Susan Mendus (Cambridge: Polity, 1994), 146–60. Baynes argues that 'MacIntyre's "highly exacting requirements" do not provide any

specific principles or criteria for determining whether a resolution is rational' (Kenneth Baynes, 'Rational Reconstruction and Social Criticism: Habermas' Model of Interpretive Science', in *Hermeneutics and Critical Theory in Ethics and Politics*, ed. Michael Kelly [Cambridge, MA: MIT Press, 1990], 132). Conversely, one could also assume a substantive conception of rationality that provides clear criteria shared by all traditions. But then it becomes unclear why MacIntyre needs to talk about different traditions at all. For this interpretation, see Amy Allen, 'MacIntyre's Traditionalism', *Journal of Value Inquiry* 31, no. 4 (1997): 511–25.

127. MacIntyre, *Whose Justice? Which Rationality?*, 349.

128. 'Philosophical theories give organized expression to concepts and theories already embodied in forms of practice and types of community' (MacIntyre, *Whose Justice? Which Rationality?*, 90).

129. 'There is no other way to engage in the formulation, rational justification, and criticism of accounts of practical rationality and justice except from some one particular tradition in conversation, cooperation, and conflict with those who inhabit the same tradition' (MacIntyre, *Whose Justice? Which Rationality?*, 350).

CHAPTER 4: IMMANENT CRITIQUE AND THE CRITICAL THEORY OF SOCIETY

1. Max Horkheimer, 'Traditional and Critical Theory', in *Critical Theory: Selected Essays*, trans. Matthew J. O'Connell (New York: Continuum, 1975), 212. For the idea of immanent critique in Habermas, see also David Held, *Introduction to Critical Theory* (London: Hutchinson, 1980), 183.

2. Held, *Introduction to Critical Theory*, 213.

3. For this debate, see Jürgen Habermas, 'Labor and Interaction: Remarks on Hegel's Jena Philosophy of Mind', in *Theory and Practice*, trans. John Viertel (Boston: Beacon Press, 1973), 142–69; Axel Honneth, 'Work and Instrumental Action', *New German Critique*, no. 26 (1982): 31–54; Ernst Michael Lange, *Das Prinzip Arbeit* (Frankfurt: Ullstein, 1980); Hans-Christoph Schmidt am Busch, *Hegels Begriff der Arbeit* (Berlin: Akademie-Verlag, 2002).

4. Jürgen Habermas, *The Theory of Communicative Action* (Boston: Beacon Press, 1984).

5. Jürgen Habermas, 'Technology and Science as "Ideology"', in *Towards a Rational Society*, trans. Jeremy J. Shapiro (Boston: Beacon Press, 1970), 101–2. See also his remark: 'In the meantime, bourgeois consciousness has become cynical; . . . it has been thoroughly emptied of binding normative contents' (Jürgen Habermas, 'Historical Materialism and the Development of Normative Structures', in *Communication and the Evolution of Society*, trans. Thomas McCarthy [Cambridge: Polity, 1979], 96–97).

6. Habermas, 'Technology and Science as "Ideology"', 113.

7. Habermas remarks: 'However, if . . . the bourgeois ideals have gone into retirement, there are no norms and values to which an immanent critique might appeal with [the expectation of] agreement' (Habermas, 'Historical Materialism', 97). Axel

Honneth writes, 'For Habermas, critique is possible only as immanent criticism' (Luc Boltanski, Axel Honneth and Robin Celikates, 'Sociology of Critique or Critical Theory? Luc Boltanski and Axel Honneth in Conversation with Robin Celikates', in *The Spirit of Luc Boltanski: Essays on the 'Pragmatic Sociology of Critique'*, ed. Simon Susen and Bryan S. Turner, trans. Simon Susen [London: Anthem Press, 2014], 569). See also Benhabib, *Critique, Norm, and Utopia*, 225; Herbert Schnädelbach, 'The Transformation of Critical Theory', in *Communicative Action: Essays on Jürgen Habermas's Theory of Communicative Action*, ed. Axel Honneth and Hans Joas, trans. Jeremy Gaines and Doris L. Jones (Cambridge: Polity, 1991), 7–22. For the time being, I neglect the later shifts in Habermas's work from a reconstruction of concrete practices to an analysis of the forms of practices. While the first strategy is clearly one of immanent critique, the second strategy depends on the assumption that the norms reconstructed from forms of practices are empirically effective in social reality. For Habermas as an immanent critic, see also Cooke, *Re-presenting the Good Society*; James G. Finlayson, *Habermas: A Very Short Introduction* (Oxford: Oxford University Press, 2005), 9.

8. See Peter Dews, 'Introduction: Habermas and the Desublimation of Reason', in *Habermas: A Critical Reader*, ed. Peter Dews (Oxford: Blackwell, 1999), 1–25.

9. Habermas, *Theory of Communicative Action*, 1:386–92.

10. Habermas, *Theory of Communicative Action*, 1:288.

11. Habermas, *Theory of Communicative Action*, 1:101.

12. Jürgen Habermas, *The Philosophical Discourse of Modernity: Twelve Lectures*, trans. Frederick G. Lawrence, rep. ed. (Cambridge, MA: MIT Press, 1990), 322.

13. Habermas, *Theory of Communicative Action*, 1:305.

14. Jürgen Habermas, 'Some Further Clarifications of the Concept of Communicative Rationality', in *On the Pragmatics of Communication*, trans. Maeve Cooke (Cambridge, MA: MIT Press, 1998), 327.

15. Habermas, *Theory of Communicative Action*, 2:77.

16. Habermas, *Theory of Communicative Action*, 2:117.

17. Habermas, *Theory of Communicative Action*, 2:117.

18. Habermas, *Theory of Communicative Action*, 2:131.

19. Habermas, *Theory of Communicative Action*, 2:135–43, in particular 142–3. See also Habermas, *Philosophical Discourse of Modernity*, 343; Baynes, 'Rational Reconstruction and Social Criticism', 135; Benhabib, *Critique, Norm, and Utopia*, 239.

20. Habermas, *Theory of Communicative Action*, 2:354–5.

21. Finlayson, *Habermas*, 53.

22. Jürgen Habermas, 'An Avantgardistic Instinct for Relevances: The Role of the Intellectual and the European Cause', in *Europe: A Faltering Project* (Cambridge: Polity, 2009), 51.

23. 'This road is the transcendental-pragmatic justification of a rule of argumentation with normative content. This rule ... is not compatible with all substantive legal and moral principles, but it does not prejudge substantive regulations, as it is a rule of argumentation only. All contents, no matter how fundamental the action

norm involved may be, must be made to depend on real discourses (or advocatory discourses conducted as substitutes for them)' (Jürgen Habermas, 'Discourse Ethics: Notes on a Program of Philosophical Justification', in *Moral Consciousness and Communicative Action* [Cambridge, MA: MIT Press, 1990], 94).

24. Jürgen Habermas, 'What Is Universal Pragmatics?', in *On the Pragmatics of Communication*, trans. Maeve Cooke (Cambridge, MA: MIT Press, 1998), 22–23.

25. Habermas, 'What Is Universal Pragmatics?', 88.

26. Habermas, 'What Is Universal Pragmatics?', 24.

27. Habermas, 'What Is Universal Pragmatics?', 25.

28. For more on this interpretation, see also Cooke, *Re-presenting the Good Society*, 51.

29. Habermas, 'Discourse Ethics', 92–93.

30. Jürgen Habermas, 'Remarks on Discourse Ethics', in *Justification and Application: Remarks on Discourse Ethics*, trans. Ciaran Cronin (Cambridge, MA: MIT Press, 1993), 31.

31. James G. Finlayson, 'Does Hegel's Critique of Kant's Moral Theory Apply to Discourse Ethics?', in *Habermas: A Critical Reader*, ed. Peter Dews (Oxford: Blackwell, 1999), 33.

32. Habermas, 'Discourse Ethics', 65–66; Finlayson, 'Does Hegel's Critique', 43–45.

33. Jürgen Habermas, *Between Facts and Norms: Contributions to a Discourse Theory of Law and Democracy* (Cambridge: Polity, 1996), 459. See also Habermas, 'Discourse Ethics', 92–93.

34. Iser, *Empörung und Fortschritt*, 123–29; Ruth Sonderegger, 'Wie diszipliniert ist (Ideologie-)Kritik? Zwischen Philosophie, Soziologie und Kunst', in *Was Ist Kritik?*, ed. Rahel Jaeggi and Tilo Wesche (Frankfurt: Suhrkamp, 2009), 55–80.

35. Habermas, 'Remarks on Discourse Ethics', 81. Iser and Finlayson agree that the validity of discourse-external norms does not follow from the justification of the norms of discourse (see Finlayson, 'Does Hegel's Critique', 33; Iser, *Empörung und Fortschritt*, 116).

36. For an extended version of the argument of this section, see Titus Stahl, 'Habermas and the Project of Immanent Critique', *Constellations* 20, no. 4 (2013): 533–52.

37. Habermas, *Theory of Communicative Action*, 2:117.

38. Habermas, *Theory of Communicative Action*, 2:139–40.

39. Habermas, *Theory of Communicative Action*, 2:139.

40. Habermas, *Theory of Communicative Action*, 2:133–34.

41. Habermas, *Theory of Communicative Action*, 2:141–42.

42. Habermas, *Theory of Communicative Action*, 2:126.

43. Axel Honneth, *The Critique of Power: Reflective Stages in a Critical Social Theory*, trans. Kenneth Baynes (1985; repr., Cambridge, MA: MIT Press, 1993), 271; William Outwaithe, *Habermas: A Critical Introduction* (Cambridge: Polity, 1994), 113–14.

44. Jürgen Habermas, 'A Reply', in *Communicative Action: Essays on Jürgen Habermas's Theory of Communicative Action*, ed. Axel Honneth and Hans Joas,

trans. Jeremy Gaines and Doris L. Jones (Cambridge: Polity, 1991), 245–46; Jürgen Habermas, 'Actions, Speech Acts, Linguistically Mediated Interactions and the Lifeworld', in *Philosophical Problems Today / Problèmes Philosophiques d'Aujourd'hui*, ed. Guttorm Fløistad, International Institute of Philosophy / Institut International de Philosophie (Dordrecht: Springer Netherlands, 1994), 68–74; see also Habermas, *Theory of Communicative Action*, 1:125–26.

45. Habermas, *Theory of Communicative Action*, 2:149.
46. Habermas, *Theory of Communicative Action*, 2:135–36.
47. Habermas, *Theory of Communicative Action*, 2:137.
48. Schnädelbach, 'Transformation of Critical Theory', 17–18; Simone Dietz, *Lebenswelt und System* (Würzburg: Königshausen & Neumann, 1993), 98–103.
49. Habermas, *Theory of Communicative Action*, 2:137.
50. Cooke, 'Avoiding Authoritarianism', 394.
51. Johannes Weiß, 'Die "Bindungseffekte kommunikativen Handelns": Einige skeptische Bemerkungen', in *Kommunikatives Handeln: Beiträge zu Jürgen Habermas' 'Theorie des Kommunikativen Handelns'*, ed. Axel Honneth and Hans Joas (Frankfurt: Suhrkamp, 2002), 447; Honneth, *Critique of Power*, 299–300.
52. Habermas, *Theory of Communicative Action*, 2:93–94, 107. As I neglected to remark in the German version of this book, it must be emphasized that Habermas changes his mind on this point later.
53. Jürgen Habermas, 'Handlungen, Sprechakte, sprachlich vermittelte Interaktionen und Lebenswelt', in *Nachmetaphysisches Denken: Philosophische Aufsätze* (Frankfurt: Suhrkamp, 1992), 97–98 (this passage is missing in the English translation).
54. Honneth, *Critique of Power*, 244, 293.
55. These levels should not be confused with those that Habermas introduces in his analysis of specifically communicative norms. See Habermas, 'Discourse Ethics', 87.
56. As Ruth Sonderegger rightly notes, only a very weak program of critique follows from the normative analysis of norms of communication. See Sonderegger, 'Wie Diszipliniert Ist (Ideologie-)Kritik?', 59.
57. Habermas, *Theory of Communicative Action*, 2:304.
58. Habermas, *Theory of Communicative Action*, 2:304–5.
59. Habermas, *Theory of Communicative Action*, 2:329.
60. Habermas, *Theory of Communicative Action*, 2:329.
61. Habermas, *Theory of Communicative Action*, 2:307.
62. Habermas, *Theory of Communicative Action*, 2:327.
63. Habermas, *Theory of Communicative Action*, 2:324.
64. Habermas, *Theory of Communicative Action*, 2:375, 386.
65. Habermas, *Theory of Communicative Action*, 2:370.
66. Habermas, *Between Facts and Norms*, 351–59.
67. This is particularly the case because the point at which the communicative lifeworld is too damaged depends on a view that emerges from public debate.
68. Habermas, 'Handlungen, Sprechakte', 97–98 (this passage is missing in the English translation); see also Honneth, *Critique of Power*, 298–99.
69. See Habermas, *Theory of Communicative Action*, 2:355, 232, 327, 375.

70. Habermas, *Theory of Communicative Action*, 2:372–73; Jürgen Habermas, *Legitimation Crisis*, trans. Thomas McCarthy (Boston: Beacon Press, 1975), 48–50; Timo Jütten, 'The Colonization Thesis: Habermas on Reification', *International Journal of Philosophical Studies* 19, no. 5 (2011): 701–27.

71. Cooke, *Re-presenting the Good Society*, 53.

72. See Maeve Cooke, *Language and Reason: A Study of Habermas's Pragmatics* (Cambridge, MA: MIT Press, 1997), 111.

73. Axel Honneth, *Reification: A New Look at an Old Idea* (Oxford: Oxford University Press, 2008), 55; Jütten, 'Colonization Thesis', 710–12.

74. On the concept of self-relation, see Ernst Tugendhat, *Self-Consciousness and Self-Determination* (Cambridge, MA: MIT Press, 1986).

75. Honneth states explicitly: 'The replacement of the paradigm of communication by the paradigm of recognition is meant to provide access to the immanent standards of social critique' (Boltanski, Honneth and Celikates, 'Sociology of Critique or Critical Theory?', 573).

76. Honneth, *Critique of Power*, 242.

77. Honneth, *Critique of Power*, 251.

78. Honneth, *Critique of Power*, 255.

79. Honneth, *Critique of Power*, 286.

80. Honneth, *Critique of Power*, 268–69.

81. Axel Honneth, 'Moral Consciousness and Class Domination: Some Problems in the Analysis of Hidden Morality', in *Disrespect: The Normative Foundations of Critical Theory* (Cambridge: Polity, 2007), 80–95.

82. Honneth, 'Moral Consciousness and Class Domination', 87.

83. Honneth, 'Moral Consciousness and Class Domination', 89.

84. This is also his conclusion in the essay: see Honneth, 'Moral Consciousness and Class Domination', 94–95.

85. Axel Honneth, *The Struggle for Recognition*, trans. Joel Anderson (Cambridge: Polity, 1995).

86. Axel Honneth, 'Integrity and Disrespect: Principles of a Conception of Morality Based on the Theory of Recognition', *Political Theory* 20, no. 2 (1992): 187–201.

87. Honneth, 'Moral Consciousness and Class Domination', 92.

88. This is thus the claim, against Habermas, 'that moral experiences are not aroused by a restriction of linguistic capabilities, but by a violation of identity claims acquired in socialization' (Axel Honneth, 'The Social Dynamics of Disrespect: On the Location of Critical Theory Today', in *Disrespect: The Normative Foundations of Critical Theory* [Cambridge: Polity, 2007], 70).

89. See also his Axel Honneth, 'A Society without Humiliation?', *European Journal of Philosophy* 5, no. 3 (1997): 306–24.

90. Honneth, *Struggle for Recognition*, 132.

91. Honneth, *Struggle for Recognition*, 135.

92. Honneth, *Struggle for Recognition*, 136–37.

93. 'Should . . . actions that adhere to specific norms rebound in certain situations owing to a violation of the norms that are assumed to be valid, then this leads to "moral" conflicts in the social life-world' (Honneth, 'Integrity and Disrespect', 198).

94. One can refer here again to Honneth's criticism that Habermas does not understand 'social interaction also as a struggle between social groups for the organizational form of purposive-rational action' (Honneth, *Critique of Power*, 269). For a conflict-theoretic reading of Honneth, see also Robin Celikates, 'Nicht bersöhnt: Wo bleibt der Kampf im 'Kampf um Anerkennung'?', in *Socialité et Reconnaissance: Grammaires de l'humain*, ed. Georg W Bertram et al. (Paris: L'Harmattan, 2007), 213–28; Jean-Philippe Deranty, 'Injustice, Violence and Social Struggle: The Critical Potential of Axel Honneth's Theory of Recognition', *Critical Horizons* 5, no. 1 (2004): 297–322; James Tully, 'Struggles over Recognition and Distribution', *Main* 7, no. 4 (2000): 469–82. It is often overlooked, however, that Honneth does not see conflict as foundational but rather describes a dialectic between struggles and presupposed potentials of justification.

95. See also Jean-Philippe Deranty, *Beyond Communication: A Critical Study of Axel Honneth's Social Philosophy* (Leiden: Brill, 2009), 321.

96. Axel Honneth, 'Redistribution as Recognition: A Response to Nancy Fraser', in *Redistribution or Recognition? A Political-Philosophical Exchange*, ed. Nancy Fraser and Axel Honneth (London: Verso, 2003), 131, emphasis added.

97. See Nancy Fraser, 'Distorted beyond All Recognition: A Response to Axel Honneth', in *Redistribution or Recognition? A Political-Philosophical Exchange*, ed. Nancy Fraser and Axel Honneth (London: Verso, 2003), 203.

98. Axel Honneth, 'The Point of Recognition: A Rejoinder to the Rejoinder', in *Redistribution or Recognition? A Political-Philosophical Exchange*, ed. Nancy Fraser and Axel Honneth (London: Verso, 2003), 247.

99. Even some of Honneth's formulations suggest this interpretation – for example, his reference to a 'pre-theoretical fact' (Honneth, 'Social Dynamics of Disrespect', 72). But even here, one can read this as referring to a violation of a normative expectation that has not yet been theorized rather than as a brute fact that is independent of social negotiation. See also Cooke, *Re-presenting the Good Society*, 42.

100. Iser, *Empörung und Fortschritt*, 173.

101. The ambiguity between these two approaches is reflected in his demand that a theory of recognition needs 'social-ontological and social-anthropological persuasiveness' (Honneth, 'Point of Recognition', 245).

102. Axel Honneth, 'Pathologies of the Social: The Past and Present of Social Philosophy', in *Disrespect: The Normative Foundations of Critical Theory*, trans. Joseph Ganahl (Cambridge: Polity, 2007), 41–42, but see Axel Honneth, 'Grounding Recognition: A Rejoinder to Critical Questions', *Inquiry* 45 (2002): 503.

103. Naturalness is certainly one of the weakest ideals in social philosophy (see Dieter Birnbacher, *Naturalness: Is the 'Natural' Preferable to the 'Artificial'?* [London: Rowman & Littlefield, 2014]), but it has never been completely abandoned. See also Honneth, 'Pathologies of the Social', 29.

104. Honneth, 'Pathologies of the Social', 35.

105. A similar argument is made by Christoph Menke, 'Das Nichtanerkennbare: Oder warum das moderne Recht keine "Sphäre der Anerkennung" ist', in *Sozialphilosophie und Kritik*, ed. Rainer Forst et al. (Frankfurt: Suhrkamp, 2009), 88.

106. Honneth often uses the studies by Barrington Moore (*Injustice: The Social Bases of Obedience and Revolt* [London: Palgrave Macmillan, 1978]) and Edward P. Thompson (*The Making of the English Working Class* [New York: Pantheon, 1964]) as illustrations of his claims. The forms of resistance discussed there are clearly an expression not of individual feelings but of collective experiences of disrespect. See Honneth, *Struggle for Recognition*, 164.

107. Compare the idea of a 'subcultural horizon of interpretation' in Honneth, *Struggle for Recognition*, 164.

108. Axel Honneth, 'A Social Pathology of Reason: On the Intellectual Legacy of Critical Theory', in *Pathologies of Reason: On the Legacy of Critical Theory* (New York: Columbia University Press, 2009), 26, emphasis added.

109. Honneth, 'Redistribution as Recognition', 157.

110. Axel Honneth, 'Democracy as Reflexive Cooperation: John Dewey and the Theory of Democracy Today', *Political Theory* 26 (1998): 763–83.

111. For the implied critique of Habermas, see Honneth, 'Democracy as Reflexive Cooperation', 778–80.

112. Axel Honneth, *Suffering from Indeterminacy*, trans. Jack Ben-Levi, Spinoza Lectures (Amsterdam: Van Gorcum, 2000), 42.

113. 'Muster' (Axel Honneth, *Leiden an Unbestimmtheit: Eine Reaktualisierung der Hegelschen Rechtsphilosophie* [Stuttgart: Reclam, 2001], 87). The third chapter was added to the German translation of *Suffering from Indeterminacy* and has not been translated into English.

114. 'Netz' (Honneth, *Leiden an Unbestimmtheit*, 89).

115. Honneth, *Suffering from Indeterminacy*, 42.

116. 'Sprachspiele' (Honneth, *Leiden an Unbestimmtheit*, 100, 116).

117. There seems to be a tension between these claims and Honneth's earlier critique of Habermas. In Honneth, 'Work and Instrumental Action', it is still production that carries normative content, although again in a way that relies on anthropology (see for an analysis Nicholas H. Smith, 'Work and the Struggle for Recognition', *European Journal of Political Theory* 8, no. 1 [2009]: 46–60). This conception has been revised by Honneth to the effect that the norms of distribution of social recognition for achievements in the sphere of social reproduction can be derived no longer from the activity of production itself but from the social norms of the organization of work. These norms are justified if they fulfil a social integrative function in the context of the society as a whole (see Axel Honneth, 'Arbeit und Anerkennung: Versuch einer Neubestimmung', *Deutsche Zeitschrift für Philosophie* 56, no. 3 [2008]: 327–41).

118. The present work was completed before the publication of Honneth's *Freedom's Right*, in which Honneth spells out the social ontological constitution of practice-based normativity in yet another way.

119. Honneth, *Struggle for Recognition*, 165.

120. He thus argues for the necessity of a 'shared semantics' that acts as a counterweight to the suppression of experiences of injustice. See Honneth, *Struggle for Recognition*, 163.

121. Axel Honneth, 'Recognition as Ideology', in *Recognition and Power: Axel Honneth and the Tradition of Critical Social Theory*, ed. Bert van den Brink and David Owen (Cambridge: Cambridge University Press, 2007), 323–48.

122. Patchen Markell, *Bound by Recognition* (Princeton, NJ: Princeton University Press, 2003).

123. Andreas Kalyvas, 'Critical Theory at the Crossroads: Comments on Axel Honneth's Theory of Recognition', *European Journal of Social Theory* 2, no. 1 (1999): 99–108, 103; Honneth, 'Social Dynamics of Disrespect', 77; Iser, *Empörung und Fortschritt*, 174.

124. Honneth, 'Grounding Recognition', 508.

125. Honneth, 'Moral Consciousness and Class Domination', 94.

126. See Jean-Philippe Deranty and Emmanuel Renault, 'Politicizing Honneth's Ethics of Recognition', *Thesis Eleven* 88, no. 1 (2007): 92–111, and (critically) Markell, *Bound by Recognition*.

127. See Deranty and Renault, 'Politicizing Honneth's Ethics of Recognition'; Tully, 'Struggles over Recognition'.

128. Honneth, 'Grounding Recognition', 513.

129. An extensive discussion of Honneth's relation to communitarianism can be found in Deranty, *Beyond Communication*, 383–93.

130. Honneth, *Struggle for Recognition*, 85–86, 118, 169; Axel Honneth and Titus Stahl, 'Wandel der Anerkennung: Überlegungen aus gerechtigkeitstheoretischer Perspektive', in *Strukturwandel der Anerkennung: Paradoxien sozialer Integration in der Gegenwart*, ed. Axel Honneth, Ophelia Lindemann and Stephan Voswinkel (Frankfurt: Campus, 2013), 275–300; Honneth, 'Redistribution as Recognition', 184–85. In parallel to this, Honneth also develops a model of critique that refers to the notion of social pathology (Honneth, 'Pathologies of the Social'; Axel Honneth, 'Rekonstruktive Gesellschaftskritik unter genealogischem Vorbehalt', in *Pathologien der Vernunft: Geschichte und Gegenwart der Kritischen Theorie* [Frankfurt: Suhrkamp, 2007], 57–69; Axel Honneth, 'The Possibility of a Disclosing Critique of Society: The Dialectic of Enlightenment in Light of Current Debates in Social Criticism', *Constellations* 7, no. 1 [2000]: 116–27) and to distorted self-relations. A third model, which Honneth also sometimes gestures towards, draws on the idea of legitimate social integration (Axel Honneth, 'Philosophy as Social Research: David Miller's Theory of Justice', in *The I in We: Studies in the Theory of Recognition* [Cambridge: Polity, 2012], 119–33).

131. Honneth, 'Grounding Recognition', 511.

132. This objection does not apply to the criterion of legitimate social integration. This has not yet been developed by Honneth sufficiently to evaluate whether it is indeed a separate criterion.

133. Iser, *Empörung und Fortschritt*, examines further potential reasons for this model of progress in detail.

134. Axel Honneth, 'The Irreducibility of Progress: Kant's Account of the Relationship between Morality and History', *Critical Horizons* 8, no. 1 (2007): 16. Honneth systematically develops this thought in Axel Honneth, 'The Normativity

of Ethical Life', trans. Felix Koch, *Philosophy & Social Criticism* 40, no. 8 (2014): 817–26 (which appeared after the German original of this book was published).

135. Axel Honneth, 'Reconstructive Social Critique with a Genealogical Reservation: On the Idea of Critique in the Frankfurt School', *Graduate Faculty Philosophy Journal* 22, no. 2 (2001): 9.

136. Honneth, 'Recognition as Ideology', 326.

137. These criteria are developed in Honneth, 'Recognition as Ideology', 337–47.

138. Habermas, *Philosophical Discourse of Modernity*, 316–21.

139. See p. 23, section 2.3.1.

CHAPTER 5: COLLECTIVE INTENTIONALITY

1. The expression 'social ontology' – which is largely used in the current debate without any clear picture of either the relationship between social ontology and philosophical ontology in general or the relationship between current theorizing and the classic accounts of social ontology in the early twentieth century – will be employed here in the minimal sense suggested by Quine. A social theory will be taken to be committed to the existence of those entities to which the bound variables in its positive claims refer (W. V. O. Quine, 'On What There Is', in *Quintessence: Basic Readings from the Philosophy of W. V. Quine* [Cambridge, MA: Harvard University Press, 2004], 177–93). Of course, this does not mean that all other parts of the Quinean picture are endorsed as well.

2. Taylor, 'Interpretation and the Sciences of Man', 34–37; Taylor, 'Irreducibly Social Goods', 127–45.

3. Taylor, 'Interpretation and the Sciences of Man', 36.

4. On the difficulties of using 'we', see Margaret Gilbert, *On Social Facts* (London: Routledge, 1989), 167–84; Hans Bernhard Schmid, *Wir-Intentionalität: Kritik des ontologischen Individualismus und Rekonstruktion der Gemeinschaft*, Alber-Reihe Praktische Philosophie 75 (Freiburg im Breisgau: Karl Alber, 2005), 41–42.

5. See Taylor, 'Theories of Meaning', 259.

6. I will use the concept of an 'attitude' in a somewhat wider sense than is usual in the philosophical debate, covering all intentional attitudes rather than merely beliefs and intentions.

7. I will use 'collective commitments' relatively loosely as covering collective beliefs, intentions and other attitudes. The debate in analytic philosophy focuses – except for Margaret Gilbert and Raimo Tuomela – on intentions and actions. For my argument, however, a generic concept of a joint attitude towards events or states of affairs is necessary.

8. Margaret Thatcher, 'Interview for Woman's Own', interview by Douglas Keay, *Woman's Own Magazine*, 31 October 1987, cited in Wikiquote Contributors, 'Margaret Thatcher', *Wikiquote*, https://secure.wikimedia.org/wikiquote/en/wiki/Margaret_Thatcher.

9. Schmid, *Wir-Intentionalität*, 35.

10. Robert Sugden, 'Thinking as a Team: Towards an Explanation of Nonselfish Behaviour', *Social Philosophy and Policy* 10 (1993): 69–89.

11. Philip Pettit, 'Groups with Minds of Their Own', in *Socializing Metaphysics*, ed. F. Schmitt (Lanham, MD: Rowman & Littlefield, 2003), 172–75.

12. Pettit does not draw this conclusion from his argument, however. See also Philip Pettit and David Schweikard, 'Joint Actions and Group Agents', *Philosophy of the Social Sciences* 36, no. 1 (2006): 18–39.

13. Max Weber, *Economy and Society*, ed. Guenther Roth and Claus Wittich (Berkeley: University of California Press, 1978), 5.

14. This has become a commonplace observation following Davidson. For a related argument regarding normative ascription, see Simon Blackburn, *Ruling Passions* (Oxford: Oxford University Press, 1998), 72. In other frameworks as well, understanding in general depends on the ascription of intentional states that are consistent with the observed actions. As Dennett argues (Daniel C. Dennett, 'Intentional Systems', *Journal of Philosophy* 68, no. 4 [1971]: 94), we can also ascribe attitudes in the case of nonhuman agents (such as nonhuman animals, machines beyond a certain threshold of complexity, etc.) that allow us to ascribe rationally to them.

15. For a similar strategy, see Deborah Tollefsen, 'Organizations as True Believers', *Journal of Social Philosophy* 33, no. 3 (2002): 395–410. Turner's objection against theories of practice (Stephen Turner, *The Social Theory of Practices: Tradition, Tacit Knowledge and Presuppositions* [Cambridge: Polity, 1994], 32) depends on ignoring this distinction.

16. Robert B. Brandom, *Making It Explicit* (Cambridge, MA: Harvard University Press, 1994), 13; Gideon Rosen, 'Who Makes the Rules around Here?', *Philosophy and Phenomenological Research* 52 (1997): 163–71; for an even stronger version of the link between normativity and intentionality, see Ralph Wedgwood, *The Nature of Normativity* (Oxford: Clarendon Press, 2007), 158–65.

17. I take this example from Gilbert, *On Social Facts*, 156.

18. Maybe both of them are members of the G. E. Moore Society (Margaret Gilbert, 'Walking Together: A Paradigmatic Social Phenomenon', *Midwest Studies in Philosophy* 15 [1990]: 5).

19. See also Raimo Tuomela, *The Philosophy of Sociality* (Oxford: Oxford University Press, 2007), 259, n. 17.

20. Margaret Gilbert, 'Obligation and Joint Commitment', *Utilitas* 11, no. 2 (1999): 143–63.

21. 'Genuine travelling together involves rights and duties that are something other than moral rights and duties' (Gilbert, *On Social Facts*, 162).

22. For these expressions, see Gilbert, *On Social Facts*, 238.

23. I take this name from David Schweikard, '"You'll Never Walk Alone": Gemeinsames Handeln und soziale Relationen', *Deutsche Zeitschrift für Philosophie* 55, no. 3 (2007): 425–40.

24. Jane Heal, 'Common Knowledge', *Philosophical Quarterly* 28 (1978): 116–31; Gilbert, *On Social Facts*, 188–91; David K. Lewis, *Convention: A Philosophical Study* (Cambridge: Cambridge University Press, 1969).

25. For problems with this view, see Schmid, *Wir-Intentionalität*, 143–45.

26. John R. Searle, 'Collective Intentions and Actions', in *Intentions in Communication*, ed. P. Cohen, J. Morgan and M. E. Pollack (Cambridge, MA: MIT Press, 1990), 401–15. For a critique of this argument, see Seumas Miller, *Social Action: A Teleological Account* (Cambridge: Cambridge University Press, 2001), 84.

27. Michael E. Bratman, 'Shared Cooperative Activity' and 'Shared Intention', in *Faces of Intention* (Cambridge: Cambridge University Press, 1999), 93–108 and 109–29, respectively.

28. Bratman, 'Shared Cooperative Activity', 96; Bratman, 'Shared Intention', 117.

29. Bratman, 'Shared Cooperative Activity', 98; Bratman, 'Shared Intention', 120.

30. Bratman, 'Shared Cooperative Activity', 102; Bratman, 'Shared Intention', 117.

31. Bratman, 'Shared Intention', 126.

32. Bratman, 'Shared Cooperative Activity', 104.

33. Michael E. Bratman, 'Shared Intention and Mutual Obligation', in *Faces of Intention* (Cambridge: Cambridge University Press, 1999), 130–41.

34. Thomas M. Scanlon, 'Promises and Practices', *Philosophy & Public Affairs* 19, no. 3 (1990): 199–226.

35. Searle, 'Collective Intentions and Actions', 404.

36. John R. Searle, *The Construction of Social Reality* (New York: Penguin, 1995), 24.

37. See Anthonie Meijers, 'Can Collective Intentionality Be Individualized?', *American Journal of Economics and Sociology* 62, no. 1 (2003): 167–83.

38. Searle, 'Collective Intentions and Actions', 407.

39. See also Dan Fitzpatrick, 'Searle and Collective Intentionality: The Self-Defeating Nature of Internalism with Respect to Social Facts', *American Journal of Economics & Sociology* 62 (2003): 45–66.

40. Tuomela, *Philosophy of Sociality*, 33.

41. Tuomela, *Philosophy of Sociality*, 37.

42. Tuomela, *Philosophy of Sociality*, chap. 8.

43. The main elements of Gilbert's theory are to be found in Margaret Gilbert, *A Theory of Political Obligation: Membership, Commitment, and the Bonds of Society* (Oxford: Oxford University Press, 2006); Margaret Gilbert, *Living Together: Rationality, Sociality and Obligation* (Lanham, MD: Rowman & Littlefield, 1996); and Gilbert, *On Social Facts*.

44. Gilbert, *On Social Facts*, 241.

45. Gilbert, 'Walking Together'.

46. Bratman also tries to integrate this phenomenon into his theory (Michael E. Bratman, 'Shared Intention', *Ethics* 104, no. 1 [1993]: 97–113). In his theory, the participants' commitment is to their own subplans, which have to be compatible with those of others in order for successful cooperation to occur. For example, A and B intend to paint a house together if A and B are committed to subplans (such as painting a specific side of the house) that are mutually compatible. In this way, A and B are both committed to their own plans and the joint project at once. The fact that they can only execute their intention if the other also does so leads to a commitment to the plans of others. However, such a commitment is still ultimately a commitment

to one's own plans. Therefore, the obligations to others derive from instrumental rationality, and there are no obligations that could overrule prudential considerations.

47. See, for example, Gilbert, 'Walking Together'.

48. Gilbert, 'Walking Together'; Gilbert, *On Social Facts*, 161–64.

49. Margaret Gilbert, 'Acting Together', in *Social Facts and Collective Intentionality*, ed. Georg Meggle (Frankfurt: Hänsel-Hohenhausen, 2002), 53–72; Margaret Gilbert, 'Social Rules: Some Problems for Hart's Account, and an Alternative Proposal', *Law and Philosophy* 18 (1999): 141–71.

50. I will show later that a discussion of the well-known problems of rule-following can lead to a better understanding of the role of these social norms, which will also be discussed in chapters 6 and 7. See also Titus Stahl, 'Practices, Norms and Recognition', *Human Affairs* 17, no. 1 (2007): 10–21.

51. See primarily Gilbert, 'Obligation and Joint Commitment'.

52. The existence of a variety of kinds of 'standing' to criticize irrational attitudes is widely acknowledged in other debates, even if there are no systematic attempts to explain this variety. Darwall, for example, argues as follows: 'We are under a requirement of reason, for example, not to believe propositions that contradict the logical consequences of known premises. But it is only in certain contexts, say, when you and I are trying to work out what to believe together, that we have any standing to demand that we each reason logically' (Stephen Darwall, *The Second-Person Standpoint* [Cambridge, MA: Harvard University Press, 2006], 13–14) and 'the authority comes not just from the requirement of reason' (Darwall, *Second-Person Standpoint*, 14, n. 26).

53. It is not always easy to determine what the relevant group is. One can also argue that the members of the other team or the spectators have a standing, as they form a larger group bound by a commitment to engage in the specific practice of having matches. This problem does not affect the overall argument, however.

54. Gilbert, *Living Together*, 348.

55. Gilbert, 'Acting Together', 65; Gilbert, *Theory of Political Obligation*, 138–39.

56. Gilbert, *On Social Facts*, 198.

57. Gilbert, 'Obligation and Joint Commitment', 146.

58. Gilbert, *Living Together*, 11; Gilbert, 'Obligation and Joint Commitment' 145–47.

59. 'These commitments are seen to flow from the joint commitment' (Margaret Gilbert, 'Agreements, Coercion, and Obligation', *Ethics* 103 [1993]: 693).

60. Kenneth Shockley, 'The Conundrum of Joint Commitment', *Social Theory and Practice* 30 (2004): 538.

61. Gilbert, *On Social Facts*, 198.

62. Shockley, 'Conundrum of Joint Commitment'.

63. Shockley, 'Conundrum of Joint Commitment', 552.

64. For this distinction, see Robert B. Brandom, *Reason in Philosophy: Animating Ideas* (Cambridge, MA: Harvard University Press, 2009), 71.

65. For an extended discussion of this argument, see Titus Stahl, 'The Conditions of Collectivity: Joint Commitments and the Shared Norms of Membership',

in *Institutions, Emotions, and Group Agents*, ed. Hans-Bernhard Schmid and Anita Konzelmann Ziv (Dordrecht: Springer, 2013), 229–44.

66. Here (and in what follows), we should not interpret the idea that commitments and the obligations attached to them ultimately rest on the acceptance of norms to exclude power and coercion. Indeed, the opposite is the case: social power often includes the ability to force others to join certain normative projects and to thereby accept obligations towards others.

67. In contrast to individual intentionality, ascriptions of collective intentional states have different normative implications when considered from the perspective of an observer who ascribes those states to the group as a unified collective subject, and when considered from the perspective of group members who are also entitled to take other members as being subject to further obligations. The two kinds of ascription are interconnected, of course, as the internal point of view must be accepted to a minimal degree among group members to make the external ascription appropriate.

68. This is one of the basic claims in Brandom, *Making It Explicit*.

69. It must be emphasized here as well that such recognition need not always be given voluntarily in a strong sense: people can be induced to recognize others' normative authority by a variety of means, including coercion, threats and other exercises of power. The fact that collective attitudes (in contrast to individual attitudes that people can be forced to adopt by such means) also involve mutual recognition and thus shared authority with regard to a norm does not mean that all participants are free to decide the content of the norm or whether they want to participate in the joint attitude in the first place.

70. For the significance of this, see Gilbert, *On Social Facts*, 198; Bratman, 'Shared Intention', in *Faces of Intention*, 126.

71. The following argument is more extensively discussed in Titus Stahl, 'Institutional Power, Collective Acceptance, and Recognition', in *Recognition and Social Ontology*, ed. Heikki Ikäheimo and Arto Laitinen (Leiden: Brill, 2011), 349–72.

72. This means that we can consistently imagine a person's accepting an obligation without acting so as to fulfil it or even believing that she has accepted it, but we cannot consistently imagine a person's accepting an obligation without accepting criticism and sanctions regarding her nonfulfilment – this would be a bizarre sense of 'acceptance'.

73. The notion of acceptance is used here in a weaker sense than in Joseph Raz, *Practical Reason and Norms* (London: Hutchinson, 1975), 124ff., for example. There, acceptance is defined as a person's taking a rule as binding for herself. By contrast, this account does without any explicitly cognitive attitude towards the norm and merely requires a practical attitude. The attitude of acceptance, however, implies not only that people will not resist sanctions but also that they will not develop a practical attitude that is directed against such sanctions. The matter is thus one of dispositions to accept sanctions even in those cases where the agent could theoretically successfully resist.

74. For the connection between normativity and sanctions, see Heinrich Popitz, *Soziale Normen* (Frankfurt: Suhrkamp, 2006), 69.

75. For an analysis of the concept of default authority, see p. 210, section 7.1.4.

76. That is, as long as no other desires interfere, but without needing a supporting desire itself.

CHAPTER 6: NORMS AND SOCIAL PRACTICES

1. See Pirmin Stekeler-Weithofer, 'Die holistische Verfassung von Praxisformen', in *Institutionen und Regelfolgen*, ed. Ulrich Baltzer and Gerhard Schönrich (Paderborn: Mentis, 2002), 59–80.

2. For a history of this idea, see Charles Taylor, *Hegel* (Cambridge: Cambridge University Press, 1975), 3–29.

3. Max Horkheimer, 'Traditional and Critical Theory', in *Critical Theory: Selected Essays*, trans. Matthew J. O'Connell (New York: Continuum, 1975), 188–243; Jürgen Habermas, *Knowledge and Human Interests*, trans. Jeremy J. Shapiro (Boston: Beacon Press, 1972); for Adorno, see David Held, *Introduction to Critical Theory* (London: Hutchinson, 1980), 217; Honneth, 'Social Dynamics of Disrespect', 255–69.

4. Turner, *Social Theory of Practices*, 1.

5. Theodore R. Schatzki, *The Site of the Social: A Philosophical Account of the Constitution of Social Life and Change* (University Park: Pennsylvania State University Press, 2002), 80–82.

6. Schatzki, *Site of the Social*, 68–70.

7. Ludwig Wittgenstein, *Philosophical Investigations* (Oxford: Blackwell, 1958); Ludwig Wittgenstein, *Remarks on the Foundations of Mathematics*, ed. Georg Henrik von Wright, Rush Rhees and G. E. M. Anscombe, trans. G. E. M. Anscombe (Cambridge, MA: MIT Press, 1967).

8. See Robert B. Brandom, 'Freedom and Constraint by Norms', *American Philosophical Quarterly* 16, no. 3 (1979): 187–96.

9. This implies, as I will argue in chapter 7, that the status of following a rule is itself, in a sense, an institutional status.

10. In what follows, I will use this slightly inelegant phrase as shorthand for the ascription of a status that makes it appropriate to treat someone as following a rule.

11. It goes without saying that 'wrong' is not used here in any moral sense but merely in the sense of 'wrong according to a rule'. Moral rules are but one subtype of such rules.

12. One can see that standards and other kinds of rules share these functions because we can use them in the same way as prescriptive rules in such contexts.

13. Philip Pettit, *The Common Mind: An Essay on Psychology, Society and Politics* (Oxford: Oxford University Press, 1993), 82–83.

14. Saul A. Kripke, *Wittgenstein on Rules and Private Language: An Elementary Exposition* (Oxford: Blackwell, 1982).

15. Kripke, *Wittgenstein on Rules*, 8–10.

16. 'But if it [the hypothesis] is false, there must be some fact about my past usage that can be cited to refute it' (Kripke, *Wittgenstein on Rules*, 9).

17. Kripke, *Wittgenstein on Rules*, 16–17.

18. Kripke, *Wittgenstein on Rules*, 22–38.
19. Kripke, *Wittgenstein on Rules*, 43.
20. Kripke, *Wittgenstein on Rules*, 13.
21. G. P. Baker and P. M. S. Hacker, 'Critical Study: On Misunderstanding Wittgenstein: Kripke's Private Language Argument', *Synthese* 58 (1984): 407–50; Colin McGinn, *Wittgenstein on Meaning: An Interpretation and Evaluation* (Oxford: Basil Blackwell, 1984).
22. To cite but one example: John McDowell, 'Wittgenstein on Following a Rule', *Synthese* 58 (1984): 325–63.
23. 'Kripke argues, in effect, by elimination' (Paul A. Boghossian, 'The Rule-Following Considerations', *Mind* 98, no. 392 [1989]: 508).
24. Kripke, *Wittgenstein on Rules*, 21.
25. For this well-known distinction, see for example T. M. Scanlon, *What We Owe to Each Other* (Cambridge, MA: Belknap Press, 2000), 18.
26. As Pippin argues, this pragmatist perspective was first developed by Hegel (Robert B. Pippin, *Hegel's Practical Philosophy: Rational Agency as Ethical Life* [Cambridge: Cambridge University Press, 2008], 247).
27. Similar arguments are advanced by Stanley Cavell, who links participation in a practice to the ability to provide excuses and justificatory reasons. See Stanley Cavell, *The Claim of Reason* (Oxford: Oxford University Press, 1979), 310–12.
28. This conception of a rule is immune to the objection that Pierre Bourdieu advances against 'intellectualist' theories (Pierre Bourdieu, *The Logic of Practice* [Cambridge: Polity, 1990], 30–42), even if Bourdieu underestimates the practical significance of explicit reference to rules. See also Robin Celikates, *Critique as Social Practice: Critical Theory and Social Self-Understanding*, trans. Naomi van Steenbergen (Lanham, MD: Rowman & Littlefield International, 2018), 44.
29. See Jasper Liptow, *Regel und Interpretation* (Weilerswist, Germany: Velbrück Wissenschaft, 2004), 91, and Philip Pettit, 'The Reality of Rule-Following', *Mind*, n.s., 99 (1990): 3.
30. At first glance, this seems to be the well-known Humean problem of induction (David Hume, *An Enquiry Concerning Human Understanding* [Mineola, NY: Dover, 2004], 20). However, as Crispin Wright (*Wittgenstein on the Foundations of Mathematics* [Cambridge, MA: Harvard University Press, 1980], 25–26) explains, Kripke's problem is of a different nature. Similarly, Nelson Goodman's ('The New Riddle of Induction', in *Fact, Fiction, and Forecast*, 2nd ed. [Indianapolis: Bobbs-Merril, 1965], 59–83) 'new riddle', which is often cited in this context, is not identical to Kripke's constitutive problem. See also Ruth Garrett Millikan, 'Truth Rules, Hoverflies, and the Kripke-Wittgenstein Paradox', in *Rule-Following and Meaning*, ed. Alexander Miller and Crispin Wright (Chesham, UK: Acumen, 2002), 218, n. 219.
31. See also Wittgenstein's remark that in following the rule, the future applications are in some sense present (Wittgenstein, *Philosophical Investigations*, 79, §195; see also Wittgenstein, *Remarks on the Foundations of Mathematics*, 116, §III.8.
32. This is what Boghossian calls the 'ordinary conception of following a rule' (Boghossian, 'Rule-Following Considerations', 516–17); see also Brandom on the 'intellectualist conception' (Brandom, *Making It Explicit*, 20).

33. Wittgenstein, *Philosophical Investigations*, 81, §201.

34. Other classic formulations of this argument are to be found in Kant (*Critique of Pure Reason*, ed. Paul Guyer and Allen W. Wood, The Cambridge Edition of the Works of Immanuel Kant [Cambridge: Cambridge University Press, 1998], 268, A133/B172) and Wilfrid Sellars ('Some Reflections on Language Games', *Philosophy of Science* 21, no. 3 [1954]: 204).

35. For Kripke's own argument, see Kripke, *Wittgenstein on Rules*, 15–17. I forego a detailed examination of the regress argument, which is amply discussed in the relevant literature.

36. Kripke, *Wittgenstein on Rules*, 41.

37. See Liptow, *Regel und Interpretation*, 123, and Wright, *Wittgenstein on the Foundations of Mathematics*.

38. 'It is taking refuge in obscurity' (McGinn, *Wittgenstein on Meaning*, 101); see also Wittgenstein on intuition as 'unnecessary shuffle' (Wittgenstein, *Philosophical Investigations*, 84, §213).

39. Wittgenstein, *Philosophical Investigations*, 81, §202.

40. At some points, Wittgenstein seems to consider dispositional theories of understanding and meaning (see Ludwig Wittgenstein, *Remarks on the Philosophy of Psychology*, vol. 2 [Oxford: Blackwell, 1980], 9–10, §35). On dispositional solutions in general, see Paul A. Boghossian, 'Review: Wittgenstein on Meaning by Colin McGinn', *Philosophical Review* 98, no. 1 (1989): 83–92; Graeme Forbes, 'Skepticism and Semantic Knowledge', in *Rule-Following and Meaning*, ed. Alexander Miller and Crispin Wright (Chesham, UK: Acumen, 2002), 16–27; Warren Goldfarb, 'Kripke on Wittgenstein on Rules', *Journal of Philosophy* 82, no. 9 (1985): 471–88; and McGinn, *Wittgenstein on Meaning*.

41. Brandom, *Making It Explicit*, 26.

42. For problems with a simple analysis of dispositions, see David K. Lewis, 'Finkish Dispositions', *Philosophical Quarterly* 47 (1997): 143–58, and C. B. Martin, 'Dispositions and Conditionals', *Philosophical Quarterly* 44 (1994): 1–8. But for the purposes of my discussion, these difficulties can be neglected.

43. See Simon Blackburn, 'The Individual Strikes Back', *Synthese* 58 (1984): 281–301.

44. Crispin Wright, 'Kripke's Account of the Argument against Private Language', *Journal of Philosophy* 81, no. 12 (1984): 759–78.

45. Kripke, *Wittgenstein on Rules*, 28–30.

46. Wittgenstein, *Philosophical Investigations*, 80–81, §§198–202; Wittgenstein, *Remarks on the Foundations of Mathematics*, 334, §VI.32.

47. For various competing interpretations, see Baker and Hacker, 'Critical Study', 407–50, 420; G. P. Baker and P. M. S. Hacker, *Wittgenstein: Rules, Grammar, and Necessity* (Oxford: Basil Blackwell, 1985), 170–79; McGinn, *Wittgenstein on Meaning*, 191–95.

48. Karin Glüer, 'Explizites und Implizites Regelfolgen', in *Institutionen und Regelfolgen*, ed. Ulrich Baltzer and Gerhard Schönrich (Paderborn: Mentis, 2002), 185, my translation.

49. Bloor provides evidence for this in David Bloor, *Wittgenstein, Rules and Institutions* (New York: Routledge, 1997), 63.

50. This issue can be helpfully compared to how the relation between empirical and rational motivations are treated in moral philosophy. For a connection to the rule-following debate, see Peter Railton, 'Normative Force and Normative Freedom: Hume and Kant, but Not Hume versus Kant', *Ratio* 12, no. 4 (1999): 320–53.

51. David Bloor, 'Wittgenstein and the Priority of Practice', in *The Practice Turn in Contemporary Theory*, ed. Karin Knorr-Cetina, Theodore R. Schatzki and Eike von Savigny (London: Routledge, 2001), 101.

52. In regard to the orienting function, Searle's remarks in *Construction of Social Reality*, 144–46, are interesting. Searle does neglect the autonomy of the normative dimension, however.

53. Bloor, 'Wittgenstein and the Priority of Practice', 104. Bloor also formulates this idea as follows: 'Normative standards come from the consensus generated by a number of interactive rule followers, and it is maintained by collectively monitoring, controlling and sanctioning their individual tendencies. Consensus makes norms objective, that is a source of external and impersonal constraint on the individual. It gives substance to the distinction between rule followers thinking they have got it right, and their having really got it right' (Bloor, *Wittgenstein, Rules and Institutions*, 17).

54. The most prominent exposition can be found in John Haugeland, 'The Intentionality All-Stars', *Philosophical Perspectives* 4, Action (1990): 383–427, but the basic idea was first formulated in John Haugeland, 'Heidegger on Being a Person', *Noûs* 16 (1982): 15–26.

55. Haugeland, 'Intentionality All-Stars', 404. Regarding Heidegger – to whose position Haugeland seems to be committed – this categorization is relativized later (see John Haugeland, 'Truth and Rule-Following', in *Having Thought: Essays in the Metaphysics of Mind* [Cambridge, MA: Harvard University Press, 1998], 305–61).

56. Haugeland, 'Intentionality All-Stars', 404.

57. Haugeland, 'Intentionality All-Stars', 404.

58. In sociology, the central function of sanctioning norms is discussed in Heinrich Popitz, *Soziale Normen* (Frankfurt: Suhrkamp, 2006), 111.

59. See Liptow, *Regel und Interpretation*, 129.

60. There is empirical evidence in Ozgür Gürerk, Bernd Irlenbusch and Bettina Rockenbach, 'The Competitive Advantage of Sanctioning Institutions', *Science* 312, no. 5770 (2006): 108–11, that the binding nature of rules is supported by this reflexive structure.

61. See p. 192, section 6.5.4, for a discussion of Brandom's normative phenomenalism.

62. Haugeland, 'The Intentionality All-Stars', 405.

63. See also my 'Practices, Norms and Recognition'.

64. Brandom, *Making It Explicit*, 36.

65. This is how Liptow, *Regel und Interpretation*, 141, reads Haugeland's objection in Haugeland, 'Truth and Rule-Following', 355–56.

66. Compare this to the discussion in Robert M. Axelrod, 'An Evolutionary Approach to Norms', *American Political Science Review* 80, no. 4 (1986): 1095–1111.

67. Both objections are raised by Kathrin Glüer, *Sprache und Regeln* (Berlin: Akademie-Verlag, 1999), 108, against Kripke's social solution.

68. Haugeland, 'Truth and Rule-Following', 313.

69. H. L. A. Hart, *The Concept of Law*, 2nd ed. (Oxford: Oxford University Press, 1994), 23.

70. Boghossian, 'Review: Wittgenstein on Meaning', 534.

71. McDowell, 'Wittgenstein on Following a Rule', 335.

72. See also: 'But isn't this just what interests you about this multiplication – how the generality of men will calculate? No – at least not usually – even if I am running to a common meeting point with everybody else' (Wittgenstein, *Remarks on the Foundations of Mathematics*, 95e, §II.69).

73. See Sabina Lovibond, *Realism and Imagination in Ethics* (Oxford: Blackwell, 1983), 89, and 'Our language game only works, of course, when a certain agreement prevails, but the concept of agreement does not enter into the language-game' (Ludwig Wittgenstein, *Zettel*, 2nd ed. [Oxford: Blackwell, 1967], 75, §430).

74. Wittgenstein, *Philosophical Investigations*, 79, §195, emphasis original.

75. Wittgenstein, *Philosophical Investigations*, 81, §201.

76. Ludwig Wittgenstein, *On Certainty*, ed. G. E. M. Anscombe and G. H. von Wright (Oxford: Blackwell, 1969), 17, §110, and 28, §204.

77. Wittgenstein, *Philosophical Investigations*, 85, §217.

78. Wittgenstein remarks on this: 'Disputes do not break out (among mathematicians, say) over the question whether a rule has been obeyed or not. People don't come to blows over it, for example' (Wittgenstein, *Philosophical Investigations*, 88, §240). See also the more general remark in Wittgenstein, *Remarks on the Foundations of Mathematics*, 323, §VI.21. This assessment might be true regarding the practice of mathematics (although even there perhaps not without exception) but is not warranted for other areas of social life, where the meaning of concepts is always disputed – as in politics and religion. Wittgenstein admits that there are gradual differences between areas of discourse but always assumes that agreement forms a background for every sort of conflict. Blackburn remarks on this: 'I was aware of the colonial ambitions of the rule-following considerations, but I had thought that the territory of ethics was safe from annexation.... [T]he passages in Wittgenstein explicitly concern only cases where ... "disputes do not break out". By contrast ethical evaluations ... do provoke disputes' (Simon Blackburn, 'Reply: Rule-Following and Moral Realism', in *Wittgenstein: To Follow a Rule*, ed. Steven H. Holtzman and Christopher M. Leich [London: Routledge, 1981], 170). In general, this problem is overlooked by the more conservative proponents of an ethics of 'Sittlichkeit', as Lovibond shows with the example of Bradley (Lovibond, *Realism and Imagination in Ethics*, 191).

79. 'Wittgensteinian philosophy has not led towards any sort of concern with social change, with power relations, or with conflict in society' (Anthony Giddens, *Central Problems in Social Theory: Action, Structure and Contradiction in Social Analysis* [London: Macmillan, 1979], 50). An interpretation of Wittgenstein with more room for conflicts can be found in James Tully, 'Wittgenstein and Political

Philosophy: Understanding Practices of Critical Reflection', *Political Theory* 17, no. 2 (1989): 172–204.

80. As Dreyfus argues convincingly, this is one of the most important contributions by Heidegger to the social ontology of institutional normativity (Hubert Dreyfus, *Being-in-the-World: A Commentary on Heidegger's Being and Time, Division I* [Cambridge, MA: MIT Press, 1991]).

81. On 'normative phenomenalism', see also Ronald Loeffler, 'Normative Phenomenalism: On Robert Brandom's Practice-Based Explanation of Meaning', *European Journal of Philosophy* 13, no. 1 (2005): 32–69, and David Lauer, 'Genuine Normativity, Expressive Bootstrapping, and Normative Phenomenalism', *Ethics & Politics* 11, no. 1 (2009): 321–50.

82. Brandom, *Making It Explicit*, 25.

83. Brandom, *Making It Explicit*, 62–63.

84. Brandom, *Making It Explicit*, 46. This idea is elaborated in Robert B. Brandom, *Between Saying and Doing: Towards an Analytic Pragmatism* (Oxford: Oxford University Press, 2008).

85. Brandom, *Making It Explicit*, 648. That we should treat a community as following a rule whenever we can do so is justified pragmatically (Brandom, *Making It Explicit*, 644).

86. Brandom, *Making It Explicit*, 626, 628.

87. The second half of this paragraph was added to the English translation for the purpose of clarification.

88. See also pp. 203–5, section 7.1.2.

89. Brandom, *Making It Explicit*, 39, 62, 508.

90. Brandom, *Making It Explicit*, 67. Brandom to a large extent reduces this attitude to the individual disposition to display certain kinds of reactions.

91. Brandom emphasizes this feature of his theory when contrasting it with that of Habermas (Robert B. Brandom, 'Facts, Norms, and Normative Facts: A Reply to Habermas', *European Journal of Philosophy* 8, no. 3 [2000]: 363).

92. This is of course not an objection to Brandom's theory as it does not aspire to do so. As he says, he wants to describe only the 'very weakest, most primitive sort of social normativity possible' in *Making It Explicit* (see Robert B. Brandom, 'Responses to Pippin, Macbeth and Haugeland', *European Journal of Philosophy* 13, no. 3 [2005]: 432).

93. See Antje Gimmler, 'Handeln und Erfahrung – Überlegungen zu einer pragmatischen Theorie des Handelns', in *Handeln und Technik – Mit und ohne Heidegger*, ed. Christoph Hubig, Andreas Luckner and Nadia Mazouz (Berlin: Lit, 2007).

94. Brandom, *Making It Explicit*, 643–45.

95. Because Brandom's theory is discussed here exclusively in relation to its significance for models of immanent critique, I will not discuss a number of issues that concern the relation between social practices and semantics, such as McDowell's objection that Brandom cannot explain why the normative practices he identifies have any significance for discourse (John McDowell, 'Motivating Inferentialism: Comments on Chapter 2 of Making It Explicit', *Pragmatics and Cognition* 13, no. 1 [2005]: 121–40). My question starts from the assumption that normative, social

CHAPTER 7: THE IMMANENT NORMS OF SOCIAL PRACTICES

1. This chapter introduction was added to the English translation.
2. See p. 186, section 6.5.2.
3. See p. 187, section 6.5.2.
4. See p. 188, section 6.5.2.
5. This is thus a 'strong consensus theory' as classified by Ulrich Baltzer, *Gemeinschaftshandeln: Ontologische Grundlagen einer Ethik sozialen Handelns* (Freiburg: Alber, 1999), 248, but at the level of evaluations.
6. This does not mean that the authority of a community as a whole cannot be put into question. It merely means that rule-following is only possible if, in concrete interactions, the authority of the relevant community to settle the correctness of actions or reactions on some level is not always challenged.
7. Habermas, *Theory of Communicative Action*, 2:18.
8. In some sense, the concept of recognition answers the question of the justification of intersubjective expectations which, for example, Shwayder's conventionalism (David S. Shwayder, *The Stratification of Behaviour* [London: Routledge & Kegan Paul, 1965], 253) still fails to answer.
9. The concept of default authority goes beyond Habermas's idea and will be discussed more explicitly later (see section 7.1.4).
10. See p. 187, section 6.5.2.
11. See also for a comparison to Brandom pp. 192–95, section 6.5.5.
12. This is also a thought that Habermas takes from Mead but unfortunately does not pursue further. See his remark: 'The authority with which the generalized other is outfitted is that of a general group will; it is not the same as the force of the generalized will of all individuals, which expresses itself in the sanctions the group applies to deviations' (Habermas, *Theory of Communicative Action*, 2:38). For the connection between rules and collective phenomena, see also Gerald J. Postema, 'Morality in the First Person Plural', *Law and Philosophy* 14 (1995): 35–64; Christine M. Korsgaard, *The Sources of Normativity* (Cambridge: Cambridge University Press, 1996); Stephen Darwall, *The Second-Person Standpoint* (Cambridge, MA: Harvard University Press, 2006), 144.
13. Brandom, *Making It Explicit*, 37.
14. Brandom, *Making It Explicit*, 38.
15. This is thus effectively an objection that relies on the pretence of many collectivist theories to offer a reductive explanation of social normativity and does not affect theories that make no such pretence.
16. Gilbert's own discussion of this topic, in particular her response to a review by John Greenwood (Margaret Gilbert, 'More on Social Facts', in *Living Together: Rationality, Sociality and Obligation* [Lanham, MD: Rowman & Littlefield International, 1996], 69ff.), is not very informative. She seems to assume that collective

phenomena are paradigmatic cases of the social but does not assume a constitutive relationship between them and other social facts.

17. See p. 154, section 5.7.4.

18. See the discussion of this concept as relating to collective intentionality in section 5.7.3.

19. See p. 200, section 7.1.

20. Here again it must be emphasized that the relation of symmetric recognition does not exclude phenomena of power and coercion. The idea that social norms always presuppose recognition does not entail that individuals need to be able to 'freely' decide about the relations of recognition in which they stand with others in any sense or about the norms that govern these relations. Normativity is only incompatible with absolutely arbitrary power, where one side has the ability to determine the content of the 'norm' ad hoc for any given case.

21. A certain foundationalism can even be detected in Wittgenstein. He indeed argues against the reductionist view that one can explain normative phenomena in nonnormative vocabulary once one has reached the 'bedrock' (Wittgenstein, *Philosophical Investigations*, 85, §217) of behaviour. But this language still distinguishes between foundations and superstructures. It is unclear whether his view is really compatible with a thoroughgoing holism.

22. For this reason, not every kind of dissent can be used as evidence for the lack of existence of a social norm, as Dworkin assumes in his criticism of Hart (Ronald Dworkin, *Taking Rights Seriously* [Cambridge, MA: Harvard University Press, 1977], 54–58). Rather, dissent only signals a breakdown of norms if the mutual ascription of authority breaks down as well. Therefore, the solution proposed here is still 'conventionalist' in the sense in which Dworkin uses the term, but less strongly so than Hart's model.

23. This model therefore traces the empirically effective and socially enforceable content of norms back to actually realized attitudes and is therefore 'conventionalist' in the sense that there is no social norm if the people involved are not capable of designating, at some level, some reaction as justified. This conventionalism – which explicitly does not explain the content but merely the existence of social norms – is acceptable in the case of generically social norms. It remains an open question, admittedly, whether it is also sufficient to explain the specific features of legal or semantic norms, for example.

24. See MacCullagh's argument to the effect that a practice theory can only elucidate not explain rule-following (Mark McCullagh, 'Wittgenstein on Rules and Practices', *Journal of Philosophical Research* 27 [2002]: 83–100).

25. See p. 150, section 5.7.2.

26. A 'higher-order norm' is operative if individual agents recognize each other as competent regarding a norm that regulates the correctness of evaluations regarding lower-order norms. Even when A sanctions B for violating a rule R, A must still presuppose that B can competently apply a higher-order rule R' which determines what counts as a violation of R (for example, a rule determining the meaning of terms in a definition). In contrast to the model of interpretation that leads to a regress problem, this argument does not assume that *every* application of a rule presupposes

another application of a higher-order rule. It merely assumes that such applications are embedded in a practice in which higher-order rules *can* become thematic once differences in interpretation arise.

27. See p. 210, section 7.1.4.

28. Giddens emphasizes the processual character of this kind of reflexivity as 'reflexively monitoring the flow of interaction with one another' (Anthony Giddens, *The Constitution of Society* [Cambridge: Polity, 1984], 30).

29. This is another argument for the claim that a plausible theory of normative social practices cannot be reductionist. A reductionist theory cannot explain how the idea that one is following a norm can become a point of orientation for the actual behaviour. This is not only emphasized by Hart; one can find similar arguments in Giddens's critique of Parsons and Althusser. Giddens particularly emphasizes that, in order to have a competent grasp of norms in the first place, subjects cannot completely internalize them to the degree that both functionalism and structuralism seem to assume (see Giddens, *Constitution of Society*, 30).

30. Bloor, 'Wittgenstein and the Priority of Practice', 101.

31. Neil MacCormick, 'Norms, Institutions, and Institutional Facts', *Law and Philosophy* 17, no. 3 (1998): 305.

32. Bloor, 'Wittgenstein and the Priority of Practice', 101.

33. The practices of interpretation that are emphasized by the hermeneutical models of social critique presume precisely this: that individuals agree that they are following some norm without there being a shared explicit belief about what that norm is.

34. See p. 180, section 6.5.1.

35. See p. 188, section 6.5.2.

36. See section 7.1.6.

37. This argument is already to be found in John R. Searle, 'How to Derive "Ought" From "Is"', *Philosophical Review* 73, no. 1 (1964): 55.

38. This issue is taken up and more extensively discussed in section 8.5.

39. See Liptow, *Regel und Interpretation*, 102 and 228–29. See also the distinction between 'connotation' and 'import' in John Ransdell, 'Constitutive Rules and Speech-Act Analysis', *Journal of Philosophy* 68, no. 13 (1971): 385–400; on the same issue, see Giddens, *Constitution of Society*, 19–20. For an overview of the debate, see Frank Hindriks, 'Constitutive Rules, Language, and Ontology', *Erkenntnis* 71, no. 2 (2009): 253–75.

40. See again section 8.5 for a more extensive discussion.

41. For this weak sense, see section 7.1.6.

42. See section 7.1.4.

43. But, in contrast to constitutive rules, it is not necessary to conform to these rules for the behaviour to count as part of the practice.

44. Schatzki, *Site of the Social*, 80.

45. See section 5.7.4.

46. Joseph Rouse, *Engaging Science* (Ithaca, NY: Cornell University Press, 1996), 141.

47. Hart, *Concept of Law*, 117–23.

48. The connection between this concept of pathology and the concept of anomie in Durkheim's discussion in The Division of Labour must be analysed as follows: Durkheim first links solidarity and law – law is the symbol of solidarity, and solidarity is the basis of law. Therefore, the solidarity that is brought about by social interaction is normally congruent with the rules of law. Only in 'rare, pathological cases' (Emile Durkheim, *The Division of Labour in Society*, ed. Steven Lukes [Houndmills, UK: Palgrave Macmillan, 2013], 53) are solidarity and law opposed to each other – and these are precisely the cases that Hart discusses. We must distinguish between such pathologies in a narrow sense and the case of anomie that is more prominent in Durkheim (Durkheim, *Division of Labour in Society*, 277). Anomie becomes prevalent if social relationships change too quickly or are deficient in another way, such that either no legal rules can emerge or such rules lose their power without being replaced by better alternatives. For this reason, it is not crime as such that is indicative of anomie (Emile Durkheim, *The Rules of Sociological Method, and Selected Texts on Sociology and Its Method*, ed. Steven Lukes [New York: Free Press, 2014], 60–64) but a lack of solidarity – that is, a lack of commitment to the law due to a lack of support of the law by solidarity.

49. This is also how Christopher F. Zurn ('Social Pathologies as Second-Order Disorders', in *Axel Honneth: Critical Essays*, ed. Danielle Petherbridge [Leiden: Brill, 2011], 345–70) and Robin Celikates (*Critique as Social Practice*, 122–26) use the concept of a 'second-order disorder', even if at least Celikates uses the concept in a different way, namely, as referring to reflexivity deficits of individual people. Honneth also refers to this concept in *Freedom's Right: The Social Foundations of Democratic Life*, trans. Joseph Ganahl (Cambridge: Polity Press, 2014), which appeared after the present work was completed.

50. Zurn ('Social Pathologies as Second-Order Disorders') also describes lack of recognition as a social pathology, but in cases like ideology or reification, the pathology consists in the fact that the recognition order is not visible as such or cannot be treated as socially constituted.

51. At this point, I will merely sketch a model of social change without presupposing a normative standard with which one could evaluate such conflicts. It is obvious, however, that one cannot do without such a standard if one wants to make a substantive claim about what forms of social critique are desirable.

CHAPTER 8: THE POSSIBILITY OF IMMANENT CRITIQUE

1. See section 7.2.2.

2. This draws on Brandom's idea that normative vocabulary serves to make implicit normative commitments explicit. See Brandom, *Making It Explicit* and *Between Saying and Doing*.

3. 'Hence one main cultural task facing any oppressed group is to undermine or explode the justification of the dominant stratum' (Moore, *Injustice*, 84).

4. The critic must then go beyond a merely moral critique of individual behaviour and towards a political social critique that is 'of larger scope and scale, addressed to

a larger audience, cast in a more general and impersonal mode' (Hannah Pitkin, *Wittgenstein and Justice* [Berkeley: University of California Press, 1972], 204).

5. Lovibond, *Realism and Imagination in Ethics*, 127. For a similar argument, see also Naomi Scheman, 'Forms of Life: Mapping the Rough Ground', in *The Cambridge Companion to Wittgenstein*, ed. Hans Sluga and David G. Stern (Cambridge: Cambridge University Press, 1996), 384.

6. Lovibond, *Realism and Imagination in Ethics*, 173.

7. Moving towards a sociologically informed social critique – a project that, for example, the first generation of the Frankfurt School pursued – is not to be equated with cutting critique off from everyday experience, however. It has often been objected that the critical models of the Bourdieu school have done so (see Celikates, *Critique as Social Practice*). Instead of seeing ordinary agents as 'dupes', a methodologically founded model of critique can make attempts to mobilize normative power transparent.

8. See Popitz, *Soziale Normen*, 72.

9. See p. 321, section 8.1.

10. On the level at which practical attitudes find expression, this can take up the model of a competition between orders of justification as developed in Luc Boltanski and Laurent Thévenot, *On Justification: Economies of Worth* (Princeton, NJ: Princeton University Press, 2006).

11. See Scheman, 'Forms of Life', 398.

12. Frank Parkin, *Class Inequality and Political Order* (New York: Praeger, 1971), 93.

13. For a similar argument (although not one concerning social groups), see Alan Gibbard, *Wise Choices, Apt Feelings: A Theory of Normative Judgment* (Cambridge, MA: Harvard University Press, 1990), 176–79.

14. Thompson, *Making of the English Working Class*, 77.

15. Joas interprets the notion of progress in American pragmatism as follows: 'the innovative individual thus deviates cognitively or normatively from the collective's received notions but uses arguments in an attempt to win support for his new view of the world. . . . For such a [discursive] relation to exist, not only must the innovator rise above the old norms, but the collective must also be able to create some sort of hypothetical distance between itself and its own norms' (Hans Joas, *The Creativity of Action* [New York: Wiley, 1996], 48).

16. Wittgenstein, *Philosophical Investigations*, 85, §218.

17. Wittgenstein, *Remarks on the Foundations of Mathematics*, 34, §I.116.

18. See section 3.3.2.

19. See, both in relation to Hegel and in relation to the general structure of discursive rationality, Brandom, 'Sketch of a Program for a Critical Reading of Hegel', 131–61; Brandom, *Reason in Philosophy*, 84.

20. For a different interpretation of Hegel, see Jaeggi, *Critique of Forms of Life*, e.g., 244.

21. See section 2.3.2.

22. See pp. 31–32, section 2.3.2. The early work of the Frankfurt Institute of Social Research can also productively be analyzed using this model. See the remarks of Horkheimer cited by Held, *Introduction to Critical Theory*, 186–87.

23. Compare the discussion in section 7.2.1.

24. Constitutive rules 'play a regulative role indirectly, because when combined with regulative rules concerning the use of our terms they do entail obligations' (Hindriks, 'Constitutive Rules, Language, and Ontology', 258). See also the distinction between 'connotation' and 'import' in Ransdell, 'Constitutive Rules and Speech-Act Analysis'.

25. See also p. 217, section 7.2.1.

26. Schatzki, *Site of the Social*, 80.

27. A similar account (without the reference to rules) can be found in Korsgaard's discussion of constitutive standards (Christine M. Korsgaard, *Self-Constitution: Agency, Identity and Integrity* [Oxford: Oxford University Press, 2009], 27–29).

28. Following Andrew J. Jones and Marek Sergot ('A Formal Characterisation of Institutionalised Power', *Logic Journal of IGPL* 4 [1996]: 427–43), I assume that the relation of institutional constitution is transitive. If one makes this assumption and also assumes that rules that prescribe orientations that are constitutive of a practice are themselves (indirectly) constitutive, then it follows that if there is a set of rules that prescribes that agents must orient themselves towards satisfying another set of rules, and if that second orientation is constitutive of membership in the practice, then the first set of rules is also constitutive of the practice.

29. In a parallel case of individual action orientations, one could also speak of practical irrationality.

30. There is a parallel here to a remark by Wittgenstein: 'The procedure of putting a lump of cheese on a balance and fixing the price by the turn of the scale would lose its point if it frequently happened for such lumps to suddenly grow or shrink for no obvious reason' (Wittgenstein, *Philosophical Investigations*, 56, §142, see also Pitkin, *Wittgenstein and Justice*, 124). In contrast to what this example suggests, however, the point to which critique refers need not always be the 'good' functioning of the practice according to external standards – after all, a practice of weighing this kind of cheese could still work out well for the people involved – but that such a practice would frustrate normative orientations that are constitutive of it.

31. Marx, 'Critical Marginal Notes', 198.

CHAPTER 9: THE CRITIQUE OF REIFICATION

1. For a more detailed explanation of this assumption, see section 7.1.6.

2. Here there is once again the parallel to which the idea of metacritique in Celikates, *Critique as Social Practice*, lends itself. Zurn ('Social Pathologies as Second-Order Disorders') also assumes a variety of 'second-order disorders', including invisibility, ideology, pathologies of reason and reification.

3. Zurn states: 'We can see that ideological beliefs are second-order disorders by comparing them with ordinary instances of mistaken beliefs. In both cases, there is an

error at the first-order level: the person holds a false belief about something. But only in the case of ideology is the mistaken belief systematically tied to social formations, and social formations that affect belief formation and stabilization at the second-order level' (Zurn, 'Social Pathologies as Second-Order Disorders', 347).

4. See Taylor, *Sources of the Self*, 500–501.

5. Hauke Brunkhorst, 'Paradigm-Core and Theory-Dynamics in Critical Social Theory: People and Programs', trans. Peter Krockenberger, *Philosophy & Social Criticism* 24, no. 6 (1998): 67–110.

6. An attempt to further systematize and expand on the ideas presented here can be found in Titus Stahl, 'Verdinglichung als Pathologie zweiter Ordnung', *Deutsche Zeitschrift für Philosophie* 59 (2011): 731–46.

7. In the English edition, this is often misleadingly translated as 'the objective form of things' (Georg Lukács, 'Reification and the Consciousness of the Proletariat', in *History and Class Consciousness: Studies in Marxist Dialectics*, trans. Rodney Livingstone [Cambridge, MA: MIT Press, 1971], 88).

8. On these four aspects, see also Stahl, 'Verdinglichung als Pathologie zweiter Ordnung', 731–33.

9. Searle, *Construction of Social Reality*, 8.

10. For example, Peter L. Berger and Thomas Luckmann describe reification as a 'modality of consciousness' (Peter L. Berger and Thomas Luckmann, *The Social Construction of Reality: A Treatise in the Sociology of Knowledge* [Garden City, NY: Doubleday, 1967], 107). See also Peter Berger and Stanley Pullberg, 'Reification and the Sociological Critique of Consciousness', *History and Theory* 4, no. 2 (1965): 196–211, and for a critique, Hannah Pitkin, 'Rethinking Reification', *Theory and Society* 16, no. 2 (1987): 263–93.

11. This intuition was perhaps most clearly expressed in Heidegger's philosophy, which does not only relate the breakdown of the relationship of subjects to their environment to the relationship of production and certainly does not regard this pathology as an epistemic error. With its distinctions between the modes of being of 'ready-to-hand' and the mode of being described as 'present-to-hand', he is not concerned with describing a particular attitude on the part of the subject. Rather, he is much more concerned with understanding how a mutually related mode of the existence of objects and persons can change in a context of practical significance. Cf. Martin Heidegger, *Being and Time*, trans. John Macquarrie and Edward Robinson (Oxford: Blackwell, 1962), 95–102; Dreyfus, *Being-in-the-World*, chap. 4. On Heidegger's relation to the critique of reification, see also Titus Stahl, 'Verdinglichung und Herrschaft: Technikkritik als Kritik sozialer Praxis', in *Ding und Verdinglichung: Technik- und Sozialphilosophie nach Heidegger und der kritischen Theorie*, ed. Hans Friesen, Christian Lotz, Jakob Meier and Markus Wolf (Munich: Wilhelm Fink, 2012), 319–23.

12. Cf. Rahel Jaeggi, 'Verdinglichung – ein aktueller Begriff?', *Jahrbuch der Internationalen Georg-Lukács-Gesellschaft* 3 (2003): 68–72.

13. Karl Marx, 'Economic and Philosophic Manuscripts of 1844', in *Collected Works: May 1874–1883*, Marx & Engels: Collected Works 3 (New York: International Publishers, 1975), 272.

14. Marx, 'Economic and Philosophic Manuscripts', 272.
15. Marx, 'Economic and Philosophic Manuscripts,' 277.
16. On this problem, cf. Habermas, *Knowledge and Human Interests*, 43–63; Axel Honneth, 'Work and Instrumental Action', *New German Critique*, no. 26 (1982): 31–54. For a general critique of this Hegelian model see Ernst Michael Lange, *Das Prinzip Arbeit* (Frankfurt: Ullstein, 1980), and Hans-Christoph Schmidt am Busch, *Hegels Begriff der Arbeit* (Berlin: Akademie-Verlag, 2002).
17. Christoph Demmerling, *Sprache und Verdinglichung* (Frankfurt: Suhrkamp, 1994), 30–31.
18. Marx, *Capital*, 1:149.
19. Marx, *Capital*, 1:162.
20. 'It is nothing but the definite social relation between men themselves which assumes here, for them, the fantastic form of a relation between things' (Marx, *Capital*, 1:165).
21. 'To the producers, therefore, the social relations between their private labours appear *as what they are*, i.e. they do not appear as direct social relations between persons in their work, but rather as material [*dinglich*] relations between persons and social relations between things' (Marx, *Capital*, 1:165–66, emphasis added).
22. Marx, *Capital*, 1:166–67; Rüdiger Dannemann, *Das Prinzip Verdinglichung: Studie zur Philosophie Georg Lukács'* (Frankfurt: Sendler, 1987), 43–47.
23. Marx, *Capital*, 1:166–67.
24. Honneth, 'Work and Instrumental Action', 33–36.
25. Lukács, 'Reification and the Consciousness of the Proletariat', 87.
26. Lukács, 'Reification and the Consciousness of the Proletariat', 88.
27. Lukács, 'Reification and the Consciousness of the Proletariat', 89, 98.
28. Lukács, 'Reification and the Consciousness of the Proletariat', 87; for the connection between subjective and objective aspects, see Pitkin, 'Rethinking Reification'.
29. Lukács, 'Reification and the Consciousness of the Proletariat', 95.
30. On the problems with Lukács's reception of Weber, see Dannemann, *Das Prinzip Verdinglichung*, 83–96.
31. Lukács, 'Reification and the Consciousness of the Proletariat', 100.
32. Lukács, 'Reification and the Consciousness of the Proletariat', 100.
33. Lukács, 'Reification and the Consciousness of the Proletariat', 105–6.
34. Lukács, 'Reification and the Consciousness of the Proletariat', 164.
35. Lukács, 'Reification and the Consciousness of the Proletariat', 149.
36. 'The desire to leave behind the immediacy of empirical reality and its no less immediate rationalist reflections must not be allowed to become an attempt to abandon immanent (social) reality.... Thus the category of mediation ... is ... the manifestation of [its] authentic objective structure' (Lukács, 'Reification and the Consciousness of the Proletariat', 162).
37. Lukács, 'Reification and the Consciousness of the Proletariat', 174, 206.
38. Cf. the following passages: 'since consciousness here ... is the self-consciousness of the object the act of consciousness overthrows the objective form of its object' and 'this process begins when the proletariat becomes conscious of its own

class point of view' (Lukács, 'Reification and the Consciousness of the Proletariat', 187, 189).

39. Habermas, *Theory of Communicative Action*, 1:364.

40. Habermas, *Philosophical Discourse of Modernity*, 19–22, 412–44.

41. Georg Lukács, 'Preface to the New Edition (1967)', in *History and Class Consciousness: Studies in Marxist Dialectics*, trans. Rodney Livingstone (Cambridge, MA: MIT Press, 1971), xxii–xxv; Martin Jay, *Marxism and Totality: The Adventures of a Concept from Lukács to Habermas* (Berkeley: University of California Press, 1984), 114–15.

42. Theodor W. Adorno, *Negative Dialectics*, trans. E. B. Ashtom (London: Routledge, 1973), 191. On the rejection of the reification paradigm in Adorno's aesthetics, see Fredric Jameson, *Late Marxism: Adorno, or the Persistence of the Dialectic* (London: Verso, 1990), 177–81. The reception of the theory of reification in Adorno's sociology is highlighted in Gillian Rose, *The Melancholy Science* (London: Macmillan, 1976), 40–50.

43. 'In Marx, however, and this distinguishes him from Hegel's ultimate idealism, the material of nature is never totally incorporated in the modes of its theoretico-practical appropriation' (Alfred Schmidt, *The Concept of Nature in Marx* [London: NLB, 1971], 136). Cf. Marx, *Capital*, 1:283, 3:959.

44. Jay, *Marxism and Totality*, 115.

45. Honneth, *Reification*, 26.

46. Honneth, *Reification*, 28.

47. The lack of a theory of practice is lamented by many interpreters of Lukács, for example, Stephen E. Bronner, *Of Critical Theory and Its Theorists* (New York: Routledge, 2002), 53.

48. Here I turn to Taylor's suggestion regarding the interdependence of normative distinctions and the vocabulary of practice. See Taylor, 'Interpretation and the Sciences of Man', 35.

49. On reification as a consequence of social domination, see Stahl, 'Verdinglichung und Herrschaft', 315.

50. For a further discussion of this example, see Stahl, 'Verdinglichung als Pathologie zweiter Ordnung', 740.

51. Here my thoughts coincide with those of Georg Lohmann, 'Authentisches und verdinglichtes Leben: Neuere Literatur zu Georg Lukács' "Geschichte und Klassenbewußtsein"', *Philosophische Rundschau* 30 (1983): 253–71, in that I also attempt to map out a more formal conception of reification that does not lead to a substantive 'theory of the good life'.

52. Andrew Arato and Paul Breines, *The Young Lukács and the Origins of Western Marxism* (New York: Seabury Press, 1979), 122.

53. There is, of course, a certain parallel here to the concept of the 'forgetting of recognition' proposed by Axel Honneth as a reformulation of the concept of reification (cf. Honneth, *Reification*, 57–61). This is only a limited resemblance. Honneth also suggests that we give the concept of reification a social ontological foundation (Honneth, *Reification*, 26), but he understands the basic attitude of recognition, which is opposed to reification, as a constitutive attitude of subjects towards one another that

determines their relation. Thus, he still remains within the paradigm of a theory of subjectivity. According to this account, only another subject can be reified. Reification can only apply to things, social practices or one's own self in a derivative way (Honneth, *Reification*, 63). However, this changes the content of the concept of reification so strongly that Lukács's original social theoretical intuition can only appear in the form of an (implausible) assertion of causality (Honneth, *Reification*, 75–79) that describes the destructive effects of capitalism on interpersonal relationships. Furthermore, the idea that reification is a 'forgetting' is too strongly tied to a model of decay of an original, intact state to avoid the criticism of romanticism levelled at Lukács by Honneth himself and – as Geuss has pointed out (Raymond Geuss, 'Philosophical Anthropology and Social Criticism', in *Reification: A New Look at an Old Idea*, ed. Martin Jay (Oxford: Oxford University Press, 2008), 127) – also implausible as a description.

54. On the relationship between Heidegger and Lukács, see Lucien Goldmann, *Lukács and Heidegger: Towards a New Philosophy* (London: Routledge & Kegan Paul, 1979).

CHAPTER 10: CONCLUSION: SOCIAL CONFLICT AND SOCIAL HOPE

1. Richard Rorty, Consequences of Pragmatism (Minneapolis: University of Minnesota Press, 1982), 208; see also Nicholas H. Smith, 'Hope and Critical Theory', Critical Horizons 6, no. 1 (2005): 45–61.

2. Richard Rorty, 'Truth without Correspondence to Reality', in Philosophy and Social Hope (London: Penguin, 1999), 39.

3. Marx, 'Letter to Ruge', 144.

Bibliography

Adorno, Theodor W. *Negative Dialectics*. Translated by E. B. Ashtom. London: Routledge, 1973.
———. *Prisms*. Translated by Samuel Weber and Shierry Weber. Cambridge, MA: MIT Press, 1983.
Allen, Amy. 'MacIntyre's Traditionalism'. *Journal of Value Inquiry* 31, no. 4 (1997): 511–25.
Allen, Jonathan. 'The Situated Critic or the Loyal Critic? Rorty and Walzer on Social Criticism'. *Philosophy & Social Criticism* 24, no. 6 (1998): 25–46. https://doi.org/10.1177/019145379802400602.
Arato, Andrew, and Paul Breines. *The Young Lukács and the Origins of Western Marxism*. New York: Seabury Press, 1979.
Axelrod, Robert M. 'An Evolutionary Approach to Norms'. *American Political Science Review* 80, no. 4 (1986): 1095–1111.
Baker, G. P., and P. M. S. Hacker. 'Critical Study: On Misunderstanding Wittgenstein; Kripke's Private Language Argument'. *Synthese* 58 (1984): 407–50.
———. *Wittgenstein: Rules, Grammar, and Necessity*. Oxford: Basil Blackwell, 1985.
Baltzer, Ulrich. *Gemeinschaftshandeln: Ontologische Grundlagen einer Ethik sozialen Handelns*. Freiburg: Alber, 1999.
Barry, Brian. 'Social Criticism and Political Philosophy'. *Philosophy and Public Affairs* 19 (1990): 360–73.
Baynes, Kenneth. 'Rational Reconstruction and Social Criticism. Habermas's Model of Interpretive Science'. In *Hermeneutics and Critical Theory in Ethics and Politics*, edited by Michael Kelly, 122–45. Cambridge, MA: MIT Press, 1990.
Benhabib, Seyla. *Critique, Norm, and Utopia: A Study of the Foundations of Critical Theory*. New York: Columbia University Press, 1986.
———. 'The Marxian Method of Critique: Normative Presuppositions'. *PRAXIS International* 4, no. 3 (1984): 284–98.

———. 'Normative Voraussetzungen von Marx' Methode der Kritik'. In *Ethik und Marx: Moralkritik und normative Grundlagen der Marxschen Theorie*, edited by Emil Angehrn and Georg Lohmann, 83–102. Königstein im Taunus: Hain/ Athenäum, 1986.
Berger, Peter L., and Thomas Luckmann. *The Social Construction of Reality: A Treatise in the Sociology of Knowledge*. Garden City, NY: Doubleday, 1967.
Berger, Peter, and Stanley Pullberg. 'Reification and the Sociological Critique of Consciousness'. *History and Theory* 4, no. 2 (1965): 196–211. https://doi.org/10.2307/2504151.
Birnbacher, Dieter. *Naturalness: Is the 'Natural' Preferable to the 'Artificial'?* Lanham, MD: Rowman & Littlefield, 2014.
Blackburn, Simon. 'The Individual Strikes Back'. *Synthese* 58 (1984): 281–301.
———. 'Reply: Rule-Following and Moral Realism'. In *Wittgenstein: To Follow a Rule*, edited by Steven H. Holtzman and Christopher M. Leich, 163–87. London: Routledge, 1981.
———. *Ruling Passions*. Oxford: Oxford University Press, 1998.
Bloor, David. 'Wittgenstein and the Priority of Practice'. In *The Practice Turn in Contemporary Theory*, edited by Karin Knorr-Cetina, Theodore R. Schatzki and Eike von Savigny, 95–106. London: Routledge, 2001.
———. *Wittgenstein, Rules and Institutions*. New York: Routledge, 1997.
Boghossian, Paul A. 'Review: *Wittgenstein on Meaning* by Colin McGinn'. *Philosophical Review* 98, no. 1 (1989): 83–92.
———. 'The Rule-Following Considerations'. *Mind* 98, no. 392 (1989): 507–49.
Boltanski, Luc, Axel Honneth and Robin Celikates. 'Sociology of Critique or Critical Theory? Luc Boltanski and Axel Honneth in Conversation with Robin Celikates'. In *The Spirit of Luc Boltanski: Essays on the 'Pragmatic Sociology of Critique'*, edited by Simon Susen and Bryan S. Turner, translated by Simon Susen, 561–89. London: Anthem Press, 2014.
Boltanski, Luc, and Laurent Thévenot. *On Justification: Economies of Worth*. Princeton, NJ: Princeton University Press, 2006.
Bourdieu, Pierre. *The Logic of Practice*. Cambridge: Polity, 1990.
Brandom, Robert B. *Between Saying and Doing: Towards an Analytic Pragmatism*. Oxford: Oxford University Press, 2008.
———. 'Facts, Norms, and Normative Facts: A Reply to Habermas'. *European Journal of Philosophy* 8, no. 3 (2000): 356–74. https://doi.org/10.1111/1468-0378.00115.
———. 'Freedom and Constraint by Norms'. *American Philosophical Quarterly* 16, no. 3 (1979): 187–96.
———. *Making It Explicit*. Cambridge, MA: Harvard University Press, 1994.
———. *Reason in Philosophy: Animating Ideas*. Cambridge, MA: Harvard University Press, 2009.
———. 'Responses to Pippin, Macbeth and Haugeland'. *European Journal of Philosophy* 13, no. 3 (2005): 429–41. https://doi.org/10.1111/j.1468-0378.2005.00238.x.
———. 'Sketch of a Program for a Critical Reading of Hegel: Comparing Empirical and Logical Concepts'. *Internationales Jahrbuch des Deutschen Idealismus* 3 (2005): 131–61.

Bratman, Michael E. 'Shared Cooperative Activity'. In *Faces of Intention*, 93–108. Cambridge: Cambridge University Press, 1999.

———. 'Shared Intention'. *Ethics* 104, no. 1 (1993): 97–113.

———. 'Shared Intention'. In *Faces of Intention*, 109–29. Cambridge: Cambridge University Press, 1999.

———. 'Shared Intention and Mutual Obligation'. In *Faces of Intention*, 130–41. Cambridge: Cambridge University Press, 1999.

Bronner, Stephen E. *Of Critical Theory and Its Theorists*. New York: Routledge, 2002.

Brunkhorst, Hauke. 'Paradigm-Core and Theory-Dynamics in Critical Social Theory: People and Programs'. Translated by Peter Krockenberger. *Philosophy & Social Criticism* 24, no. 6 (1998): 67–110. https://doi.org/10.1177/019145379802400604.

Buchwalter, Andrew. 'Hegel, Marx, and the Concept of Immanent Critique'. *Journal of the History of Philosophy* 29, no. 2 (1991): 253–79.

Cavell, Stanley. *The Claim of Reason*. Oxford: Oxford University Press, 1979.

Celikates, Robin. *Critique as Social Practice: Critical Theory and Social Self-Understanding*. Translated by Naomi van Steenbergen. Lanham, MD: Rowman & Littlefield International, 2018.

———. 'Nicht versöhnt: Wo bleibt der Kampf im 'Kampf um Anerkennung'?' In *Socialité et Reconnaissance: Grammaires de l'humain*, edited by Georg W. Bertram, Robin Celikates, Christophe Laudou and David Lauer, 213–28. Paris: L'Harmattan, 2007.

Cohen, Joshua. 'Spheres of Justice by Michael Walzer'. *Journal of Philosophy* 83, no. 8 (1986): 457–68.

Cooke, Maeve. 'Avoiding Authoritarianism: On the Problem of Justification in Contemporary Critical Social Theory'. *International Journal of Philosophical Studies* 13, no. 3 (2005): 379–404. https://doi.org/10.1080/09672550500169182.

———. *Language and Reason: A Study of Habermas's Pragmatics*. Cambridge, MA: MIT Press, 1997.

———. *Re-presenting the Good Society*. Cambridge, MA: MIT Press, 2006.

Dannemann, Rüdiger. *Das Prinzip Verdinglichung: Studie zur Philosophie Georg Lukács'*. Frankfurt: Sendler, 1987.

Darwall, Stephen. *The Second-Person Standpoint*. Cambridge, MA: Harvard University Press, 2006.

Demmerling, Christoph. *Sprache und Verdinglichung*. Frankfurt: Suhrkamp, 1994.

Dennett, Daniel C. 'Intentional Systems'. *Journal of Philosophy* 68, no. 4 (1971): 87–106.

Deranty, Jean-Philippe. *Beyond Communication: A Critical Study of Axel Honneth's Social Philosophy*. Leiden: Brill, 2009.

———. 'Injustice, Violence and Social Struggle: The Critical Potential of Axel Honneth's Theory of Recognition'. *Critical Horizons* 5, no. 1 (2004): 297–322.

Deranty, Jean-Philippe, and Emmanuel Renault. 'Politicizing Honneth's Ethics of Recognition'. *Thesis Eleven* 88, no. 1 (2007): 92–111. https://doi.org/10.1177/0725513607072459.

Dews, Peter. 'Introduction: Habermas and the Desublimation of Reason'. In *Habermas: A Critical Reader*, edited by Peter Dews, 1–25. Oxford: Blackwell, 1999.
Dietz, Simone. *Lebenswelt und System*. Würzburg: Königshausen & Neumann, 1993.
Dreyfus, Hubert. *Being-in-the-World: A Commentary on Heidegger's Being and Time, Division I*. Cambridge, MA: MIT Press, 1991.
Durkheim, Emile. *The Division of Labour in Society*. Edited by Steven Lukes. Houndmills, UK: Palgrave Macmillan, 2013.
———. *The Rules of Sociological Method, and Selected Texts on Sociology and Its Method*. Edited by Steven Lukes. New York: Free Press, 2014.
Dworkin, Ronald. *Taking Rights Seriously*. Cambridge, MA: Harvard University Press, 1977.
———. 'To Each His Own'. *New York Review of Books* 30, no. 6 (1983): 4–6.
Finlayson, James G. 'Does Hegel's Critique of Kant's Moral Theory Apply to Discourse Ethics?' In *Habermas: A Critical Reader*, edited by Peter Dews. Oxford: Blackwell, 1999.
———. *Habermas: A Very Short Introduction*. Oxford: Oxford University Press, 2005.
———. 'Morality and Critical Theory: On the Normative Problem of Frankfurt School Social Criticism'. *Telos* 2009, no. 146 (2009): 7–41. https://doi.org/10.3817/0309146007.
Fitzpatrick, Dan. 'Searle and Collective Intentionality: The Self-Defeating Nature of Internalism with Respect to Social Facts'. *American Journal of Economics & Sociology* 62 (2003): 45–66.
Forbes, Graeme. 'Skepticism and Semantic Knowledge'. In *Rule-Following and Meaning*, edited by Alexander Miller and Crispin Wright, 16–27. Chesham, UK: Acumen, 2002.
Forst, Rainer. *Contexts of Justice: Political Philosophy beyond Liberalism and Communitarianism*. Translated by John M. M. Farrell. Berkeley: University of California Press, 2002.
Fraser, Nancy. 'Distorted beyond All Recognition: A Response to Axel Honneth'. In *Redistribution or Recognition? A Political-Philosophical Exchange*, edited by Nancy Fraser and Axel Honneth, 198–236. London: Verso, 2003.
Geuss, Raymond. *The Idea of a Critical Theory*. Cambridge: Cambridge University Press, 1981.
———. 'Philosophical Anthropology and Social Criticism'. In *Reification: A New Look at an Old Idea*, edited by Martin Jay, 120–30. Oxford: Oxford University Press, 2008.
Gibbard, Alan. *Wise Choices, Apt Feelings: A Theory of Normative Judgment*. Cambridge, MA: Harvard University Press, 1990.
Giddens, Anthony. *Central Problems in Social Theory: Action, Structure and Contradiction in Social Analysis*. London: Macmillan, 1979.
———. *The Constitution of Society*. Cambridge: Polity, 1984.
Gilbert, Margaret. 'Acting Together'. In *Social Facts and Collective Intentionality*, edited by Georg Meggle, 53–72. Frankfurt: Hänsel-Hohenhausen, 2002.
———. 'Agreements, Coercion, and Obligation'. *Ethics* 103 (1993): 679–706.

———. *Living Together: Rationality, Sociality and Obligation*. Lanham, MD: Rowman & Littlefield, 1996.
———. 'More on Social Facts'. In *Living Together: Rationality, Sociality and Obligation*, 263–78. Lanham, MD: Rowman & Littlefield, 1996.
———. 'Obligation and Joint Commitment'. *Utilitas* 11, no. 2 (1999): 143–63.
———. *On Social Facts*. London: Routledge, 1989.
———. 'Social Rules: Some Problems for Hart's Account, and an Alternative Proposal'. *Law and Philosophy* 18 (1999): 141–71.
———. *A Theory of Political Obligation: Membership, Commitment, and the Bonds of Society*. Oxford: Oxford University Press, 2006.
———. 'Walking Together: A Paradigmatic Social Phenomenon'. *Midwest Studies in Philosophy* 15 (1990): 3–14.
Gimmler, Antje. 'Handeln und Erfahrung – Überlegungen zu einer pragmatischen Theorie des Handelns'. In *Handeln und Technik – Mit und ohne Heidegger*, edited by Christoph Hubig, Andreas Luckner, and Nadia Mazouz. Berlin: Lit, 2007.
Glüer, Kathrin. 'Explizites und Implizites Regelfolgen'. In *Institutionen und Regelfolgen*, edited by Ulrich Baltzer and Gerhard Schönrich, 157–76. Paderborn: Mentis, 2002.
———. *Sprache und Regeln*. Berlin: Akademie-Verlag, 1999.
Goldfarb, Warren. 'Kripke on Wittgenstein on Rules'. *Journal of Philosophy* 82, no. 9 (1985): 471–88.
Goldmann, Lucien. *Lukács and Heidegger: Towards a New Philosophy*. London: Routledge & Kegan Paul, 1979.
Goodman, Nelson. 'The New Riddle of Induction'. In *Fact, Fiction, and Forecast*, 2nd ed., 59–83. Indianapolis: Bobbs-Merril, 1965.
Gürerk, Özgür, Bernd Irlenbusch and Bettina Rockenbach. 'The Competitive Advantage of Sanctioning Institutions'. *Science* 312, no. 5770 (2006): 108–11. https://doi.org/10.1126/science.1123633.
Habermas, Jürgen. 'Actions, Speech Acts, Linguistically Mediated Interactions and the Lifeworld'. In *Philosophical Problems Today / Problèmes Philosophiques d'Aujourd'hui*, edited by Guttorm Fløistad, 45–74. International Institute of Philosophy / Institut International de Philosophie. Dordrecht: Springer Netherlands, 1994. https://doi.org/10.1007/978-94-017-4522-2_3.
———. 'An Avantgardistic Instinct for Relevances: The Role of the Intellectual and the European Cause'. In *Europe: A Faltering Project*, 49–58. Cambridge: Polity, 2009.
———. *Between Facts and Norms: Contributions to a Discourse Theory of Law and Democracy*. Cambridge: Polity, 1996.
———. 'Discourse Ethics: Notes on a Program of Philosophical Justification'. In *Moral Consciousness and Communicative Action*, 43–115. Cambridge, MA: MIT Press, 1990.
———. 'Handlungen, Sprechakte, sprachlich vermittelte Interaktionen und Lebenswelt'. In *Nachmetaphysisches Denken: Philosophische Aufsätze*, 63–104. Frankfurt: Suhrkamp, 1992.

———. 'Historical Materialism and the Development of Normative Structures'. In *Communication and the Evolution of Society*, translated by Thomas McCarthy, 95–129. Cambridge: Polity, 1979.

———. *Knowledge and Human Interests*. Translated by Jeremy J. Shapiro. Boston: Beacon Press, 1972.

———. 'Labor and Interaction: Remarks on Hegel's Jena Philosophy of Mind'. In *Theory and Practice*, translated by John Viertel, 142–69. Boston: Beacon Press, 1973.

———. *Legitimation Crisis*. Translated by Thomas McCarthy. Boston: Beacon Press, 1975.

———. *The Philosophical Discourse of Modernity: Twelve Lectures*. Translated by Frederick G. Lawrence. Cambridge, MA: MIT Press, 1990.

———. 'Remarks on Discourse Ethics'. In *Justification and Application: Remarks on Discourse Ethics*, translated by Ciaran Cronin, 19–112. Cambridge, MA: MIT Press, 1993.

———. 'A Reply'. In *Communicative Action: Essays on Jürgen Habermas's Theory of Communicative Action*, edited by Axel Honneth and Hans Joas, translated by Jeremy Gaines and Doris L. Jones, 214–64. Cambridge: Polity, 1991.

———. 'Some Further Clarifications of the Concept of Communicative Rationality'. In *On the Pragmatics of Communication*, translated by Maeve Cooke, 307–42. Cambridge, MA: MIT Press, 1998.

———. 'Technology and Science as "Ideology"'. In *Towards a Rational Society*, translated by Jeremy J. Shapiro, 81–122. Boston: Beacon Press, 1970.

———. *The Theory of Communicative Action*. Boston: Beacon Press, 1984.

———. 'What Is Universal Pragmatics?' In *On the Pragmatics of Communication*, translated by Maeve Cooke, 21–104. Cambridge, MA: MIT Press, 1998.

Hart, H. L. A. *The Concept of Law*. 2nd ed. Oxford: Oxford University Press, 1994.

Haugeland, John. 'Heidegger on Being a Person'. *Noûs* 16 (1982): 15–26.

———. 'The Intentionality All-Stars'. *Philosophical Perspectives* 4, Action (1990): 383–427.

———. 'Truth and Rule-Following'. In *Having Thought: Essays in the Metaphysics of Mind*, 305–61. Cambridge, MA: Harvard University Press, 1998.

Heal, Jane. 'Common Knowledge'. *Philosophical Quarterly* 28 (1978): 116–31.

Hegel, Georg Wilhelm Friedrich. *Elements of the Philosophy of Right*. Translated by Allen W. C. Wood and H. B. Nisbet. Cambridge Texts in the History of Political Thought. Cambridge: Cambridge University Press, 1991.

———. *Encyclopedia of the Philosophical Sciences in Basic Outline*. Translated by Klaus Brinkmann and Daniel O. Dahlstrohm. Cambridge: Cambridge University Press, 2010.

Heidegger, Martin. *Being and Time*. Translated by John Macquarrie and Edward Robinson. Oxford: Blackwell, 1962.

Held, David. *Introduction to Critical Theory*. London: Hutchinson, 1980.

Hindriks, Frank. 'Constitutive Rules, Language, and Ontology'. *Erkenntnis* 71, no. 2 (2009): 253–75.

Honneth, Axel. 'Arbeit und Anerkennung Versuch einer Neubestimmung'. *Deutsche Zeitschrift für Philosophie* 56, no. 3 (2008): 327–41.

———. *The Critique of Power: Reflective Stages in a Critical Social Theory*. Translated by Kenneth Baynes. Cambridge, MA: MIT Press, 1993.

———. 'Democracy as Reflexive Cooperation: John Dewey and the Theory of Democracy Today'. *Political Theory* 26 (1998): 763–83.

———. 'Formen der Gesellschaftskritik'. In *Desintegration: Bruchstücke einer soziologischen Zeitdiagnose*, 71–79. Frankfurt: Fischer, 1994.

———. *Freedom's Right: The Social Foundations of Democratic Life*. Translated by Joseph Ganahl. Cambridge: Polity, 2014.

———. 'Grounding Recognition: A Rejoinder to Critical Questions'. *Inquiry* 45 (2002): 499–519.

———. 'Integrity and Disrespect: Principles of a Conception of Morality Based on the Theory of Recognition'. *Political Theory* 20, no. 2 (1992): 187–201. https://doi.org/10.1177/0090591792020002001.

———. 'The Irreducibility of Progress: Kant's Account of the Relationship between Morality and History'. *Critical Horizons* 8, no. 1 (2007): 1–17. https://doi.org/10.1558/crit.v8i1.1.

———. *Leiden an Unbestimmtheit: Eine Reaktualisierung der Hegelschen Rechtsphilosophie*. Stuttgart: Reclam, 2001.

———. 'Moral Consciousness and Class Domination: Some Problems in the Analysis of Hidden Morality'. In *Disrespect: The Normative Foundations of Critical Theory*, translated by Joseph Ganahl, 80–95. Cambridge: Polity, 2007.

———. 'The Normativity of Ethical Life'. Translated by Felix Koch. *Philosophy & Social Criticism* 40, no. 8 (2014): 817–26. https://doi.org/10.1177/0191453714541538.

———. 'Pathologies of the Social: The Past and Present of Social Philosophy'. In *Disrespect: The Normative Foundations of Critical Theory*, translated by Joseph Ganahl, 3–48. Cambridge: Polity, 2007.

———. 'Philosophy as Social Research: David Miller's Theory of Justice'. In *The I in We: Studies in the Theory of Recognition*, 119–33. Cambridge: Polity, 2012.

———. 'The Point of Recognition. A Rejoinder to the Rejoinder'. In *Redistribution or Recognition? A Political-Philosophical Exchange*, edited by Nancy Fraser and Axel Honneth, 237–68. London: Verso, 2003.

———. 'The Possibility of a Disclosing Critique of Society: The Dialectic of Enlightenment in Light of Current Debates in Social Criticism'. *Constellations* 7, no. 1 (2000): 116–27. https://doi.org/10.1111/1467-8675.00173.

———. 'Recognition as Ideology'. In *Recognition and Power: Axel Honneth and the Tradition of Critical Social Theory*, edited by Bert van den Brink and David Owen, 323–48. Cambridge: Cambridge University Press, 2007.

———. 'Reconstructive Social Critique with a Genealogical Reservation: On the Idea of Critique in the Frankfurt School'. *Graduate Faculty Philosophy Journal* 22, no. 2 (2001): 3–11.

———. 'Redistribution as Recognition: A Response to Nancy Fraser'. In *Redistribution or Recognition? A Political-Philosophical Exchange*, edited by Nancy Fraser and Axel Honneth, 110–97. London: Verso, 2003.

———. *Reification: A New Look at an Old Idea*. Oxford: Oxford University Press, 2008.

———. 'Rekonstruktive Gesellschaftskritik unter genealogischem Vorbehalt'. In *Pathologien der Vernunft: Geschichte und Gegenwart der kritischen Theorie*, 57–69. Frankfurt: Suhrkamp, 2007.

———. 'The Social Dynamics of Disrespect: On the Location of Critical Theory Today'. *Constellations* 1, no. 2 (1994): 255–69.

———. 'The Social Dynamics of Disrespect: On the Location of Critical Theory Today'. In *Disrespect: The Normative Foundations of Critical Theory*, 63–79. Cambridge: Polity, 2007.

———. 'A Social Pathology of Reason: On the Intellectual Legacy of Critical Theory'. In *Pathologies of Reason: On the Legacy of Critical Theory*, 19–42. New York: Columbia University Press, 2009.

———. 'A Society without Humiliation?' *European Journal of Philosophy* 5, no. 3 (1997): 306–24. https://doi.org/10.1111/1468-0378.00042.

———. *The Struggle for Recognition*. Translated by Joel Anderson. Cambridge: Polity, 1995.

———. *Suffering from Indeterminacy*. Translated by Jack Ben-Levi. Spinoza Lectures. Amsterdam: Van Gorcum, 2000.

———. 'Work and Instrumental Action'. *New German Critique*, no. 26 (1982): 31–54.

Honneth, Axel, and Titus Stahl. 'Wandel der Anerkennung: Überlegungen aus gerechtigkeitstheoretischer Perspektive'. In *Strukturwandel der Anerkennung: Paradoxien sozialer Integration in der Gegenwart*, edited by Axel Honneth, Ophelia Lindemann and Stephan Voswinkel, 275–300. Frankfurt: Campus, 2013.

Horkheimer, Max. 'Traditional and Critical Theory'. In *Critical Theory: Selected Essays*, translated by Matthew J. O'Connell, 188–243. New York: Continuum, 1975.

Hume, David. *An Enquiry Concerning Human Understanding*. Mineola, NY: Dover, 2004.

Iser, Mattias. *Empörung und Fortschritt: Grundlagen einer kritischen Theorie der Gesellschaft*. Frankfurt: Campus, 2008.

———. 'Gesellschaftskritik'. In *Politische Theorie: 22 umkämpfte Begriffe zur Einführung*, edited by Gerhard Göhler and Mattias Iser, 155–72. Wiesbaden: VS (UTB), 2004.

Jaeggi, Rahel. *Critique of Forms of Life*. Cambridge, MA: Belknap Press, 2018.

———. 'Rethinking Ideology'. In *New Waves in Political Philosophy*, edited by Boudewijn de Bruin and Christopher F. Zurn, 63–86. London: Palgrave Macmillan UK, 2009. https://doi.org/10.1057/9780230234994_4.

———. 'Verdinglichung—Ein aktueller Begriff?' *Jahrbuch der internationalen Georg-Lukács-Gesellschaft* 3 (2003): 68–72.

Jameson, Fredric. *Late Marxism: Adorno, or the Persistence of the Dialectic*. London: Verso, 1990.
Jay, Martin. *Marxism and Totality: The Adventures of a Concept from Lukács to Habermas*. Berkeley: University of California Press, 1984.
Joas, Hans. *The Creativity of Action*. New York: Wiley, 1996.
Jones, Andrew J., and Marek Sergot. 'A Formal Characterisation of Institutionalised Power'. *Logic Journal of IGPL* 4 (1996): 427–43.
Jütten, Timo. 'The Colonization Thesis: Habermas on Reification'. *International Journal of Philosophical Studies* 19, no. 5 (2011): 701–27. https://doi.org/10.1080/09672559.2011.629672.
Kalyvas, Andreas. 'Critical Theory at the Crossroads: Comments on Axel Honneth's Theory of Recognition'. *European Journal of Social Theory* 2, no. 1 (1999): 99–108.
Kant, Immanuel. *Critique of Pure Reason*. Edited by Paul Guyer and Allen W. Wood. The Cambridge Edition of the Works of Immanuel Kant. Cambridge: Cambridge University Press, 1998. https://doi.org/10.1017/CBO9780511804649.
Kauppinen, Antti. 'Reason, Recognition, and Internal Critique'. *Inquiry* 45, no. 4 (2002): 479–98.
Kelly, Michael, ed. *Hermeneutics and Critical Theory in Ethics and Politics*. Cambridge, MA: MIT Press, 1990.
Korsgaard, Christine M. *Self-Constitution: Agency, Identity and Integrity*. Oxford: Oxford University Press, 2009.
———. *The Sources of Normativity*. Cambridge: Cambridge University Press, 1996.
Kripke, Saul A. *Wittgenstein on Rules and Private Language: An Elementary Exposition*. Oxford: Blackwell, 1982.
Lange, Ernst Michael. *Das Prinzip Arbeit*. Frankfurt: Ullstein, 1980.
Lauer, David. 'Genuine Normativity, Expressive Bootstrapping, and Normative Phenomenalism'. *Ethics & Politics* 11, no. 1 (2009): 321–50.
Lewis, David K. *Convention: A Philosophical Study*. Cambridge: Cambridge University Press, 1969.
———. 'Finkish Dispositions'. *Philosophical Quarterly* 47 (1997): 143–58.
Liptow, Jasper. *Regel und Interpretation*. Weilerswist, Germany: Velbrück Wissenschaft, 2004.
Loeffler, Ronald. 'Normative Phenomenalism: On Robert Brandom's Practice-Based Explanation of Meaning'. *European Journal of Philosophy* 13, no. 1 (2005): 32–69.
Lohmann, Georg. 'Authentisches und verdinglichtes Leben. Neuere Literatur zu Georg Lukács' "Geschichte und Klassenbewußtsein"'. *Philosophische Rundschau* 30 (1983): 253–71.
———. 'Gesellschaftskritik und normativer Maßstab: Überlegungen zu Marx'. In *Arbeit, Handlung, Normativität*, edited by Axel Honneth and Urs Jaeggi, 234–99. Frankfurt: Suhrkamp, 1980.
Lovibond, Sabina. *Realism and Imagination in Ethics*. Oxford: Blackwell, 1983.
Löw-Beer, Martin. 'Living a Life and the Problem of Existential Impossibility'. *Inquiry* 34, no. 2 (1991): 217–36.

Lukács, Georg. 'Preface to the New Edition (1967)'. In *History and Class Consciousness: Studies in Marxist Dialectics*, translated by Rodney Livingstone. Cambridge, MA: MIT Press, 1971.

———. 'Reification and the Consciousness of the Proletariat'. In *History and Class Consciousness: Studies in Marxist Dialectics*, translated by Rodney Livingstone, 83–222. MIT Press, 1971.

MacCormick, Neil. 'Norms, Institutions, and Institutional Facts'. *Law and Philosophy* 17, no. 3 (1998): 301–45.

MacIntyre, Alasdair C. *After Virtue*. 3rd ed. Notre Dame, IN: University of Notre Dame Press, 2007.

———. 'Epistemological Crises, Dramatic Narrative, and the Philosophy of Science'. In *The Task of Philosophy: Selected Essays*, 1:3–23. Cambridge: Cambridge University Press, 2006.

———. *Three Rival Versions of Moral Enquiry: Encyclopedia, Genealogy, and Tradition*. Notre Dame, IN: University of Notre Dame Press, 1990.

———. *Whose Justice? Which Rationality?* Notre Dame, IN: University of Notre Dame Press, 1988.

Markell, Patchen. *Bound by Recognition*. Princeton, NJ: Princeton University Press, 2003.

Martin, C. B. 'Dispositions and Conditionals'. *Philosophical Quarterly* 44 (1994): 1–8.

Marx, Karl. *Capital: A Critique of Political Economy*. Edited by Ernest Mandel. Translated by Ben Fowkes and David Fernbach. 3 vols. New York: Penguin, 1990–1993.

———. 'Contribution to the Critique of Hegel's Philosophy of Law'. In *Karl Marx/Friedrich Engels: March 1843–August 1844*, 3:3–129. Marx & Engels: Collected Works. New York: International Publishers, 1975.

———. 'Critical Marginal Notes on the Article "The King of Prussia and Social Reform. By a Prussian"'. In *Karl Marx/Friedrich Engels: March 1843–August 1844*, 3:189–206. Marx & Engels: Collected Works. New York: International Publishers, 1975.

———. 'Economic and Philosophic Manuscripts of 1844'. In *Collected Works: May 1874–1883*, 3:229–346. Marx & Engels: Collected Works. New York: International Publishers, 1975.

———. 'Letter to Ferdinand Lassalle, 22 February 1858'. In *Letters 1856–1859*, 40:268–72. Marx & Engels: Collected Works. New York: International Publishers, 1983.

———. 'Letter to Ruge, September 1843'. In *Karl Marx/Friedrich Engels: March 1843–August 1844*, 3:141–45. Marx & Engels: Collected Works. New York: International Publishers, 1975.

McCullagh, Mark. 'Wittgenstein on Rules and Practices'. *Journal of Philosophical Research* 27 (2002): 83–100.

McDowell, John. 'Motivating Inferentialism: Comments on Chapter 2 of Making It Explicit'. *Pragmatics and Cognition* 13, no. 1 (2005): 121–40.

———. 'Wittgenstein on Following a Rule'. *Synthese* 58 (1984): 325–63.

McGinn, Colin. *Wittgenstein on Meaning: An Interpretation and Evaluation*. Oxford: Basil Blackwell, 1984.
Meijers, Anthonie. 'Can Collective Intentionality Be Individualized?' *American Journal of Economics and Sociology* 62, no. 1 (2003): 167–83. https://doi.org/10.1111/1536-7150.t01-1-00006.
Menke, Christoph. 'Das Nichtanerkennbare. Oder warum das moderne Recht keine "Sphäre der Anerkennung" ist'. In *Sozialphilosophie und Kritik*, edited by Rainer Forst, Martin Hartmann, Rahel Jaeggi and Martin Saar, 87–108. Frankfurt: Suhrkamp, 2009.
Miller, David. 'Virtues, Practices, and Justice'. In *After MacIntyre*, edited by John Horton and Susan Mendus, 245–64. Oxford: Polity, 1994.
Miller, Seumas. *Social Action: A Teleological Account*. Cambridge: Cambridge University Press, 2001.
Millikan, Ruth Garrett. 'Truth Rules, Hoverflies, and the Kripke-Wittgenstein Paradox'. In *Rule-Following and Meaning*, edited by Alexander Miller and Crispin Wright, 209–33. Chesham, UK: Acumen, 2002.
Moore, Barrington. *Injustice: The Social Bases of Obedience and Revolt*. London: Palgrave Macmillan, 1978.
Nagel, Thomas. *The View from Nowhere*. Oxford: Oxford University Press, 1986.
O'Neill, Onora. 'Starke und schwache Gesellschaftskritik in einer globalisierten Welt'. *Deutsche Zeitschrift für Philosophie* 48 (2000): 719–28.
Outwaithe, William. *Habermas: A Critical Introduction*. Cambridge: Polity, 1994.
Parkin, Frank. *Class Inequality and Political Order*. New York: Praeger, 1971.
Pettit, Philip. *The Common Mind: An Essay on Psychology, Society and Politics*. Oxford: Oxford University Press, 1993.
———. 'Groups with Minds of Their Own'. In *Socializing Metaphysics*, edited by F. Schmitt, 172–75. Lanham, MD: Rowman & Littlefield, 2003.
———. 'The Reality of Rule-Following'. *Mind*, n.s., 99 (1990): 1–21.
Pettit, Philip, and David Schweikard. 'Joint Actions and Group Agents'. *Philosophy of the Social Sciences* 36, no. 1 (2006): 18–39. https://doi.org/10.1177/0048393105284169.
Pinkard, Terry P. *Hegel's Phenomenology: The Sociality of Reason*. New York: Cambridge University Press, 1996.
Pippin, Robert B. *Hegel's Practical Philosophy: Rational Agency as Ethical Life*. Cambridge: Cambridge University Press, 2008.
Pitkin, Hannah. 'Rethinking Reification'. *Theory and Society* 16, no. 2 (1987): 263–93.
———. *Wittgenstein and Justice*. Berkeley: University of California Press, 1972.
Popitz, Heinrich. *Soziale Normen*. Frankfurt: Suhrkamp, 2006.
Postema, Gerald J. 'Morality in the First Person Plural'. *Law and Philosophy* 14 (1995): 35–64.
Quine, W. V. O. 'On What There Is'. In *Quintessence: Basic Readings from the Philosophy of W. V. Quine*, 177–93. Cambridge, MA: Harvard University Press, 2004.

Railton, Peter. 'Normative Force and Normative Freedom: Hume and Kant, but Not Hume versus Kant'. *Ratio* 12, no. 4 (1999): 320–53. https://doi.org/10.1111/1467-9329.00098.

Ransdell, John. 'Constitutive Rules and Speech-Act Analysis'. *Journal of Philosophy* 68, no. 13 (1971): 385–400.

Raz, Joseph. 'Morality as Interpretation'. *Ethics* 101, no. 2 (1991): 392–405.

———. *Practical Reason and Norms*. London: Hutchinson, 1975.

Redding, Paul. *Analytic Philosophy and the Return of Hegelian Thought*. Cambridge: Cambridge University Press, 2007.

Rorty, Richard. *Consequences of Pragmatism*. Minneapolis: University of Minnesota Press, 1982.

———. *Contingency, Irony and Solidarity*. Cambridge: Cambridge University Press, 1989.

———. 'Truth without Correspondence to Reality'. In *Philosophy and Social Hope*, 23–46. London: Penguin, 1999.

Rosa, Hartmut. 'Cultural Relativism and Social Criticism from a Taylorian Perspective'. *Constellations* 3, no. 1 (1996): 39–60. https://doi.org/10.1111/j.1467-8675.1996.tb00042.x.

———. *Identität und kulturelle Praxis: Politische Philosophie nach Charles Taylor*. Frankfurt: Campus, 1998.

Rose, Gillian. *The Melancholy Science*. London: Macmillan, 1976.

Rosen, Gideon. 'Who Makes the Rules around Here?' *Philosophy and Phenomenological Research* 52 (1997): 163–71.

Rössler, Beate. 'Kommunitaristische Sehnsucht und liberale Rechte: Zu Michael Walzers politischer Theorie der Gesellschaft'. *Deutsche Zeitschrift für Philosophie* 41, no. 6 (1993): 1035–48.

Rouse, Joseph. *Engaging Science*. Ithaca, NY: Cornell University Press, 1996.

Saar, Martin. *Genealogie als Kritik: Geschichte und Theorie des Subjekts nach Nietzsche und Foucault*. Frankfurt: Campus, 2007.

Scanlon, Thomas M. 'Promises and Practices'. *Philosophy & Public Affairs* 19, no. 3 (1990): 199–226.

———. *What We Owe to Each Other*. Cambridge, MA: Belknap Press, 2000.

Schatzki, Theodore R. *The Site of the Social: A Philosophical Account of the Constitution of Social Life and Change*. University Park: Pennsylvania State University Press, 2002.

Scheman, Naomi. 'Forms of Life: Mapping the Rough Ground'. In *The Cambridge Companion to Wittgenstein*, edited by Hans Sluga and David G. Stern, 383–410. Cambridge: Cambridge University Press, 1996.

Schmid, Hans Bernhard. *Wir-Intentionalität: Kritik des ontologischen Individualismus und Rekonstruktion der Gemeinschaft*. Alber-Reihe Praktische Philosophie 75. Freiburg im Breisgau: Karl Alber, 2005.

Schmidt, Alfred. *The Concept of Nature in Marx*. London: NLB, 1971.

Schmidt am Busch, Hans-Christoph. *Hegels Begriff der Arbeit*. Berlin: Akademie-Verlag, 2002.

Schnädelbach, Herbert. 'The Transformation of Critical Theory'. In *Communicative Action: Essays on Jürgen Habermas's Theory of Communicative Action*, edited by Axel Honneth and Hans Joas, translated by Jeremy Gaines and Doris L. Jones, 7–22. Cambridge: Polity, 1991.

Schweikard, David. '"You'll Never Walk Alone": Gemeinsames Handeln und soziale Relationen'. *Deutsche Zeitschrift für Philosophie* 55, no. 3 (2007): 425–40.

Searle, John R. 'Collective Intentions and Actions'. In *Intentions in Communication*, edited by P. Cohen, J. Morgan and M. E. Pollack, 401–15. Cambridge, MA: Bradford Books, 1990.

———. *The Construction of Social Reality*. New York: Penguin, 1995.

———. 'How to Derive "Ought" From "Is"'. *Philosophical Review* 73, no. 1 (1964): 43–58.

Sellars, Wilfrid. 'Some Reflections on Language Games'. *Philosophy of Science* 21, no. 3 (1954): 204–28. https://doi.org/10.1086/287344.

Shapiro, Ian. *Political Criticism*. Berkeley: University of California Press, 1990.

Shockley, Kenneth. 'The Conundrum of Joint Commitment'. *Social Theory and Practice* 30 (2004): 535–57.

Shwayder, David S. *The Stratification of Behaviour*. London: Routledge & Kegan Paul, 1965.

Smith, Nicholas H. *Charles Taylor: Meaning, Morals and Modernity*. Cambridge: Polity, 2002.

———. 'Hope and Critical Theory'. *Critical Horizons* 6, no. 1 (2005): 45–61.

———. *Strong Hermeneutics: Contingency and Moral Identity*. London: Routledge, 1997.

———. 'Work and the Struggle for Recognition'. *European Journal of Political Theory* 8, no. 1 (2009): 46–60.

Sonderegger, Ruth. 'Wie diszipliniert ist (Ideologie-)Kritik? Zwischen Philosophie, Soziologie und Kunst'. In *Was ist Kritik?*, edited by Rahel Jaeggi and Tilo Wesche, 55–80. Frankfurt: Suhrkamp, 2009.

Stahl, Titus. 'The Conditions of Collectivity: Joint Commitments and the Shared Norms of Membership'. In *Institutions, Emotions, and Group Agents*, edited by Hans-Bernhard Schmid and Anita Konzelmann Ziv, 229–44. Dordrecht: Springer, 2013.

———. 'Habermas and the Project of Immanent Critique'. *Constellations* 20, no. 4 (2013): 533–52. https://doi.org/10.1111/1467-8675.12057.

———. 'Institutional Power, Collective Acceptance, and Recognition'. In *Recognition and Social Ontology*, edited by Heikki Ikäheimo and Arto Laitinen, 349–72. Leiden: Brill, 2011.

———. 'Practices, Norms and Recognition'. *Human Affairs* 17, no. 1 (2007): 10–21. https://doi.org/10.2478/v10023-007-0002-0.

———. 'Verdinglichung als Pathologie zweiter Ordnung'. *Deutsche Zeitschrift für Philosophie* 59 (2011): 731–46. https://doi.org/10.1524/dzph.2011.59.5.731.

———. 'Verdinglichung und Herrschaft: Technikkritik als Kritik sozialer Praxis.' In *Ding und Verdinglichung: Technik- und Sozialphilosophie nach Heidegger und der kritischen Theorie*, edited by Hans Friesen, Christian Lotz, Jakob Meier and Markus Wolf, 299–324. Munich: Wilhelm Fink, 2012.

Stekeler-Weithofer, Pirmin. 'Die holistische Verfassung von Praxisformen'. In *Institutionen und Regelfolgen*, edited by Ulrich Baltzer and Gerhard Schönrich, 59–80. Paderborn: Mentis, 2002.

———. *Hegels analytische Philosophie: Die Wissenschaft der Logik als kritische Theorie der Bedeutung*. Paderborn: Schöningh, 1992.

Stern, Robert. 'MacIntyre and Historicism'. In *After MacIntyre*, edited by John Horton and Susan Mendus, 146–60. Cambridge: Polity, 1994.

Sugden, Robert. 'Thinking as a Team: Towards an Explanation of Nonselfish Behaviour'. *Social Philosophy and Policy* 10 (1993): 69–89.

Taylor, Charles. 'Explanation and Practical Reason'. In *The Quality of Life*, edited by Martha Nussbaum and Amartya Sen, 208–31. Oxford: Oxford University Press, 1993.

———. *Hegel*. Cambridge: Cambridge University Press, 1975.

———. 'Interpretation and the Sciences of Man'. In *Philosophy and the Human Sciences: Philosophical Papers 2*, 15–57. Cambridge: Cambridge University Press, 1985.

———. 'Irreducibly Social Goods'. In *Philosophical Arguments*, 127–45. Cambridge, MA: Harvard University Press, 1995.

———. 'Language and Human Nature'. In *Human Agency and Language: Philosophical Papers 1*, 215–47. Cambridge: Cambridge University Press, 1985.

———. 'Legitimation Crisis?' In *Philosophy and the Human Sciences: Philosophical Papers 2*, 248–88. Cambridge: Cambridge University Press, 1985.

———. 'Neutrality in Political Science'. In *Philosophy and the Human Sciences: Philosophical Papers 2*, 58–90. Cambridge: Cambridge University Press, 1985.

———. *A Secular Age*. Cambridge, MA: Belknap Press, 2007.

———. 'Self-Interpreting Animals'. In *Human Agency and Language: Philosophical Papers 1*, 45–76. Cambridge: Cambridge University Press, 1985.

———. 'Social Theory as Practice'. In *Philosophy and the Human Sciences: Philosophical Papers 2*, 91–115. Cambridge: Cambridge University Press, 1985.

———. *Sources of the Self: The Making of the Modern Identity*. Cambridge, MA: Harvard University Press, 1989.

———. 'Theories of Meaning'. In *Human Agency and Language: Philosophical Papers 1*, 248–92. Cambridge: Cambridge University Press, 1985.

———. 'What Is Human Agency?' In *Human Agency and Language: Philosophical Papers 1*, 15–44. Cambridge: Cambridge University Press, 1985.

Theunissen, Michael. *Sein und Schein: Die kritische Funktion der Hegelschen Logik*. Frankfurt: Suhrkamp, 1978.

Thompson, Edward P. *The Making of the English Working Class*. New York: Pantheon, 1964.

Tollefsen, Deborah. 'Organizations as True Believers'. *Journal of Social Philosophy* 33, no. 3 (2002): 395–410. https://doi.org/10.1111/0047-2786.00149.

Tugendhat, Ernst. *Self-Consciousness and Self-Determination*. Cambridge, MA: MIT Press, 1986.

Tully, James. 'Struggles over Recognition and Distribution'. *Main* 7, no. 4 (2000): 469–82.

———. 'Wittgenstein and Political Philosophy: Understanding Practices of Critical Reflection'. *Political Theory* 17, no. 2 (1989): 172–204.

Tuomela, Raimo. *The Philosophy of Sociality*. Oxford: Oxford University Press, 2007.

Turner, Stephen. *The Social Theory of Practices: Tradition, Tacit Knowledge and Presuppositions*. Cambridge: Polity, 1994.

Wallace, James D. *Norms and Practices*. Ithaca, NY: Cornell University Press, 2009.

Walzer, Michael. *The Company of Critics: Social Criticism and Political Commitment in the Twentieth Century*. New York: Basic Books, 1988.

———. *Interpretation and Social Criticism*. Cambridge, MA: Harvard University Press, 1987.

———. 'Mut, Mitleid und ein gutes Auge: Tugenden der Sozialkritik und der Nutzen der Gesellschaftstheorie'. *Deutsche Zeitschrift für Philosophie* 48, no. 5 (2000): 709–18.

———. 'Nation and Universe'. In *The Tanner Lectures on Human Values XI*, edited by Grethe B. Peterson, 509–57. Salt Lake City: University of Utah Press, 1990.

———. 'Objectivity and Social Meaning'. In *The Quality of Life*, edited by Martha Nussbaum and Amartya Sen, 165–77. Oxford: Oxford University Press, 1993.

———. *Spheres of Justice*. New York: Basic Books, 1983.

———. *Thick and Thin: Moral Criticism at Home and Abroad*. Notre Dame, IN: University of Notre Dame Press, 1994.

Walzer, Michael, and Ronald Dworkin. '"Spheres of Justice": An Exchange'. *New York Review of Books* 30, no. 12 (1983).

Warnke, Georgia. 'Social Interpretation and Political Theory: Walzer and His Critics'. In *Hermeneutics and Critical Theory in Ethics and Politics*, edited by Michael Kelly, 204–26. Cambridge, MA: MIT Press, 1990.

Weber, Max. *Economy and Society*. Edited by Guenther Roth and Claus Wittich. Berkeley: University of California Press, 1978.

Wedgwood, Ralph. *The Nature of Normativity*. Oxford: Clarendon Press, 2007.

Weiß, Johannes. 'Die "Bindungseffekte kommunikativen Handelns": Einige skeptische Bemerkungen'. In *Kommunikatives Handeln: Beiträge zu Jürgen Habermas' 'Theorie des Kommunikativen Handelns'*, edited by Axel Honneth and Hans Joas, 433–54. Frankfurt: Suhrkamp, 2002.

Wikiquote Contributors. 'Margaret Thatcher'. *Wikiquote*. https://secure.wikimedia.org/wikiquote/en/wiki/Margaret_Thatcher.

Wittgenstein, Ludwig. *On Certainty*. Edited by G. E. M Anscombe and G. H. von Wright. Oxford: Blackwell, 1969.

———. *Philosophical Investigations*. Oxford: Blackwell, 1958.

———. *Remarks on the Foundations of Mathematics*. Edited by Georg Henrik von Wright, Rush Rhees and G. E. M. Anscombe. Translated by G. E. M. Anscombe. Cambridge, MA: MIT Press, 1967.

———. *Remarks on the Philosophy of Psychology*. Vol. 2. Oxford: Blackwell, 1980.

———. *Zettel*. 2nd ed. Oxford: Blackwell, 1967.

Wright, Crispin. 'Kripke's Account of the Argument against Private Language'. *Journal of Philosophy* 81, no. 12 (1984): 759–78.
———. *Wittgenstein on the Foundations of Mathematics*. Cambridge, MA: Harvard University Press, 1980.
Zurn, Christopher F. 'Social Pathologies as Second-Order Disorders'. In *Axel Honneth: Critical Essays*, edited by Danielle Petherbridge, 345–70. Leiden: Brill, 2011.

Index

Adorno, Theodor W., 160, 261, 272–73
anthropology, 45, 57, 99–109, 202
articulation, 43–56, 63, 66, 95–98, 233, 239, 242
authority, 58, 60, 68, 137, 142, 149–55, 158, 182, 194–95, 199, 203–7, 212, 216, 221–26, 231, 232, 235, 238, 240, 246, 250, 276; default, 152, 194, 198, 201, 205, 207–10, 216–19, 226, 234, 238–39, 286

Boghossian, Paul, 188
Bourdieu, Pierre, 160
Brandom, Robert, 160, 175, 170, 183–85, 189–99, 204–5
Bratman, Michael, 134–38

Cohen, Joshua, 39
collective commitment. *See* joint commitment
collective intentionality, 117–55, 205–9, 217; individualist theories of, 119, 124–27, 133–38, 145; and justification, 121, 130–32, 138, 142, 151, 154; normative dimensions of, 125–33, 135, 137–39, 141–46, 150–51, 154–55, 205–7
colonization of the lifeworld, 90–93
common knowledge, 134–35, 139, 143

community. *See* group, social
conflict: interpretive, 34, 40, 48, 49, 52, 62, 64–74, 250; about justification, 172, 186, 192, 199, 201, 203, 213–16, 219, 222, 238–45, 277; between norms, 224–26; social, 16, 29, 34, 39, 73–74, 92, 95–97, 107, 110, 213, 230–37, 283–86. *See also* inconsistency
conformism, 180–92, 194–95, 198–203, 209–10, 232–33, 235
conservatism, 38, 45, 64, 235–37, 250, 261
contradiction, social, 29–32, 77, 251–56, 259, 276, 281
cooperation, 21, 48, 59, 61, 64, 72, 102–4, 107, 110–12, 132–36, 139, 140, 269
crisis, 28, 57, 68–71, 270
critical theory, 2, 5, 20–21, 24–25, 75–76, 90–92, 102, 111, 160, 180, 216, 238, 257–59, 261, 266
critique: aesthetic, 12–14; dogmatic (*see* dogmatism); external, 14–17, 20, 278; internal, 16–22, 30, 37, 56, 60, 231, 241, 256; justification of, 3–6, 14–23, 31, 36–40, 49–54, 64–74, 83, 91, 98–106, 109, 199–215, 219–20, 225, 237, 239–51, 257, 283–87;

345

radical, 5, 7, 36, 45, 70, 236; and reasons, 3, 10, 11–20, 22, 33, 38–40, 54, 71, 113, 230, 233–37, 245–41, 257; reflexive, 12–13, 17, 27, 247, 258–60; transcendent, 4–5, 21, 24, 29, 33, 43, 45, 65, 110, 245, 281

default authority. *See* authority, default
Dewey, John, 98–100, 103–4, 107
disagreement, 37, 41, 72–73, 76, 201. *See also* conflict
disposition, 10, 16, 21, 24, 128–29, 141, 151, 153, 161, 169, 175–78, 181–89, 193–95, 197, 201, 203, 209, 213–15, 219–20, 245–48, 264
disrespect, 95–99, 101–15
dogmatism, 1–4, 30
Dreyfus, Herbert, 160
duality of social practice, 181, 215
Durkheim, Emile, 85, 224

Enlightenment, 14, 63, 260
epistemology, 25, 34, 68–69, 81, 96–97, 105, 110–14, 170–71, 237–41

Foucault, Michel, 20
Fraser, Nancy, 99, 102, 108

Giddens, Anthony, 160
Gilbert, Margaret, 124, 125, 133, 139–48, 155
Glüer, Karin, 178
Gramsci, Antonio, 36, 39, 111
group, social, 3, 5, 10, 13, 16–17, 22–23, 34–35, 39–40, 46–47, 60, 63, 68, 101–2, 105, 107, 118–27, 131–32, 136–38, 140–55, 164, 170–71, 182–89, 194, 198, 200–201, 204–8, 216, 219, 223, 226, 231, 235–36, 240–41, 248

Habermas, Jürgen, 6, 76–97, 100–102, 105, 110–19, 158, 160, 202, 229–30, 272, 274
Hart, H. L. A, 188, 222–25, 230

Haugeland, John, 180, 183–88, 190, 194, 198, 203–4, 209–10
Hegel, Georg Wilhelm Friedrich, 5, 25–30, 96–97, 102–7, 111, 251, 261, 266, 267–73, 284
Heidegger, Martin, 183, 261, 280
hermeneutics, 6, 22–24, 33–35, 42–74, 77, 80, 87, 93, 97, 100, 111–14, 117, 155, 229, 239–41, 246, 250, 285
Honneth, Axel, 6, 20, 76, 94–115, 119, 158, 229–30, 261, 273, 284
Horkheimer, Max, 75, 102, 160
human right, 16, 125

ideology, 4, 22, 37, 39, 40, 49, 76–77, 87, 105–7, 122, 125, 244, 246, 259, 269–73
inconsistency between norms and behaviour, 17–18, 22, 38, 95, 231, 239, 242, 246
individualism, 163, 179–80, 185–86, 194, 198, 213. *See also* collective intentionality, individualist theories of
injustice, 4, 40, 95–98, 100, 105, 107, 114, 246

joint commitment, 6, 118, 122–25, 129, 137–47, 151–55, 158, 201, 206–7
justification: in collective intentionality (*see* collective intentionality and justification); of critique (*see* critique, justification of); Hegel's model of, 26–28; and rules (*see* rules, justificatory dimension)

Kripke, Saul, 164, 168–81, 190–91, 238

labor. *See* work
lifeworld, 78–93, 112–15, 263
Lohmann, Georg, 3
Lukács, Georg, 261–80

MacIntyre, Alasdair, 6, 34, 52, 56–73, 110, 118, 249, 251

manipulation, 18, 54
market, 21, 76, 80, 267–69, 278–79
Marx, Karl, 1–5, 23, 25, 26, 28–31, 76, 77, 251, 256, 261, 265–70, 273, 278, 284, 287
McDowell, John, 160, 189
Mead, George Herbert, 85, 96, 97
moral reasons. *See* reasons, moral
motivation, 10–15, 18–22, 36, 51, 54, 56, 97–98, 101, 155, 163, 168, 221, 227

narrative, 38, 62–71, 80, 210, 229, 280
Nietzsche, Friedrich, 20, 261
normative epistemology, 25, 81–82, 97, 105, 110–14, 237–41
normative force, 5, 25, 42, 83–88, 106, 115, 118, 123, 137, 143, 146, 155, 163, 201, 205–6, 210, 213, 219, 223–24, 229, 235, 238, 244–48
normative phenomenalism, 189–92, 209
normative potential, 4–6, 23–25, 41, 75, 78, 81, 88, 93–98, 112, 160
norms: critique of, 3, 20, 30, 86–87; explicitly accepted, 4–5, 14, 16, 17, 20–21, 33, 38, 41, 58, 65, 66, 72, 81, 97, 160, 163–64, 170, 195, 199, 222–27, 230–31, 240–44, 247; immanent, 1–2, 4–6, 22–23, 24–25, 26, 28, 29, 42, 57–58, 62, 74, 75, 77, 81, 87–89, 91, 93, 95–96, 99–103, 106, 110–17, 119–20, 157–59, 161, 163–64, 170, 185, 187, 195, 197–200, 207, 209, 212, 219, 222–27, 230–32, 238–51, 257–59; moral, 16, 34–35, 45, 59; shared 39–43, 46–50, 68, 117–18, 120, 122–23, 171, 186–88, 194, 198, 226–27

objectivity, 35, 36, 41, 49–50, 58–60, 64, 77, 92, 160–63, 167, 190–93, 210, 256, 262–80, 285–87
obligation, 4, 17, 21, 49, 82, 87, 89, 111, 118–24, 129–55, 157, 162–63, 205, 208, 211–12, 215, 223, 237; collective, 149; individual, 132, 144–47, 153–55
oppression, 4, 22, 106, 237

Parkin, Frank, 243
pathology, social, 48, 50, 56, 70, 81, 89–92, 97–98, 103, 106, 107, 114, 222–25, 230, 242, 265–66, 276
personal identity, 47–49, 100. *See also* subjectivity
Pettit, Philip, 126–27
phenomenology, 126, 173, 267, 279
Platonism, 176–77, 215
practice: moral, 34, 41, 54, 70; social, 3–7, 9–13, 19–24, 27–31, 39–44, 47–52, 58–62, 71–75, 78, 84, 87–88, 93, 98, 101–7, 110–16, 119–20, 141, 159–64, 180–83, 190, 193, 210–27, 229, 232–37, 250–56, 258–59, 274–80
progress, 23–25, 37–38, 49–53, 56, 62, 64–74, 91–94, 105–10, 112–14, 226, 230, 247–51, 283–84
protest, 91–92, 105, 243, 246, 260, 277

racism, 4, 18, 248
rationality, 26, 29, 49, 56, 63–71, 77–78, 81, 95, 104, 129, 131–32, 141–42, 151; communicative, 78, 80, 87–91, 101, 104; instrumental, 78, 90, 104, 259–62; standard of, 63–64, 66–71, 77, 132, 151
Rawls, John, 3, 35
realism, normative or moral, 15, 106–7
reasons: in critique (*see* critique and reasons); exonerating 152–53, 216; moral, 3, 13, 34, 136
recognition, 5–7, 94–112, 120, 146–54, 190, 194–95, 198–216, 219–26, 229, 233, 236, 242, 247, 250, 258, 275–80, 284–86
reductionism, 127, 136, 185, 189, 208

reflexivity: of critique (*see* critique, reflexive); of rule-following, 185, 188, 199, 213–20, 223
regularism, 177, 189, 215
regulism, 175, 215
reification, 90, 94, 257–81
Rorty, Richard, 20, 285–89
Rössler, Beate, 40
rules: constitutive, 27, 99, 217–18, 221, 235, 251–55, 265, 277, 284; infinity of, 173–75, 177–79, 183, 209; justificatory dimension, 165–74, 178–79, 180–83, 189–93; normativity of, 173–79, 181, 185–86, 188–90, 193, 195, 198, 203–5, 215, 225; orientation function, 166–68, 171, 173–77, 180–84, 188, 189, 199, 201, 203, 209, 213–19; and reasons, 172, 191–92, 215, 216

sanction, 138, 149–53, 162, 184–88, 204, 208, 213–15, 218, 233, 240, 244, 246, 248, 254
Scanlon, Thomas M., 136
scepticism, 168–175, 180, 190–93, 199
Schatzki, Theodore R., 221, 254
Schiller, Friedrich, 261
science, social, 23–24, 87, 116, 160–63
Searle, John R., 133, 136–38, 217–18, 254, 263
self-understanding, 11, 15, 17, 19, 20–24, 28–29, 33–34, 38–40, 44–55, 59–60, 68–71, 74–75, 96, 98, 100, 113–19, 229, 239–43, 247, 249
sexism, 4, 106, 248
Shockley, Kenneth, 145–46
Simmel, Georg, 261–62, 270
social ontology, 5–6, 24–25, 84–89, 105, 117–20, 123–24, 204, 216, 229

social theory, 42–43, 57, 60, 62, 72–76, 78, 84–85, 92, 98, 102, 123, 128, 158, 163, 243, 262, 272
sociology, 120, 159, 160, 273. *See also* science, social
status, normative, 83, 132–33, 147, 161–66, 170–73, 181–86, 190–95, 199–203, 209–12, 215–25, 236, 252–55
Sugden, Robert, 126
subjectivity, 99–101, 119, 262, 265, 270–73, 280

Taylor, Charles, 6, 22, 34, 42–57, 63, 65, 66, 69–74, 110, 118, 155, 160, 239, 251
tradition, 35–37, 40, 56–73, 109, 117–19, 126, 246, 249–51, 275
transcendental arguments, 51, 89, 108, 119, 245
Tuomela, Raimo, 133, 137–38

universal pragmatics, 81–84, 114

validity (Geltung), 12–15, 17, 40, 141, 149, 154, 160, 172, 202, 207–8, 222, 223, 235, 243, 267, 275; claim, 78–88, 95, 101, 107, 111; of interpretations, 49–50, 54–55, 66, 249; surplus, 36, 129
vocabulary, 20, 47, 59–60, 65–66, 71, 110, 118, 124–28, 239, 264

Walzer, Michael, 3, 6, 16, 17, 22, 34–43, 47, 55–58, 63, 65, 66, 69–70, 73–74, 155
Weber, Max, 78, 128, 261, 269–70
Wittgenstein, Ludwig, 7, 120, 158–59, 164–70, 175–78, 189–92, 216
work, 75–76, 95, 263–70, 273

www.ingramcontent.com/pod-product-compliance
Lightning Source LLC
Chambersburg PA
CBHW022008300426
44117CB00005B/89